Focus on Learning
A Learning College Reader

Terry O'Banion and Cynthia D. Wilson, Editors

League for Innovation in the Community College

Published with generous support from

The League for Innovation in the Community College is an international organization dedicated to catalyzing the community college movement. The League hosts conferences and institutes, develops web resources, conducts research, produces publications, provides services, and leads projects and initiatives with more than 800 member colleges, 160 corporate partners, and a host of other government and nonprofit agencies in a continuing effort to make a positive difference for students and communities. Information about the League and its activities is available at www.league.org.

The opinions expressed in this book are those of the authors and do not necessarily reflect the views of the League for Innovation in the Community College or WebStudy, Inc.

Terry O'Banion is President Emeritus of the League for Innovation in the Community College and Director of the Community College Leadership Program at Walden University.

Cynthia D. Wilson is Vice President for Learning and Research at the League for Innovation in the Community College.

Contents

Preface

Terry O'Banion
Cynthia D. Wilson

Asking precisely when American education seemed to forget that its most important, most urgent, most commendable goal was to ensure that the students in its care were actually learning, or that the essential business of education was to support and enhance student learning, would likely prompt a range of answers—including among them denials that the forgetting ever happened. Refutations aside, two decades ago the widely held perceptions of educational decline were genuine, and they resulted in dramatic calls for extensive institutional reform, from Kindergarten through the baccalaureate degree and beyond.

For the community college, the most enduring response to those calls for change came from thought leaders who advocated a concept so seemingly simple, pure, and obvious that an educational reform movement focused on learning and a concept called "the Learning College" are frequently met with bewildered inquiries by those outside the field: "Wait a minute," begins the common question from baffled family, friends, acquaintances, even strangers, "isn't learning what schools are for?"

The simple answer, of course, is, "Yes," and the Learning Paradigm and Learning College concepts have undoubtedly promoted and strengthened the community college field's focus on learning. The simple answer becomes more complex—"Yes, *but...*"—when reform moves from urgent call to meaningful action. Institutional transformation can be a slow, complicated process, as those involved in making their colleges more learning centered have discovered. Still, community college educators continue to choose the path that willfully and visibly puts learning at the heart of the institution's work.

The overarching
question that frames
the Learning Paradigm and the Learning College is a simple one: Does this action improve and expand student learning?

In its ongoing support for colleges that make this choice, the League for Innovation in the Community College provides a number of resources through its publications, conferences, and other service to the field. In *Focus on Learning: A Learning College Reader*, the League for Innovation brings together in one volume a compilation of works that represent some of the foremost thinking on the Learning Paradigm and Learning College. In making selections for the book, the editors sought advice from leaders in the movement, many of whom are represented in the pages that follow.

Part I is a review of early calls for action and conceptual responses to those calls. The following two sections feature processes for leading, implementing, assessing, and evaluating the Learning College. These works include reports on independent research, grant-funded projects, and individual college efforts. The widening interest in the physical space for learning is addressed in Part IV, as is a revisiting of the Wingspread Group's recommendation that the entire architecture of higher education be transformed. The book ends with a look at the continuing challenges for the Learning College, including questions still to be asked and answered.

The overarching question that frames the Learning Paradigm and the Learning College is a simple one: Does this action improve and expand student learning? If this question can surface and be addressed in the daily activities of a college engaged in a journey to become more learning centered, the culture of an institution will begin slowly to change, and the mindsets of its leaders will begin to grasp new perspectives: Does this new advising program improve and expand student learning? Do these learning outcomes for the fine arts department improve and expand student learning? Do these new attempts to create community and connectedness through this new technology improve and expand student learning? Does this staff development program for classified staff improve and expand student learning? Does this budget improve and expand student learning? These are the kinds of questions faculty and administrators need to ask about everything we do in the institution, because everything we do should in some way be related to improving and expanding student learning—or maybe we shouldn't be doing it.

Once college stakeholders learn how to ask this fundamental question in its various forms, a follow-up question takes center stage: How do we know this action improves and expands student learning? If this reform effort is to be different than those that have come before, then we must become more astute at collecting, analyzing, and applying evidence that what we do is effective and efficient. We must become cynics of our own romanticism; we must balance our passion with caution and rationality. We must be able to explain to our students and our colleagues, to our supporters and detractors, to those who govern and fund us—and ultimately to ourselves—that we are on the right journey to make a substantive difference in the lives of our students, our communities, and our world by placing learning as the core process and product of all our efforts.

The collected articles and reports in this book are only a fraction of the thought, research, and action that has been prompted by the concepts of the Learning Paradigm and Learning College, but they are a valuable resource for colleges that begin, or continue, to address the core questions: Does this action improve and expand student learning? How do we know? This volume contains a number of answers to those questions, and some selections are sure to prompt even more questions as the journey unfolds.

Focus on Learning: The Core Mission of Higher Education

— Terry O'Banion

Institutions of higher education in the United States have achieved worldwide recognition in pursuit of three key missions: research, teaching, and service—missions valued by their stakeholders primarily in that order. The great centers of university research have produced breakthroughs in every field of science that have made our universities the envy of the world. Because of their success, "research" has become embedded as one of the cardinal values and purposes of higher education. Leading four-year colleges and community colleges have established "teaching" as a second cardinal value as many four-year colleges provide ideal residential communities for selected groups of students, and community colleges provide innovative approaches to assist great numbers of underprepared students in achieving success. All levels of institutions ascribe to "service" as an expression of their core values as they work to improve society at the local, state, national, and international level. Research, teaching, and service have provided a rich harvest from the higher education enterprise for American society and the world.

At the end of the 20th century another key mission or purpose—a corollary of research, teaching, and service—began to sprout in the landscape of higher education. The new mission was not new at all, but it had not been as visible as research, teaching, and service in the policies, programs, and practices of institutions. Awakened from its dormancy, it began to claim territory that could establish it as more than a graft or a mutation of the historical missions rooted for decades. As the 21st century got under way, it became increasingly clear that "learning" had broken through the traditional hardpan of higher education and had established its own patch in the Groves of Academe. For some who toil in the vineyards of higher education, "learning" will be no more than an upstart, an inconsequential sprout destined to wither and die. For others "learning" is the core business of all educational institutions—a transcendent value that arches over research, teaching, and service—providing a sharply focused perspective that will greatly enrich the work of the educational community.

As a newly articulated mission of higher education, "learning" has been cited by several leaders as part of the triumvirate of traditional missions. In a letter to the editor of *Change* in May of 2000, James Bess, Professor of Higher Education at New York University, said, "Institutions of higher education must maintain their unique roles in society—as extraordinary places where *teaching, learning, and research* can unfold, unfettered by the crass, short-term expectations of profit" (p. 6, emphasis added). Two years later, in the lead article of the Association of Governing Board's newsletter, Berberet and McMillin stated, "It doesn't take a Ph.D. to know that a college or university fulfills its multiple missions—*student learning, discovery of new knowledge, and community engagement*—chiefly through its faculty" (p. 1, emphasis added). Perhaps "learning" is being incorporated as a key mission of higher education, even supplanting some of the established missions, more rapidly than we realized.

The Emerging Focus on Learning

Learning is, of course, the transcendent value that undergirds almost all educational activity. The purpose of research is to build on past learning to create new learning. The purpose of teaching is to improve and expand student learning. The purpose of service is to translate learning and provide learning to improve communities and citizens. All educators strongly value learning as a continuing activity for themselves and as the outcome for others of their efforts. *But learning has been more of an implied mission in higher education than a visible mission.* It is the visible missions—research, teaching, and service—that determine the policies, practices, programs, and uses of personnel in our institutions. And it is the visible missions on which all rewards are based.

One of the highest honors that can be bestowed on a university professor is that of Distinguished Research Chair. Ernest Boyer's seminal work, *Scholarship Reconsidered*, was an attempt to right the balance that had tilted too far in the direction of traditional research over other forms of scholarship. Boyer hoped to establish "teaching" as an equal to "research" in the reward systems of universities, but the hope is fading fast. In a review of teaching and learning practices in higher education between 1980 and 2000, the authors concluded, "With few exceptions, teaching changes have not been tied to higher education's incentive and reward system. Research remains the primary avenue to individual and institutional prestige" (p. 13).

> **Learning is,** of course, the transcendent value that undergirds almost all educational activity.

Aping the university's value system, community colleges, in the 1990s, created the concept of the Endowed Teaching Chair, identifying teachers for their teaching prowess rather than for their ability to help students learn. The following excerpts are cited from a description of an endowed teaching program at a leading community college: "The purpose of the endowed chair program is threefold: to recognize and promote teaching excellence at the college; to spotlight outstanding members of the college's teaching faculty; and to provide the college with financial resources needed to support teaching excellence….The program enables the college to honor outstanding members of the teaching faculty and provide resources needed for the advancement of teaching….The criteria for selection of a faculty member for an endowed chair includes a faculty committee's judgment of the candidate's record of teaching excellence, contribution to the advancement of instruction within his or her field, and the degree of esteem expressed by his or her colleagues." In this program, teaching trumps learning at every turn.

Even so, there is an emerging focus on learning at all levels of education and in an increasing number of countries that suggests a possible transformation in core educational practice, and, perhaps, even in the traditional missions of higher education.

The Learning Revolution

In the last fifteen years a Learning Revolution has spread rapidly across all levels of American higher education. In 1994, the cover of *Business Week* declared a Learning Revolution in progress; in 1995, a special section in *TIME* announced the developing Learning Revolution. In 1996, the first national conference on "The Learning Paradigm" was held in San Diego, California, and the Association of Community College Trustees released a special issue of the *Trustee Quarterly* devoted entirely to *The Learning Revolution: A Guide for Community College Trustees.*

> ## The Learning
> ### Revolution, "in a matter
> of decades," has the potential
> to fundamentally change the
> education enterprise....

In 1997, the American Council on Education and the American Association of Community Colleges jointly published *A Learning College for the 21st Century,* by Terry O'Banion which, for the first time, outlined the principles and practices of a Learning College. In 1997 and 1998, the League for Innovation and the Public Broadcasting Service (PBS) sponsored three national teleconferences on the Learning Revolution and the Learning College. In a few short years, the Learning Revolution had taken American higher education by storm and had found community colleges—the American version of colleges of further education—to be particularly interested in implementing the Learning Revolution. In a 1998 survey by the League for Innovation in the Community College, 73 percent of the nation's community college presidents indicated they had undertaken an initiative for their institutions to become more learning-centered community colleges.

From 2000 to 2010 the League for Innovation has continued to champion the Learning Revolution. The League coordinated two major million-dollar grants at the beginning of the decade, one to create vanguard learning colleges and the other to create models of learning outcomes. In addition, the League launched a monthly series of *Learning Abstracts* and began to sponsor an annual Learning College Summit. Now, in 2010, the League is publishing this volume, *Focus on Learning: A Learning College Reader,* as the Learning Revolution continues to impact and change higher education.

The Learning Revolution in education is part of a larger social transformation going on in the United States and in the world. Peter Drucker, in *Managing for the Future,* succinctly captures this special period of change: "Every few hundred years throughout Western history, a sharp transformation has occurred. In a matter of decades, society altogether rearranges itself—its world view, its basic values, its social and political structures, its arts, its key institutions. Fifty years later a new world order exists...our age is such a period of transformation." The Learning Revolution, "in a matter of decades," has the potential to fundamentally change the education enterprise in the United States, Canada, Scotland, Australia, Jamaica, Turkey, and other countries where it is taking hold.

A Revolution With a Purpose

In a nutshell, the purpose of the Learning Revolution is to "place learning first" in every policy, program, and practice in higher education by overhauling the traditional architecture of education. In a seminal work, *An American Imperative,* the Wingspread Group on Education (1993) said, "We must redesign all our learning systems to align our entire education enterprise for the personal, civic, and workplace needs of the twenty-first century." The Wingspread Group went a step further and indicated the challenge institutions of higher education will face if they are to implement the Learning Revolution: "Putting learning at the heart of the academic enterprise will mean overhauling the conceptual, procedural, curricular, and other architecture of postsecondary education on most campuses."

While there seems to be a revolution or reform movement about every decade in American education, the Learning Revolution is quite different from reform efforts of the past. The Learning Revolution has two distinct goals that make it different: (1) to place learning first in every policy, program, and practice in higher education, and (2) to overhaul the traditional architecture of education.

Placing Learning First

It is generally inferred that learning is the primary purpose of education, but policies, practices, and value statements often reflect other priorities. Any student of education can cite the three primary missions most often articulated for American universities as noted earlier: research, teaching, and service. In many universities, however, the reward system places higher value on research over teaching and service. New tenure-track faculty are often warned by colleagues and mentors against investing too much energy and time in their teaching assignments. Universities have established distinguished research chairs as a clear designation of the primacy placed on research.

In contrast, the community college places such strong value on teaching that the institution is often referred to as "the teaching college." For example, in community colleges, the value placed on teaching is clearly reflected in their mission statements. Robert Barr (1994), former director of institutional research and planning at Palomar College in California, says: "It is revealing that virtually every mission statement contained in the catalogs in California's 107 community colleges fails to use the word learning in a statement of purpose. When it is used, it is almost always bundled in the phrase *teaching and learning* as if to say that, while learning may indeed have something to do with community colleges, it is only present as an aspect of teaching."

One of the most significant documents ever written on the community college in the U.S., *Building Communities,* the 1988 report of the Commission on the Future of Community Colleges, repeatedly highlights the central value placed on teaching in the community college: "Building communities dedicated to teaching is the vision and inspiration of this report. Quality instruction should be the hallmark of the movement. The community college should be the nation's premier teaching institution." As noted earlier, aping the university's propensity to place its highest value on research by establishing distinguished research chairs, the community college has established distinguished teaching chairs as a clear symbol of the primacy it places on teaching.

When research and teaching are the most visible values in an educational institution, the policies, practices, programs, and personnel in that institution are aligned to reflect those values. If learning is placed first to become the most important value, the policies, practices, programs, and personnel will be realigned to reflect the change in focus. Recognition by key stakeholders in the institution that learning should be placed first as a key mission is the beginning of the Learning Revolution.

Overhauling the Traditional Architecture

Every faculty member and administrator in education has been frustrated at some time or another with the traditional architecture of education that limits how they can teach or manage and how students can learn. Roger Moe, former majority leader of the Minnesota State Senate, has said, "Higher education is a thousand years of tradition wrapped in a hundred years of bureaucracy." The current system is time-bound, place-bound, efficiency-bound, and role-bound. These traditional limits on the architecture of education apply to American education but may differ in other countries depending on their educational history and the extent to which they have implemented reforms in recent years.

The educational system in the U. S. is *time-bound* by credit hours and semester courses. College students are learning in blocks of time that are artificial. Excellent teachers know that learning is not constrained to one-hour meetings held on Monday, Wednesday, and Friday, and they have been frustrated in teaching within these prescribed boundaries.

The system is *place-bound*. Learning is initiated, nurtured, monitored, and certified primarily by teachers in classrooms on a campus. We have experimented with distance education that takes courses off campus, but while it has increased student access, it retains the old model of education. Distance education, for the most part, is a nontraditional delivery system for traditional education. Work-based learning was supposed to break up that model, but it doesn't—it extends the model and is controlled by it because work-based learning is built around the current structure of the school. It still binds the student to a place.

The system is *efficiency-bound*. Our model of education reflects in great part the adjustment to an agricultural and industrial economy of an earlier era. Public school students are still dismissed early in the afternoon and in the summers so they can work on farms that no longer exist. Reflecting the industrial economy, education responded by creating a lock-step, put-them-in-boxes, factory model—the basis of American education today. Academic credit, based on time in class, makes learning appear orderly. This model creates an efficiency system to award credentials. Grades are collected and turned into credits, and these compilations are supposed to represent profound learning.

Finally the system is *role-bound,* which may be its greatest weakness. In education, we make the assumption that one human being, the teacher, can ensure that thirty very different human beings, one hour a day, three days a week for sixteen weeks, can learn enough to become enlightened citizens, productive workers, and joyful lifelong learners. Then we assume that this one human being can repeat this miracle three more times in the same sixteen-week period for ninety additional individuals. We provide little comfort and support when teachers fail to live up to this role-bound myth.

Reformers have been consistent in their criticism of the constraints on learning reflected in the industrial model of schooling in the United States. In 1962, John Dewey argued, "Nature has not adapted the young animal to the narrow desk, the crowded curriculum, the silent absorption of complicated facts." More than 20 years ago, K. Patricia Cross, a leading advocate for educational reform throughout her career, observed: "After some two decades of trying to find answers to the question of how to provide education for all the people, I have concluded that our commitment to the lock-step, time-defined structures of education stands in the way of lasting progress." More recently, the Tofflers have noted that, "America's schools...still operate like factories, subjecting the raw material (children) to standardized instruction and routine inspection." Today, this inherited architecture of education places great limits on a system struggling to redefine itself. The school system, from kindergarten through graduate school, is time-bound, place-bound, efficiency-bound, and role-bound.

If learning is placed first to become the most important value, the policies, practices, programs, and personnel will be realigned to reflect the change in focus.

The Learning College

As the Learning Revolution spread throughout all levels of education in the United States, innovators and reformers began to create programs and practices to reflect the emerging focus on learning. Learning communities were being created everywhere, and research established their potency as an effective new program to retain students and improve their performance. Learning outcomes became the coin of the realm for organizing and focusing what needed to be learned; the accrediting associations began to require learning outcomes of all institutions. Peter Senge's learning organization captured the imaginations of scores of leaders who tried to transform their organizational structures and practices to reflect the new emphasis on learning. Studies on the brain were translated into educational practice to expand students' potential for learning. Learning portfolios were designed to capture the substance of what students were learning. And a host of learning-centered innovations flooded the journals and conference forums: classroom assessment techniques, project-based learning, contextual learning, work-based learning, authentic learning, first-year experience, service learning, active learning, and collaborative learning are examples.

However, these innovations, programs, and practices tended to operate in a vacuum. Many were quite effective, but they seldom unfolded as part of an overall strategy to place learning first and overhaul the traditional architecture of education. It was business as usual for American education—piecemeal reform. But, as reported in *The Progress of Educational Reform* (1995), "While piecemeal implementation of reforms may lead to progress, it will not be the same magnitude as a systemic strategy focused on student learning." What was needed was an overall framework, a systemic design, of what a college would look like if it placed learning first and overhauled the traditional architecture of education. The Learning College was the first such effort to fill that bill.

The Learning College places learning first and provides educational experiences for learners anyway, anyplace, anytime. The model is based on the assumption that educational experiences are designed for the convenience of learners rather than for the convenience of institutions and their staffs. The term "The Learning College" is used as a generic reference for all educational institutions.

The Learning College is based on six key principles:

- The Learning College creates substantive change in individual learners.

- The Learning College engages learners as full partners in the learning process with learners assuming primary responsibility for their own choices.

- The Learning College creates and offers as many options for learning as possible.

- The Learning College assists learners to form and participate in collaborative learning activities.

- The Learning College defines the roles of learning facilitators by the needs of the learners.

- The Learning College and its learning facilitators succeed only when improved and expanded learning can be documented for learners.

Principle I: The Learning College creates substantive change in individual learners. The need for colleges to support this first principle is a self-evident, general truth, easily verifiable in personal experience. It is so elementary that it is often unstated and overlooked. This first principle must be stated and restated until it becomes an embedded value undergirding all other principles.

At its best, formal schooling is every society's attempt to provide a powerful environment that can create substantive change in individuals. But formal schooling is no longer at its best in many societies. In the Learning College, this first principle must form the framework for all other activities. The learners and the learning facilitators in the Learning College must be aware of the awesome power that can be released when learning works well. Learning in the Learning College will not be business as usual. Powerful processes will be at work; substantive change will be expected. Learners will be exploring and experimenting with new and expanded versions of what they can become. And it is important for educational leaders planning to initiate major change to become more learning centered, to realize and to make visible to all of their stakeholders and constituents that what they are about to do will create substantive change in individual learners.

Principle II: The Learning College engages learners as full partners in the learning process, with learners assuming primary responsibility for their own choices. At the point a learner chooses to engage the Learning College, a series of services will be initiated to prepare the learner for the experiences and opportunities to come. Until there is a seamless system of education across all sectors of education based on the principles of the Learning College, the services will be heavily focused on orienting the learner to the new experiences and expectations of the Learning College, which are not usually found in traditional schools. Two key expectations will be communicated to new learners at the first stage of engagement: (1) Learners are full partners in the creation and implementation of their learning experiences, and (2) Learners will assume primary responsibility for making their own choices about goals and options.

The services will include assessing the learner's abilities, achievements, values, needs, goals, expectations, resources, and environmental and situational limitations. A personal profile will be constructed by the learner in consultation with an expert assessor to illustrate what this learner knows, wants to know, and needs to know. A personal learning plan will be constructed from this personal profile, and the learner will negotiate a contract that outlines responsibilities of both the learner and the Learning College. The Learning College will also provide orientation and experimentation for learners who are unfamiliar with the new learning environment of the Learning College. Some learners will need training in using the technology, in developing collaborations, in locating resources, and in navigating learning systems. Specialists will monitor these services carefully and will be responsible for approving a learner's readiness to fully engage the learning opportunities provided.

It will be the Learning College's responsibility to provide clear and easily accessible information in a variety of formats. This information should include guidelines for making decisions about dates, workloads, resources, and learning options; details about processes and options new to the learner; and agreements regarding expectations and responsibilities. It will be the learner's responsibility to review and provide information, experiment with processes and options, make choices, and commit to full engagement in the choices made.

Principle III. The Learning College creates and offers as many options for learning as possible. The learner will review and experiment with options regarding time, place, structure, and methodology. Entry vouchers will be exchanged for the selected options and exit vouchers will be held for completion.

Each learning option will include specific goals and competency levels needed for entry as well as specific outcome measures of competency levels achieved. Learning Colleges will constantly create additional learning options, including prescribed, preshrunk portable modules; stand-alone technological expert systems; opportunities for collaboration with other learners in small groups and through technological links; and tutor-led groups, individual reading programs, project-based activities, service learning opportunities, lectures, and laboratories. It is important that traditional options needed by some students be retained to provide for the multiple needs of students.

A major goal of the Learning College will be to create as many learning options as possible in order to provide successful learning experiences for all learners. If the learner's goal is to become competent in English as a second language, there should be four or five learning options available to achieve the goal. If the learner's goal is to become competent in welding a joint, there should be four or five learning options available to achieve that goal.

To manage the activities and progress of thousands of learners engaged in hundreds of learning options at many different times, at many different levels, in many different locations, the Learning College will rely on expert systems using advanced technology. Without these complex systems, the Learning College cannot function. These systems reflect the breakthrough that will free education from the time-bound, place bound, and role-bound systems that currently manage the educational enterprise.

Principle IV. The Learning College assists learners to form and participate in collaborative learning activities. To transform a traditional institution into a Learning College is to turn the university ideal of a "community of scholars" into a new ideal of "communities of learners." More than just cute word play, the focus on creating communities among all participants in the Learning College—including not only students but also the faculty and other learning specialists—on creating student cohorts, and developing social structures that support individual learning is a requirement of a Learning College.

It has become increasingly clear from research that learning is a social activity. The constructivists Abel, Cennamo, and Chung, say, "Learning is a social enterprise. Through social interaction, as well as through action on objects, learners make sense of the world." In the United States, "learning communities" is a specific phrase for a curricular intervention that enhances collaboration and expands learning, and these communities have taken hold in hundreds of institutions across the country. There are many other forms of collaborative learning including project-based learning, electronic forums (e.g., Twitter and Facebook), and collaborative problem-solving activities that illustrate this principle.

In a Learning College, staff will form and recruit students into cohorts of common interest or circumstances. Process facilitators will orient individuals and form them into groups or communities of learners. Resource specialists will attend to the resource needs of both individuals and groups of learners. Learning facilitators will design experiences that build upon and use group strengths and other dynamics.

Assessment specialists will design and implement authentic assessments that can occur both individually and in the context of collaborative learning. The Learning College will be designed not only around the unique needs of individual learners but also around their needs for association. The Learning College will foster and nourish learning communities as an integral part of its design.

Principle V. The Learning College defines the roles of learning facilitators by the needs of the learners. If learners have varied and individual needs that require special attention, then it follows that the personnel employed in this enterprise must be selected on the basis of what learners need. Everyone employed in the Learning College will be a learning facilitator. Every employee will be directly linked to learners in the exercise of his or her duties, although some activities, such as accounting, may be more indirectly related. The goal is to have every employed person thinking about how his or her work facilitates the learning process.

The learners and the learning facilitators in the Learning College must be aware of the awesome power that can be released when learning works well.

The Learning College will contract with many specialists to provide services to learners. Specialists will be employed on a contractual basis to produce specific products or to deliver specific services; some will work full time, but many will work part time, often from their homes, linked to learners through technology. A number of specialists will be scattered around the world providing unique services and special expertise.

The Board of Regents for the State of Ohio calls for learning consultants who will be mentors, facilitators of inquiry, architects of connection, and managers of collaboration and integration. The groundwork is already being prepared for the new role of the learning facilitator to support the goals and purposes of the Learning College.

Principle VI. The Learning College and its learning facilitators succeed only when improved and expanded learning can be documented for learners. "What does this learner know?" and "What can this learner do?" provide the framework for documenting outcomes, both for the learner and for the learning facilitators. If the ultimate goal of the Learning College is to promote and expand learning, then this will be the yardstick by which the Learning College faculty and staff are evaluated. Conventional information may be assembled for students (retention rates and achievement scores) and for faculty (service and observation by students, peers, and supervisors), but the goal will be to document what students know and what they can do, and to use this information as the primary measure of success for the learning facilitators and the Learning College.

All learning options in the Learning College will include the competencies required for entrance and for exit. These competencies will reflect national and state standards when available, or they will be developed by specialists on staff or on special contract. Assessing a learner's readiness for a particular learning option will be a key part of the initial engagement process and thereafter a continuing process embedded in the culture of the institution.

A New Beginning

These six principles form the core of the Learning College. They refer primarily to process and structure, and are built on the basic philosophy that the student is central in all activities within the scope of the educational enterprise. There are certainly other principles that must be considered in creating a new paradigm of learning. The kind of content to be addressed, how colleges are funded, and how institutions are governed are examples of key issues that must be resolved and for which principles must be designed. In these six principles, there is at least a beginning direction for those who wish to create a Learning College that places learning first and provides educational experiences for learners anyway, anyplace, anytime. Such a college is designed to help students make passionate connections to learning.

References

Abel, S.K, Cennamo, K. S. & Chung, M. (1996). A "Layers of Negotiation" Model for Designing Constructivist Learning Material. *Educational Technology*, 36 (4) 39-48.

Barr, R. (1994 February). A New Paradigm for Community Colleges. *The News*. San Marcos, CA: Research and Planning Group of the California Community Colleges.

Berberet, J. & McMillin, L. (2002). The American Professoriate in Transition. AGB Priorities. Spring (18), 1-15. Washington, DC: Association of Governing Boards of Universities and Colleges.

Boyer, E. (1990). *Scholarship Reconsidered: Priorities of the Professoriate*. New York: Carnegie Foundation for the Advancement of Teaching.

Commission on the Future of Community Colleges. (1988). *Building Communities: A Vision for a New Century*. Washington, DC: American Association of Community Colleges.

Cross, K. P. (1976). *Accent on Learning: Improving Instruction and Reshaping the Curriculum*. San Francisco: Jossey-Bass.

Dewey, J. & Dewey, E. (1962), *Schools of Tomorrow*. New York: E.P. Dutton and Company, Inc.

Drucker, P. T. (1992). *Managing for the Future: The 1990s and Beyond*. New York: Penguin Books.

Moe, R., cited in Armajani, Babak, et al. (1994 January). *A Model for the Reinvented Higher Education System: State Policy and College Learning*. Denver: Education Commission of the States.

O'Banion, T. (1997). *A Learning College for the 21st Century*. Phoenix: Oryx Press.

O'Banion, T. (1997). The Learning Revolution: A Guide for Community College Trustees. (Special Issue). *Trustee Quarterly*, 1.

Ohio Technology in Education Steering Committee. (1996 March). *Technology in the Learning Communities of Tomorrow: Beginning the Transformation*. Ohio Board of Regents.

Senge, P. (1990). *The Fifth Discipline: The Art and Practice of the Learning Organization*. New York: Doubleday.

Toffler, A. & Toffler, H. (1995 March/April). Getting Set for the Coming Millennium. *The Futurist*.

Wingspread Group on Higher Education. (1993). *An American Imperative: Higher Expectations for Higher Education*. Racine, WI: The Johnson Foundation, Inc.

Part I.

The Learning College: A Historical Perspective

When George Boggs delivered his opening-day speech at Palomar College on September 3, 1985, his remarks foreshadowed the development of the concept of the "learning paradigm" that was born on that campus and that was the genesis of Terry O'Banion's work on the Learning College. The text of that speech, "A People Place" (pages 11-14) seems an appropriate way to open Part I of this volume, "The Learning College: A Historical Perspective." Reminding his audience that Palomar students are, "pretty important people on this campus" who "should not be treated as intrusions in our job; they are our job," Boggs, who served as president of the college at the time, urged his colleagues to show students "we care about them, that we are glad to have them here, and that we will help them succeed." He talked about collective responsibility for student success, a collective that includes all members of the college community—student services professionals, classified staff, and administrators as well as faculty and students. Near the end of the speech, he also talked about the interdependence of the various sectors of the college in helping to ensure the success of students and of the institution. Most tellingly, though, he began the speech by asking a single, overarching question: "Are the needs of the target population compatible with our central mission: student learning?" In that question, George Boggs reflected values and a vision that set the stage for what would become the Learning College Movement. In retrospect and alongside Terry O'Banion's six principles of the Learning College, these comments seem prescient, but they also reflect the mood of a country that was deeply engaged in re-examining its educational institutions.

Ultimately, though, the Wingspread Group's

message is not one of doom and gloom; instead, it is one of hope.

The fall 1985 term at Palomar and other American colleges and universities opened while the country's K-12 institutions were still reeling from publication of *A Nation at Risk*, spinning inside the whirlwind of dramatic reform efforts it spawned. Higher education had a few more years before *An American Imperative* (pages 15-27) sent it into a similar kind of reform-driven storm. The Wingspread Group on Higher Education's open letter to the American people called for extensive transformation in the nation's colleges and universities, opening with the provocative—and well-founded—claim that, "A disturbing and dangerous mismatch exists between what American society needs of higher education and what it is receiving." The first paragraphs continue this theme and seem, sadly, still current: "...the nation's colleges and universities appear to live by an unconscious educational rule of thumb that their function is to weed out, not to cultivate, students for whom they have accepted responsibility"; "Education is in trouble, and with it our nation's hopes for the future"; and "...an increasingly skeptical public expresses the same sense of sticker shock about college costs that is now driving health care reform." Ultimately, though, the Wingspread Group's message is not one of doom and gloom; instead, it is one of hope. It is also a call to action, and to that end, the open letter's appendices include a self-assessment checklist (page 26) that is as relevant today as it was almost two decades ago. College leaders might do well to pose the questions from 1993 to today's faculty and staff, facilitating conversation and perhaps developing action agendas around today's responses.

Of course, *An American Imperative* caused a stir in higher education, much as its predecessor, *A Nation at Risk*, caused in the K-12 sector. It definitely stirred thinking, some of which, occurring concurrently, emerged as what Robert Barr and John Tagg called, "a paradigm shift...taking hold in American higher education." In their seminal article, "From Teaching to Learning: A New Paradigm for Undergraduate Education" (pages 28-37), they explained:

> In its briefest form, the paradigm that has governed our colleges is this: A college is an institution that exists *to provide instruction*. Subtly but profoundly we are shifting to a new paradigm: A college is an institution that exists to *produce learning*.

In the first paragraph of this 1995 article in *Change*, Barr and Tagg crystallized and distilled the reform-focused discussions springing out of *An American Imperative* and contemporary writings on learning and organizational theory.

They spent the rest of the article juxtaposing the Instruction Paradigm and the Learning Paradigm, offering an argument for the latter that was so compelling it generated what Terry O'Banion and others dubbed a Learning Revolution (see p. 4).

O'Banion molded the ideas of the Learning Paradigm into the concept of the Learning College, consciously moving away from earlier distinctions between teaching and learning while focusing instead on the role of the entire institution in fostering effective teaching and other practices to improve and expand student learning. In his 1997 groundbreaking book, *A Learning College for the 21st Century*, O'Banion defines the Learning College as "placing learning first and providing learning opportunities anyway, anyplace, and anytime," and he establishes its six fundamental principles. The same year, the League for Innovation published the O'Banion monograph, *Creating More Learning-Centered Community Colleges* (pages 38-54), in which he describes the Learning College principles and reviews common themes culled from six community colleges "beginning to experiment with new approaches to placing learning first." In the monograph, he also explores issues and challenges colleges pursuing this work may face as well as various conditions that may either impede or support the change effort.

As more and more college leaders became interested in the ideas of the Learning College and more and more questions were asked, O'Banion wrote several shorter articles clarifying distinctions between the Learning College and other related movements. Two of these articles, both originally published in the League for Innovation's *Leadership Abstracts* series, are included in this volume: a 1996 article, "Learning Communities, Learning Organizations, and Learning Colleges" (pages 55-56), and a 1999 article, "The Learning College: Both Learner and Learning Centered" (pages 57-58). The section concludes with a 1999 article by Cynthia Wilson, "Faculty of the Future in Learning Colleges," that began an exploration of the role of faculty in this new movement and became the foundation for one of the first doctoral dissertations written on the Learning College (pages 59-62).

A People Place

— George Boggs

Boggs, George. *A People Place.* Orientation Day Speech at Palomar College, September 3, 1985.

Question: "Are the needs of the target population compatible with our central mission: student learning?"

Within the last year, at least three national reports on postsecondary education have been issued, each highly critical of the current state of higher education in our country. The National Institute of Education report, *Involvement in Learning,* and the Association of American Colleges report, *Integrity in the College Curriculum,* focused on perceived weaknesses in higher education.

No less critical is *A Study of California's Community Colleges,* prepared for the California Roundtable by Berman, Weiler Associates, issued last April. According to that study, community colleges, in negotiating a transition from local autonomy to a higher degree of state control, "have received mixed signals from the California public. The colleges have been asked to impose higher student standards but told to continue to ensure maximum access for all students. They have been criticized for ignoring the transfer function, but given strong financial incentives to weaken transfer programs and associated student services. And they have been encouraged to pursue all of their traditional missions, while being told that they may be trying too much." Related to those "mixed signals," community colleges have had to react to funding instability, a growing percentage of part-time and underprepared or disadvantaged students, and, most recently, enrollment decline.

We have been, as institutions, like ships at sea, buffeted by unexpected waves, reacting to stay afloat, and drifting rather than setting our own course. As I see it, our overriding goal will be to gain control of our own destiny.

In *Opportunity for Excellence: The Lessons Learned by Five Colleges,* published in March of 1985, the experiences of five very different kinds of colleges led to common findings or lessons.

Lesson 1. "Opportunity is implicit in adversity. Good times have meant business as usual for higher education, continued growth accomplished largely by adding the new to what already exists.

"In contrast, hard times necessitate reappraisal. They have forced some institutions to develop new visions to guide their futures.

"Colleges are talking more and more about excellence. Quality takes on a special urgency during hard times. Excellence becomes more than appealing rhetoric: it becomes a pragmatic necessity for colleges that want to attract serious students and financial support.

"Today, institutions that know themselves and are confident of their directions have the potential to make big strides. There is greater opportunity now than in the past, the potential for achievement is higher, and the rewards for succeeding are larger. Never in recent memory have colleges had a greater opportunity to reach for excellence."

Lesson 2. "Sound management is essential for colleges today. Its consequences are a clear sense of institutional direction and collegiate character, and a heightened accent on quality."

Lesson 3. "Focusing on education is the best remedy for the challenges facing colleges and universities today."

In the August/September issue of the *AACJC Journal,* John Roueche and George Baker report, in an article titled, "The Success Connection," how the staff at Miami-Dade Community College were able to transform their institution from one suffering from lack of direction, low expectations for students, and unstable financing to one that was identified last year as the best community college in the country. The selection panel was asked to identify community colleges that

1. Were recognized nationally for their ability to maximize student success (and document it);

2. Were able to develop and pursue policies and standards that combine open-door admissions with an emphasis on quality in academic programs;

3. Enjoyed strong and dedicated leadership; and

4. Selected, evaluated, rewarded, and developed exceptional teachers in all aspects of the comprehensive mission of the community college.

Miami-Dade invested considerable energy and time in mission analysis, in sustaining a healthy dialogue to ensure that the college mission was updated and understood both internally and externally. Implicit in mission analysis is the often misunderstood issue of college marketing. Marketing should not be equated with "the search for ADA," nor should it be thought of as just the job of the public information office. Marketing Palomar College is everybody's job.

One of the many good lessons pointed out in Peters and Waterman's book, *In Search of Excellence,* is that companies that are the most successful and that make the most money are not those with the stated goal of making money, but those which emphasize service to customers or quality of product. Lee Noel, formerly with AC, now with Selection Research Incorporated, states that student retention should not be a goal of an institution, but rather a by-product of effective teaching and effective student services. In line with these observations, we need to keep in mind that ADA is not the goal of Palomar College, but a by-product of effective teaching, effective student services, effective support, effective administration, and effective marketing.

> **Never in recent** memory have colleges had a greater opportunity to reach for excellence.

Effective marketing involves strategic planning. A principal task of marketing is not so much to be skillful in making the organization do what suits the interest of the customer. A first step in strategic marketing is to gather data, to identify our target populations, to do accurate environmental and needs assessment. For example, let's suppose that one of our identified target populations is recent high school graduates in our service area. It would be helpful, then, to have data showing future projections of numbers of high school graduates and past trends in the percentage of recent graduates who chose Palomar College. Why did they choose Palomar? Why did some select other institutions over Palomar? What are their goals—transfer education, vocational education? What are their needs—help in determining goals, remedial services, counseling services, tutorial services, transportation, financial aid?

Recent high school graduates represent but one of the target populations we need to identify. The demographic makeup of our area is changing, and we need to be prepared to meet the educational needs of our community.

The second step in strategic marketing is to review the goals and needs of the target populations along with the institutional mission, goals, and values. Is there a match? Are the needs of the target population compatible with our central mission—student learning? Can we modify programs and services and shift resources to meet the needs of our clientele? Can we maintain a healthy balance in the curricula and services we provide?

Students are
pretty important people
on this campus.

The next step in marketing is the presentation of our institution to the public. It is a statement of what we are. I noticed, in reviewing a report from a Palomar committee on strengthening transfer and vocational programs, that we already recognize the importance of the image that this advertising aspect of marketing creates.

Finally, the key to any marketing plan is the quality of the services and the product. If an institution cannot deliver quality, no amount of advertising can compensate. Moreover, we must be able to demonstrate that our programs are effective.

Every step of this marketing process requires the involvement of all segments of the college staff. We must find out together what the educational needs of our community are. Together, we must review our mission in light of these needs. Every one of us represents Palomar College, and each of us shapes the image that the public has of our institution. And every one of us is responsible for quality control.

Let us review, for a moment, the student as a customer. It's an appropriate analogy; we wouldn't be in business without them. Think of yourself as a customer. Why do we shop where we do? Why do you bank where you do? Why do you get your hair cut where you do? Why do you get your car fixed where you do? Is it just the price, or is quality important? Is an attractive environment important? Are

friendly people important? How do you feel when you have to deal with people who don't care about you as a customer, or who don't care about their jobs, or who don't appear confident in what they are doing?

The message here is obvious. Students are pretty important people on this campus. We are here because they have chosen to come to Palomar College to learn. They should not be treated as intrusions in our job; they are our job.

A college campus can be a pretty intimidating place for some students. We need to show them we care about them, that we are glad to have them here, and that we will help them succeed. The responsibility for creating an environment which attracts and retains students is one we all share. It is every employee's job to care for students. That includes secretaries, custodians, faculty members, administrators, counselors, etc. If you can't answer their questions, find out who can and direct them or take them to the people who can help them. Be pleasant, even if you have heard the same question 100 times.

Students, of course, are more than just passive customers. They must be active participants in the institution. And, in the final analysis, they are the people who are most responsible for learning and for their own goal attainment. The NIE study, *Involvement in Learning*, reports that the more intensely students engage in their own education, the greater will be their growth, their satisfaction with their educational experiences, and their persistence in college. That involvement, then, must be encouraged.

Tomorrow morning, those of you who are teachers will face a new group of students. The beginning of a term was always the most exciting for me as a teacher because I always had new ideas that I wanted to try out and high hopes for a good experience for both me and my students. The promise of the new term being better than the last was always there.

What are the conditions for excellence in the classroom? Research findings reveal no surprises here: Teachers must care about their students, care about their subjects, be able to show the relevancy of their subjects, communicate high expectations, and care about good teaching. Caring is more than just rhetoric. If you care, your behavior reflects it. Ray Dahlin told me last week that he tells his students on the first day that "this is going to be one of the best classes they will take in college." I hope you all feel that way about your subjects and that you do communicate it to your students, and further, that you continue to communicate it in the things you do.

Research studies reveal that the single most important predictor of student success in the classroom is the expectation of the teacher. Communicate your high expectations to students clearly. Expect quality work. Demand it. Support it. Reward it.

The Association of American Colleges, in *Integrity in the College Curriculum*, tells us we need to focus less on content and knowledge in our courses and more on how knowledge is created and methods and styles of inquiry that lead to creation of knowledge. Tests should measure the higher levels of cognitive skills and not simple recall of information. Writing should be required in every course. Requiring students to be literate is not just the responsibility of the English Department. Library assignments should be given to develop research skills.

Teacher behaviors communicate powerful messages about expectations to students. Starting class late or dismissing class early communicates that class time is not valuable. On the other hand, requiring regular attendance communicates that important information is presented and discussed in class. Assigning reading from the textbook and testing from those assignments communicates that reading the textbook is important for understanding your subject. Providing frequent and timely feedback communicates that the instructor cares about student learning. Referring students who need help in basic skills to tutors or remedial classes communicates that basic skills competencies are important for success in your class. Using student names in class communicates that the teacher knows students well enough to know how much work they are doing in class.

Judith Eaton, president of the Community Colleges of Philadelphia and past chairperson of the board of directors of the American Association of Community and Junior Colleges, says, "Every faculty member and every administrator is a role model for every student. Therefore, we have a commitment in the classroom not only to reflect competency in an individual field, but to reflect high standards of academic education and technological sophistication. It is important to be articulate; it is important to be analytical; it is important to be aware—no matter your instructional area, your background, your discipline, your program."

The Center for Improvement of Teaching and Learning for the City Colleges of Chicago last year published a research report titled, *Attendance and Achievement*, which described strategies for student success that might be good to review with your students. There are no surprises. Successful students are highly involved in class; they pay attention, ask questions, contribute to discussion, and take notes. Outside of class, they study in quiet environments, avoid distractions, and take advantage of college resources to assist them in their studies. The Chicago study found a direct correlation between student attendance in class and final course grade. Attendance at the beginning of the semester was most critical.

Is it possible to have high expectations of students and to care about them at the same time? I have to reflect and tell you about one of my most demanding high school teachers. I suppose we all have favorite teacher stories, and this is one of mine. She taught junior and senior English, and she was serious about it. Despite her reputation for holding to high standards in her courses, students nicknamed her "mamma Lynch" (although no one had the boldness to address her with that title). The fact that she cared about her students was obvious. I still remember her asking whether I had a date for the prom (I was a typical shy teenager). When I indicated that I hadn't, she reminded me

that Mary Golden didn't have one either and how much it would mean for her to be able to go. I remember Mrs. Lynch asking whether I'd heard yet about college acceptance, and I remember her going with me to help me get a part-time job to earn money for college.

Caring doesn't mean you have to find dates for your students, but caring is what you do to convey to people that they are important and that it's important to you that they succeed in your class and at Palomar College.

Teacher
behaviors
communicate powerful messages about expectations to students.

Caring also means doing some mundane, unexciting kinds of things like turning in roll sheets on time to be sure students are properly registered for your class, turning grade sheets in on time to be sure students receive grades and transcripts when they need them, following final examination schedules so that student examinations are scheduled properly, and attending graduation ceremonies to recognize student achievement.

Caring should not stop with students. Palomar College is a people place. We need to care about one another and let each other know we care. We need to value what each of us does. We need to be available to one another. We need to communicate across departmental and segmental lines. We need to give a high priority to staff development and growth. We need to share successful practices. We need to recognize each other's accomplishments. We all need to be involved in the success of our college.

In an *Innovation Abstracts* article called "Sandboxes and Honeybees" published last September, Roland Barth pointed out some striking similarities in how nursery school children play and how college professionals often behave. "Two three-year-olds are busily engaged in opposite corners of a sandbox. One has a shovel and a bucket; one has a rake and a hoe. At no time do they borrow each other's toys. Although in close proximity, having much to offer one another, each works and plays pretty much in isolation. College professors, staff, and administrators, likewise, often seem to be groups of isolated individuals connected only by common heating systems and parking lots."

I hope we realize how interdependent we are, that the Chemistry Department can't be excellent if the Mathematics Department isn't, that quality in student services is as important as quality in instruction, that vocational education is as important to our mission as transfer education, and that none of us would be able to function well without the support of an effective classified staff and the leadership provided by a competent administration.

In closing, I want to let you know that the door to my office is open to you—and I should tell you it's located in a new place, the symbolic center of any learning on many campus, the library building. I hope you will feel free to come by, and I hope you can invite me to visit your areas and show me the programs I know you are proud of.

References

Association of American Colleges. (1985). *Integrity in the College Curriculum: A Report to the Academic Community.* The Findings and Recommendations of the Project on Redefining the Meaning and Purpose of Baccalaureate Degrees. Washington, DC: Author. ED251059.

Berte, N., et al. (1985). *Opportunity for Excellence: The Lessons Learned by Five Colleges.* Ford Foundation Conference on the Future of the Undergraduate College. Bradford, MA. ED260647.

Peters, T., and Waterman, R. H. Jr. (1982). *In Search of Excellence: Lessons From America's Best-Run Companies.* New York: Harper & Row.

Rouche, J. E., and Baker, G. H. (1985 Aug/Sept). The Success Connection: Creating a Culture of Excellence. *Community and Junior College Journal 56*(1): 20-26.

Study Group on the Conditions of Excellence in American Higher Education. (1984). *Involvement in Learning: Realizing the Potential of American Higher Education.* Final Report. National Institute of Education: Washington, DC.

Weiler, D., et al. (1985). *A Study of California's Community Colleges.* Prepared for the California Roundtable, San Francisco.

An American Imperative: Higher Expectations for Higher Education

— Wingspread Group on Higher Education

Wingspread Group on Higher Education. (1993). *An American Imperative: Higher Expectations for Higher Education*. Racine, WI: The Johnson Foundation.

Chairman's Preface

The world our children inhabit is different, radically so, than the one we inherited. An increasingly open, global economy requires—absolutely requires—that all of us be better educated, more skilled, more adaptable, and more capable of working collaboratively. These economic considerations alone mean that we must change the ways we teach and learn.

But an increasingly diverse society, battered (and that is not too strong a term) by accelerating change, requires more than workplace competence. It also requires that we do a better job of passing on to the next generation a sense of the value of diversity and the critical importance of honesty, decency, integrity, compassion, and personal responsibility in a democratic society. Above all, we must get across the idea that the individual flourishes best in a genuine community to which the individual in turn has an obligation to contribute.

None of us is doing as well as we should in this whole business. We are all part of the problem, if only because we acquiesce in a formal education system that is not meeting our needs.

We must not forget that no nation can remain great without developing a truly well-educated people. No nation can remain good without transmitting the fundamental values of a civil society to each new generation. No nation can remain strong unless it puts its young people at the forefront of its concerns. America is falling short on each of these counts. It has much to do.

Believing these things, I was very pleased when in January 1993 the president of The Johnson Foundation suggested that I chair a working group sponsored by four leading private foundations—The William and Flora Hewlett Foundation, The Johnson Foundation, Inc., Lilly Endowment, Inc., and The Pew Charitable Trusts—to examine the question: "What Does Society Need from Higher Education?"

The foundations assembled a working group of talented and experienced men and women (Appendix C) and provided us with a remarkable collection of essays written for our use by 32 individuals representing diverse social, professional, and economic perspectives. Indeed, we found the essays so helpful that we have appended them to this report for the benefit of others (Appendix D).* The Johnson Foundation made the magnificent setting of its Wingspread facilities and, more importantly, the talents of its staff available to us. We were encouraged to define our own agenda and to begin our work.

Some of what we have to say in the attached open letter will not be easy reading for our friends and colleagues in higher education. We understand that; some of it was not easy writing, either. We have, however, tried to avoid finding fault and pointing fingers. Our comments should be understood as an effort by close and affectionate friends to express concern and to offer suggestions to colleagues whose labors we respect and badly need.

An additional point: there is no single silver bullet cure. Much as it would simplify our national task, no single act will transform the incredibly diverse world of higher education into an enterprise routinely producing graduates with all of the qualities, competences, and attitudes we would hope for them.

An additional point: there is no single silver bullet cure.

Rather, our suggestions and our questions will require of each institution—campus by campus—honest introspection and some very hard and even controversial new thinking about its roles and responsibilities, principles, and priorities.

I want to express our gratitude to all those who have assisted our work in so many thoughtful and gracious ways, beginning with the four sponsoring foundations. I should note that their support and the assistance of others (including the scores of individuals from education, business, public life, and philanthropy who offered helpful comments on a preliminary draft of this document) does not imply that any of them subscribe to the conclusions we have reached or the challenges we advance.

Finally, I think it only fair to point out that although every member of our group supports the major themes of our open letter, none of us necessarily subscribes to every detail. That should be little surprise. The Wingspread Group was composed of 16 accomplished, thoughtful individuals, all with strongly held views. On the big questions—the conviction that American education faces serious problems, the belief that we need to develop new ways of thinking about higher education, and the conclusions and challenges in this document—we are unanimous.

We hope this open letter to those of our fellow Americans who share our concern for the future will stimulate the national debate about higher education that we consider essential.

William E. Brock
Chairman

---

* Editors' note: Space limitations restrict inclusion of all appendices in this volume; however, a full copy of the original publication, including all appendices, is available at www.eric.ed.gov as ED364144.

An American Imperative: Higher Expectations for Higher Education

"Everything has changed but our ways of thinking, and if these do not change we drift toward unparalleled catastrophe." **Albert Einstein**

A disturbing and dangerous mismatch exists between what American society needs of higher education and what it is receiving. Nowhere is the mismatch more dangerous than in the quality of undergraduate preparation provided on many campuses. The American imperative for the 21st century is that society must hold higher education to much higher expectations or risk national decline.

Establishing higher expectations, however, will require that students and parents rethink what too many seem to want from education: the credential without the content, the degree without the knowledge and effort it implies.

In the past, our industrial economy produced many new and low-skill jobs and provided stable employment, often at high wages, for all. Now the nation faces an entirely different economic scenario: a knowledge-based economy with a shortage of highly skilled workers at all levels and a surplus of unskilled applicants scrambling to earn a precarious living. Many of those unskilled applicants are college graduates, not high school dropouts.

Like much of the rest of American education, the nation's colleges and universities appear to live by an unconscious educational rule of thumb that their function is to weed out, not to cultivate, students for whom they have accepted responsibility. An unacceptably high percentage of students leaks out of the system at each juncture in the education pipeline. This hemorrhaging of our human resources occurs despite the low standards prevalent in American education and the existence of a wide diversity of institutions offering many options for students. It is almost as though educators take failure for granted.

Education is in trouble, and with it our nation's hopes for the future. America's ability to compete in a global economy is threatened. The American people's hopes for a civil, humane society ride on the outcome. The capacity of the United States to shoulder its responsibilities on the world stage is at risk. We understand the explanations offered when criticisms are leveled at higher education: entrants are inadequately prepared; institutional missions vary; we are required by law to accept all high school graduates; students change their minds frequently and drop out of school; controlling costs is difficult in the labor-intensive academy; cutting-edge research consumes the time of senior faculty. All of these things are true.

But the larger truth is that the explanations, no matter how persuasive they once were, no longer add up to a compelling whole. The simple fact is that some faculties and institutions certify for graduation too many students who cannot read and write very well, too many whose intellectual depth and breadth are unimpressive, and too many whose skills are inadequate in the face of the demands of contemporary life.

These conclusions point to the possibilities for institutional decline given that an increasingly skeptical public expresses the same sense of sticker shock about college costs that is now driving health care reform. The withdrawal of public support for higher education can only accelerate as students, parents, and taxpayers come to understand that they paid for an expensive education without receiving fair value in return.

The seeds for national disaster are also there: the needs of an information- and technology-based global economy, the complexities of modern life, the accelerated pace of change and the growing demands for competent, high-skill performance in the workplace require that we produce much higher numbers of individuals—whether high school, community college or four-year graduates—prepared to learn their way through life. Most Americans and their policymakers, concerned about the quality of pre-collegiate education, take heart in the large numbers of Americans who receive associate's and bachelor's degrees every year. The harsh truth is that a significant minority of these graduates enter or reenter the world with little more than the knowledge, competence, and skill we would have expected in a high school graduate scarcely a generation ago.

What does our society NEED from higher education? It needs stronger, more vital forms of community. It needs an informed and involved citizenry. It needs graduates able to assume leadership roles in American life. It needs a competent and adaptable workforce. It needs very high quality undergraduate education producing graduates who can sustain each of these goals. It needs more first-rate research pushing back the important boundaries of human knowledge and less research designed to lengthen academic résumés. It needs an affordable, cost-effective educational enterprise offering lifelong learning. Above all, it needs a commitment to the American promise—the idea that all Americans have the opportunity to develop their talents to the fullest. Higher education is not meeting these imperatives.

A Changing America and a Changing World

American society has never been static, but now change is accelerating. The United States is becoming more diverse: by the year 2020, about one-third of Americans will be members of minority groups, traditionally poorly served by education at all levels. New information and technologies are accelerating change: with a half life of less than five years, they are reshaping the way the world lives, works, and plays. Our society is aging: in 1933, 17 Americans were employed for every Social Security recipient; by 2020, the ratio will have dropped from 17-to-1 to 3-to-1. In 1950, the Ford Motor Company employed 62 active workers for every retiree; by 1993, the ratio dropped to 1.2-to-1. These statistics are a stark reminder of our need to assure that American workers are educated to levels that maximize their productivity and, hence, our collective economic well-being.

A generation ago, Americans were confident that the core values which had served our nation well in the past could guide it into the future. These values were expressed in homey statements such as: "Honesty is the best policy"; "Serve your country"; "Be a good neighbor." Today we worry that the core values may be shifting and that the sentiments expressed are different: "Don't get involved"; "I gave at the office"; "It's cheating only if you get caught." Too many of us today worry about "me" at the expense of "we."

A generation ago, our society and its institutions were overseen by white males. Immigration policy favored peoples from Northern Europe. The television images of Ozzie and Harriet were thought to reflect the middle-class American family. Almost all of that has changed as women and members of minority groups increasingly have assumed their place at the table, and immigrants and refugees from once-distant lands have remade the face of the United States.

A generation ago, computers took up entire rooms; punch cards for data processing were the cutting edge of technology; operators stood by to help with transatlantic calls; many families watched the clock each afternoon until local television stations began their evening broadcasts. Today, microprocessors, miniaturization, and fiber optics have made information from the four corners of the world instantaneously available to anyone with a computer, transforming the way we manage our institutions, the way we entertain ourselves, and the way we do our business.

A generation ago, our society was affluent, richer than it had ever been, with the prospect that its wealth would be more widely and deeply shared than ever before. The American economy—our assembly lines, our banks and farms, our workers and managers—dominated the global economy. Ours was the only major economy to emerge intact from World War II. Trade barriers limited global competition. Our industrial plant and national infrastructure were the envy of the world. As a people, we believed we could afford practically anything, and we undertook practically everything.

Those days are behind us. Global competition is transforming the economic landscape. Fierce competitors from abroad have entered domestic markets, and one great American industry after another has felt the effects. We have watched with growing concern as our great national strengths have been challenged, as the gap between rich and poor has widened, and as the nation's economic energy has been sapped by budget and trade deficits. We have struggled—so far unsuccessfully—to set the country back on the confident, spirited course we took for granted a generation ago.

We can regain that course only if Americans work smarter. Otherwise, our standard of living will continue the enervating erosion that began two decades ago. Individual economic security in the future will depend not on job or career stability, but on employability, which itself will be a function of adaptability and the willingness to learn, grow, and change throughout a lifetime.

Americans may be aware of all of this, but we are prisoners of our past. Our thinking and many of our institutions, including our educational institutions, are still organized as though none of these changes had occurred.

The 3,400 institutions of higher learning in America come in all shapes and sizes, public and private. They include small liberal arts institutions, two-year community colleges, and technical institutions, state colleges and universities, and flagship research universities. In each of these categories, models of both excellence and mediocrity exist. Despite this diversity, most operate as though their focus were still the traditional student of days gone by: a white, male, recent high school graduate, who attended classes full-time at a four-year institution and lived on campus. Yesterday's traditional student is, in fact, today's exception.

There are more women than men among the 13.5 million students on today's campuses. Forty-three percent of today's students are over the age of 25, including 300,000 over the age of 50. Minority Americans now make up about 20 percent of enrollments in higher education. Almost as many students attend part-time and intermittently as attend full-time and without interruption. More college students are enrolled in community colleges than in four-year institutions. And there are more students living at home or off-campus than there are in dormitories. Fixed in our mind's eye, however, the image of the traditional student blocks effective responses to these new realities.

These demographic, economic, and technological changes underscore the mismatch between what is needed of higher education and what it provides. Because we are now a more diverse people, society needs a much better sense of the things that unite us. Because the global economy has had such a profound effect on American standards of living, individuals in our society and the economy as a whole need to be much better prepared for the world of work.

Institutions, like organisms,

must respond to changes in their environment if they are to survive.

In short, we need to educate more people, educate them to far higher standards, and do it as effectively and efficiently as possible.

Warning Signs

Institutions, like organisms, must respond to changes in their environment if they are to survive. Not surprisingly, given higher education's slow adaptation, real problems shadow the real successes of the nation's colleges and universities.

Crisis of Values. The nation's colleges and universities are enmeshed in, and in some ways contributing to, society's larger crisis of values. Intolerance on campus is on the rise; half of big-time college sports programs have been caught cheating in the last decade; reports of ethical lapses by administrators, faculty members and trustees, and of cheating and plagiarism by students are given widespread credence.

From the founding of the first American colleges 300 years ago, higher education viewed the development of student character and the transmission of the values supporting that character as an essential responsibility of faculty and administration. The importance of higher education's role in the transmission of values is, if anything, even greater today than it was 300 or even 50 years ago. The weakening of the role of family and religious institutions in the lives of young people, the increase in the number of people seeking the benefits of higher education, and what appears to be the larger erosion of core values in our society make this traditional role all the more important.

In this context, it is fair to ask how well our educational institutions are transmitting an understanding of good and bad, right and wrong, and the compelling core of values any society needs to sustain itself. While there is a paucity of concrete data, enough anecdotal evidence exists to suggest that there is too little concerted attention, on too many campuses, to this responsibility.

In the final analysis, a society is not simply something in which we find ourselves. Society is "we." It is our individual and collective integrity, our commitment to each other and to the dignity of all. All of the other accomplishments of higher education will be degraded if our colleges and universities lose their moral compass and moral vocation.

The Costs of Weeding. Few thoughtful observers believe that our K-12 schools are adequate for today's needs. About half our high school students are enrolled in dead-end curricula that prepare them poorly for work, life, or additional learning. Too many of the rest are bored and unchallenged. Too few are performing to standards that make them competitive with peers in other industrialized countries. Half of those entering college full-time do not have a degree within five years. Half of all students entering Ph.D. programs never obtain the degree. In short, our education system is better organized to discourage students—to weed them out—than it is to cultivate and support our most important national resource, our people.

The Uneducated Graduate. The failure to cultivate our students is evident in a 1992 analysis of college transcripts by the U.S. Department of Education, which reveals that 26.2 percent of recent bachelor's degree recipients earned not a single undergraduate credit in history; 30.8 percent did not study mathematics of any kind; 39.6 percent earned no credits in either English or American literature; and 58.4 percent left college without any exposure to a foreign language. Much too frequently, American higher education now offers a smorgasbord of fanciful courses in a fragmented curriculum that accords as much credit for "Introduction to Tennis" and for courses in pop culture as it does for "Principles of English Composition," history, or physics, thereby trivializing education—indeed, misleading students by implying that they are receiving the education they need for life when they are not.

The original purpose of an undergraduate education, the development of a broadly educated human being, prepared, in the words of Englishman John Henry Cardinal Newman, "to fill any post with credit", has been pushed to the periphery. That purpose, restated, was the essential message of a commission convened by President Harry S Truman 45 years ago. According to the Truman Commission, higher education should help students acquire the knowledge, skills, and attitudes to enable them "to live rightly and well in a free society." The 1992 transcript analysis cited above suggests that educators need to ask themselves how well their current graduates measure up to the standards of Newman and the Truman Commission, and to the needs of American society for thoughtful citizens, workers, and potential leaders.

For without a broad liberal education, students are denied the opportunity to engage with the principal ideas and events that are the source of any civilization. How then are they to understand the values that sustain community and society, much less their own values? Educators know better, but stand silent.

There is further disturbing evidence that graduates are unprepared for the requirements of daily life. According to the 1993 National Adult Literacy Survey (NALS), surprisingly large numbers of two- and four-year college graduates are unable, in everyday situations, to use basic skills involving reading, writing, computation, and elementary problem-solving.*

The NALS tasks required participants to do three things: read and interpret prose, such as newspaper articles, work with documents like bus schedules and tables and charts, and use elementary arithmetic to solve problems involving, for example, the costs of restaurant meals or mortgages. The NALS findings were presented on a scale from low (Level 1) to high (Level 5) in each of the three areas. The performance of college graduates on these scales is distressing:

- in working with documents, only eight percent of all four-year college graduates reach the highest level;

- in terms of their ability to work with prose, only 10 percent of four-year graduates are found in Level 5; and

- with respect to quantitative skills, only 12 percent of four-year graduates reach the highest level.

In fact, only about one-half of four-year graduates are able to demonstrate intermediate levels of competence in each of the three areas. In the area of quantitative skills, for example, 56.3 percent of American-born, four-year college graduates are unable CONSISTENTLY to perform simple tasks, such as calculating the change from $3.00 after buying a 60 cent bowl of soup and a $1.95 sandwich. Tasks such as these should not be insuperable for people with 16 years of education.

Growing Public Concern. Opinion polls leave no doubt that Americans have a profound respect for higher education. They consider it essential to the nation's civility and economic progress, and to advances in science, technology, and medicine. Americans are convinced that an undergraduate degree is as important to success in today's world as a high school diploma was in yesterday's.

But, simultaneously, the polls reveal deep public concern about higher education. The public is overwhelmed by sticker shock when it considers college costs. According to the polls, the overwhelming majority of the American people believes that colleges and universities—both public and private—are overpriced and lie increasingly beyond the reach of all but the wealthy. Public confidence in the "people running higher education" has declined as dramatically with respect to education leaders as it has with respect to the leadership of medicine, government, and business.

---

* Results of the NALS survey, conducted by the Educational Testing Service for the U.S. Department of Education, were released in September 1993. The largest effort of its type ever attempted, the survey offers a comprehensive analysis of the competence of American adults (both college- and non-college-educated) based on face-to-face interviews with 26,000 people. We note with concern that the 1993 survey findings reflect a statistically significant decline from those of an earlier survey conducted in 1985.

While the public is most interested in achievement, costs, and management, it believes that the academy focuses instead on advanced study and research. Several of the essays written for our study echo a number of the conclusions of the 1992 report of the President's Advisory Council on Science and Technology. Both remind us that the academic culture and rewards system too frequently encourages graduate education and research at the expense of undergraduate education. What emerges is a picture of academic life which only grudgingly attends to undergraduate learning, and to the advice, counseling, and other support services students need. The dominant academic attitude, particularly on large campuses enrolling most American students, is that research deserves pride of place over teaching and public service, in part because many senior faculty prefer specialized research to teaching, and in part because institutions derive much of their prestige from faculty research. Indeed, the ideal model in the minds of faculty members on campuses of all kinds is defined by what they perceive to be the culture and aspirations of flagship research universities.

Three Central Issues

It is hard not to conclude that too much undergraduate education is little more than secondary school material—warmed over and reoffered at much higher expense, but not at correspondingly higher levels of effectiveness. The United States can no longer afford the inefficiencies, or the waste of talent, time, and money, revealed by these warning signs. Indeed, the nation that responds best and most rapidly to the educational demands of the Age of the Learner will enjoy a commanding international advantage in the pursuit of both domestic tranquility and economic prosperity. To achieve these goals for our country, we must educate more people, and educate them far better. That will require new ways of thinking.

Given the diversity of American higher education, there can be no single formula for change common to all, but we do believe that there are at least three fundamental issues common to all 3,400 colleges and universities:

- taking values seriously;
- putting student learning first;
- creating a nation of learners.

The nation's colleges and universities can respond to the agenda defined in this open letter. They can do so by reaffirming their conviction that the moral purpose of knowledge is at least as important as its utility. They can do so by placing student learning at the heart of their concerns. They can do so by working toward what educator John Goodlad has called "a simultaneous renewal" of higher education and the nation's K-12 schools as one continuous learning system.

To focus what we hope will be a vigorous, widespread national debate, we have distilled the results of six-months' work and discussion into a compact document designed to make our line of reasoning as clear as possible. Our purpose is not so much to provide answers. Rather, we hope to raise some of the right questions and thus encourage Americans and their colleges and universities

to consider and adopt a new direction. That is why we close this document not with a set of recommendations, but with a set of challenges for American higher education, for the public, and for its representatives.

We begin our discussion in the pages that follow with an argument for putting first things first: the need for a rigorous liberal education that takes values seriously and acknowledges that value-free education has proven a costly blind alley for society.

Taking Values Seriously

"The Holocaust reminds us forever that knowledge divorced from values can only serve to deepen the human nightmare; that a head without a heart is not humanity."
President Bill Clinton

Democratic societies need a common ground, a shared frame of reference within which to encourage both diversity and constructive debate about the common good. A free people cannot enjoy the fruits of its liberty without collaborative efforts in behalf of community. Higher education has a central obligation to develop these abilities.

There are some values, rooted in national experience, even defined in the Constitution, that Americans share. These "constitutional" values have evolved into a set of civic virtues:

- respect for the individual and commitment to equal opportunity;
- the belief that our common interests exceed our individual differences;
- concern for those who come after us;
- support for the freedoms enunciated in the Bill of Rights, including freedom of religion, of the press, of speech, and of the right to assemble;
- the belief that individual rights and privileges are to be exercised responsibly;
- respect for the views of others; and
- the conviction that no one is above the law.

If values are to be taken seriously, the place to start is by reaffirming the primacy of the visions of Newman and the Truman Commission: liberal education is central to living "rightly and well in a free society." We do not believe that a history major needs to know as much chemistry as a forest management major, that an engineering major needs to know as much literature as an English major. But every student needs the knowledge and understanding that can come only from the rigors of a liberal education. Such an education lies at the heart of developing both social and personal values. If the center of American society is to hold, a liberal education must be central to the undergraduate experience of all students. The essentials of a liberal education should be contained in a rigorous, required curriculum defined on each campus.

We believe, too, that every institution of higher education should ask itself—NOW—what it proposes to do to assure that next year's entering students will graduate as individuals of character more sensitive to the needs of community, more competent in their ability to contribute to society, and more civil in their habits of thought, speech, and action.

We are also convinced that each educational institution must, openly and directly, begin the kinds of discussions that promise to build campus consensus on the civic virtues it most treasures. The questions concluding this section, and repeated in Appendix A, define some of the issues that need to be addressed.

What do these issues mean in practice? Several implications appear obvious: campuses must model the values they espouse; they must help students experience society and reflect on it as an integral part of their education; they must act on their understanding that matters of the spirit reflect such a profound aspect of the human condition that they cannot be ignored on any campus.

With respect to modeling values, a former president of Yale University, A. Bartlett Giamatti, once said: "[A]n educational institution teaches far, far more, and more profoundly, by how it acts than by anything anyone within it ever says." Mr. Giamatti was echoed by one of our essayists, Robert Rosenzweig, who wrote, "American society needs colleges and universities to be active exemplars of the values they have always professed...." In both statements, the critical emphasis is on ACTING and EXEMPLIFYING, not simply proclaiming. On campus, as elsewhere, the dictum "Do as I say, not as I do" is an invitation to cynicism among our citizens, particularly students.

We want also to stress that society's needs will be well served if colleges and universities wholeheartedly commit themselves to providing students with opportunities to experience and reflect on the world beyond the campus. Books and lectures provide an intellectual grounding in the realities of the marketplace and of the nation's social dilemmas. But there is no substitute for experience. Academic work should be complemented by the kinds of knowledge derived from first-hand experience, such as contributing to the well-being of others, participating in political campaigns, and working with the enterprises that create wealth in our society.

Last but not least, we want to suggest that matters of the spirit have a far more important role to play in institutions of higher education than has been encouraged in recent years. We do not argue for one system of belief or another, one denomination or another, or for compulsory religious observance of any kind. Certainly we understand that campuses must be dedicated to free inquiry, ungoverned by either faddish orthodoxy or intolerant ideology. But we do argue that faith and deep moral conviction matter in human affairs. Because they do, they must matter on campus.

We believe that the concept of a value-free education is a profoundly misleading contradiction in terms, a blind alley with very high costs to personal life, community, and even workplace. A campus community whose members cannot readily give answers to the following questions* is a campus without a purpose:

- What kind of people do we want our children and grandchildren to be?

- What kind of society do we want them to live in?

- How can we best shape our institution to nurture those kinds of people and that kind of society?

Initiating and sustaining discussions and initiatives of the sort suggested above will be difficult on large campuses, but not impossible. Organizing and sustaining community service programs for large numbers of students both inside and outside the classroom is difficult, but not impossible. Encouraging collaborative learning is perhaps more difficult than grading on the curve, but it is not impossible. Yet activities such as these both model and teach the skills of community.

The questions raised in the realm of values may, on occasion, be deeply troubling. In our view that is all to the good. If the journey is too comfortable, the right questions are probably not being asked, and asking the right questions is essential if higher education is to rise to Pericles' standards:

> Pericles knew that any successful society must be an educational institution. However great its commitment to individual freedom and diversity, it needs a code of civic virtue and a general devotion to the common enterprise without which it cannot flourish or survive.

> It must transmit its understanding of good and bad and a sense of pride, admiration, and love for its institutions and values to its citizens, especially the young. ‡

It is fashionable to decry the quality of American leadership, public and private. Yet virtually all our leadership emerges from one institution of higher education or another.

As students are groomed on campus, so shall they live and lead. Pericles understood. Do we?

Taking Values Seriously

- How does our educational program match the claims of our recruiting brochures, and where is it falling short?

- How does our core curriculum of required courses respond to the needs of our students for a rigorous liberal education enabling them to "live rightly and well in a free society"? Where does it fall short?

- In what ways does our institution model the values and skills expected in our community? Where and how are we falling short?

- What steps might we take to improve the general climate of civility on our campus?

- How comprehensive and effective is the code of professional conduct and ethics for our faculty and staff? When was it last reviewed?

---

* Questions taken from Howard Bowen, *The State of the Nation and the Agenda for Higher Education.* San Francisco: Jossey-Bass, 1982.

‡ Donald Ragan, *Pericles of Athens and the Birth of Democracy.* New York: Simon & Schuster, 1991.

- In what ways does our institution and its educational program promote the development of shared values, specifically the civic virtues listed below, among our students?
    o respect for the individual and commitment to equal opportunity in a diverse society;
    o the belief that our common interests exceed our individual differences;
    o support for the freedoms enunciated in the Bill of Rights, including freedom of religion, of the press, of speech, and of the right to assemble;
    o the belief that individual rights and privileges are accompanied by responsibilities to others;
    o respect for the views of others; and
    o the conviction that no one is above the law.
- What moral and ethical questions should we be putting to the student groups and organizations we sanction on campus? What standards of conduct do we expect of these groups? How have we made these standards clear?
- How do the activities of our athletic programs square with our institution's stated values, and where do they fall short?
- What steps will we take to assure that next year's entering students will graduate as individuals of character more sensitive to the needs of community, more competent to contribute to society, more civil in their habits of thought, speech, and action?
- What other related questions should we address at our institution?

Putting Student Learning First

"The future now belongs to societies that organize themselves for learning." **Ray Marshall and Marc Tucker**

If it is time to take values seriously on campus, it is also time to redress the imbalance that has led to the decline of undergraduate education. To do so, the nation's colleges and universities must for the foreseeable future focus overwhelmingly on what their students learn and achieve. Too much of education at every level seems to be organized for the convenience of educators and the institution's interests, procedures and prestige, and too little focused on the needs of students.

Putting students at the heart of the educational enterprise requires that we face a difficult truth: academic expectations and standards on many campuses are too low, and it shows. Institutions that start with learning will set higher expectations for all students, then do a much more effective job of helping them meet those expectations, points to which we return below.

Putting learning at the heart of the enterprise means campuses must:

- understand their mission clearly and define the kinds of students they can serve best;
- define exactly what their entering students need to succeed;
- start from where the students begin and help them achieve explicitly stated institutional standards for high achievement;
- tailor their programs—curriculum, schedules, support services, office hours—to meet the needs of the students they admit, not the convenience of staff and faculty;
- systematically apply the very best of what is known about learning and teaching on their campuses;
- rigorously assess what their students know and are able to do in order to improve both student and institutional performance; and
- develop and publish explicit exit standards for graduates, and grant degrees only to students who meet them.

Interestingly, steps such as these are among the recommendations recently advanced by some of this nation's most distinguished African-American leaders.* As they note, their recommendations for improving the learning environment for minorities will inevitably work to the advantage of all students, including disadvantaged MAJORITY learners. We were struck by how congruent their analysis and recommendations are to our own.

Putting learning at the heart of the academic enterprise will mean overhauling the conceptual, procedural, curricular, and other architecture of postsecondary education on most campuses. For some students this will mean greater independence. For others, the academic experience may change little outwardly; internally, it will be far more challenging and exciting. For many others—particularly those whose learning needs are being served poorly now—academic life will be more directive, more supportive, and more demanding. It will be more directive on the assumption that institutions are responsible for evaluating and responding to the learning needs of students. It will be more supportive because it will be focused on what students need in order to succeed. It will be far more demanding because it will be aimed at producing graduates who demonstrate much higher levels of knowledge and skills.

Skills. Traditionally, the acquisition of skills essential to life and work has been considered a by-product of study, not something requiring explicit attention on campus. We know of only a handful of the nation's colleges and universities that have developed curricular approaches similar to, for example, the list of critical skills developed by the Secretary of Labor's Commission on Achieving Necessary Skills (SCANS—see Appendix E). But skills such as these—written and oral communication, critical analysis, interpersonal competence, the ability to obtain and use data, the capacity to make informed judgments, and the skills

* John Hope Franklin, et al., *The Inclusive University: A New Environment for Higher Education*. Washington: Joint Center for Political and Economic Studies, 1993.

required in community life—are essential attributes of a liberal education when they are accompanied by discipline-based knowledge. These skills can be learned. If they are to be learned, however, they must be taught and practiced, not merely absorbed as a result of unplanned academic experience. We believe that the modern world requires both knowledge AND such skills and competences. Neither is adequate without the other.

Student Achievement. There is growing research evidence that all students can learn to much higher standards than we now require. When they do not, the flaw is most likely to be in the system, not the individual. We agree with those who make the important point that the truly outstanding educational institution graduates students who achieve more than would have been predicted on entry. (This is a standard, incidentally, that challenges even the most prestigious of our great universities and small liberal arts colleges, the institutions routinely enrolling the best secondary school graduates.)

There is a growing body of knowledge about learning and the implications of that knowledge for teaching. What is known, however, is rarely applied by individual teachers, much less in concert by entire faculties. We know that teaching is more than lecturing. We know that active engagement in learning is more productive than passive listening. We know that experiential learning can be even more so. We know we should evaluate institutional performance against student outcomes. We know all of this, but appear unable to act on it. It is time to explore the reasons for our failure to act.

No group has a greater stake in the new evidence relative to student achievement than socially and economically disadvantaged students, particularly disadvantaged minority Americans. At the elementary and secondary levels, the achievement gap separating minority and majority students is slowly closing. These results appear to reflect a combination of factors including minimum competency standards, ongoing assessment, and programs to provide the special support many of these young Americans need. These were vitally important steps, but we share the distress of many Americans, including educators, that they have not gone far enough: minimum competency is not enough. Many minority Americans are still being left behind by an education system that is not serving their needs.

We also know that support services work. From a host of small experiments it is clear that when students—particularly those less advantaged in life—know their institution is unambiguously committed to their success, performance rises dramatically. Yet too few campuses have done much more than offer perfunctory, often inconvenient, student-support services. Too few have created one-stop "success centers" where students can find assistance with the full range of their concerns when they most need help—which is frequently before 9 a.m. and after 5 p.m. In the most impressive of these centers, a student enters into a relationship with a single individual who becomes an advocate for the student, responsible for marshaling all of the institution's assets and focusing them on the student's success.

Assessment. Finally, our vision calls for new ways of thinking about assessing what students know and are able to do. In medicine, testing and assessment are used to define the best course for future action. They provide data for both doctor (the teacher) and patient (the student) as to what steps to take to improve the individual's health (learning). In contemporary colleges and universities, however, such use of assessment is rare.

Examinations in educational institutions (including elementary and secondary schools) normally establish competitive rankings and sort students. They rarely diagnose strengths and weaknesses, examine needs, or suggest what steps to take next. In almost no institution are a student's skills systematically assessed, developed, and then certified. This assessment issue transcends the needs of learners. In an institution focused on learning, assessment feedback becomes central to the institution's ability to improve its own performance, enhancing student learning in turn.

New forms of assessment should focus on establishing what college and university graduates have learned—the knowledge and skill levels they have achieved and their potential for further independent learning. Only a few scattered institutions have instituted exit assessments.

The sad fact is that campuses spend far more time and money establishing the credentials of applicants than they do assessing the knowledge, skills, and competences of their graduates.

Indeed, the entire system is skewed in favor of the input side of the learning equation: credit hours, library collections, percentage of faculty with terminal degrees, and the like. The output side of the equation—student achievement—requires much greater attention than it now receives. That attention should begin by establishing improved measures of student achievement, measures that are credible and valued by the friends and supporters of education, by testing and accrediting bodies, and by educational institutions themselves.

We understand that the changes we suggest will be difficult and demanding. We recognize that they will require new attitudes on the part of faculty and institutions and, most critically, new skills and ways of doing business. There will be costs associated with these changes—though relatively modest costs in the context of overall institutional budgets—notably for staff development and student support services. We believe it reasonable to suggest that campuses devote a greater percentage of revenues to these needs.

Finally, we want to stress that responsibility in a learning institution is a two-way street. Students, at any level of education, are the workers in the educational process. They have a major obligation for their own success. Too many students do not behave as though that were the case, apparently believing (as do many parents) that grades are more important for success in life than acquired knowledge, the ability to learn throughout a lifetime, and hard work on campus. Educational institutions, having accepted students and their tuition, have a positive obligation to help these students acquire the knowledge, skills, competences, and habits of intellectual self-discipline requisite to becoming productive citizens and employees. Students, parents, and community leaders will have to be willing to support the high expectations and hard work that superior student achievement will require.

Too many campuses have become co-conspirators in the game of "credentialism." Many campuses still do not offer the guidance and support all students require to reach the higher levels of achievement contemporary life requires. Too few are sufficiently engaged in effective collaboration with other learning institutions, notably K-12 schools, to assure that students arriving on campus are prepared intellectually and are received in ways which enhance their prospects for success. Institutions of higher education must reach out much more effectively to colleagues elsewhere to help create a nation of learners and reduce the barriers to their learning.

Putting Student Learning First

- How recently have we reviewed our program offerings to assure that they match our mission and the needs and goals of the students we admit?

- In what ways could we do a better job of helping our students to attain higher levels of both knowledge and skills?

- What steps should we take to establish or improve a rigorous curriculum requiring core knowledge and competences of our students?

- How have we tried to integrate curricular offerings for the benefit of students and faculty? Is "course sprawl" contributing to our budgetary problems and making it more difficult for students to register in courses required for graduation? What might be done?

- To what extent are our educational programs, class schedules, registration, and other administrative and support services organized around the needs of learners rather than the convenience of the institution? What improvements can we make?

- How do we encourage and assist students to develop the basic values required for learning, e.g., self-discipline, perseverance, responsibility, hard work, intellectual openness?

- In what ways are we assessing learning to diagnose needs and accomplishments? How could we improve feedback to students and faculty on student performance in order to enhance both teaching and learning?

- How does our institution assure that students have demonstrated a high level of achievement, consistent with our published standards for acquiring both knowledge and skills, as a basis for receiving our degrees or certificates? Can we raise our standards?

- In what ways are we applying what is known about learning to the teaching practices of our faculty and graduate students? How do our pedagogical approaches enhance learning, and where do they fall short?

- How do we support faculty initiatives to improve

learning and teaching? In particular, is our faculty well grounded in the available research concerning adult learning? If not, what will we do to improve our record?

- How could we do a better job of helping students learn at lower overall cost to our institution? How would we reinvest the savings?

- What other related questions should we address at our institution to improve the quality of learning?

Creating a Nation of Learners

"The fixed person for the fixed duties, who in older societies was a blessing, in the future will be a public danger." **Alfred North Whitehead**

We must redesign all of our learning systems to align our entire education enterprise with the personal, civic, and workplace needs of the 21st Century.

In the last generation, higher education has been swept up in the tide of social and economic change. The horizons and aspirations of women and members of minority groups have expanded. Older students have arrived on campus, many for the first time, seeking help to improve their skills, develop career prospects, and respond to new developments in technology. Family mobility is on the rise, and with it mobility from campus to campus. The modern workplace, open to global competition, requires levels of knowledge and skills beyond anything we have aspired to in the past, and well beyond what our schools and universities are now producing.

These changes demand that American education transform itself into a seamless system that can produce and support a nation of learners, providing access to educational services for learners as they need them, when they need them, and wherever they need them.

This is not an argument for merger or homogeneity. But colleges and universities need to understand that their business is ALL of education. They can no longer afford to concern themselves exclusively with HIGHER education. They must address themselves much more effectively to the other key pieces of the education enterprise. Americans and their educators are now handicapped by an education legacy from the past when what they need is a solution for the future. Our current educational institutions worked reasonably well in a society that had little need for large numbers of educated adults. Why question that structure when 90 percent of the population left school after 8th grade (the turn of the century); when only 50 percent of the population graduated from high school (1940); or even when only one-third of high school graduates enrolled in higher education (1950)? Now the need has changed. There can be no justification for such a system in today's world with its growing demand for better-educated people.

In this new environment many more educators must be prepared to say: "All of us, from pre-school to post-graduate, are in this together. It is not enough to complain about each other's failings. It is time to stop addressing the problem piecemeal. We must begin to work collaboratively on the system as a whole." It is no longer tolerable for so many in higher education to complain about the quality of those they admit, but do nothing to set higher standards and work with colleagues in K-12 schools to help students attain those standards. Our education system is in crisis; business-as-usual is a formula for national disaster.

Assessment and achievement are critical components of an enhanced education system. Experts today are thinking about the need for summary educational documents, not just grades, attendance records, and test scores, but data representing genuine learning achievements across a lifetime of educational and training experiences. The Educational Testing Service, the American College Testing program, and the American Council on Education are already piloting initiatives of this kind—Work Link, Work Keys, and the External Diploma Program respectively—which aim to revise quite radically how we think about and use assessment. These efforts deserve encouragement from everyone interested in improving the quality of learning, and in particular from the American business community. They will increasingly assure that learning, wherever it occurs, is valued and given credit; they will, in and of themselves, help to create a national culture encouraging lifelong formal and informal learning.

We are aware that a number of institutions work with local schools, and that some are very serious and effective in these efforts. But as one of our essayists put it, "the sum of it all adds up to considerably less than a response to an urgent need that is grounded in both self-interest and national interest."

We join others in calling for a simultaneous renewal of both higher education and the nation's K-12 schools. A serious, sustained dialogue should start by identifying shared needs and problems:

- a clear public definition of what students should know and be able to do at each educational level;

- standards of entry AND EXIT for higher education;

- increasing the use of assessment to diagnose learning needs and enhance student achievement;

- improving both the theory and practice of teaching and learning;

- recruiting and educating more effective teachers at all levels;

- bringing education's resources to bear on issues of character and its development;

- reducing the barriers to inter-institutional transfer among institutions of higher education; and

- exploring the implications for college admissions practices of the six National Education Goals established in 1989, and the potential for collaboration with K-12 schools.

The entire education establishment has a self-evident interest in this kind of collaborative dialogue and action. If a community college has developed an outstanding student support system, even the most prestigious research university should consider it as a benchmark. If a public school system has created a successful school-within-a-school to relieve the negative impact of size on students, public mega-universities should consider the possibility that they have something to learn from it. Any educational institution should want to practice existing, innovative, research-based approaches for applying to teaching what is known about learning. Where innovations in self-paced and distance learning are succeeding, any institution concerned about productivity and cost containment should examine them carefully as potential contributors to its own efficiency and effectiveness. Every campus has an interest in emulating those colleges and universities that have extended a collaborative hand to elementary and secondary education. Such collaboration can enhance course content and standards across the board, and raise the motivation and confidence of students who might otherwise not be considering postsecondary education.

Nor is the opportunity to learn from others restricted to the traditional world of education. Where a corporation has developed effective educational innovations, campuses should investigate the implications for their own work. Many museums are currently developing innovative and effective approaches to teaching and learning about science, history, and art. But all of these advances—and many others—are taking place independently of each other at a time when America needs a more collaborative, cost-effective and better-articulated way of responding to the lifelong learning needs of growing numbers of its citizens.

Creating a Nation of Learners

- In what ways have we organized our programs to develop and support a capacity for lifelong learning among our students?

- How might we provide the same level of service and support to "nontraditional" students, and students in nontraditional learning programs, as we do for traditional full-time students? Within our mission, when have we examined alternative, more flexible, and student-oriented ways to provide for student learning?

- How often do we survey employers of our recent graduates—and the graduates themselves—to discover how and under what circumstances graduates succeed or fall short? How can that process be improved?

- In what ways do we work with K-12 systems to enlarge our understanding of their difficulties, encourage teachers and administrators to see us as resources, and enlarge our own competences? In what ways have we relegated this effort to our school of education? How have we tried to involve the entire campus?

- How are we working with high schools and other educational institutions both to communicate to them the knowledge and skills that students will need to be successful in higher education and to help students meet those requirements?

- How do our departments provide graduate students and professors with training in how people learn and what that means for teaching? What needs to be done to make this institutionwide and to set institutionwide standards?

- How is our campus working with local schools and other colleges and universities to bring teaching and learning to state-of-the-art standards from kindergarten through the undergraduate years? What more can we do?

- How might we bring our teacher recruitment and teacher education programs into better alignment with the real needs of both society and students? What are our benchmarks?

- What provisions might a statewide compact contain if we wished to ease student transfer between institutions?

- In what ways are we organized to make use of educational achievements from nontraditional organizations and settings?

- What other related questions should we address in an effort to reduce the institutional barriers to learning and to make our institution more responsive to the needs of others, e.g., K-12 education, employers, and other institutions of higher education?

First Steps: Challenges for Higher Education

"For every right that you cherish, you have a duty which you must fulfill. For every hope that you entertain, you have a task that you must perform. For every good that you wish to preserve, you will have to sacrifice your comfort and your ease. There is nothing for nothing any longer." **Walter Lippmann**

Our wake-up call places a heavy burden on the shoulders of the men and women in higher education. It will require rethinking the assumptions of the education enterprise and reinventing many of its ways of doing business. Educators, particularly faculty members, must demonstrate that they have noted the warning signs, understand the potential for institutional and national decline, and are ready to act.

Solutions for the problems we have described will require vigorous, creative, and persistent leadership on campus, in the community, in state capitols, and in Washington. On the other hand, the problems of undergraduate education cannot effectively be addressed by bold strokes of state or national public policy. They can best be solved campus by campus with the active involvement of faculty, staff, students, trustees, and their friends and supporters off campus including, notably, state legislators. Hence, our solutions are cast not as recommendations for policymakers to impose from on high, but as challenges to be taken up on each of the nation's 3,400 campuses. Diversity and autonomy are among the great strengths of American higher education, as they are of American society itself. They are strengths to be respected and drawn upon as each institution decides for itself how it will respond.

As first steps in what will be a long journey, we issue five challenges.

For colleges and universities:

WE CHALLENGE you to evaluate yourselves against the questions in the attached "Self-Assessment Checklist," and to commit yourself publicly to an institutional plan that builds on the strengths and remedies the deficiencies you identify.

WE CHALLENGE you to define and publicly state your standards of entry and exit in terms of the knowledge, skills, and abilities you expect from both applicants and graduates, and to put in place measures to assure student and institutional attainment of those standards by a fixed date.

WE CHALLENGE you to develop a curriculum that will assure all graduates—our future citizens, employees, and leaders—the benefits of a liberal education.

WE CHALLENGE you to assure that next year's entering students will graduate as individuals of character more sensitive to the needs of community, more competent to contribute to society, and more civil in habits of thought, speech, and action.

For trustees, regents, legislators, alumni, and funders in particular:

WE CHALLENGE you to respond to institutions that take up the first four challenges by giving them the regulatory and financial flexibility they need to get the job done. Institutional creativity, not micro-management, is the essential precondition to change. But we do urge you to urge them on. One of the best ways to do so is to insist that the campuses for which you have stewardship responsibility undertake the attached self-assessment.

We understand that some institutions will believe it unnecessary to respond to the challenges above. Perhaps they are correct, although we suggest that even the best can be better. Institutions hesitant to undertake a comprehensive self-assessment might consider administering the National Adult Literacy Survey instrument to a representative sample of graduating seniors. By permitting comparison of institutional performance with a nationwide sample of graduates of either two- or four-year institutions, the NALS instrument can provide a minimally acceptable performance benchmark for any institution. No campus has anything to lose by turning to NALS, and it is difficult to imagine that most would not want to know where they stand. Some may be satisfied with the results, but many will be surprised.

Finally, we issue a challenge to the broader public, specifically to students, parents, employers, and citizens. This agenda for higher education is ambitious. It will not be accomplished easily or soon; nor can it bear fruit without your participation and support. All of us have contributed to the situation in which higher education today finds itself; we too must play our part in responding to the imperatives of the future. Every American must accept the fact that in an open, global economy, education is a critical national resource.

A generation ago, we told educators we wanted more people with a college credential and more research-based knowledge. Educators responded accordingly. Now we need to ask for different things. Students must value achievement, not simply seek a credential. Students (and parents) should look to the value added to their lives, not simply to the prestige of the institutions they attend. Employers must make clear to educators what they value in new employees. Without new public attitudes, higher education will find it difficult to persevere in the task ahead.

One of these difficulties is financial. Higher education's claim on public and private funds increasingly competes with a growing list of other compelling claims. One consequence is that after rising every year since the end of World War II, total state support for public higher education declined for two successive years as the 1990s began, and there is little reason to expect net new resources for the foreseeable future.

Since at least World War II, higher education's growth has been made possible by an expanding national economy. However, the post-World War II surge in productivity which fueled remarkable growth in our national wealth will not repeat itself unless educational institutions make a determined, successful effort to enhance the knowledge and skills Americans bring to the workplace. Thus, higher education's best financial hope rests on helping itself by helping expand the nation's wealth, by providing the knowledgeable and highly skilled workforce that can enhance our productivity, revitalize our communities, and rebuild our sense of "we."

We are convinced that those colleges and universities that demonstrate that they are doing more with what they have—those doing the best job of preserving strong, core programs and eliminating the less essential—will find not only that they have freed up resources to reinvest in themselves, but they will also have made a compelling case for additional external support. We also believe that institutions that defer change until new resources are available will find themselves waiting for a very long time. Financial salvation will begin on the campus, or it will probably not begin at all. But as campuses begin to respond to the kinds of challenges we issue, there must be solid public and financial support for higher education. It IS a critical national resource.

Finally . . .

Higher education and the society it serves face a fork in the road. Either educators and other Americans raise their sights and take the difficult steps described in this open letter, or we all face the certain and unpleasant prospect of national decline. No one can look squarely at the quality of our undergraduate education, and its graduates, and come to a more optimistic conclusion.

We are guardedly hopeful that higher education will respond positively to the kinds of change we believe essential to our national well-being. That hope rests on the active participation of faculty members, administrators, and the public, many of whom understand the need for change and are working to effect it.

That hope rests on the fact that so many Americans understand how critical a productive and affordable system of higher education is to the American future. Even the most severe critic of higher education understands its importance and wishes it well.

Most significantly, there is hope, because when the nation has called on colleges and universities to adapt in the past, higher education has always responded.

We cannot believe it will hesitate now.

Appendices*

Appendix A. A Self-Assessment Checklist

All those with an interest in higher education—faculty, academic leadership, trustees and regents, students, parents, state legislators, public officials, and others—will find the questions on the following pages helpful in assessing the educational institutions in which they have an interest. Additional questions and issues will, of course, arise on each campus.

Conducting this kind of self-assessment is the first step in any effort to think in different ways about the nation's colleges and universities. Each institution will want to conduct its self-assessment in its own way, but we believe committed, persistent, straightforward leadership at the institutional level, including participation by trustees and regents, is essential to a candid and useful outcome.

We also believe that each institution should develop and publish an action plan to respond to both the positive and negative conclusions if its self-assessment.

First Questions

Responses to the following three questions will provide a helpful context in which to assess one's institution.

- What kind of people do we want our children and grandchildren to be?
- What kind of society do we want them to live in?
- How can we best shape our institution to nurture those kinds of people and that kind of society? ‡

Our campus's response to these questions includes the following major points:

Taking Values Seriously

- How does our educational program match the claims of our recruiting brochures, and where is it falling short?
- How does our core curriculum of required courses respond to the needs of our students for a rigorous liberal education enabling them to "live rightly and well in a free society"? Where does it fall short?
- In what ways does our institution model the values and skills expected in our community? Where and how are we falling short?
- What steps might we take to improve the general climate of civility on our campus?
- How comprehensive and effective is the code of professional conduct and ethics for our faculty and staff? When was it last reviewed?
- In what ways does our institution and its educational program promote the development of shared values, specifically the civic virtues listed below, among our students?
    o respect for the individual and commitment to equal opportunity in a diverse society;
    o the belief that our common interests exceed our individual differences;
    o support for the freedoms enunciated in the Bill of Rights, including freedom of religion, of the press, of speech, and of the right to assemble;
    o the belief that individual rights and privileges are accompanied by responsibilities to others;
    o respect for the views of others; and
    o the conviction that no one is above the law.
- What moral and ethical questions should we be putting to the student groups and organizations we sanction on campus? What standards of conduct do we expect of these groups? How have we made these standards clear?
- How do the activities of our athletic programs square with our institution's stated values, and where do they fall short?
- What steps will we take to assure that next year's entering students will graduate as individuals of character more sensitive to the needs of community, more competent to contribute to society, more civil in their habits of thought, speech, and action?
- What other related questions should we address at our institution?

---

* Editors' note: Appendices to *An American Imperative* are reproduced in part here. The full document, including appendices, is available through ERIC, www.eric.ed.gov, ED364144.

‡ John Hope Franklin, et al., *The Inclusive University: A New Environment for Higher Education*. Washington: Joint Center for Political and Economic Studies, 1993.

Putting Student Learning First

- How recently have we reviewed our program offerings to assure that they match our mission and the needs and goals of the students we admit?

- In what ways could we do a better job of helping our students to attain higher levels of both knowledge and skills?

- What steps should we take to establish or improve a rigorous curriculum requiring core knowledge and competences of our students?

- How have we tried to integrate curricular offerings for the benefit of students and faculty? Is "course sprawl" contributing to our budgetary problems and making it more difficult for students to register in courses required for graduation? What might be done?

- To what extent are our educational programs, class schedules, registration, and other administrative and support services organized around the needs of learners rather than the convenience of the institution? What improvements can we make?

- How do we encourage and assist students to develop the basic values required for learning, e.g., self-discipline, perseverance, responsibility, hard work, intellectual openness?

- In what ways are we assessing learning to diagnose needs and accomplishments? How could we improve feedback to students and faculty on student performance in order to enhance both teaching and learning?

- How does our institution assure that students have demonstrated a high level of achievement, consistent with our published standards for acquiring both knowledge and skills, as a basis for receiving our degrees or certificates? Can we raise our standards?

- In what ways are we applying what is known about learning to the teaching practices of our faculty and graduate students? How do our pedagogical approaches enhance learning, and where do they fall short?

- How do we support faculty initiatives to improve learning and teaching? In particular, is our faculty well grounded in the available research concerning adult learning? If not, what will we do to improve our record?

- How could we do a better job of helping students learn at lower overall cost to our institution? How would we reinvest the savings?

- What other related questions should we address at our institution to improve the quality of learning?

Creating a Nation of Learners

- In what ways have we organized our programs to develop and support a capacity for lifelong learning among our students?

- How might we provide the same level of service and support to "non-traditional" students, and students in non-traditional learning programs, as we do for traditional full-time students? Within our mission, when have we examined alternative, more flexible, and student-oriented ways to provide for student learning?

- How often do we survey employers of our recent graduates—and the graduates themselves—to discover how and under what circumstances graduates succeed or fall short? How can that process be improved?

- In what ways do we work with K-12 systems to enlarge our understanding of their difficulties, encourage teachers and administrators to see us as resources, and enlarge our own competences? In what ways have we relegated this effort to our school of education? How have we tried to involve the entire campus?

- How are we working with high schools and other educational institutions both to communicate to them the knowledge and skills that students will need to be successful in higher education and to help students meet those requirements?

- How do our departments provide graduate students and professors with training in how people learn and what that means for teaching? What needs to be done to make this institution-wide and to set institution-wide standards?

- How is our campus working with local schools and other colleges and universities to bring teaching and learning to state-of-the-art standards from kindergarten through the undergraduate years? What more can we do?

- How might we bring our teacher recruitment and teacher education programs into better alignment with the real needs of both society and students? What are our benchmarks?

- What provisions might a statewide compact contain if we wished to ease student transfer between institutions?

- In what ways are we organized to make use of educational achievements from non-traditional organizations and settings?

- What other related questions should we address in an effort to reduce the institutional barriers to learning and to make our institution more responsive to the needs of others, e.g., K-12 education, employers, and other institutions of higher education?

Appendix B. Resources and Documentation
See ERIC, www.eric.ed.gov, ED364144.

Appendix C. Members of the Wingspread Group
Appendix C is reproduced in part here. Additional biographical information on each member is available in the original publication. See ERIC, www.eric.ed.gov, ED364144.

Patricia Aburdene, Author, Megatrends, Limited
Gilbert F. Amelio, President and Chief Executive Officer, National Semiconductor Corporation
Michael E. Baroody, President, National Policy Forum
William E. Brock, Chairman, The Brock Group, Ltd.
Martha Layne Collins, President, St. Catharine College
Robben W. Fleming, President Emeritus, University of Michigan
Mitchell S. Fromstein, Chairman and Chief Executive Officer, Manpower, Incorporated
Roger W. Heyns, Retired President, The William and Flora Hewlett Foundation
Robert H. McCabe, President, Miami-Dade Community College District
Constance Berry Newman, Under Secretary, The Smithsonian Institution
Sr. Joel Read, President, Alverno College
Albert Shanker, President, American Federation of Teachers
Peter Smith, Dean, School of Education and Human Development, The George Washington University
Adrienne K. Wheatley, Student, John F. Kennedy School of Government and Trustee of Princeton University
Blenda J. Wilson, President, California State University, Northridge
Joe B. Wyatt, Chancellor, Vanderbilt University

Appendix D. Contributed Essays
See ERIC, www.eric.ed.gov, ED364144.

Appendix E. The SCANS Agenda
In 1991 and 1992, the Secretary's Commission on Achieving Necessary Skills (SCANS) called on the American educational system, from pre-school through post-graduate, to attend to the responsibilities graduates assume as workers, parents, and citizens. Asserting that there is more to life than earning a living, SCANS also insisted that the following set of foundation skills and competences are essential for all in the modern world.

Foundation Skills

Competent individuals in the high-performance workplace need:

- Basic Skills—reading, writing, arithmetic and mathematics, speaking and listening.

- Thinking Skills—the ability to learn, to reason, to think creatively, to make decisions, and to solve problems.

- Personal Qualities—individual responsibility, self-esteem and self-management, sociability, and integrity.

Competences

Effective individuals can productively use:

- Resources—They know how to allocate time, money, materials, space, and staff.

- Interpersonal skills—They can work on teams, teaching others, serve customers, lead, negotiate, and work well with people from culturally diverse backgrounds.

- Information—They can acquire and evaluate data, organize and maintain files, interpret and communicate, and use computers to process information.

- Systems—They understand social, organizational, and technological systems; they can monitor and correct performance, and they can design or improve systems.

- Technology—They can select equipment and tools, apply technology to specific tasks, and maintain and troubleshoot equipment.

From Teaching to Learning: A New Paradigm for Undergraduate Education

By Robert B. Barr and John Tagg

Barr, Robert, and Tagg, John. (1995 November/December). "From Teaching to Learning: A New Paradigm for Undergraduate Education." *Change.*

The significant problems we face cannot be solved at the same level of thinking we were at when we created them.
Albert Einstein

A paradigm shift is taking hold in American higher education. In its briefest form, the paradigm that has governed our colleges is this: A college is an institution that exists *to provide instruction*. Subtly but profoundly we are shifting to a new paradigm: A college is an institution that exists *to produce learning*. This shift changes everything. It is both needed and wanted.

We call the traditional, dominant paradigm the "Instruction Paradigm." Under it, colleges have created complex structures to provide for the activity of teaching conceived primarily as delivering 50-minute lectures—the mission of a college is to deliver instruction.

Now, however, we are beginning to recognize that our dominant paradigm mistakes a means for an end. It takes the means or method—called "instruction" or "teaching" —and makes it the college's end or purpose. To say that the purpose of colleges is to provide instruction is like saying that General Motors' business is to operate assembly lines or that the purpose of medical care is to fill hospital beds. We now see that our mission is not instruction but rather that of producing learning with every student by whatever means work best.

The shift to a "Learning Paradigm" liberates institutions from a set of difficult constraints. Today it is virtually impossible for them to respond effectively to the challenge of stable or declining budgets while meeting the increasing demand for postsecondary education from increasingly diverse students. Under the logic of the Instruction Paradigm, colleges suffer from a serious design flaw: it is not possible to increase outputs without a corresponding increase in costs, because any attempt to increase outputs without increasing resources is a threat to quality. If a college attempts to increase its productivity by increasing either class sizes or faculty workloads, for example, academics will be quick to assume inexorable negative consequences for educational quality.

Just as importantly, the Instruction Paradigm rests on conceptions of teaching that are increasingly recognized as ineffective. As Alan Guskin pointed out in a September/October 1994 *Change* article premised on the shift from teaching to learning, "the primary learning environment for undergraduate students, the fairly passive lecture-discussion format where faculty talk and most students listen, is contrary to almost every principle of optimal settings for student learning." The Learning Paradigm ends the lecture's privileged position, honoring in its place whatever approaches serve best to prompt learning of particular knowledge by particular students.

The Learning Paradigm also opens up the truly inspiring goal that each graduating class learns more than the previous graduating class. In other words, the Learning Paradigm envisions the institution itself as a learner—over time, it continuously learns how to produce more learning with each graduating class, each entering student.

For many of us, the Learning Paradigm has always lived in our hearts. As teachers, we want above all else for our students to learn and succeed. But the heart's feeling has not lived clearly and powerfully in our heads. Now, as the elements of the Learning Paradigm permeate the air, our heads are beginning to understand what our hearts have known. However, none of us has yet put all the elements of the Learning Paradigm together in a conscious, integrated whole.

Lacking such a vision, we've witnessed reformers advocate many of the new paradigm's elements over the years, only to see few of them widely adopted. The reason is that they have been applied piecemeal within the structures of a dominant paradigm that rejects or distorts them. Indeed, for two decades the response to calls for reform from national commissions and task forces generally has been an attempt to address the issues *within the framework of the Instruction Paradigm*. The movements thus generated have most often failed, undone by the contradictions within the traditional paradigm. For example, if students are not learning to solve problems or think critically, the old logic says we must teach a class in thinking and make it a general education requirement. The logic is all too circular: What students are learning in the classroom doesn't address their needs or ours; therefore, we must bring them back into another classroom and instruct them some more. The result is never what we hope for because, as Richard Paul, director of the Center for Critical Thinking, observes glumly, "critical thinking is taught in the same way that other courses have traditionally been taught, with an excess of lecture and insufficient time for practice."

To see what the Instruction Paradigm is we need only look at the structures and behaviors of our colleges and infer the governing principles and beliefs they reflect. But it is much more difficult to see the Learning Paradigm, which has yet to find complete expression in the structures and processes of any college. So we must imagine it. This is what we propose to do here. As we outline its principles and elements, we'll suggest some of their implications for colleges—but only some, because the expression of principles in concrete structures depends on circumstances. It will take decades to work out many of the Learning Paradigm's implications. But we hope here that by making it more explicit we will help colleagues to more fully recognize it and restructure our institutions in its image.

That such a restructuring is needed is beyond question: the gap between what we say we want of higher education and what its structures *provide* has never been wider. To use a distinction made by Chris Argyris and Donald Schön, the difference between our espoused theory and our theory-in-use is becoming distressingly noticeable. An "espoused theory," readers will recall, is the set of principles people offer to explain their behavior; the principles we can infer from how people or their organizations actually behave is their "theory-in-use." Right now, the Instruction Paradigm is our theory-in-use, yet the espoused theories of most educators more closely resemble components of the Learning Paradigm. The more we discover about how the mind works and how students learn, the greater the disparity between what we say and what we do. Thus so many of us feel increasingly constrained by a system increasingly at variance with what we believe. To build the colleges we need for the 21st century—to put our minds where our hearts are, and rejoin acts with beliefs—we must consciously reject the Instruction Paradigm and restructure what we do on the basis of the Learning Paradigm.

The Paradigms

When comparing alternative paradigms, we must take care: the two will seldom be as neatly parallel as our summary chart suggests (Figure 1). A paradigm is like the rules of a game: one of the functions of the rules is to define the playing field and domain of possibilities on that field. But a new paradigm may specify a game played on a larger or smaller field with a larger or smaller domain of legitimate possibilities. Indeed, the Learning Paradigm expands the playing field and domain of possibilities and it radically changes various aspects of the game. In the Instruction Paradigm, a specific methodology determines the boundary of what colleges can do; in the Learning Paradigm, student learning and success set the boundary. By the same token, not all elements of the new paradigm are contrary to corresponding elements of the old; the new includes many elements of the old within its larger domain of possibilities. The Learning Paradigm does not prohibit lecturing, for example. Lecturing becomes one of many possible methods, all evaluated on the basis of their ability to promote appropriate learning.

In describing the shift from an Instruction to a Learning Paradigm, we limit our address in this article to undergraduate education. Research and public service are important functions of colleges and universities but lie outside the scope of the present discussion. Here, as in our summary chart, we'll compare the two paradigms along six dimensions: mission and purposes, criteria for success, teaching/learning structures, learning theory, productivity and funding, and nature of roles.

Figure 1. Comparing Educational Paradigms

The Instruction Paradigm	The Learning Paradigm
Mission and Purposes	**Mission and Purposes**
• Provide/deliver instruction • Transfer knowledge from faculty to students • Offer courses and programs • Improve the quality of instruction • Achieve access for diverse students	• Produce learning • Elicit student discovery and construction of knowledge • Create powerful learning environments • Improve the quality of learning • Achieve success for diverse students
Criteria for Success	**Criteria for Success**
• Inputs, resources • Quality of entering students • Curriculum development, expansion • Quantity and quality of resources • Enrollment, revenue growth • Quality of faculty, instruction	• Learning & student-success outcomes • Quality of exiting students • Learning technologies development, expansion • Quantity and quality of outcomes • Aggregate learning growth, efficiency • Quality of students, learning
Teaching/Learning Structures	**Teaching/Learning Structures**
• Atomistic; parts prior to whole • Time held constant, learning varies • 50-minute lecture, 3-unit course • Classes start/end at same time • One teacher, one classroom • Independent disciplines, departments • Covering material • End-of-course assessment • Grading within classes by instructors • Private assessment • Degree equals accumulated credit hours	• Holistic; whole prior to parts • Learning held constant, time varies • Learning environments • Environment ready when student is • Whatever learning experience works • Cross discipline/department collaboration • Specified learning results • Pre/during/post assessments • External evaluations of learning • Public assessment • Degree equals demonstrated knowledge and skills
Learning Theory	**Learning Theory**
• Knowledge exists "out there" • Knowledge comes in chunks and bits; delivered by instructors • Learning is cumulative and linear • Fits the storehouse of knowledge metaphor • Learning is teacher centered and controlled • "Live" teacher, "live" students required • The classroom and learning are competitive and individualistic • Talent and ability are rare	• Knowledge exists in each person's mind and is shaped by individual experience • Knowledge is constructed, created, and "gotten" • Learning is a nesting and interacting of frameworks • Fits learning how to ride a bicycle metaphor • Learning is student centered & controlled • "Active" learner required, but not "live" teacher • Learning environments and learning are cooperative, collaborative, and supportive • Talent and ability are abundant
Productivity/Funding	**Productivity/Funding**
• Definition of productivity: cost per hour of instruction per student • Funding for hours of instruction	• Definition of productivity: cost per unit of learning per student • Funding for learning outcomes
Nature of Roles	**Nature of Roles**
• Faculty are primarily lecturers • Faculty and students act independently and in isolation • Teachers classify and sort students • Staff serve/support faculty and the process of instruction • Any expert can teach • Line governance; independent actors	• Faculty are primarily designers of learning methods and environments • Faculty and students work in teams with each other and other staff • Teachers develop every student's competencies and talents • All staff are educators who produce student learning and success • Empowering learning is challenging and complex • Shared governance; teamwork

Mission and Purposes

In the Instruction Paradigm, the mission of the college is to provide instruction, to teach. The method and the product are one and the same. The means is the end. In the Learning Paradigm, the mission of the college is to produce learning. The method and the product are separate. The end governs the means.

Some educators may be uncomfortable with the verb "produce." We use it because it so strongly connotes that the college takes responsibility for learning. The point of saying that colleges are to produce learning—not provide, not support, not encourage—is to say, unmistakably, that they are responsible for the degree to which students learn. The Learning Paradigm shifts what the institution takes responsibility for: from quality instruction (lecturing, talking) to student learning. Students, the co-producers of learning, can and must, of course, take responsibility for their own learning. Hence, responsibility is a win-win game wherein two agents take responsibility for the same outcome even though neither is in complete control of all the variables. When two agents take such responsibility, the resulting synergy produces powerful results.

> **In this sense,**
> it is no contradiction
> to say that students, faculty,
> and the college as an institution
> can all take responsibility for
> student learning.

The idea that colleges cannot be responsible for learning flows from a disempowering notion of responsibility. If we conceive of responsibility as a fixed quantity in a zero-sum game, then students must take responsibility for their own learning, and no one else can. This model generates a concept of responsibility capable of assigning blame but not of empowering the most productive action. The concept of responsibility as a framework for action is quite different: When one takes responsibility, one sets goals and then acts to achieve them, continuously modifying one's behavior to better achieve the goals. To take responsibility for achieving an outcome is not to guarantee the outcome, nor does it entail the complete control of all relevant variables; it is to make the achievement of the outcome the criterion by which one measures one's own efforts. In this sense, it is no contradiction to say that students, faculty, and the college as an institution can all take responsibility for student learning.

In the Learning Paradigm, colleges take responsibility for learning at two distinct levels. At the organizational level, a college takes responsibility for the aggregate of student learning and success. Did, for example, the graduating class's mastery of certain skills or knowledge meet our high, public standards for the award of the degree? Did the class's knowledge and skills improve over those of prior classes? The college also takes responsibility at the individual level, that is, for each individual student's learning. Did Mary Smith learn the chemistry we deem appropriate for a degree in that field? Thus, the institution takes responsibility for both its institutional outcomes and individual student outcomes.

Turning now to more specific purposes, in the Instruction Paradigm, a college aims to transfer or deliver knowledge from faculty to students; it offers courses and degree programs and seeks to maintain a high quality of instruction within them, mostly by assuring that faculty stay current in their fields. If new knowledge or clients appear, so will new course work. The very purpose of the Instruction Paradigm is to offer courses.

In the Learning Paradigm, on the other hand, a college's purpose is not to transfer knowledge but to create environments and experiences that bring students to discover and construct knowledge for themselves, to make students members of communities of learners that make discoveries and solve problems. The college aims, in fact, to create a series of ever more powerful learning environments. The Learning Paradigm does not limit institutions to a single means for empowering students to learn; within its framework, effective learning technologies are continually identified, developed, tested, implemented, and assessed against one another. The aim in the Learning Paradigm is not so much to improve the quality of instruction—although that is not irrelevant—as it is to improve continuously the quality of learning for students individually and in the aggregate.

Under the older paradigm, colleges aimed to provide access to higher education, especially for historically underrepresented groups such as African-Americans and Hispanics. Too often, mere access hasn't served students well. Under the Learning Paradigm, the goal for underrepresented students (and all students) becomes not simply access but success. By "success" we mean the achievement of overall student educational objectives such as earning a degree, persisting in school, and learning the "right" things—the skills and knowledge that will help students to achieve their goals in work and life. A Learning Paradigm college, therefore, aims for ever-higher graduation rates while maintaining or even increasing learning standards.

By shifting the intended institutional outcome from teaching to learning, the Learning Paradigm makes possible a continuous improvement in productivity. Whereas under the Instruction Paradigm a primary institutional purpose was to optimize faculty well-being and success—including recognition for research and scholarship—in the Learning Paradigm a primary drive is to produce learning outcomes more efficiently. The philosophy of an Instruction Paradigm college reflects the belief that it cannot increase learning outputs without more resources, but a Learning Paradigm college expects to do so continuously. A Learning Paradigm college is concerned with learning productivity, not teaching productivity.

Criteria for Success

Under the Instruction Paradigm, we judge our colleges by comparing them to one another. The criteria for quality are defined in terms of inputs and process measures. Factors such as selectivity in student admissions, number of PhDs on the faculty, and research reputation are used to rate colleges and universities. Administrators and boards may look to enrollment and revenue growth and the expansion of courses and programs. As Guskin put it, "We are so wedded to a definition of quality based on resources that we find it extremely difficult to deal with the results of our work, namely student learning."

The Learning Paradigm necessarily incorporates the perspectives of the assessment movement. While this movement has been under way for at least a decade, under the dominant Instruction Paradigm it has not penetrated very far into normal organizational practice. Only a few colleges across the country systematically assess student learning outcomes. Educators in California community colleges always seem to be surprised when they hear that 45 percent of first-time fall students do not return in the spring and that it takes an average of six years for a student to earn an associate's (AA) degree. The reason for this lack of outcomes knowledge is profoundly simple: under the Instruction Paradigm, student outcomes are simply irrelevant to the successful functioning and funding of a college.

Our faculty evaluation systems, for example, evaluate the performance of faculty in teaching terms, not learning terms. An instructor is typically evaluated by her peers or dean on the basis of whether her lectures are organized, whether she covers the appropriate material, whether she shows interest in and understanding of her subject matter, whether she is prepared for class, and whether she respects her students' questions and comments. All these factors evaluate the instructor's performance in teaching terms. They do not raise the issue of whether students are learning, let alone demand evidence of learning or provide for its reward.

Many institutions construe teaching almost entirely in terms of lecturing. A true story makes the point. A biology instructor was experimenting with collaborative methods of instruction in his beginning biology classes. One day his dean came for a site visit, slipping into the back of the room. The room was a hubbub of activity. Students were discussing material enthusiastically in small groups spread out across the room; the instructor would observe each group for a few minutes, sometimes making a comment, sometimes just nodding approval. After 15 minutes or so the dean approached the instructor and said, "I came today to do your evaluation. I'll come back another time when you're teaching."

In the Instruction Paradigm, teaching is judged on its own terms; in the Learning Paradigm, the power of an environment or approach is judged in terms of its impact on learning. If learning occurs, then the environment has power. If students learn more in environment A than in environment B, then A is more powerful than B. To know this in the Learning Paradigm we would assess student learning routinely and constantly.

Institutional outcomes assessment is analogous to classroom assessment, as described by K. Patricia Cross and Thomas Angelo. In our own experience of classroom-assessment training workshops, teachers share moving stories about how even limited use of these techniques has

prompted them to make big changes in their teaching, sometimes despite years of investment in a previous practice. Mimi Steadman, in a recent study of community college teachers using classroom assessment, found that "eighty-eight percent of faculty surveyed reported that they had made changes in their teaching behaviors as a result." This at first was startling to us. How could such small amounts of information produce such large changes in teacher behavior? Upon reflection, it became clear. The information was feedback about learning, about results—something teachers rarely collect. Given information that their students were not learning, it was obvious to these teachers that something had to be done about the methods they had been using. Likewise, we think, feedback on learning results at the institutional level should have a correspondingly large impact on an institution's behavior and on the means it uses to produce learning.

Of course, some will argue, true education simply cannot be measured. You cannot measure, for example, true appreciation of the beauty of a work of art. Certainly some learning is difficult, even impossible to measure. But it does not follow that useful and meaningful assessment is impossible.

If we compare outcomes assessment with the input measures controlling policy in the Instruction Paradigm, we find that measures of outcome provide far more genuine information about learning than do measures of input. Learning outcomes include whatever students do as a result of a learning experience. Any measurement of students' products from an educational experience is a measure of a learning outcome. We could count the number of pages students write, the number of books they read, their number of hours at the computer, or the number of math problems they solve.

Of course, these would be silly methods to determine institutional incentives, and we do not recommend them. Any one of them, however, would produce more useful information on learning than the present method of measuring inputs and ignoring outcomes. It would make more sense to fund a college on the number of math problems students solve, for example, than to fund it on the number of students who sit in math classes. We suspect that any system of institutional incentives based on outcomes would lead to greater learning than any system of incentives based on inputs. But we need not settle for a system biased toward the trivial. Right now, today, we can construct a good assessment regime with the tools we have at hand.

Our faculty evaluation systems,

for example, evaluate the performance of faculty in teaching terms, not learning terms.

The Learning Paradigm requires us to heed the advice of the Wingspread Group: "New forms of assessment should focus on establishing what college and university graduates have learned—the knowledge and skill levels they have achieved and their potential for further independent learning."

Teaching/Learning Structures

By structures we mean those features of an organization that are stable over time and that form the framework within which activities and processes occur and through which the purposes of the organization are achieved. Structure includes the organization chart, role and reward systems, technologies and methods, facilities and equipment, decision-making customs, communication channels, feedback loops, financial arrangements, and funding streams.

Peter Senge, in *The Fifth Discipline*, a book about applying systems theory to organizational learning, observes that institutions and their leaders rarely focus their attention on systemic structures. They seldom think, he says, to alter basic structures in order to improve organizational performance, even though those structures generate the patterns of organizational action and determine which activities and results are possible. Perhaps the recent talk about restructuring, re-engineering, and reinvention in higher education reflects a change in focus and a heightened awareness of both the constraining and liberating power of organizational structures.

Structures
reflecting an old
paragigm can frustrate the
best ideas and innovations
of new-paradigm thinkers.

There is good reason to attend to structure. First, restructuring offers the greatest hope for increasing organizational efficiency and effectiveness. Structure is leverage. If you change the structure in which people work, you increase or decrease the leverage applied to their efforts. A change in structure can either increase productivity or change the nature of organizational outcomes. Second, structure is the concrete manifestation of the abstract principles of the organization's governing paradigm. Structures reflecting an old paradigm can frustrate the best ideas and innovations of new-paradigm thinkers. As the governing paradigm changes, so likewise must the organization's structures.

In this section, we focus on the main structures related to the teaching and learning process; funding and faculty role structures are discussed later under separate headings.

The teaching and learning structure of the Instruction Paradigm college is atomistic. In its universe, the "atom" is the 50-minute lecture, and the "molecule" is the one-teacher, one-classroom, three-credit-hour course. From these basic units the physical architecture, the administrative structure, and the daily schedules of faculty and students are built. Dennis McGrath and Martin Spear, professors at the Community College of Philadelphia, note that "education proceeds everywhere through the vehicle of the three-credit course. Faculty members [and everyone else, we might add] have so internalized that constraint that they are long past noticing that it is a constraint, thinking it part of the natural order of things."

The resulting structure is powerful and rigid. It is, of course, perfectly suited to the Instruction Paradigm task of offering one-teacher, one-classroom courses. It is antithetical to creating almost any other kind of learning experience. A sense of this can be obtained by observing the effort, struggle, and rule-bending required to schedule even a slightly different kind of learning activity, such as a team-taught course.

In the "educational atomism" of the Instruction Paradigm, the parts of the teaching and learning process are seen as discrete entities. The parts exist prior to and independent of any whole; the whole is no more than the sum of the parts, or even less. The college interacts with students only in discrete, isolated environments, cut off from one another because the parts—the classes—are prior to the whole. A "college education" is the sum the student's experience of a series of discrete, largely unrelated, three-credit classes.

In the Instruction Paradigm, the teaching and learning process is governed by the further rule that time will be held constant while learning varies. Although addressing public elementary and secondary education, the analysis of the National Commission on Time and Learning nonetheless applies to colleges:

> Time is learning's warden. Our time-bound mentality has fooled us all into believing that schools can educate all of the people all of the time in a school year of 180 six-hour days....If experience, research, and common sense teach nothing else, they confirm the truism that people learn at different rates, and in different ways with different subjects. But we have put the cart before the horse: our schools...are captives of clock and calendar. The boundaries of student growth are defined by schedules...instead of standards for students and learning.

Under the rule of time, all classes start and stop at the same time and take the same number of calendar weeks. The rule of time and the priority of parts affect every instructional act of the college.

Thus it is, for example, that if students come into college classes "unprepared," it is not the job of the faculty who teach those classes to "prepare" them. Indeed, the structure of the one-semester, three-credit class makes it all but impossible to do so. The only solution, then, is to create new courses to prepare students for the existing courses; within the Instruction Paradigm, the response to educational problems is always to generate more atomized, discrete instructional units. If business students are lacking a sense of ethics, then offer and require a course in business ethics. If students have poor study skills, then offer a "master student" course to teach such skills.

Instruction Paradigm colleges atomistically organize courses and teachers into departments and programs that rarely communicate with one another. Academic departments, originally associated with coherent disciplines, are the structural home bases for accomplishing the essential work of the college: offering courses. "Departments have a life of their own," notes William D. Schaefer, professor of English and former executive vice chancellor at UCLA. They are "insular, defensive, self-governing, [and] compelled to protect their interests because the faculty positions as well as the courses that justify funding those positions are located therein."

Those globally applicable skills that are the foundation of meaningful engagement with the world—reading, writing, calculating, reasoning—find a true place in this structure only if they have their own independent bases: the English or math or reading departments. If students cannot reason or think well, the college creates a course on reasoning and thinking. This in turn produces pressure to create a corresponding department. "If we are not careful," warns Adam Sweeting, director of the Writing Program at the Massachusetts School of Law at Andover, "the teaching of critical thinking skills will become the responsibility of one university department, a prospect that is at odds with the very idea of a university."

Efforts to extend college-level reading, writing, and reasoning "across the curriculum" have largely failed. The good intentions produced few results because, under the Instruction Paradigm, the teacher's job is to "cover the material" as outlined in the disciplinary syllabus. The instructor charged with implementing writing or reading or critical thinking "across the curriculum" often must choose between doing her job or doing what will help students learn—between doing well, as it were, or doing good.

From the point of view of the Learning Paradigm, these Instruction Paradigm teaching and learning structures present immense barriers to improving student learning and success. They provide no space and support for redesigned learning environments or for experimenting with alternative learning technologies. They don't provide for, warrant, or reward assessing whether student learning has occurred or is improving.

In a Learning Paradigm college, the structure of courses and lectures becomes dispensable and negotiable. Semesters and quarters, lectures, labs, syllabi—indeed, classes themselves—become options rather than received structures or mandatory activities. The Learning Paradigm prescribes no one "answer" to the question of how to organize learning environments and experiences. It supports any learning method and structure that works, where "works" is defined in terms of learning outcomes, not as the degree of conformity to an ideal classroom archetype. In fact, the Learning Paradigm requires a constant search for new structures and methods that work better for student learning and success, and expects even these to be redesigned continually and to evolve over time.

The transition from Instruction Paradigm to Learning Paradigm will not be instantaneous. It will be a process of gradual modification and experimentation through which we alter many organizational parts in light of a new vision for the whole. Under the Instruction Paradigm, structures are assumed to be fixed and immutable; there is no ready means for achieving the leverage needed to alter them. The first structural task of the Learning Paradigm, then, is to establish such leverage.

The key structure for changing the rest of the system is an institutionwide assessment and information system—an essential structure in the Learning Paradigm, and a key means for getting there. It would provide constant, useful feedback on institutional performance. It would track transfer, graduation, and other completion rates. It would track the flow of students through learning stages (such as the achievement of basic skills) and the development of in-depth knowledge in a discipline. It would measure the knowledge and skills of program completers and graduates. It would assess learning along many dimensions and in many places and stages in each student's college experience.

To be most effective, this assessment system would provide public institutional-level information. We are not talking about making public the status of individual students by name, but about making the year-to-year graduation rate—or the mean score of graduating seniors on a critical thinking assessment, for example—"public" in the sense that they are available to everyone in the college community. Moreover, in the Learning Paradigm college, such data are routinely talked about and acted upon by a community ever dedicated to improving its own performance.

The effectiveness of the assessment system for developing alternative learning environments depends in part upon its being external to learning programs and structures. While in the Instruction Paradigm students are assessed and graded within a class by the same instructor responsible for teaching them, in the Learning Paradigm much of the assessment would be independent of the learning experience and its designer, somewhat as football games are independent measures of what is learned in football practice. Course grades alone fail to tell us what students know and can do; average grades assigned by instructors are not reliable measures of whether the institution is improving learning.

Ideally, an institution's assessment program would measure the "value-added" over the course of students' experience at the college. Student knowledge and skills would be measured upon entrance and again upon graduation, and at intermediate stages such as at the beginning and completion of major programs. Students could then be acknowledged and certified for what they have learned; the same data, aggregated, could help shift judgments of institutional quality from inputs and resources to the value-added brought to student learning by the college.

The transition
from Instruction

Paradigm to Learning

Paradigm will not be

instantaneous.

The college devoted to learning first identifies the knowledge and skills it expects its graduates to possess, without regard to any particular curriculum or educational experiences. It then determines how to assess them reliably. It assesses graduating students, and the resulting information is then used to redesign and improve the processes and environments leading to such outcomes. In this manner, enhancing intellectual skills such as writing and problem solving and social skills such as effective team participation become the project of all learning programs and structured experiences. The whole would govern the parts.

Information from a sophisticated assessment system will gradually lead to the transformation of the college's learning environments and supporting structures. Such a system seeks out "best practice" benchmarks against which improvements in institutional performance can be measured in learning terms. It is the foundation for creating an institutional capacity to develop ever more effective and efficient ways of empowering learning. It becomes the basis for generating revenue or funding according to learning results rather than hours of instruction. Most importantly, it is the key to the college's and its staff's taking responsibility for and enjoying the progress of each student's education.

Instead of fixing the means—such as lectures and courses—the Learning Paradigm fixes the ends, the learning results, allowing the means to vary in its constant search for the most effective and efficient paths to student learning. Learning outcomes and standards thus would be identified and held to for all students—or raised as learning environments became more powerful—while the time students took to achieve those standards would vary. This would reward skilled and advanced students with speedy progress while enabling less prepared students the time they needed to actually master the material. By "testing out," students could also avoid wasting their time being "taught" what they already know. Students would be given "credit" for degree-relevant knowledge and skills regardless of how or where or when they learned them.

Many students
cruise through schools
substituting an ersatz role-

playing exercise for learning.

In the Learning Paradigm, then, a college degree would represent not time spent and credit hours dutifully accumulated, but would certify that the student had demonstrably attained specified knowledge and skills. Learning Paradigm institutions would develop and publish explicit exit standards for graduates and grant degrees and certificates only to students who met them. Thus colleges would move away from educational atomism and move toward treating holistically the knowledge and skills required for a degree.

Learning Theory

The Instruction Paradigm frames learning atomistically. In it, knowledge, by definition, consists of matter dispensed or delivered by an instructor. The chief agent in the process is the teacher who delivers knowledge; students are viewed as passive vessels, ingesting knowledge for recall on tests. Hence, any expert can teach. Partly because the teacher knows which chunks of knowledge are most important, the teacher controls the learning activities. Learning is presumed to be cumulative because it amounts to ingesting more and more chunks. A degree is awarded when a student has received a specified amount of instruction.

The Learning Paradigm frames learning holistically, recognizing that the chief agent in the process is the learner. Thus, students must be active discoverers and constructors of their own knowledge. In the Learning Paradigm, knowledge consists of frameworks or wholes that are created or constructed by the learner. Knowledge is not seen as cumulative and linear, like a wall of bricks, but as a nesting and interacting of frameworks.

Learning is revealed when those frameworks are used to understand and act. Seeing the whole of something—the forest rather than the trees, the image of the newspaper photo rather than its dots—gives meaning to its elements, and that whole becomes more than a sum of component parts. Wholes and frameworks can come in a moment—a flash of insight—often after much hard work with the pieces, as when one suddenly knows how to ride a bicycle.

In the Learning Paradigm, learning environments and activities are learner-centered and learner-controlled. They may even be "teacherless." While teachers will have designed the learning experiences and environments students use—often through teamwork with each other and other staff—they need not be present for or participate in every structured learning activity.

Many students come away from college with a false notion of what learning is and come to believe falsely that learning—at least for some subjects—is too difficult for them. Many students cruise through schools substituting an ersatz role-playing exercise for learning.

The first time I (Barr) studied calculus as a college freshman, I did well by conventional standards. However, while I could solve enough problems to get A's on exams, I really didn't feel that I understood the Limit Theorem, the derivative, or much else. But 15 years later, after having completed college and graduate school and having taught algebra and geometry in high school, I needed to relearn calculus so that I could tutor a friend. In only two, albeit intense, days, I relearned—or really learned for the first time, so it seemed—two semesters of calculus. During those days, I wondered how I ever thought calculus was difficult and why I didn't see the Limit Theorem and derivative for the simple, obvious things they are.

What was the difference between my first learning of calculus and the second? It certainly wasn't a higher IQ. And I don't think it was because I learned or remembered much from the first time. I think it was that I brought some very powerful intellectual frameworks to the learning the second time that I didn't have the first time. Having taught algebra and geometry, I had learned their basic structure, that is, the nature of a mathematical system. I had learned the lay of the land, the whole. Through many years of schooling and study, I had also learned a number of other frameworks that were useful for learning calculus. Thus learning calculus the second time within these "advanced" frameworks was easy compared to learning, or trying to learn, calculus without them as I did as a freshman.

So much of this is because the "learning" that goes on in Instruction Paradigm colleges frequently involves only rudimentary, stimulus-response relationships whose cues may be coded into the context of a particular course but are not rooted in the student's everyday, functioning understanding.

The National Council on Vocational Education summarizes the consequences in its 1991 report, *Solutions*: "The result is fractionation, or splitting into pieces: having to learn disconnected sub-routines, items, and sub-skills without an understanding of the larger context into which they fit and which gives them meaning." While such approaches are entirely consistent with educational atomism, they are at odds with the way we think and learn. The same report quotes Sylvia Farnham-Diggory's summary of contemporary research: "Fractionated instruction maximizes forgetting, inattention, and passivity. Both children and adults acquire knowledge from active participation in holistic, complex, meaningful environments organized around long-term goals. Today's school programs could hardly have been better designed to prevent a child's natural learning system from operating."

The result is that when the contextual cues provided by the class disappear at the end of the semester, so does the learning. Howard Gardner points out that "researchers at Johns Hopkins, MIT, and other well-regarded universities have documented that students who receive honor grades in college-level physics courses are frequently unable to solve basic problems and questions encountered in a form slightly different from that on which they have been formally instructed and tested."

The Learning Paradigm embraces the goal of promoting what Gardner calls "education for understanding"—"a sufficient grasp of concepts, principles, or skills so that one can bring them to bear on new problems and situations, deciding in which ways one's present competencies can suffice and in which ways one may require new skills or knowledge." This involves the mastery of functional, knowledge-based intellectual frameworks rather than the short-term retention of fractionated, contextual cues.

The learning theory of the Instruction Paradigm reflects deeply rooted societal assumptions about talent, relationships, and accomplishment: that which is valuable is scarce; life is a win-lose proposition; and success is an individual achievement. The Learning Paradigm theory of learning reverses these assumptions.

Under the Instruction Paradigm, faculty classify and sort students, in the worst cases into those who are "college material" and those who cannot "cut it," since intelligence and ability are scarce. Under the Learning Paradigm, faculty—and everybody else in the institution—are unambiguously committed to each student's success. The faculty and the institution take an R. Buckminster Fuller view of students: human beings are born geniuses and designed for success. If they fail to display their genius or fail to succeed, it is because their design function is being thwarted. This perspective is founded not in wishful thinking but in the best evidence about the real capabilities of virtually all humans for learning. As the Wingspread Group points out, "There is growing research evidence that all students can learn to much higher standards than we now require." In the Learning Paradigm, faculty find ways to develop every student's vast talents and clear the way for every student's success.

Under the Instruction Paradigm, the classroom is competitive and individualistic, reflecting a view that life is a win-lose proposition. The requirement that the students must achieve individually and solely through their own efforts reflects the belief that success is an individual accomplishment. In the Learning Paradigm, learning environments—while challenging—are win-win environments that are cooperative, collaborative, and supportive. They are designed on the principle that accomplishment and success are the result of teamwork and group efforts, even when it appears one is working alone.

Productivity and Funding

Under the Instruction Paradigm, colleges suffer from a serious design flaw—they are structured in such a way that they cannot increase their productivity without diminishing the quality of their product. In the Instruction Paradigm, productivity is defined as cost per hour of instruction per student. In this view, the very quality of teaching and learning is threatened by any increase in the student-to-faculty ratio.

Under the Learning Paradigm, productivity is redefined as the cost per unit of learning per student. Not surprisingly, there is as yet no standard statistic that corresponds to this notion of productivity. Under this new definition, however, it is possible to increase outcomes without increasing costs. An abundance of research shows that alternatives to the traditional semester-length, classroom-based lecture method produce more learning. Some of these alternatives are less expensive; many produce more learning for the same cost. Under the Learning Paradigm, producing more with less becomes possible because the more that is being produced is learning and not hours of instruction. Productivity, in this sense, cannot even be measured in the Instruction Paradigm college. All that exists is a measure of exposure to instruction.

Under the Learning Paradigm, faculty—and everybody else in the institution—are unambiguously committed to each student's success.

Given the Learning Paradigm's definition, increases in productivity pose no threat to the quality of education. Unlike the current definition, this new definition requires that colleges actually produce learning. Otherwise, there is no "product" to count in the productivity ratio.

But what should be the definition of "unit of learning" and how can it be measured? A single, permanent answer to that question does not and need not exist. We have argued above that learning, or at least the effects of learning, can be measured, certainly well enough to determine what students are learning and whether the institution is getting more effective and efficient at producing it.

The Instruction Paradigm wastes not only institutional resources but the time and energy of students. We waste our students' time with registration lines, bookstore lines, lock-step class scheduling, and redundant courses and requirements. We do not teach them to learn efficiently and effectively. We can do a lot, as D. Bruce Johnstone, former chancellor of SUNY, suggests, to reduce the false starts and aimless "drift" of students that slow their progress toward a degree. Now let's consider how colleges are funded. One of the absurdities of current funding formulas is that an institution could utterly fail its educational mission and yet its revenue would remain unaffected. For example, attendance at public colleges on the semester system is measured twice, once in the fall and again in the spring. Normally, at California community colleges, for example, about two-thirds of fall students return for the spring term. New students and returning stop-outs make up for the one-third of fall students who leave. Even if only half—or none at all—returned, as long as spring enrollments equal those of the fall, these institutions would suffer no loss of revenue.

> **In our experience,** people will suffer the turbulence and uncertainty of change if it promises a better way to accomplish work they value.

There is no more powerful feedback than revenue. Nothing could facilitate a shift to the Learning Paradigm more swiftly than funding learning and learning-related institutional outcomes rather than hours of instruction. The initial response to the idea of outcomes-based funding is likely to be "That's not possible." But, of course, it is. As the new paradigm takes hold, forces and possibilities shift and the impossible becomes the rule.

Nature of Roles

With the shift to the Learning Paradigm comes a change in roles for virtually all college employees.

In the Instruction Paradigm, faculty are conceived primarily as disciplinary experts who impart knowledge by lecturing. They are the essential feature of the "instructional delivery system." The Learning Paradigm, on the other hand, conceives of faculty as primarily the designers of learning environments; they study and apply best methods for producing learning and student success.

If the Instruction Paradigm faculty member is an actor—a sage on a stage—then the Learning Paradigm faculty member is an inter-actor—a coach interacting with a team. If the model in the Instruction Paradigm is that of delivering a lecture, then the model in the Learning Paradigm is that of designing and then playing a team game. A coach not only instructs football players, for example, but also designs football practices and the game plan; he participates in the game itself by sending in plays and making other decisions. The new faculty role goes a step further, however, in that faculty not only design game plans but also create new and better "games," ones that generate more and better learning.

Roles under the Learning Paradigm, then, begin to blur. Architects of campus buildings and payroll clerks alike will contribute to and shape the environments that empower student learning. As the role structures of colleges begin to loosen up and as accountability for results (learning) tightens up, organizational control and command structures will change. Teamwork and shared governance over time replace the line governance and independent work of the Instruction Paradigm's hierarchical and competitive organization.

In the Learning Paradigm, as colleges specify learning goals and focus on learning technologies, interdisciplinary (or nondisciplinary) task groups and design teams become a major operating mode. For example, faculty may form a

design team to develop a learning experience in which students networked via computers learn to write about selected texts or on a particular theme.

After developing and testing its new learning module, the design team may even be able to let students proceed through it without direct faculty contact except at designated points. Design teams might include a variety of staff: disciplinary experts, information technology experts, a graphic designer, and an assessment professional. Likewise, faculty and staff might form functional teams responsible for a body of learning outcomes for a stated number of students. Such teams could have the freedom that no faculty member has in today's atomized framework, that to organize the learning environment in ways that maximize student learning.

Meeting the Challenge

Changing paradigms is hard. A paradigm gives a system integrity and allows it to function by identifying what counts as information within the infinite ocean of data in its environment. Data that solve problems that the paradigm identifies as important are information; data that are irrelevant to those problems are simply noise, static. Any system will provide both channels for transmitting information relevant to the system and filters to reduce noise.

Those who want to change the paradigm governing an institution are—from the institution's point of view—people who are listening to the noise and ignoring the information. They appear crazy or out of touch. The quartz watch was invented by the Swiss. But the great Swiss watchmakers responded to the idea of gearless timepieces in essentially the same way that the premiere audience responded to Stravinsky's *The Rite of Spring*. They threw tomatoes. They hooted it off the stage.

The principle also operates in the other direction. From the point of view of those who have adopted a new paradigm, the institution comes to sound like a cacophony-generating machine, a complex and refined device for producing more and louder noise. From the perspective of the governing paradigm, the advocates of the insurgent paradigm seem willing to sacrifice the institution itself for pie-in-the-sky nonsense. But from the perspective of the insurgents, the defenders of the present system are perpetuating a system that no longer works.

But paradigms do change. The Church admits Galileo was right. *The Rite of Spring* has become an old warhorse. Paradigms can even change quickly. Look at your watch.

Paradigms change when the ruling paradigm loses its capacity to solve problems and generate a positive vision of the future. This we very much see today. One early sign of a paradigm shift is an attempt to use the tools and ideas of a new paradigm within the framework provided by the old, or to convey information intelligible in the new paradigm through the channels of the old. This, too, is now happening.

In our experience, people will suffer the turbulence and uncertainty of change if it promises a better way to accomplish work they value. The shift to the Learning Paradigm represents such an opportunity.

The Learning Paradigm doesn't answer all the important questions, of course. What it does do is lead us to a set of new questions and a domain of possible responses. What knowledge, talents, and skills do college graduates need in order to live and work fully? What must they do to master such knowledge, talents, and skills? Are they doing those things? Do students find in our colleges a coherent body of experiences that help them to become competent, capable, and interesting people? Do they understand what they've memorized? Can they act on it? Has the experience of college made our students flexible and adaptable learners, able to thrive in a knowledge society?

How do you begin to move to the new paradigm? Ultimately, changing paradigms means doing everything differently. But we can suggest three areas where changes—even small ones—can create leverage for larger change in the future.

First, you begin by speaking. You begin to speak *within* the new paradigm. As we come to understand the Learning Paradigm, we must make our understanding public. Stop talking about the "quality of instruction" or the "instructional program." Instead, talk about what it takes to produce "quality learning" and refer to the college's "learning programs." Instead of speaking of "instructional delivery," speak about "learning outcomes."

The primary reason the Instruction Paradigm is so powerful is that it is invisible. Its incoherencies and deficiencies appear as inherent qualities of the world. If we come to see the Instruction Paradigm as a product of our own assumptions and not a force of nature, then we can change it. Only as you begin to experiment with the new language will you realize just how entrenched and invisible the old paradigm is. But as you and your colleagues begin to speak the new language, you will then also begin to think and act out of the new paradigm.

Second, if we begin to talk about the "learning outcomes" of existing programs, we'll experience frustration at our nearly complete ignorance of what those outcomes are— the Learning Paradigm's most important category of information is one about which we know very little now. The place to start the assessment of learning outcomes is in the conventional classroom; from there, let the practice grow to the program and institutional levels. In the Learning Paradigm, the key structure that provides the leverage to change the rest is a system for requiring the specification of learning outcomes and their assessment through processes external to instruction. The more we learn about the outcomes of existing programs, the more rapidly they will change.

Third, we should address the legally entrenched state funding mechanisms that fund institutions on the basis of hours of instruction. This powerful external force severely constrains the kinds of changes that an institution can make. It virtually limits them to changes within classrooms, leaving intact the atomistic one-teacher, one-classroom structure. We need to work to have state legislatures change the funding formulas of public colleges

and universities to give institutions the latitude and incentives to develop new structures for learning. Persuading legislators and governors should not be hard; indeed, the idea of funding colleges for results rather than seat time has an inherent political attractiveness. It is hard to see why legislators would resist the concept that taxpayers should pay for what they get out of higher education, and get what they pay for.

Try this thought experiment. Take a team of faculty at any college—at your college—and select a group of students on some coherent principle, any group of students as long as they have something in common. Keep the ratio of faculty to students the same as it already is. Tell the faculty team, "We want you to create a program for these students so that they will improve significantly in the following knowledge and cognitive skills by the end of one year. We will assess them at the beginning and assess them at the end, and we will tell you how we are going to do so. Your task is to produce learning with these students. In doing so, you are not constrained by any of the rules or regulations you have grown accustomed to. You are free to organize the environment in any way you like. The only thing you are required to do is to produce the desired result— student learning."

We have suggested this thought experiment to many college faculty and asked them whether, if given this freedom, they could design a learning environment that would get better results than what they are doing now. So far, no one has answered that question in the negative. Why not do it?

The change that is required to address today's challenges is not vast or difficult or expensive. It is a small thing. But it is a small change that changes everything. Simply ask, how would we do things differently if we put learning first? Then do it.

Those who say it can't be done frequently assert that environments that actually produce learning are too expensive. But this is clearly not true. What we are doing now is too expensive by far. Today, learning is prohibitively expensive in higher education; we simply can't afford it for more and more of our students. This high cost of learning is an artifact of the Instruction Paradigm. It is simply false to say that we cannot afford to give our students the education they deserve. We can, but we will not as long as we allow the Instruction Paradigm to dominate our thinking. The problem is not insoluble. However, to paraphrase Albert Einstein, we cannot solve our problem with the same level of thinking that created it.

Buckminster Fuller used to say that you should never try to change the course of a great ship by applying force to the bow. You shouldn't even try it by applying force to the rudder. Rather you should apply force to the trim-tab. A trim-tab is a little rudder attached to the end of the rudder. A very small force will turn it left, thus moving the big rudder to the right, and the huge ship to the left. The shift to the Learning Paradigm is the trim-tab of the great ship of higher education. It is a shift that changes everything.

Creating More Learning-Centered Community Colleges

Terry O'Banion

O'Banion, Terry. (1997). *Creating More Learning-Centered Community Colleges*. Mission Viejo, CA: League for Innovation in the Community College.

A dip into the literature on American education at any point in this century will reveal a reform movement either flourishing in full bloom or in the early stages of emergence or decline. The impulse to improve, perhaps basic to human nature, flowers again and again in education as we refine past efforts and experiment with new practices in our continuing quest for quality.

The current
impulse to improve
what we do in education

presents a special challenge

and opportunity for

community colleges.

Throughout the 1980s, secondary and elementary schools struggled with one of the most massive reform movements in the history of education. Triggered by the 1983 publication of *A Nation at Risk* that lambasted the "rising tide of mediocrity" in the nation's schools, a wave of educational reform swept the country. Over 100 national reports and 300 state reports fueled a number of key changes: increased requirements for high school graduation, increased standards for teacher's certification, increased use of assessment, and increased application of technology. These changes, however, did not bring about the desired results of their champions, and some critics (Daggett 1992, Leonard 1992, and Marchese 1995) observed that after ten years of such reform the nation's schools were no better than at the beginning of the decade.

For the most part, institutions of higher education were largely unaffected by reform efforts in the public schools. Colleges and universities studied these reform efforts, and some assisted public schools in carrying out reforms. The policies, programs, and practices in higher education, however, were left intact until the early 1990s when the impulse to improve surfaced in a number of reform reports directed at higher education.

In 1993, *An American Imperative: Higher Expectations for Higher Education*, published as "An Open Letter to Those Concerned About the American Future," triggered a wave of reform in higher education similar to that of the public schools in the 1980s. In fact, the 1993 report echoed similar alarms sounded in the 1983 report: "A disturbing and dangerous mismatch exists between what American society needs of higher education and what it is receiving. Nowhere is the mismatch more dangerous than in the quality of undergraduate preparation provided on many campuses. The American imperative for the twenty-first century is that society must hold higher education to much higher expectations or risk national decline" (Wingspread Group on Higher Education, p. 1).

The 1983 and 1993 reports were remarkably similar in their language and in their analysis of the issues. Both reports were issued as "Open Letters" to the public; both reports indicated that the current system of education was inappropriate for the complexity of American society; both reports cited extensive data on the failures of students; both reports sounded the alarm as an "imperative" for a society at "great risk." But in their recommendations for solutions, the reports were vastly different. For the public schools, the 1983 report recommended shoring-up the current system by increasing standards, revising curricula, adding technology, and increasing spending. For higher education, the 1993 report recommended what many have come to view as a radical departure from past solutions: place learning first and change the historical architecture of education. The 1993 report stated the challenge in succinct terms: "putting learning at the heart of the academic enterprise will mean overhauling the conceptual, procedural, curricular, and other architecture of postsecondary education on most campuses" (Wingspread Group on Higher Education, p. 14).

In the last few years, the reform movement in higher education, triggered by the 1993 report, *An American Imperative*, has spread rapidly and has captured the attention of legislators, national higher education organizations, and a growing number of faculty members and administrators. Some view the reform movement as a learning revolution (*Business Week* 1994, *Time* 1995, Oblinger and Rush 1997), and others view it as a shift in paradigms (Boggs 1993, Gales 1994, Barr and Tagg 1995). Peter Drucker (1992) believes that these changes in education reflect a profound shift in the larger society.

Every few hundred years throughout Western history, a sharp transformation has occurred. In a matter of decades, society altogether rearranges itself—its world view, its basic values, its social and political structures, its arts, its key institutions. Fifty years later a new world exists...our age is such a period of transformation (*Managing for the Future*). Drucker goes on to say that "it is a safe prediction that in the next 50 years schools and universities will change more and more drastically than they have since they assumed their present form 300 years ago when they organized themselves around the printed book" (p. 97).

Regardless of how this reform movement in higher education is described—a revolution in learning, a paradigm shift, a societal transformation—the current impulse to improve what we do in education presents a special challenge and opportunity for community colleges. Community colleges resonate well with the goals of the current reform movement: (1) placing learning first, and (2) overhauling the traditional architecture of education. This monograph addresses the role of the community college in relationship to these two goals, provides basic principles for an idealized institution described as the "learning college," shares practical experiences from a number of community colleges actively engaged in becoming more learning-centered institutions, and reviews briefly some of the key issues and challenges community colleges will face if they decide to take the journey.

Placing Learning First

One of the two key goals of the current reform effort calls for institutions of higher education to place learning as their highest priority. Many educators are offended by this recommendation because they believe they have always placed learning first. Of course educators at all levels place great value on learning, but institutional statements and reward systems often reflect other priorities. Any student of education can cite the three primary missions most often articulated by universities: teaching, research, and service. However, in many universities, the reward system places higher value on research over teaching and service. "Learning" is seldom, if ever included as one of the primary missions although its relationship to teaching, research, and service is clearly implied by most educators.

Teaching is probably the most universally acclaimed mission for all levels of higher education. In the most comprehensive survey of its kind (Higher Education Research Institute, 1991) involving more than 35,000 faculty members in 392 public institutions of higher education, 99 percent of the community college faculty said they considered "being a good teacher" an essential or very important professional goal; so did 98 percent of the faculty from four-year colleges and 98 percent of the faculty from universities.

In the community college such strong value is placed on teaching that the institution is often referred to as "the teaching college." One of the most significant documents ever written on the community college, *Building Communities* (1988)—the report of the Commission on the Future of Community Colleges—highlighted over and over the central value placed on teaching in the community college: "Building communities through dedicated teaching is the vision and the inspiration of this report" (p. 8). "Quality instruction should be the hallmark of the movement" (p. 25). "The community college should be the nation's premier teaching institution" (p. 25).

The current reform effort does not ask institutions to place less value on teaching or other missions, but to review their statements and reward systems to ensure that learning is valued as visibly as teaching and other missions. In Barr's 1994 study of California community college mission statements, he noted, "It is revealing that virtually every mission statement contained in the catalogs in California's 107 community colleges fails to use the word 'learning' in a statement of purpose" (p. 2).

For community colleges that want to become more learning-centered institutions, it may make a difference in policies, programs, and practices if learning is embedded in institutional culture as the highest priority. Community colleges that wish to embed this perspective in their culture can ask two basic questions that will keep faculty, staff, trustees, and administrators focused on the major goal: (1) Does this action improve and expand learning? (2) How do we know this action improves and expands learning?

These two questions can be applied to any area of activity in an institution to help its members become more aware of the importance of learning in everyday practice:

- Does this budget improve and expand learning? How do we know?

- Does this staff development program improve and expand learning? How do we know?

- Does the purchase of these six computers improve and expand learning? How do we know? Does the remodeling of this laboratory improve and expand learning? How do we know? Does the creation of this new program improve and expand learning? How do we know? Does this service to the community improve and expand learning? How do we know?

- Does this faculty evaluation system improve and expand learning? How do we know?

- Does this system of shared governance improve and expand learning? How do we know?

Precise answers to these questions and hundreds of similar questions about every institutional action (department, division, board, etc.) will be hard to come by, but the very voicing of these questions is an expression of commitment and value that will keep the transcendent goal of becoming a more learning-centered institution clearly and constantly visible for all to see.

Overhauling the Traditional Architecture of Education

The "Carnegie unit" is a metaphor for a vast array of traditional structural elements that have provided the framework for American schooling for generations of students—a framework targeted for major overhaul as the second goal of the current reform effort. The "Carnegie unit" is equivalent to one credit students receive for a yearlong course in high school, an early attempt to measure accumulated learning in order to communicate the amount of learning received. Ideally, students earn five credits in each of four years of high school, and an accumulated 20 credits qualifies them for a high school diploma.

The Carnegie unit is but the tip of a very large iceberg that has frozen education into a structure created for an earlier social order. The current architecture of education was created at the end of the last century when 90 percent of the population left school after the eighth grade and when the industrial revolution began to replace an economy built on agriculture. In an agricultural society, students were needed by their families to work on the farms. Schools were designed to end in the middle of the afternoon so that students could be home before dark to milk the cows, gather the eggs, and feed the hogs. Summers were set aside for major farm chores: harvesting crops, tilling new land, building barns, and repairing tools and fences. In Plant City, Florida, a major strawberry-producing center, the schools, as late as the 1940s, were referred to as "strawberry schools" in recognition of their adaptation to an agricultural economy. "Everyone recognizes it [the academic calendar] for what it is: a relic of an agrarian society in which all able-bodied men and women were needed in the fields at certain times of the year" (Lovett 1995, p. Bl).

When the nation changed from an agricultural to an industrial economy, the old school structure remained but was updated and streamlined to fit the new industrial model. Scientific management and hierarchical organization, the bedrock principles of bureaucracy, were introduced in the schools, in part to socialize youth in the virtues of order and discipline. More importantly, the modern factory, pioneered by Henry Ford in the production of automobiles, appeared ideally suited to schooling that up to this point had flourished in the cottage industry of one-room schoolhouses. Using the industrial model, schools could be operated like factories with students as products moving through an assembly line. Teachers were the workers who turned out the products, and they were supervised by principals and presidents, the management bureaucracy.

Reformers have been consistent in their criticism of the constraints on learning reflected in the industrial model of schooling. John Dewey said, "Nature has not adapted the young animal to the narrow desk, the crowded curriculum, the silent absorption of complicated facts" (Dewey and Dewey 1962, p. 15). K. Patricia Cross, a leading advocate for educational reform throughout her career, observed over twenty years ago, "After some two decades of trying to find answers to the question of how to provide education for all the people, I have concluded that our commitment to the lock-step, time-defined structures of education stands in the way of lasting progress" (1976, p. 171). More recently, the Tofflers have noted that "America's schools...still operate like factories, subjecting the raw material (children) to standardized instruction and routine inspection" (1995, p. 13).

Today this inherited architecture of education places great limits on a system struggling to redefine itself. The school system, from kindergarten through graduate school, is time-bound, place-bound, bureaucracy-bound, and role-bound. (See Figure 1.)

Figure 1. Traditional Limits on Education

Time-Bound	Place-Bound
• class hours • semester course • school year	• campus • classroom • library
Bureaucracy-Bound	Role-Bound
• linear/sequential • ADA/FTE • credit/grade	• expert • lecture • sole judge

Time-Bound. "Hurry up, the bell's going to ring!" Every teacher who has ever lived knows full well the tyranny of time forced on the system by the creation of the "class hour." "Unyielding and relentless, the time available in a uniform six-hour day and a 180-day year is the unacknowledged design flaw in American education. By relying on time as the metric for school organization and curriculum, we have built the learning enterprise on a foundation of sand" (National Education Commission on Time and Learning 1994, p. 8). Herding groups of students through one-hour sessions five days a week in high schools and three days a week in college flies in the face of everything known about how learning occurs. No one believes that thirty different students arrive at the appointed hour ready to learn in the same way, on the same schedule, all in rhythm with each other.

Recognizing that schools suffer from a time-bound mentality, the United States Department of Education appointed a national commission in 1992 to study the issue. Members of the commission concluded, "Learning in America is a prisoner of time. For the past 150 years, American public schools have held time constant and let learning vary.... Time is learning's warden" (*Ibid.,* p.7). The time framework is particularly pernicious when it is extended to credit hours per course. "The vast majority of college courses have three or four hours of credit. Isn't it a coincidence of cosmic proportions that it takes exactly the same billable unit of work to learn the plays of Shakespeare and differential calculus? Or maybe the guest has been amputated to fit the bed" (Peters 1994, p. 23). The National Education Commission on Time and Learning reports that no matter how complex or simple the school subject—literature, shop, physics, gym, or algebra—the schedule assigns each an impartial national average of 51 minutes per class period, no matter how well or poorly students comprehend the material (1994, p.7).

The reliance on time as a unit of measure must be changed to reflect mastery instead of time on task, recognizing what is universally understood: human beings learn at different rates. Students should not have to serve time. Time should serve them.

Place-Bound. School is a place. It is a schoolhouse, a schoolroom, a campus, a college. Sometimes school occurs *off-campus* but obviously is defined in relationship *to campus.* Young students go *to school.* Young adults go *off to college.* Incorrigible students are kicked *out of school.* School/college, and the learning that occurs in that context, is *over* here. It is external to everything else that goes on in the learner and the society. It is cloistered, private, sacrosanct territory. Speed zones control its outer edges and liquor stores cannot be built within its perimeters. School is an ivory tower on the hill; it nestles in the gated groves of academe. Its residents do not mix with "townies." School is a place.

School as a place is deeply embedded in the collective unconscious of a people who made great sacrifices to construct their first college in 1636. This early pattern of school and schoolrooms has been stamped indelibly on each successive generation as the natural order of the world of education. "...[T]he design and practices of our childhood schoolrooms tend to be reproduced in most education and training settings, even those that aspire to be nontraditional or 'radically innovative.' Despite decades of experience with models, demonstrations, and experimental programs, the 'New American School' persistently gravitates back to our familiar models of school, classrooms, and teaching" (Perelman 1992, p. 125).

Schools are as place-bound as they are time-bound, and together these two traditions constitute a formidable barrier to change. Leonard says, "...[T]he conventional classroom...is the isolation cell, the lock-up" (1992, p. 28). If the student is to be freed for more powerful learning experiences and the teacher is to be freed to facilitate that learning in a more powerful way, then the walls must crumble, the boundaries made limitless. "The metaphor of a classroom is a powerful one. This most basic and fundamental unit of academic life—the sanctity of the classroom and the authority of the teacher within it—is about to be turned inside out" (Plater 1995, p. 27).

If reform efforts are successful, the campus, the classroom, and the library may no longer serve as the primary sites for learning. There will always be a need for these sites to accommodate some students who learn well in a place-bound context. But in many locations these place-bound constructs will become artifacts abandoned by a great many students and faculty who will embrace the open architecture created by applications of new technology and new knowledge about how human beings learn.

Bureaucracy-Bound. The adoption of business values and practices in education started in about 1900. The great business barons of the time, including Andrew Carnegie, John D. Rockefeller, and J.P. Morgan, powerfully influenced American culture, especially education. President Calvin Coolidge reflected the values of these industrial barons and much of the country when he said, in 1925, "The business of America is business." Of all the traditional architectural elements of schools, critics have been most vocal about the negative influence of the bureaucratic model.

Perelman writes, "Education developed in scale and bureaucratic density to mimic the industrial bureaucracy it was styled to serve. Education in its less than two-century-old modern form is an institution of bureaucracy, by bureaucracy, for bureaucracy" (1992, p. 118-119). Perelman believes that the bureaucratic nature of schools will lead to their ultimate downfall as society in general moves to less bureaucratic models of social interaction. "...[The disappearance of education is inevitable, not only because education itself has become a huge socialist bureaucracy, but because it is a bureaucracy designed for a bureaucratic society" (*Ibid., p. 119*).

Leonard makes much the same observation, "From the beginning it was an administrative expediency, an attempt to adapt the tutor-learner system to mass education, a crude way of handling a large number of learners with a much smaller number of teachers. We were able to get away with it in the past chiefly because our society required few academically or technically educated citizens" (1992, p. 26).

Sizer noted a decade ago that the hierarchical bureaucracies of contemporary schools are, "...paralyzing American education. The structure is getting in the way of children's learning" (1984, p. 206). And Drucker weighs in with the astute observation that, "Nothing is less productive than to make more efficient what should not be done at all" (1992, p. 29).

The negative effects of the bureaucracy-bound model can be seen in clear relief in the educational code that regulates the California community college system. For 100 years, state and federal laws and structures have been added piece-meal to regulate the delivery of education to California residents; the cumulative effect is mind-boggling.

In the California Education Code alone, there are currently over 1,200 statutes that directly regulate and affect the affairs of community colleges. This ponderous code does not even include the 640 regulations adopted by the board of governors and the hundreds and hundreds of federal statutes and regulations that govern the specific activities of colleges. (Nussbaum 1992). Roger Moe, majority leader of the Minnesota State Senate, frustrated in his attempts to bring about educational reform in his state, summed up the basic character of the bureaucratic model: "Higher education is a thousand years of tradition wrapped in a hundred years of bureaucracy" (1994, p. 1).

Role-Bound. By the end of the sixth grade a typical student has experienced at least six different teachers. With high school graduation, assuming six teachers a year for six years, the number climbs to 42. With a bachelor's degree, assuming 124 units divided by 3, the

> # If reform
> efforts are successful,
> the campus, the classroom, and
> the library may no longer serve
> as the primary sites for learning.

number of teachers for a typical student now totals 83. Ten courses for a master's degree—the minimum level of school achievement for the great majority of instructors working in community colleges today—bring the total number of teachers experienced by a student to 93, not including a vast array of teachers encountered in preschool, scouts, 4-H, Sunday school, summer camp, etc. In short, most educators with a master's degree have spent at least 17 school years under the tutelage of approximately 93 different teachers. Teaching, however, is the one profession that expects so much of its members and pays so little.

Teachers are expected to be knowledge experts, assessors, evaluators, managers, data collectors, artists, group facilitators, counselors, information processors, lecturers, problem analysts, problem solvers, coaches, mentors, behavior controllers, and value clarifiers. Their formal education is ill designed to prepare them for these multiple roles, and postal clerks and cabin personnel on airlines often receive more on-the-job training. Most new teachers are not inducted into the profession, except sometimes in an internship as part of preteaching exercises. Teachers are thrown into the profession, dumped into the classroom to sink or swim on their own. No wonder they fall back on the models they know too well. They teach as they were taught by the 93 teachers who were their models, repeating the catechism that is passed on generation after generation, bound in a role that pretends each is an up-to-date expert in some discipline, that endorses the lecture method as the primary tool of teaching, and that demands each teacher serve as sole judge and jury over the lives of his or her students.

As Kipp has said: "Having observed people teach all our lives, professors-to-be are supposed to know instinctively what to do in the classroom. We're tossed in this rolling sea with no Baywatch lifeguard around, left to sink or swim among the circling students. Small wonder, then, that the worst practices of the profession get passed along from one generation of professors to the next" (1997, p. 11).

Just as schools must be released from the architectural limits of time and place, teachers must be released from their traditional roles to focus their talents and abilities on the learner and learning as their *raison d'etre*. "Restructuring the role of faculty members will, at first, prove to be a monumental undertaking. All of the incentives seem against doing so—except, in the end, survival" (Guskin 1994, p. 16). Perelman describes the basic model of education in vivid terms: "There may be no more common and erroneous stereotype than the image of instruction as injecting knowledge into an empty head. Whether in a typical schoolroom, or a congressional hearing, or a corporate training session, the same one-way process is acted out. In each, the teacher or expert faces the learners, taking on the critical role of 'fountain of knowledge.' The learner plays the 'receiver of wisdom,' passively accepting the intelligence being dispensed, like an empty bowl into which water is poured" (1992, p. 135). More succinctly, Russell Edgerton (1997), after serving for twenty years as president of the American Association for Higher Education, said, "Professors impart knowledge. Students absorb this knowledge. Examinations test whether students can recall what they have learned. In short, teaching is telling; learning is recalling" (p. 30).

If the dominant role for teachers has been that of conveyor of information, the conveyor belt has been the lecture. "Lecturing is the overwhelming method of choice for teaching undergraduates in most institutions" (Terenzini and Pascarella 1994, p.29). Despite a large body of evidence gathered over many years regarding the limitations of the lecture method, the current educational architecture supports and encourages its continuing and widespread use. One study (Pollio 1984), for example, found that teachers in the typical classroom spent about 80 percent of their time lecturing to students who were attentive to what was being said about 50 percent of the time.

The historical architecture of education—the time-bound, place-bound, bureaucracy-bound, and role-bound model currently embedded in educational culture—presents a formidable barrier to education reform. Many faculty, administrators, and support staff succeeded as students in this environment, and many work comfortably today within these structures.

Furthermore, funding systems, work schedules, and social structures support the continuity of the current architecture. For institutions that want to become more learning-centered, however, the architecture must be changed or there will be significant limits on the extent to which learning can be placed first.

The Learning College

In major reform efforts it is helpful to review both ideal models of proposed alternatives and the experiences of vanguard institutions that are beginning to create their own models. In this section we review the idealized model; in the next section we review the practical experiences of six colleges that are on their way to becoming more learning-centered institutions. Community colleges will launch the reform efforts to become more learning centered from a variety of positions. Some will extend their current efforts in Total Quality Management to include more focus on improved and expanded learning for students. Some will use information technology as the catalyst to direct their efforts toward learning. Some community colleges will attempt to apply the experiences they have learned in their "shadow colleges," the divisions that customize education for business and industry, to other programs in the institution. Still others will launch their initiatives from a successful experiment with key innovations such as learning communities or classroom assessment. Regardless of the point of departure, it will be helpful for those community colleges making visible commitments to becoming more learning centered to create a frame of reference to serve as a guide for their journey. This frame of reference is more than a vision statement; it is a set of basic principles developed in the context of shared values among the institution's members. What do we really believe? and What can we really become? are questions that focus the institutional conversation.

From hundreds of such conversations over the past four decades, I have constructed a frame of reference that provides a point of departure for creating a more learning-centered college. It is offered here, not as a final answer or even a completely developed guide, but as an example of how the challenge can be approached. I hope this example I call "The Learning College" will serve as a catalyst to assist community colleges in creating their own sets of principles or frameworks to guide their efforts to become more learning-centered institutions.

The learning college places learning first and provides educational experiences for learners anyway, anyplace, anytime (O'Banion 1995-96, p. 22). The model is based on the assumption that educational experiences are designed for the convenience of learners rather than for the convenience of institutions and their staffs. The term "the learning college" is used as a generic reference for all institutions of higher education.

The learning college is based on six key principles:

- The learning college creates substantive change in individual learners.

- The learning college engages learners in the learning process as full partners, assuming primary responsibility for their own choices.

- The learning college creates and offers as many options for learning as possible.

- The learning college assists learners to form and participate in collaborative learning activities.

- The learning college defines the roles of learning facilitators by the needs of the learners.

- The learning college and its learning facilitators succeed only when improved and expanded learning can be documented for its learners.

Principle I: The learning college creates substantive change in individual learners. If the current reform efforts are worth the energy and time they will require, then community colleges should settle for nothing less than substantive change in individual learners. That is a goal highly desired from educational experiences for our own children and all those in our care. No faculty member, administrator, support staff, or trustee will argue with this principle, but it is not often held up visibly as a principle to guide action. Stated up front and stated often it can become embedded in the institutional culture, undergirding all other principles.

Institutional priorities, however, usually focus on organizing data on the more obvious outcomes of learning and are most often reported for groups: rates of graduation, persistence, or employment for selected cohorts. This is important information and must be collected by all institutions to satisfy external constituencies and to gauge average institutionwide success.

But this general information provides only a rudimentary measure of institutional effectiveness. At some point in their efforts to become more learning-centered institutions, community college staff members will engage in a series of rich conversations about other definitions of learning. There will be discussions regarding the differences among training, education, and learning. Complex constructs regarding basic learning, hardy learning, and more powerful learning will emerge from the discussion of personal values and experience in education.

In my definition, learning kindles new ways of seeing, thinking, and doing that lead to changed behavior. If that definition is even partially correct, then the institutional participants engaged in a conversation about learning may encounter new ways of seeing, thinking, and doing— leading to changes in their behavior. In the learning college, substantive change in individual learners occurs in administrators, faculty, support staff, and trustees, as well as in students. Making learning a central topic of institutional conversation and agreeing that substantive change in individual learners is a basic institutional principle make the current reform effort a great deal more than business as usual.

Principle II: The learning college engages learners in the learning process as full partners, assuming primary responsibility for their own choices. At the point a learner chooses to engage the learning college, a series of services will be initiated to prepare the learner for the experiences and opportunities to come. Until there is a seamless system of education for lifelong learning based on principles similar to those of the learning college, these services will be heavily focused on orienting the learner to new experiences and expectations that are not usually found in traditional schools. Two key expectations will be communicated to new learners at the first stage of engagement: 1) learners are full partners in the creation and implementation of their learning experiences, and 2) learners will assume primary responsibility for making their own choices about goals and options.

The services will include assessing the learner's abilities, achievements, values, needs, goals, expectations, resources, and environmental or situational limitations. A personal profile will be constructed by the learner in consultation with an expert assessor to illustrate what this learner knows, wants to know, and needs to know. The learner's self-assessment will be a key activity. A personal learning plan will be constructed from this personal profile, and the learner will negotiate a contract that outlines responsibilities of both the learner and the learning college.

As part of the contract, the learner will be responsible for selecting from among the learning options provided by the learning college. The assessment information, the terms of the contract, historical records from previous learning experiences, external evaluations, work experience, and all other pertinent information will be recorded on the learner's smart card, which serves as a portfolio of information, a lifelong record of lifelong educational experiences. The smart card, similar to an Automated Teller Machine (ATM) card already widely used by banks, will belong to the learner, who will be responsible for keeping it current with assistance from specialists in the learning college. In addition to the smart card, other educational institutions and employers will develop their own systems to verify what they need to know about the learner.

The learning college will also provide orientation and experimentation for learners who are unfamiliar with the learning environment of the learning college. Some learners will need training in using technology, in developing collaborations, in locating resources, and in navigating learning systems. Specialists will monitor these services carefully and will be responsible for approving a learner's readiness to fully engage the learning opportunities provided.

> **Complex** constructs regarding basic learning, hardy learning, and more powerful learning will emerge from the discussion of personal values and experience in education.

In the learning college, the orientation and experimentation process will take as much time as necessary to meet the needs of each learner. Some learners seeking minimal learning experiences about which they are very clear can begin their activities immediately following their first point of engagement. Some learners will want to participate in the orientation and experimentation process for a few days or a few weeks. Some learners may be engaged in the process for several months. Since there will be no restrictions on time and place for the engagement, there will be no limitations governing the activities except the needs of the learner. There will be many options for learners to engage the learning college, including self-guided print and video modules, live and Internet-based activities, classes and laboratories on campus, and individual consultations with a variety of specialists. Continuing learners will soon learn to navigate the learning college system and use it to their full advantage.

The student will not, however, drive all the choices regarding learning. Colleges are collections of wise educators who know a great deal about the larger values associated with a college education. Faculty may want to require selected liberating experiences for students. A college might, for example, require all students to provide some service to the community, examine their views on diversity, develop special skills such as how to access the Internet, express their creativity in some art form, or understand some special feature of their culture. A college has the right, perhaps even the responsibility, to provide the fullest education possible for its students. Its goal is not always best achieved if the collegiate experience is reduced to a K-Mart in which the customers select only the items with which they are already familiar.

Community colleges attempt to provide experiences that will broaden and deepen the thinking of their students through such programs as critical thinking across the curriculum or a required general education core of courses. And community college faculty and administrators should continue to struggle with what constitutes a common core of learning for all their students. However, in a more learning-centered college the options for how individuals will learn the common core will be greatly increased. The goal is to provide liberating experiences agreed upon by the faculty that are free of the constraints of the historical educational architecture.

Principle III: The learning college creates and offers as many options for learning as possible. In the learning college there are many options for the learner in initial engagement and in continuing educational activities— options regarding time, place, structure, staff support, and methods of delivery. The learner has reviewed these options and experimented with some that are unfamiliar.

Each learning option includes specific goals and competency levels needed for entry, as well as specific outcome measures of competency levels needed for exit. Learning colleges are constantly creating additional learning options for learners, many of them suggested by learners from their own experiences. A major goal of the learning college is to create as many learning options as possible in order to provide successful learning experiences for all learners. If one option does not work, the learner should be able to navigate a new path to an alternative learning option at any point.

Practitioners,
as well as researchers,
know that group interaction can be very helpful to individual learning.

If a learning college had to develop a full array of options from scratch, the task would be overwhelming and too costly. Fortunately, there is a tremendous variety of resources available, many of them field tested and free. Thousands of individual faculty members have designed improved or alternative learning materials as part of their sabbaticals, on released time during regular terms, on summer projects, with innovation grants from various institutions, and with support from federal and foundation grants. Individual colleges have initiated programs to design and develop new learning opportunities for students, sometimes with a considerable commitment of college resources. Colleges have initiated consortia to work in collaboration with each other and with agencies and companies to produce new learning programs. State and federal agencies, and most especially the military, have created hundreds of learning options that are free. Business and industry have spent billions on training materials. Educational entrepreneurs such as book publishers, testing agencies, information networks, training organizations, and computer corporations are in the specific business of developing training materials often available to educational institutions for a fee paid by the students.

To manage the activities and progress of thousands of learners engaged in hundreds of learning options at many different times, at many different levels, in many different locations, the learning college will rely on expert systems based on early developments such as General Motors' Computer-Aided Maintenance System or Miami-Dade Community College's Synergy Integrator. Without these complex technological systems, the learning college cannot function. These learning management systems are the breakthroughs that will free education and educators from the time-bound, place-bound, and role-bound systems that currently manage the educational enterprise.

Principle IV: The learning college assists learners to form and participate in collaborative learning activities. In the learning college, the university ideal of a "community of scholars" is transformed into a "community of learners." More than just cute word play, the focus on creating communities among participants in the learning process— including not just students but also the faculty, administrators, and support staff—on creating student cohorts, and on developing social structures that support individual learning is a requirement of a learning college.

Practitioners, as well as researchers, know that group interaction can be very helpful to individual learning. There are examples of effective collaborative learning models at all levels of education. We also know from experience that programs designed to build cohorts of students and then to engage them in a common experience or curriculum greatly increase retention and ultimately program completion. Nursing programs in community colleges have some of the highest success rates in all of education, in part because they are often highly selective, but also because a cohort is guided together through a rigorous competency-based curriculum. Nursing students study together and support each other, and there is no disincentive for all to succeed at high levels because students are not graded relative to each other (as on a Bell curve) but relative to a performance standard.

The most widespread form of collaborative learning in the community college takes place in "learning communities," a specific term that is a curricular intervention to enhance collaboration and expand learning. "Learning communities…purposefully restructure the curriculum to link together courses or course work so that students find greater coherence in what they are learning, as well as increased intellectual interaction with faculty and fellow students" (Gablenick et al., 1990, p. 5). These collaborations are also referred to as learning clusters, triads, federated learning communities, coordinated studies, and integrated studies; but "learning communities" has emerged as the favorite descriptor. When the same 30 students enroll for nine credit hours in a sequence of courses under the rubric of "Reading, Writing, and Rats," they have enrolled in a learning community.

In the learning college some learning communities and collaborative learning activities will not look very much like classrooms, and many will have dynamics defined by characteristics of pace, distance, membership, and means of communication. For instance, as the number of adult workers returning to college for education and training continues to grow, a likely venue for establishing learning communities will be in the workplace. Workplaces that value and encourage lifelong learning—whether because of altruism or enlightened self-interest—will make ideal sites for communities of learners, as common interest may be easier to determine and the level of resources available to support the community may be very high. For instance, video-on-demand can distribute information, including interactive training modules, directly to the desktop of employees; information resources can be concentrated at a common work location; and assessment services or learning specialists can be housed at the work site as desired.

Powerful networking technology can also help nurture a learning community by assisting its members to communicate with each other regularly in both synchronous and asynchronous modes. Certainly if courtship can be accomplished in cyberspace, then learning communities can be formed there. The electronic forums established in the Maricopa Community Colleges are pioneering efforts to create communities of learners through technology networks.

The roles that college educators will play in forming and supporting learning communities are yet to be thoroughly defined. However, in a learning college, staff will form and recruit students into cohorts of common interests or circumstances. Process facilitators will orient individuals and help them form groups or communities of learners. Resource specialists will attend to the resource needs of both individuals and groups of learners. Learning facilitators will design experiences that build upon and use group strengths and other dynamics.

Assessment specialists will design and implement authentic assessments that can occur both individually and in the context of the learning community. The learning college will be designed not only around the unique needs of individual learners but also around their needs for association. The learning college will foster and nourish communities of learners as an integral part of its design and as a key process for creating substantive change in individual learners.

Principle V: The learning college defines the roles of learning facilitators by the needs of the learners. Everyone employed in the learning college will be a learning facilitator, including categories formerly designated administration or support staff. Trustees will also be considered learning facilitators as they exercise their responsibilities for governance and policy development in creating a more learning-centered institution. Every employee will be directly linked to learners in the exercise of his or her duties, although some activities such as accounting may be more indirectly related. The goal is to have every employee thinking about how his or her work facilitates the learning process.

When the current members of the staff do not have the skills to meet the needs of the learners, the learning college will contract with specialists to provide the needed services. Specialists will be employed on a contract basis to produce specific products or deliver specific services; some will work full time, but many will work part time, often from their homes, linked to the institution and to learners through technology. A number of specialists will be scattered around the world providing unique services and special expertise.

The groundwork is already being prepared for these new roles to emerge. A 1996 report by the Ohio Technology in Education Steering Committee recommended the term "learning consultant" to best describe the educator of the future. "As learning consultants, educators will play many roles:

- Learning consultants will be mentors—guiding each learner to his or her own chosen goals.

- Learning consultants will be facilitators of inquiry—coaching learners and helping them remove barriers as they move toward discovery.

- Learning consultants will be architects of connection—observing the needs of individual learners and joining them to information experiences, resources, experts, and teams.

- Learning consultants will be managers of collaboration and integration—combining the needs and abilities of *their* learning communities with the needs and abilities of *other* learning communities" (1996, p. 13).

Learners will also participate as learning facilitators, and this role could be made part of the options negotiated in the orientation process. Many will not have time, but others will welcome the opportunity to offer their experience and knowledge to assist other learners. Colleges already use students as lab assistants and tutors to facilitate learning. In the learning college, these roles and opportunities will be expanded to capitalize on the resources students bring.

The goal of Principle V is to use the resources of the institution to better meet the needs of students, but it is also designed to free faculty from the restrictions placed on them by the historical role-bound architecture of education. In actual practice, colleges try to implement this principle by employing specialists (counselors, librarians, instructional designers, staff development trainers, etc.) and releasing selected teaching faculty from a class or two to conduct special projects. But the common denominator of the traditional role-bound model—one full-time faculty member teaching four or five courses each term—continues to dominate most of the thinking and most of the action in the institution. An audit of the great variety of skills and expertise residing in the current faculty would be mind-boggling in its richness and complexity. Changing the historical architecture of education to allow the skills and expertise of the faculty to be better matched to the needs of learners would be an overwhelmingly complex task, but a task that could lead to more satisfied and successful faculty and students.

Principle VI: The learning college and its learning facilitators succeed only when improved and expanded learning can be documented for its learners. "What does this learner know?" and "What can this learner

Guiding the
portfolio assessment

process will be one of the

primary functions of learning

facilitators.

do?" are questions that provide the framework for documenting outcomes, both for the learner and the learning facilitators. If the ultimate goal of the learning college is to promote and expand learning, then these

questions mark the yardstick by which the learning college and staff are measured. Conventional information may be assembled for students (retention rates and achievement scores) and for faculty (ratings by students, peers, and supervisors, and community service), but the goal will be to document what students know and what they can do and to use this information as the primary measure of success for the learning facilitators and the learning college.

All learning options in the learning college utilize competency requirements for entrance and for exit. These competencies reflect national and state standards when available, or they have been developed by specialists on staff or on special contract. Assessing a learner's readiness for a particular learning option is a key part of the initial engagement process and thereafter a continuing process embedded in the culture of the institution.

Learners negotiate and sign contracts for overall programs (general education core, basic skills, workplace skills, etc.) and may need to negotiate specific contracts for some learning options whether part of a program or not. Moreover, learners will be encouraged to add competencies and goals beyond those established in the standards.

Portfolio assessment will be one of the primary means by which learning is documented. A portfolio is a systematic and organized collection of evidence of what the learner knows and what the learner can do. It builds on prior information, is in constant use through revision and updates, and provides continuity for future learning activities. Specific benchmarks of achievement may be applied to determine credits earned if credits continue to be the hallmarks for moving learners along a seamless path of education.

Guiding the portfolio assessment process will be one of the primary functions of learning facilitators. Since many of the learning options will be stand-alone, student-led collaborations, contracts with specialists, or facilitated by tutors and coaches, learning facilitators will have more time for the portfolio assessment. It may be possible to codify some of the assessment process for easier management, and advances in technology will provide some assistance.

These six principles form the core of the learning college. They refer primarily to process and structure and are built on the basic philosophy that the student is central in all activities of the educational enterprise. There are certainly other principles that must be considered in creating a new paradigm of learning, loosely coupled here into a concept designated "the learning college." Content, funding, and governance are examples of pertinent issues that must be addressed and for which principles must be designed. Still, these six principles provide a starting point for those who wish to create a more learning-centered college, a college that places learning first and provides educational experiences for learners anyway, anyplace, anytime.

Six Colleges Take Their First Steps

A small vanguard of leading community colleges is beginning to experiment with new approaches to placing learning first, implementing new practices and programs to make their institutions more learning centered. Six community colleges have been identified by the author that are committed to institutionwide efforts to place learning and learners as central to all their efforts: Community College of Denver (Colorado), Jackson Community College (Michigan), Lane Community College (Oregon), Maricopa Community Colleges (Arizona), Palomar College (California), and Sinclair Community College (Ohio).

The early experiences of these colleges are informative for other colleges that plan on exploring how to respond to the new emphasis on learning. Although each college initiated its activities in terms of its own culture, there are common elements that reflect beginning steps or practices that may be useful to other colleges. The common elements are listed here as four first steps on the journey to become a more learning-centered institution; more detail on additional steps and individual practices and policies of the six colleges can be found in *A Learning College for the 21st Century* (O'Banion 1997).

Recast Statements of Mission and Values to Focus on Learning. There will often be months of institutional thrashing about before some key leaders begin to speak about the need to better assess outcomes or the need to better serve customers or the need to re-engineer programs to reflect declining resources. Every institution begins its journey based on its own character, culture, and community; at some point, however, it becomes clear that the kind of institutional change called for in the current situation is so substantive that a review of mission and basic values is required.

If learning is to be the central focus of a learning-centered institution, then learning must be the central focus of mission and value statements. When college members engage this issue, there will be a great deal of discussion and frustration, but it is an early step that cannot be avoided. Revised or new statements are created after much soul-searching and reflect new values held in common by very different groups. These statements are not easily developed, but once college members travel the long, hard road leading to consensus, they will have a vision to guide them for the rest of their journey.

The following brief excerpts from several new mission statements reveal the new focus on learning:

- *Jackson Community College IS a community of learners.*

- *Lane Community College provides quality learning experiences in a caring environment. Above all, Lane must put the learner first by shifting more and more to a learner-focused organization.*

- *Learning is a process which is lifelong for everybody and should be measured in a consistent, ongoing manner focused on improvement.* (Maricopa Community Colleges)

- *We see ourselves as a learning institution in both our object and our method.* (Palomar College)

These statements are taken out of context and do not do justice to the complete and more elegant statements developed by the colleges, but they do provide a flavor of the new ideas beginning to percolate in community colleges. Any community college planning to become more learning centered will eventually be involved in a review and revision, if not complete overhaul, of its mission and values statements.

Realign Current Structures to Accommodate Collaboration and Teamwork Within the College Community. Many community colleges are involved in restructuring and re-engineering their institutions in response to changing conditions. The increasing use of technology, the expanding diversity of students, the demand for a better prepared work force, and declining support of education are only some of the reasons institutions of higher education are involved in reviewing their missions, their programs, and their practices. More and more, leaders in higher education are beginning to realize there is more involved than realigning the existing institution to improve on current practice. Leaders are beginning to realize they are engaged in a major reform that transcends the efforts to tinker with and tweak a few programs here and there. The entire system of higher education, and its supportive architecture, is being called into question; answers lead to a major change that places learning front and center. Jerry Moskus, president of Lane Community College, recognized this challenge in 1993 and said to the faculty and staff, "Lane must rethink nearly everything it does."

Leaders at Lane initiated their institutionwide effort to become a learning-centered college by examining in great detail their current organizational structure. All faculty and staff were invited to participate, and eventually a new organizational structure was created based upon a new vision that placed learning at the center of all their activities.

Community colleges that begin the journey to become more learning centered will almost always reorganize their current structure to ensure more collaboration and teamwork among institutional members. Traditional hierarchical structures designed for control and efficiency do not elicit the kind of creativity and commitment required for learning-centered institutions. Colleges that are reorganizing to become more learning-centered reflect the ideas of Deming, Juran, Senge, and Wheatley regarding the

need to flatten organizations, empower individuals, and involve all stakeholders. Community colleges are finding their own voice regarding structural changes, as noted in the following:

- *To leverage structural change, Maricopa agreed that changing the learning paradigm from a traditional one to a current, more learner-centered approach was the vehicle to more comprehensive, and even profound, structural change.*

- *Organizations that move routine decision making and problem solving to work teams are better able to adapt to continued change. We must break down the walls between departments by designing our processes and services around work teams that cut across artificial organizational lines.* (Lane Community College)

- *Palomar College empowers our educational team— faculty, staff, and administration—to create powerful learning environments.*

- *Effective organization change is really the relationship between structure, strategy, systems, style, skills, and staff, and something called shared values.* (Sinclair Community College)

The form of the new organizational structure created by community colleges moving toward a more learning-centered paradigm is not nearly as important as the long and sometimes chaotic processes colleges use to create new structures. And more important than the processes used are the new values that emerge from the willingness to engage in the processes. Community colleges that plan to reorganize to become more learning centered will learn little from the diagrams and charts that illustrate new structures developed by other colleges. All of the essence lies between the lines and around the boxes and can be understood and appreciated only through direct experience applied to one's own situation.

Involve All Stakeholders. In a community college the key stakeholders include administrators, full-time faculty, students, support staff, and trustees. Depending on the culture of the institution and its capacity to manage complexity, part-time faculty and community representatives should be included as well. Determining the groups to be represented in creating a more learning-centered institution is a crucial first step.

The new "science" of management and leadership that prescribes flattened organizations, open communication, and empowered participation makes a strong case for involving all stakeholders in major reform efforts. Margaret Wheatley, a consultant on organizational change, says, "Any change program that insists on defining how things ought to be done, that tries to impose a structure on everyone—without their involvement—works against our natural tendencies" (in Brown 1994, p. 24).

Wheatley goes on to explain:

> You need deep and meaningful involvement of the whole organization. This seems like an insurmountable barrier, to involve the whole organization, but I believe the starting point for real

change is to focus energy and direction on this one key question: "Can we involve the expertise and experience of everyone in the organization?" We can't ignore that question. We've got to figure out how we can avoid the temptation to design things for people instead of engaging them in creating their own responses to change (Ibid., p. 26).

Few community college leaders will argue against the importance of involving all stakeholders in the process of creating a learning-centered institution, but many will be challenged about how to do this. It is more practical to set a goal of involving everyone who wants to participate by providing numerous opportunities for their participation. Staff members can participate in institutionwide convocations, workshops and seminars, and special-training sessions. Staff development programs can be reengineered to focus on activities related to learning-centered efforts. In-house newsletters can provide important information regarding project activities. In some cases, a special publication will need to be created to carry the message for the learning initiative. Copies of key documents, such as the vision statement and the framework of guiding principles, and later documents, such as new policies for assessing students or selecting faculty or rewarding and promoting support staff that will evolve from project activities, will need to be sent to every member of the college community for review and response. Universal agreement is not the goal; universal opportunity to participate is, and some changes may need to be put to a vote.

Community colleges often take

great pride in comparing their commitment to teaching to the university's commitment to research.

Create an Open System of Communication. Convening a single meeting and distributing one key paper about the initiative to become more learning-centered as the only strategies for change will doom the effort to an early death. This is not an undertaking that can succeed by tossing one stone in the pond and following up on the ripples. Creating a learning-centered institution means tossing hundreds of stones into the pond, dumping boulders into the pond, and perhaps even filling in the pond and digging a new one.

This kind of change will not occur unless the members of the community college are kept fully and constantly informed about what is happening and unless there are mechanisms provided whereby they can communicate across the entire community of participants. Fortunately, technological innovations such as listserv now exist, and these are being put in place in many community colleges, allowing for a rich exchange of information and opportunities for connecting individuals and groups that usually function in the margins.

Wilson says, "If a vision is to shape the future and drive action, then the leader—and others in executive positions—must communicate it broadly, consistently, and continuously, until it becomes an integral part of the organization's culture" (1996, p. 5). The message must be driven home again and again through speeches, newsletters, meetings, articles, interviews, surveys, and actions.

As college constituents become convinced that the leadership is engaged in a serious commitment to become more learning centered, there will be a tremendous release of creativity and ideas that individuals will want to share. There must be highly visible and readily accessible mechanisms in place to allow for this outpouring of ideas. Mechanisms must also be in place to link people with common suggestions and concerns, to capture and record suggestions and ideas, and to incorporate these perspectives in creating a new culture that is learning centered.

A project manager is often appointed to ensure that mechanisms are in place for the communication that is needed. In some community colleges, a task force with representation from all groups will ensure institutionwide communication. The CEO of the college will need to take responsibility for many official roles in communicating about the project activities, as well as many unofficial ones. Leaders in the faculty and support staff must be involved and speak out in support of project activities. As the project emerges and matures, more and more participants will take responsibility for communicating their needs and their ideas if they see that these are taken seriously.

These four initial steps appear to be common for all community colleges that begin the journey to become more learning centered. The specifics of these steps are idiosyncratic to the culture of the institution and the character and abilities of its leaders. The steps are not as linear or formulaic as they appear to be in these written descriptions. In actuality, all four steps occur simultaneously and are often not even identifiable until they are almost completed. All four steps appear as guidelines or practices to follow, and at the same time, they are explicit value statements. For a college ready to launch an initiative to become more learning centered, these four steps are a good place to begin.

Key Issues and Challenges

The kind and amount of change called for in becoming a more learning-centered community college—the complete overhaul of the traditional architecture of education to place learning first—will be a formidable task, even for the most healthy and best-endowed institutions. Change always creates tension, and major change creates major tension. Educational leaders who embrace the learning-centered concept can expect a life filled with tension, and a review of some of the key issues and challenges that lie ahead will help them prepare for the long haul. These key issues and challenges should be reviewed and discussed in depth—perhaps as a series of organized staff development seminars—early in the creation of an institutionwide initiative to become a more learning-centered college. If faculty, administrators, and support staff can come to an early understanding of and perhaps even agreement about some of the obstacles they will face, their efforts will have a greater chance for success.

The Teaching Versus Learning Red Herring. Many reform efforts never get beyond heated discussions of differences in perceptions of the meaning of core concepts. The most volatile concept in the language of the new emphasis on learning appears when teaching and learning are cast as "teaching versus learning." In the early days of the current reform efforts, only a few years ago, a number of writers and speakers—including this one—tried to frame the issue in terms of teaching versus learning. The argument was made that the community college places more value on teaching than it does on learning, and it is easy to cite evidence to support the argument (*Building Communities* 1988, Barr 1994, Barr and Tagg 1995).

Community colleges often take great pride in comparing their commitment to teaching to the university's commitment to research. To drive the point home, community college advocates often note the university's propensity to use graduate students to staff large lecture sessions while they, more committed to quality teaching, make teaching the priority of professional staff. In the early 1990s, community colleges began to establish endowed teaching chairs, their version of the university's endowed research chairs. Endowed teaching chairs have now been established in dozens of community colleges across the country as one of the most visible expressions of the community college's commitment to teaching.

In retrospect, the community college has placed great value on teaching, but that does not mean that the community college does not also place great value on learning. To the contrary, every community college teacher understands that the basic purpose of teaching is to help students learn. Learning is the end, and teaching is the primary means to that end. Even the California State University System's Academic Senate defines "*learning*, the product of teaching" (1996).

The teaching versus learning debate is a red herring that serves only to divide and create rancor. It unnecessarily puts faculty on the defensive and unfairly demeans their commitments and contributions to the educational enterprise. The debate has no value in the conversations that must occur about the core concepts of teaching and learning and should be locked away in some Pandora's box where it belongs.

Having said that is not to deny that the language of teaching may overwhelm the language of learning in current mission statements, job descriptions, and program statements. It will be the task of those engaged in creating a more learning-centered perspective to right the balance and to examine whether practices, programs, and policies are influenced when learning takes a more visible place alongside that of teaching. There is ample room and great need for both in educational institutions of the twenty-first century.

Learning Organizations. Learning organization is a term popular in business and industry that is becoming increasingly adapted to institutions of higher education. Garvin suggests that "A learning organization is an organization skilled at creating, acquiring, and transferring knowledge, and at modifying its behavior to reflect new knowledge and insights" (1993, p. 80). The goal is to create a "community of commitment" among the members of an organization so they can function more fully and more openly to achieve the goals of the organization.

Peter Senge chartered the territory of the learning organization in his 1990 book, *The Fifth Discipline: The Art and Practice of the Learning Organization*. Senge describes the learning organization as one in which "people continually expand their capacity to create the results they truly desire, where new and expansive patterns of thinking are nurtured, where collective aspiration is set free, and where people are continually learning how to learn together" (p. 3). According to Senge, a learning organization depends upon five disciplines: systems thinking, personal mastery, mental models, building shared vision, and team learning. Through these disciplines, a college will flatten its organization; develop models of collaboration for faculty, administrators, and support staff; develop processes for evaluating and reviewing its goals; and involve all stakeholders in learning better how to do their jobs.

Faculty are
fully aware of
administrators who trot out new language that is not fortified with new beliefs and new behaviors.

A number of community colleges are attracted to the concept of the learning organization and have begun to apply some of the processes developed by Senge and his colleagues. Because they are familiar with the language of the learning organization, many community college leaders, especially presidents, assume they are engaged in creating more learning-centered institutions as a result of their interest in and compliance with the processes of the learning organization. It is quite possible, however, for a college to flatten its hierarchy, open the information flow, focus on whole systems, work together in teams, and develop flexible structures designed to enhance the continuing involvement of all members of the college's community and still retain models of the historical architecture of education. In some ways, a learning organization is designed for the staff of the institution, while a learning-centered institution is designed for the students. There is no guarantee that a learning organization will become a learning-centered institution placing learning first for students unless those values are made clearly visible as the primary goal of a learning organization.

The basic concept of the learning organization, however, provides a powerful foundation on which to build a learning-centered institution. The concepts and processes of the learning organization are highly compatible with the concepts and processes of a learning-centered institution. Community colleges engaged in creating a learning organization have established an excellent foundation for launching an institutionwide initiative to become a more learning-centered college.

The Language of Learning. At the present time, many colleges use the terms "learning communities," "learning organizations," and "learning colleges"—along with "learner-centered " and learning-centered"—as if they all meant the same thing. These terms do have a great deal in common as reflections of various aspects of the new emphasis on learning, but individuals do apply different meanings to these terms. It will be helpful if participants within an institution can agree on a common vocabulary to guide the institutional conversation.

One of the pitfalls of glibly adopting a new language is that it can give the appearance of change while old beliefs and behaviors are retained. Seasoned community college educators can spot with ease those who do not "walk the talk." Faculty are fully aware of administrators who trot out new language that is not fortified with new beliefs and new behaviors. Such action is a vacuous exercise that serves only to harden existing layers of cynicism. All members of the college community engaged in helping their institution to become more learning-centered should work hard to ensure that new practices, programs, and policies reflect the language they all agree best reflects these values and intentions.

As community colleges explore and experiment with becoming more learning-centered institutions, there is an opportunity to create a new language about learning, a community college-specific language. In the past, community colleges have borrowed a great deal of language from universities and four-year colleges to describe their values and their practices. Currently, community colleges are busy adapting language from business and industry. Surely there is a special language of learning embedded in the idiosyncratic experiences of community college faculty and staff as they continue decade after decade to provide learning opportunities for the most challenging learners in all of higher education. Among institutions of higher education, community colleges have long been one of the institutions most committed to learning. The creative mavericks who will lead community colleges to a new emphasis on learning should give some thought to creating their own language to reflect the unique perspectives they will bring to the task of building more learning-centered institutions.

If guardians are to become advocates,

leaders of the change initiative must engage a core of devoted faculty members who will champion change.

We Are Already Innovating as Fast as We Can. Faculty members, administrators, and support staff in community colleges take great pride in their innovations and in the innovative spirit with which they approach problems and opportunities. Innovation has become such an important value in the community college that it is often listed along with the open-door philosophy, student-centeredness, and teaching as an identifying characteristic of the community college movement.

Innovations can now be understood as the struggles of creative faculty and administrators to change the historical architecture of education that acts as a barrier to change. The effort to break down the traditional architecture of education is probably the motivating impulse for most educational innovation. It can be amply illustrated that many current innovations have been designed as specific interventions to address the limitations placed on teaching and learning by the time-bound, place-bound, bureaucracy-bound, and role-bound architecture inherited from earlier times.

In summary, open-entry/open-exit programs, distance learning, and computerized assessment testing are good illustrations of innovations designed to change the time-bound architecture. Many creative faculty have been trying to break out of the classroom for years, recognizing that the classroom and the campus are architectural constructs that can limit a student's and a faculty member's access to learning. Again, distance learning is a boundary breaker, but so are innovations in service learning and school-to-work programs. Learning communities, project-based education, and electronic forums are good examples of recent innovations designed to change the bureaucracy-bound model of education. Customized training programs, classroom assessment, and peer tutors are innovations that aim to break down historical restrictions on the role of faculty.

A case can be made that innovations in general are designed to bring about change and are, therefore, important elements in reform efforts. Many innovations certainly do create improved opportunities for students to learn and expanded opportunities for teachers to teach in new and creative ways. Most innovations, however, do not create major institutionwide change. In fact, most innovations emerge in isolation as stand-alone programs or practices championed by a select group whose members are often unaware of or uninterested in other innovations percolating throughout the institution. Even when innovators are encouraged with special institutional grants and institutional recognition, they still operate largely in isolation in terms of bringing about any institutionwide change. Few individual innovators are able to transcend the insular, bureaucratic structure of the college to connect their work and their energy to substantive, institutionwide change.

The moment waits for a visionary leader to create a new framework from existing innovations by cobbling together these innovative practices and programs into a newly assembled gestalt. If the energy and creativity of an institution's innovators could be channeled into a common cause and focused on changing the historical architecture prevalent everywhere in education, substantial educational reform could become a reality for many community colleges.

Can Guardians Become Advocates? Most educators are familiar with the observation that changing the curriculum (or making any major change in education for that matter) is as difficult as moving a cemetery: you get no help from the residents. All successful guardians of a process, a program, an institution tend to protect what has been created. And that is a central challenge for today's educators, for most educators have been successful within the framework of the traditional architecture of education. Why would instructors or administrators want to make major changes in a system that has rewarded them for performing well as students or has provided them with fairly attractive jobs? Educators are successful navigators of the current educational system, and while they recognize it is not a perfect system, many believe they work effectively for change within the existing boundaries.

It is generally acknowledged that the creators or guardians of a program or institution will find the task of making changes formidable. The following quotation on this challenge is attributed to George Washington:

> One of the difficulties in bringing about change in an organization is that you must do so through the persons who have been successful in that organization, no matter how faulty the system or organization is. To such persons, you see, it is the best of all possible organizations, because look

who was selected by it and look who succeeded most within it. Yet these are the very people through whom we must bring about improvements.

If guardians are to become advocates, leaders of the change initiative must engage a core of devoted faculty members who will champion change. This group will likely include a number of faculty who are frustrated with the lack of change and lack of leadership to date and other faculty who are active change agents in the institution. Who selects the core members, who is selected, and how they are selected can be very delicate processes depending on the institutional culture, especially the trust levels that exist among the various groups. The formation of this group of advocates is a beginning step in helping other guardians in the institution become advocates.

Institutional leaders can also encourage guardians to become advocates by not making scapegoats of past leaders or previous actions. William Bridges (1993), a management consultant, suggests:

> Never denigrate the past. Many managers, in their enthusiasm for a future that is going to be better than the past, ridicule or talk slightingly about the old way of doing things. In doing so they consolidate the resistance against the transition because people identify with the way things use to be and thus feel their self-worth is at stake when the past is attacked. (p. 30)

This is tricky business, of course. Changes of the magnitude called for in becoming a more learning-centered institution require giving up much that is familiar and creating much that is new. Leaders must strike a careful balance between these goals. They are likely to be more successful in encouraging change if they can offer rational explanations for ending some practices and creating new ones, rather than beating up on the past in which individuals in the institution may have considerable personal investment.

Funding Learning. It would make a great deal of sense to fund the educational enterprise in terms of the kind and amount of learning that is produced, that is, to implement learning-based funding. However, neither external funding formulas nor internal resource allocation and workload systems in community colleges tend to be sensitive to what and how much students actually learn.

Current state funding formulas for community colleges generally allocate funds on the basis of average daily attendance or some other accepted calculation of full-time student equivalence—formulas designed for an industrial factory model of education. There are modest efforts under way in states such as Florida, Ohio, Tennessee, Illinois, Missouri, and Colorado to fund colleges based upon their performance in producing certain outcomes, including student learning. However, the debate in these states over what kind of learning outcomes to fund, how to measure learning, and what formula to use to best match funding to learning outcomes is fairly indicative of the difficulty involved in any attempt to institute learning-based funding. To date, attempts to reward learning by earmarking special funds to encourage certain practices and programs have been minor, and most institutional officials seek to ensure that any performance-based state funding is either limited

to a small percentage of their total institutional allocations or sought in addition to, not as a replacement for, traditional attendance-based funding.

So, other than as a modest and symbolic spur towards desired practice, states are not likely to contribute much to institutional movement toward learning-based funding. Rather, it appears that states contribute most to institutional flexibility by using funding models that are neutral, namely, that do not require institutions to maintain traditional place-bound, time-bound, and role-bound models of higher education. Perhaps the best public policy stance for a state to take that wishes to encourage a learning-centered focus in its publicly supported institutions—and for institutional leaders to recommend and lobby in support of—is to provide base appropriations to community colleges that are not directly tied to the production of credit hours. States such as Missouri, that have decoupled credit hours and funding, at least tacitly permit learning-centered innovation without the threat of lost funding.

Regardless of external funding mechanisms, internal resource allocation systems, especially those associated with workload calculations, are where the rubber meets the road for learning-based funding models. As long as colleges allocate their funds and human resources by the rules of the industrial model, little learning-centered movement is likely to occur. As long as the basic workload model is one full-time faculty member assigned to teach four or five classes of 120-150 students, as much as 80 percent of all of the institutional funds will be tied up in that model, leaving little with which to innovate toward learning-centeredness.

It would make a great deal of sense to fund the educational enterprise in terms of the kind and amount of learning that is produced,

The challenge for colleges serious about becoming more learning centered is to develop alternative workload models, and only a very few workable examples have yet to be applied broadly in many institutions. However, there are hints of solutions to this funding bottleneck. One alternative funding approach has been employed in support of learning communities. Instead of loading one faculty member with three separate sections of English composition, another with three sections of American history, and a third with three sections of psychology, colleges engaged in building learning communities have instead assigned these three same faculty to the total 75-90 students enrolled in the learning cohort defined by these three courses. While the workload calculations are the same, the freedom to provide learners with multiple learning options within the context of a three-course block are greatly expanded, and the faculty are still paid by a recognizably comfortable model. This model could also be extended to include funding, for instance, five faculty to provide multiple learning options to 250 full-time students, support by learning specialists, student development professionals, and other support staff—achieving similar ratios to the traditional workload formula but with greatly increased flexibility and ability to focus on the individual needs and constraints of different learners.

Another workload model that might be adapted to support learning-centered initiatives is that used in many hands-on and clinical-based occupational programs—and in some technical colleges—the 35-hour faculty work week. Rather than loading faculty on the basis of classes taught, many colleges routinely make assignments that conform to an overall contact hour standard, usually about 35 hours per week. While some faculty would abhor such a schedule, others find its simplicity and flexibility to support learners in whatever way appears appropriate during fixed hours without concern for complex load calculations to be liberating. Some faculty would be even more supportive of 35-hour weeks if these could be extended into eleven or twelve month contracts at prorated pay, rather than limited to nine months, increasing their earning opportunities substantially.

Other more complicated and radical models are possible. For example, a college could attempt to develop a model to provide as many learning options as possible for 150 students who needed to succeed in achieving the learning outcomes of freshman composition. One possibility would be to assign one faculty member with the responsibility to assist these 150 students to earn the required competencies by whatever means the college could arrange. The instructor could meet some of these 150 students in a traditional class; others could work through course competencies over the Internet; others might use resource systems that are either text, video, or computer based to achieve the required outcomes—with all of the various options managed by the lead faculty member but also supported by multiple learning specialists and support staff. Instead of building loads upon classes taught, the college could build loads based upon student learning outcomes.

Creative community colleges committed to becoming more learning centered will be able to come up with better models than this one. It will be very important to consider different approaches to work load because the reallocation of resources is generally the only realistic option available to colleges to make some of the changes recommended in this monograph. However, reallocation will not be easy, for there is a great deal of mistrust on this issue. Nonetheless, resource allocation and reallocation, changed workload formulas, and alternative funding models must be faced early on in most community colleges if any real progress is to occur. There simply must be some breakthrough on how to make more effective use of the most critical and most expensive resource in the institution: the full-time faculty.

The Territorial Imperative: We Versus They. The most formidable barrier to change in education today is the divide that grows ever wider between key groups in the institution. Full-time faculty, part-time faculty, administrators, support staff, trustees, and students stake out their territory and defend their turf. Their struggles are usually over resources or rights or power; the struggles are seldom about learning.

Educational institutions are a microcosm of the larger society and reflect the loss of community noted by Bellah and Associates in *Habits of the Heart* in which we limit our communication with each other primarily to a vocabulary of individualism. In 1981, K. Patricia Cross wrote an article suggesting that community colleges were on "a plateau between two periods of high energy and a sense of mission in the community colleges. The old ideals that sparked enthusiasm and the sense of common purpose in community colleges have receded, and new ideals have not yet emerged to take their place" (Cross 1981, p. 113).

More recently (1997) Cross reexamined the extent community college faculty rallied around a common purpose and discovered that faculty still feel a great sense of loss regarding community.

> When I asked the various constituencies of 18 geographically dispersed community colleges to rate the Is and Should be importance of 20 institutional goals, faculty (N=1064) rated the creation of a sense of community the most important goal for their college (First on "should be" goals) and near the bottom in actual accomplishment (18th out of 20 goals on "is" goals). The discrepancy between what existed and what was thought desirable was far greater on "community" than on any of the other 19 institutional goals (p.30).

In some institutions of higher education, the loss of community and the open belligerence between some groups is such that there is no possibility of reasonable discourse on the institution becoming more learning centered. The kind of change called for in the current reform effort cannot occur in unhealthy institutions where battle lines have been drawn between we and they.

Even in healthy institutions, the task of overhauling the entire architecture of education to place learning first will be so difficult that all members of the college need to be aware of the pitfalls they will encounter. They also need to be aware of the positive elements working in their favor that can provide the foundation for creating a more learning-centered institution.

It might be helpful for college members to review the conditions that impede and conditions that support their efforts, especially in terms of the we-versus-they challenge. A visible listing of these sometimes invisible forces may improve communication and keep the initiative from floundering. Even the process of identifying these seven conditions can begin to build a common understanding and vocabulary that can expand the trust and commitment among key constituents. Every institution needs to compile its own list, but the following may offer some guidance as a point of departure.

Conditions That May Impede Change

1. Even when individuals recognize the need for change, they are often overwhelmed about how to articulate the framework for change that will be required.

2. Many of those who desire change doubt the ability of their colleagues to manage the transformation. At some point, because of the overwhelming nature of the task, everyone doubts his or her own ability.

3. Everyone complains about the time required to continue the present structure while they are also involved in creating a new structure. The task is to continue to serve three meals a day while the kitchen is being completely remodeled.

4. Many attempts at substantive change fail because college members have had few opportunities to develop the skills and knowledge required for major change. A massive in-house training program is required for all groups if the change process is to be understood and managed well.

5. Many colleges are trying to change the way they operate and how they communicate internally at the same time they launch major initiatives to change the way they educate their students. Some want to use the principles of Senge's "learning organization" to become a more learning-centered institution. These can be complementary or very separate goals; both require an extraordinary amount of time and effort and new learning.

6. Vested interests prevail and provide islands of comfort for many. Power struggles among divisions and campuses and between individual leaders increase the tension.

7. Once the change initiative begins to infiltrate the culture of the college, it is exceedingly difficult for any one individual to understand and articulate the big picture of what is going on.

Conditions That May Support Change

1. An overwhelming majority of college staff recognize the need for change. College staff are generally well read, up-to-date, and rational; they have a good understanding that the world in general and education in particular are going through a significant period of change.

2. Staff members like being part of a college culture where the need for change and an emerging vision for that change has begun to be articulated by its leaders. No faculty, administrator, or support staff wants to be part of a community college that proclaims, "There is no need for change here."

3. Those who work in community colleges are strongly committed to the basic values that undergird a learning-centered institution. They are rightly cynical about quick fixes and simplistic solutions, but every faculty member in a community college wants to be a better teacher; every administrator and member of the support staff wants to do a better job; everyone in the community college wants students to learn more; everyone in the community college wants the institution to improve its services to students and to the community.

4. Community colleges take great pride in their commitment to teaching, but not as an end in itself. Community college teachers and administrators have always understood that the purpose of teaching is to improve and expand learning. Because of its historical commitment to quality teaching, the community college is the ideal crucible in which to create a more learning-centered institution.

5. Community colleges have struggled for decades to teach the most diverse and most underprepared students ever to attend college. In the right situation, any improvement and support to perform these tasks more effectively will be welcomed.

6. New tools have emerged in the last decade in the form of improved assessment practices, new research on learning, and an expanding application of information technology. These new tools will help community college innovators to transform their colleges into more learning-centered institutions.

7. Community colleges have matured as institutions of higher education and are not as defensive as they were in earlier decades. Holding a well-deserved seat at the table of higher education, they are now positioned to take on national leadership in the continuing transformation of their culture toward a more learning-centered system.

Epilogue

The amount and kind of change going on in education today is enormous, and no institution is untouched by that change. Even if there were no major reform effort in progress, there would be major changes in the use of information technology, in governance and control, in student demographics, in funding and resources, in alliances and partnerships, and in innovations in teaching and management. But it is important not to mistake these related changes for the new emphasis on learning. These other changes will happen whether championed or not because they are natural processes reflecting transformations in the larger society. But it is possible for all these changes to develop over the next decade without a new emphasis on learning. A decade from now great changes in education will be clearly evident, but the traditional architecture of education could be pretty much in place, and learning could still not be the primary mission and outcome of educational institutions.

A new emphasis on learning must transcend all other changes in education and provide an overarching framework for the changes needed to place learning first. If two key goals guide the change process—1) overhauling the traditional architecture of education and 2) placing learning as the primary mission and outcome of education—then substantive change will be the result.

Finally, the measure of whether or not community colleges have been successful in becoming more learning centered can be gauged by embedding two questions in the culture of the institution: *Does this action improve and expand learning?* and *How do we know this action improves and expands learning?* The educational institution that consciously and visibly links every action with learning and consciously and visibly evaluates the outcome of those linkages will be an institution engaged in becoming more learning centered.

References

Barr, Robert B. "A New Paradigm for the Community Colleges," *The News*, Published by the Research and Planning Group for California Community Colleges. San Diego Community College District, February 1994.

Barr, Robert B. and Tagg, John. "A New Paradigm for Undergraduate Education," *Change*, Vol. 27, No. 6, November/December 1995.

Boggs, George R. "Community Colleges and the New Paradigm," *Celebrations*. Austin, Texas: National Institute for Staff and Organizational Development, September 1993.

Bridges, William. Managing Transition: *Making the Most of Change*. Reading, MA: Addison-Wesley, 1993.

Brown, Tom. An Interview with Margaret Wheatley. *Industry Week*, April 18, 1994.

California State University Academic Senate. "Faculty Productivity and Accountability." Unpublished paper, May 1996.

Commission on the Future of Community Colleges. Building Communities: *A Vision for a New Century*. Washington, DC: American Association of Community Colleges, 1988.

Cross, K. Patricia. *Accent on Learning: Improving Instruction and Reshaping the Curriculum*. San Francisco: Jossey-Bass, 1976.

Cross, K. Patricia. "Community Colleges on the Plateau," *Journal of Higher Education* Vol. 52, No. 2, March/April 1981.

Cross, K. Patricia. "Developing Professional Fitness," *The Cross Papers*, No.1, Mission Viejo: League for Innovation in the Community College, September 1997.

Daggett, Willard R. "Preparing Students for the 1990s and Beyond." Unpublished paper from the International Center for Leadership in Education, January 1992.

Dewey, John and Dewey, Evelyn. *Schools of Tomorrow*. New York: E.P. Dutton and Company, Inc., 1962.

Drucker, Peter T. *Managing for the Future: The 1990s and Beyond*. New York: Penguin, 1992.

Edgerton, Russell. Higher Education White Paper. Philadelphia: The Pew Charitable Trusts, September 1997.

Gabelnick, Faith et. al. *Learning Communities: Creating Connections Among Students, Faculty, and Disciplines*. New Directions for Teaching and Learning, Number 41. San Francisco: JosseyBass, Inc., Spring 1990.

Gales, R. "Can Colleges Be Reengineered?" Across the Board: *The Conference Board Magazine*, March 1994, pp. 31, 16-22.

Garvin, David A. "Building a Learning Organization," *Harvard Business Review*, July/ August 1993.

Guskin, Alan E. "Restructuring the Role of Faculty," *Change*, September/October 1994.

Higher Education Research Institute. "The American College Teacher: National Norms for the 1989-90 HER Faculty Survey." Los Angeles: University of California at Los Angeles. In *The Chronicle of Higher Education*, August 26, 1992, p. 30.

Kirp, David L. "Those Who Can't: 27 Ways of Looking at a Classroom." *Change*, Vol. 29, No.3, May/June 1997.

Leonard, George. "The End of School," *The Atlantic*, Vol. 269, No.5, May 1992.

Lovett, Clara M. "Small Steps to Achieve Big Changes," *The Chronicle of Higher Education*, November 24, 1995.

"The Learning Revolution," *Business Week*, February 28,1994, pp. 80-88.

"The Learning Revolution," *Time*, Spring 1995, p. 49-51.

Marchese, Ted. "Getting Smarter about Teaching," *Change*, September/October 1995.

Moe, Roger. Cited in Armajani, Babak, et al. *A Model for the Reinvented Higher Education System: State Policy and College Learning*. Denver: Education Commission of the States, January 1994.

The National Commission on Excellence in Education. A Nation at Risk: *The Imperative for Educational Reform*. Washington, DC: U.S. Government Printing Office, April 1983.

National Education Commission on Time and Learning. *Prisoners of Time*. Washington DC: U.S. Government Printing Office, April 1994.

Nussbaum, Thomas J. "Too Much Law...Too Much Structure: Together We Can Cut the Gordian Knot." Paper delivered at the 1992 Annual Convention of the Community College League of California.

O'Banion, Terry. *A Learning College for the 21st Century*. Phoenix: Oryx Press, 1997.

O'Banion, Terry. "A Learning College for the 21st Century," *Community College Journal*, December/January 1995-96.

Oblinger, Diana G. and Rush, Sean C. (Eds.) *The Learning Revolution*. Boston, MA: Anker Publishing Company, Inc., 1997.

Ohio Technology in Education Steering Committee. *Technology in the Learning Communities of Tomorrow: Beginning the Transformation*. Ohio Board of Regents, March 1996.

Perelman, Lewis J. *School's Out: A Radical New Formula for the Revitalization of America's Educational System*. New York: Avon Books, 1992.

Peters, Roger. "Some Snarks Are Boojums: Accountability and the End(s) of Higher Education," Change, November/December 1994.

Plater, William M. "Future Work: Faculty Time in the Twenty-First Century," *Change*, May /June 1995.

Pollio, H. *What Students Think About and Do in College Lecture Classes*. Teaching-Learning Issues, No. 53, Knoxville, TN: University of Tennessee, Learning Research Center, 1984.

Senge, Peter M. *The Fifth Discipline: The Art and Practice of the Learning Organization*. New York: Doubleday, 1990.

Sizer, Theodore R. *Horace's Compromise: The Dilemma of the American High School*. Boston: Houghton, 1984.

Terenzini, Patrick T. and Pascarella, Ernest T. "Living With Myths: Undergraduate Education in America," Change, Januaryl February 1994.

Toffler, Alvin and Toffler, Heidi. "Getting Set for the Coming Millennium," *The Futurist*, March/April 1995.

Wilson, Ian. "The Practical Power of Vision," On *the Horizon* Vol. 4, No. 2, March/April 1996.

Wingspread Group on Higher Education. *An American Imperative: Higher Expectations for Higher Education*. Racine, Wisconsin: The Johnson Foundation, Inc., 1993.

Learning Communities, Learning Organizations, and Learning Colleges

— Terry O'Banion

O'Banion, Terry. (1996). Learning Communities, Learning Organizations, and Learning Colleges, *Leadership Abstracts 9*(8).

A learning revolution appears to be spreading rapidly across the higher education landscape. Triggered by the 1983 report, *A Nation at Risk*, that warned "the educational foundations of our society are presently being eroded by a rising tide of mediocrity," the revolution was energized by a second wave of reform reports that began appearing in the early 1990s. These reports focused the reform efforts on a common theme: to place learning first. A 1993 report, *An American Imperative*, called for "putting student learning first" and "creating a nation of learners." In 1994 the Education Commission of the States urged a reinvented higher education system that would reflect a new paradigm shift centered on learning. In 1995 the Association of American Colleges and Universities issued a paper titled, "The Direction of Educational Change: Putting Learning at the Center."

Community colleges and their leaders have also joined the revolution. Myran and Zeiss predict, "We are entering a period of profound and fundamental change for community colleges.... We are becoming learner-based colleges." George Boggs says, "The mission is student learning. The most important people in the institution are the learners. Everyone else is there to facilitate and support student learning." The Board of Governors of the California Community Colleges in its 1995 New Basic Agenda announces, "Student learning is essential to the social and economic development of multicultural California."

And a handful of community colleges, soon to number in the hundreds, are busy redrafting statements of values and mission, redesigning organizational structures and processes, developing outcome measures, and applying information technology, all in the name of making their institutions more learner centered. As community colleges embrace the learning revolution, there is some understandable confusion regarding a number of terms that have appropriated the word "learning" as part of their nomenclature. Terms in current use include learning communities, learning organizations, and learning colleges.

Learning Communities

A curricular intervention designed to enhance collaboration and expand learning, a learning community "purposefully restructures the curriculum to link together courses or course work so that students find greater coherence in what they are learning, as well as increased intellectual interaction with faculty and fellow students." The structures are also referred to as learning clusters, triads, federated learning communities, coordinated studies, and integrated studies; but the term "learning communities" has emerged as the favorite descriptor. When the same 30 students enroll for nine credit hours in a sequence of courses under the rubric of "Reading, Writing, and Rats," they have enrolled in a learning community.

The first learning community was offered in the Experimental College at the University of Wisconsin in 1927. There have been numerous variations on the learning community in higher education for the last 70 years, and the first such experiments in a community college occurred at Santa Fe Community College (Florida) in 1966. More recently, the community colleges in Washington State, Daytona Beach Community College (Florida), and LaGuardia Community College (New York) have been leaders in developing new and expanded forms of learning communities.

As community colleges embrace the learning revolution, there is some understandable confusion regarding a number of terms that have appropriated the word "learning" as part of their nomenclature.

Learning communities are powerful curricular innovations and certainly help revolutionize the learning process, but they are not a necessary construct in the learning revolution. Learning communities would have emerged with or without a learning revolution; it is not likely they would have by themselves created a learning revolution. In some colleges in which they exist, the rest of the institution maintains business as usual in which learning is not always first. But since learning communities do exist, it would be wise to incorporate them into the architecture of the current learning revolution.

Learning Organizations

Garvin suggests that, "A learning organization is an organization skilled at creating, acquiring, and transferring knowledge, and at modifying its behavior to reflect new knowledge and insights." The goal is to create a "community of commitment" among the members of an organization so they can function more fully and more openly to achieve the goals of the organization.

Peter Senge charted the territory of the learning organization in his 1990 book, *The Fifth Discipline: The Art and Practice of the Learning Organization*. Senge describes the learning organization as one in which "people continually expand their capacity to create the results they truly desire, where new and expansive patterns of thinking are nurtured, where collective aspiration is set free, and where people are continually learning how to learn together." According to Senge, a learning organization depends upon five disciplines: systems thinking, personal mastery, mental models, shared vision, and team learning. Through these disciplines, a college will flatten its organization, develop models of collaboration for faculty and administrators, develop processes for evaluating and reviewing its goals, and involve all stakeholders in learning better how to do their jobs.

A number of community colleges are attracted to the concept of the learning organization and have begun to apply some of the processes developed by Senge and his colleagues. Because they are familiar with the language of the learning organization, many community college leaders assume they are engaged in creating learning-centered institutions as a result of their interest in and compliance with the processes of the learning organization. It is quite possible, however, for a college to reduce its hierarchy, open the information flow, focus on whole systems, work together in teams, and develop flexible structures designed to enhance the continuing involvement of all stakeholders and still retain models of classrooms, lecturing, and teacher-as-sage as has been true in past practice. In some ways, a learning organization is designed for the staff of the institution, while a learning-centered institution is designed for the students. There is no guarantee that a learning organization will become a learning-centered institution placing learning first for students unless those values are made clearly visible as the primary goal of a learning organization.

The basic concept of the learning organization, however, provides a powerful foundation on which to build a learning-centered institution. The concepts of the learning organization are philosophically compatible with the concepts of a learning-centered institution, and the processes of learning organizations are compatible with the processes of learning-centered institutions.

Learning Colleges

A new term has emerged in the last several years, specifically tailored for the community college, that reflects the goals and purposes of the learning revolution in action. The term "learning college" is much more useful in describing the comprehensive nature of a community college committed to placing learning first than are the terms "learning communities" and "learning organizations." The learning college places learning first and provides educational experiences for learners any way, any place, any time. The learning college is based on six key principles:

- The learning college creates substantive change in individual learners.

- The learning college engages learners as full partners in the learning process, assuming primary responsibility for their own choices.

- The learning college creates and offers as many options for learning as possible.

- The learning college assists learners to form and participate in collaborative learning activities.

- The learning college defines the roles of learning facilitators by the needs of the learners.

- The learning college and its learning facilitators succeed only when improved and expanded learning can be documented for its learners.

The key challenge for those who wish to launch learning colleges is to redesign the current learning environment inherited from an earlier agricultural and industrial society—an environment that is time bound, place bound, efficiency bound, and role bound. Roger Moe, Majority Leader for the Minnesota State Senate, has described higher education as "a thousand years of tradition wrapped in a hundred years of bureaucracy." Education today is not very different than education was one hundred years ago.

The learning revolution aims toward creating a new culture and a new architecture of education, a new system in which the learner is placed at the center of everything that occurs in the educational enterprise. The learning community is a curricular innovation that can help achieve that purpose when it is included in an institutionwide plan. The learning organization is a concept that contributes to an institutional culture in which discussions regarding student learning are more likely to take place. The learning college is a comprehensive approach incorporating both learning communities and learning organizations in helping community colleges to fulfill the aim of the learning revolution, which is to place learning first.

The Learning College: Both Learner and Learning Centered

— Terry O'Banion

O'Banion, Terry. (1999). The Learning College: Both Learner and Learning Centered. *Leadership Abstracts 2*(2).

As the Learning Revolution spreads rapidly throughout education, a new language on learning is beginning to appear. Every new book, conference program, and website is peppered with learning terms: learning college, learning communities, learning organizations, learning outcomes, brain-compatible learning, surface learning, deep learning, and learning facilitators.

The term "learning college" is beginning to be used to designate a new direction in education and provides an umbrella to shelter many of the concepts in current use. Two key concepts are "learner centered" and "learning centered." These terms are often used interchangeably, but they do not mean the same thing. While different, however, both concepts are deeply embedded in the history of education and are equally valuable in providing a foundation for the Learning College.

Learner Centered

Seasoned educators can easily remember the Humanistic Education Movement nourished by humanistic and phenomenological psychologists and one of the movement's key leaders, Carl Rogers, who gave us "client-centered therapy." Institutes in dozens of universities in the 1960s, with funds from the National Defense Education Act, trained school and college counselors in client-centered approaches to counseling, and "client centered" set the tone in many schools for the interactions between counselors and students and sometimes between teaching faculty and students.

The Student Development Movement, launched at the beginning of the 1970s, urged colleges and universities to become more "student centered." Student development champions, in their many statements, would not settle for counselors and student personnel professionals alone to become student centered; they wanted everyone in the institution to do so, and they achieved modest success in their goals.

In the late 1980s and 1990s, the purveyors of Total Quality Management asked educators to become more "customer centered," another variation on the theme. For the most part, educators have rejected the terminology of customer centered because it smacks too much of the business world and implies that the customer is always right, a sentiment few educators hold.

Client centered, student centered, customer centered, and learner centered all mean essentially the same thing—institutions and their employees attempt to focus on the special needs of the individuals they exist to serve through their policies, programs, and practices. Learner centered is but the most recent manifestation of the impulse to respond to individual needs, and it carries the added value of suggesting via the word "learner" the reason for the relationship between the institution and the client, or student, or customer it serves.

Learning Centered

Schools and colleges are by definition centers of learning, and faculty often bridle with appropriate righteous indignation if anyone suggests they are not learning centered. In the last forty years the impulse to place learning more firmly at the center of the educational enterprise has had a number of manifestations. Learning contracts were widely used during the Progressive Education Movement to stipulate for both student and teacher the specific goals and grades the student would achieve. Learning contracts carried the added value of making it clear that it was the student's responsibility to live up to the contract he/she had signed, an old value and practice regaining popularity in the Learning Revolution.

> # Two key concepts
> are "learner centered" and "learning centered." These terms are often used interchangeably, but they do not mean the same thing.

In the 1960s and early 1970s, spurred by the work of Bloom, Postlethwaite, Mager, and others, behavioral objectives became the common currency for learning-centered education. In this period there were major attempts to codify what learning meant by creating banks of specific objectives for courses and programs. Faculty could access these banks of objectives and select those most pertinent to their goals, their teaching styles, and the levels of competency of their students. Some community college leaders were so attracted to the promise of behavioral objectives they even attempted "management by objectives," and for a while in the 1960s MBO was as popular as TQM has been in more recent years.

The attempt to focus on learning-centered practices emerged again in the 1970s and 1980s under the banner of competency-based education. Community colleges created entrance and exit competencies, especially for selected vocational programs. In some cases students were allowed to enter these programs on demand and exit when they had mastered the required competencies, a practice heralding one of the key goals of the current Learning Revolution. Today, some community colleges, such as the Community College of Denver and Johnson County Community College, have developed exit competencies for every course and program in the catalog.

A flurry of interest in assessment, championed by the American Association for Higher Education, reaching its apogee at Alverno College (WI) in the 1980s and continuing today, has helped focus attention on learning outcomes. Several of the regional accrediting associations have provided leadership in assisting colleges to become more learning centered by requiring more attention to learning outcomes and outcomes assessment. The national effort to establish skill standards and the various state efforts to implement performance-based funding are more recent manifestations of the continuing goal of colleges to become learning centered.

Learning contracts, behavioral objectives, competency-based education, learning outcomes, skill standards, and performance-based funding are all variations on the theme of the notion of learning centeredness. The vision statement of Palomar College (CA) captures the essence of what it means to be learning centered:

> Our new vision statement reflects a subtle but nonetheless profound shift in how we think of the college and what we do. We have shifted from an identification with process to an identification with results. We are no longer content with merely providing quality instruction. We will judge ourselves henceforth on the quality of student learning we produce. And further, we will judge ourselves by our ability to produce ever greater and more sophisticated student learning and meaningful educational success with each passing year, each exiting student, and each graduating class.

The Difference

As stated earlier, even though there have been two distinctive streams in education—one learner centered and the other learning centered—many educators still treat the concepts as if they were synonymous. An illustration may clarify the difference.

A client (student, customer, learner) decides to go to an expensive spa for a week to lose five pounds (behavioral objective, learning outcome, exit competency). The client is treated exceedingly well in keeping with the high fees paid.

Facials and body wraps are provided daily along with a special diet of spa cuisine. The surroundings are beautifully landscaped; soft music plays in the background; the hectic pace of the outside world is soon forgotten. There are many options to choose from including aerobics, hip-hop classes, guided walks, meditation, and quiet moments of reading. The client is pampered beyond his wildest dreams. The spa is truly client centered, student centered, customer centered, learner centered.

At the end of the week the client packs to leave the spa and, as a final act of self-assessment, steps on the scale in his well-appointed bathroom. To his dismay not one pound has been lost. He has paid a high price for a learner-centered experience but did not achieve his learning-centered goal of losing five pounds.

It is not enough to make students feel good about the environment on the campus or the services they receive. It is not enough to impress students with the dazzling performance of great lecturers. It is not enough to provide all the latest in information technology. If we cannot document expanded or improved learning—however defined and however measured—we cannot say with any assurance that learning has occurred. And it is much more likely that we will be able to document learning when we place high value on learning-centered policies, programs, and practices and when we employ personnel who know how to create learning outcomes, learning options, and learning-centered activities.

Fortunately, we do not have to choose between learner-centered and learning-centered perspectives. In a Learning College it is important for faculty and staff to be both. The Learning College integrates these concepts and requires both care and service for the individual and attention to quality learning outcomes.

Faculty of the Future in Learning Colleges

— Cynthia D. Wilson

Wilson, Cynthia D. (1999 Spring). Faculty of the Future in Learning Colleges. *Michigan Community College Journal* 5(1), 75-84.

During the past decade, significant forces have risen that question the effectiveness of the typical community college instructor. These forces drive a movement for reform in higher education, and pressure from various groups is forcing community colleges to become accountable for their mission (Roueche, Johnson, & Roueche, 1997).

Legislators across the nation are demanding that colleges establish and measure student outcomes, and in some states, funding is based on performance. By tying funding to performance, legislatures are pressuring colleges to improve their success rates and their methods of measuring success. In addition, employers are calling for workers who enter the marketplace with stronger skills than were needed in the past. In part, the push is driven by rapid developments in technology, in part by increased competition in the global marketplace. As the number of competing industries increases, employers seek well-trained workers to improve efficiency and productivity (Institute for Future Studies, 1994; O'Banion, 1994).

Changing demographics also create a need for transformation in the community college. Some futurists predict that an increasing number of workers will need more education than a high school diploma but less than a bachelor's degree. The community college associate degree and certificate programs are in place to meet this demand.

Increased diversity among workers in the United States also calls for change. Differences in age, ethnicity, language, and life experiences create a diverse group of students whose needs, desires, and expectations vary (Baker, 1998). In addition to their educational pursuits, many community college students have work and family obligations, and the educational needs of these students differ from those of traditional college and university students. If community colleges are to survive and succeed, their leaders must address the calls for change by transforming the institutions they serve.

Transforming the Community College to a Learning Institution

One answer to the challenge transforms community colleges from teaching to learning institutions (Barr & Tagg, 1995; Boggs, 1995-1996; O'Banion, 1997). In *An American Imperative* (1993), the Wingspread Group on Higher Education recommends the student be the center of all activity in higher education. The learning college is an excellent model for creating student-centered institutions. To ensure the transformation, faculty must support and facilitate the development of the learning college. A clearly defined role for faculty in community colleges of the future may help ease the transition for employees. Faculty job descriptions that list the qualifications and skills necessary to succeed in a learning environment may ensure that personnel are trained to lead the learning process. A review of scholarly literature on the creation of community college learning environments provides a profile of roles for faculty in a learning college.

Faculty Roles

The faculty of the future will need to possess skills that complement the learning college—a student-centered institution in which every aspect of the college focuses on student success (Boggs, 1995-96). Administrative departments are designed to encourage student use, while academic divisions are focused on developing programs and activities that facilitate student learning (Barr & Tagg, 1995). According to O'Banion (1997), "the learning college places learning first and provides educational experiences for learners anyway, anyplace, anytime" (p. 47). When faculty members shift from a teaching to a learning paradigm, their roles change in several ways. An examination of faculty roles reveals changes in relationships with students and colleagues as well as with public and private organizations.

To ensure the transformation, faculty must support and facilitate the development of the learning college.

In the future, the relationship between faculty and students changes when educators make the transition from teacher to learning facilitator. At the same time, calls for accountability from legislators, taxpayers, community members, employers, and students compel community college leaders to address student outcomes when determining institutional effectiveness. If professional educators do not take responsibility for determining desired outcomes, then legislators will likely mandate accountability criteria (Roueche, 1998). The Futures Commission (1988) report recommends that faculty help define educational outcomes for students. At Sinclair Community College in Dayton, Ohio, and the Community College of Denver, faculty members have directed the process of defining measurable learning outcomes (McClenney, 1997a; Ponitz, 1997). In addition, the Council for Higher Education Accreditation is developing quality assessment instruments to assist community college leaders in determining student outcomes (Eaton, 1998).

Factors such as age, employment, culture, life experience, and educational preparation must be considered when faculty members develop learning activities for community college students (O'Banion, 1994). To document student progress, faculty members need standard, professional instruments for measuring desired outcomes (O'Banion, 1997). The information can then be used to evaluate student and program success, action plans for revision and improvement (Ewell, 1994), or requests for expansion of course offerings.

In its 1988 report, the Futures Commission recommended the creation of learning communities and other collaborative learning experiences for students (p. 25). Learning communities provide quality, holistic learning experiences for students while fostering ideas of team-building and individual responsibility. Within such a broadened perspective, learning becomes more meaningful and lasting than in traditional courses. Student success rates increase (Matthews, 1994), and "[b]y implication, learning communities enhance the quality of campus life, contribute to the development of connections beyond the college, and help prepare students for the challenges of leadership" (p. 181). At Palomar College in San Marcos, California, research shows that learning community students demonstrate improved critical thinking skills and increased confidence in motivational, social, and writing skills. In addition, retention rates among learning community students are higher than rates among other students (Boggs & Michael, 1997).

Course Connections to Life

To promote student success, faculty members can include learning activities that demonstrate the relationship between content and the career/life experiences of students, subsequently allowing students to experience the practical reason for learning. In addition, internships, employee/employer "shadowing," and mentors allow learners to apply classroom knowledge to real-life situations. Under the tutelage of experts in the field and learning facilitators in the classroom, students encounter safe, nurturing environments in which to learn and grow. Students leave a course, program, or institution with "value added" to their lives; finding the connection between learning and life achieves the goal (Alfred, 1994). At Valencia Community College in Orlando, Florida, the internship program provides students with "an opportunity to gain hands-on experience in a training-related work environment" (Turning students into employees, n.d.). Valencia is also involved with public schools in Orange and Osceola Counties in the local "School 2 Work" initiative. In an effort to strengthen job skills among students, businesses provide speakers, equipment, field trips, internships, apprenticeships, and scholarships to schools. Furthermore, business leaders participate on advisory committees and host workshops and seminars (School 2 Work, n.d.). Service learning is a valuable tool to enhance student interest in community development (Parnell, 1990) and adds practical humanism to the educational experience through student assistance to community service agencies (O'Banion, 1997).

Technology

Technology has the potential to assist the transformation from teaching to learning (O'Banion, 1997). The Maricopa Community College District leaders in Phoenix, Arizona, recognizing the potential of technology, have supported faculty efforts to use "electronic forums and Internet protocols as the central learning scaffold to build a cyber-learning system" (Elsner, 1997, p. 184). Such learning activities provide examples of how faculty members at Maricopa use technology to create a "learner-centered system" (Elsner, 1997, p. 184). Advancements such as interactive video and electronic mail are used routinely by faculty members to serve the needs of distant students. By using some forms of technology-based learning, students can be released from time and location constraints, and in some cases, students can direct their own learning.

Interaction Among Colleagues

Collaborative skills will enable faculty to work effectively in learning communities and elsewhere with students, colleagues, community members, and business leaders (Future Faculty Task Force, 1995). Collaboration skills help faculty develop learning communities among themselves as they work together to create a rich learning environment for students (Future Faculty Task Force, 1995). Collaborative activities build community among faculty members and help eliminate "the isolation of faculty and the essential loneliness of teaching as currently conceived and executed" (Matthews, 1994, p. 187).

While remaining expert and current in their disciplines, faculty members will be able to "cross discipline and departmental barriers" (Future Faculty Task Force, 1995, p. 5), particularly as they develop learning communities for students. The role of the future faculty member requires both a commitment to learning and the ability to develop innovative and creative learning activities for students. Faculty members will take advantage of professional learning centers located on their campuses to improve their skills and services to clients, to share ideas and activities with colleagues, and to participate in accountability processes (Lauridsen, 1994). Teaching and learning centers are "a fairly recent phenomena" in community colleges, in large part a response to pressures for educational reform (Lauridsen, 1994, p. 231). Supported by the institution and led by the faculty, these centers will grow in number, quality, and use as they work to improve the caliber of the learning environment.

Student, Mission, Purpose

Future faculty members will understand and be committed to the community college student, mission, and purpose. They will also understand their professional responsibilities and the policies and practices of the college (Future Faculty Task Force, 1995). The number of students who are employed has increased the need for scheduling alternatives to meet the needs of those who cannot attend traditional day classes (Wingspread, 1993, p. 13). To meet the needs of these students, faculty members will work in evening and weekend colleges, open entry-open exit programs, and fast-track degree programs.

Shared Governance

As accountability becomes tied to funding, faculty members will take part in college governance. Shared governance requires that "authority is delegated to each party to make decisions appropriate to its responsibility and to accept consequences of those decisions" (Future Faculty Task Force, 1995, pp. 2-3). Faculty members will have the right and the responsibility to participate in the development of the learning environment (Jenrette & Napoli, 1994). They will be involved in decisions that determine the direction and scope of the learning environment and of all parts of student life as it is associated with the college. At the Community College of Denver, faculty members are already an integral part of the process through which priorities are determined (McClenney, 1997b). Through the Quality Initiatives and other Continuous Quality Improvement programs at Brookhaven (Farmers Branch, TX), faculty members have a direct, active part in self-assessment and campus improvement (Bumphus, 1997). In the future, faculty members will be involved in consensus building, quality management and improvement, and decisions affecting their roles in the institution (Cross, 1994).

Committed to improving student success, the future faculty members will understand "how learning occurs" so they can help "[create] a sustainable system that fosters it" (learning@maricopa, 1997, p. 5). Aware of the diversity of populations and learning styles, faculty will be better prepared to provide a variety of experiences designed to improve student learning and add value to student lives (Future Faculty Task Force, 1995). One method of demonstrating their commitment to student success will be through participation in recruiting and advising activities (Richardson & Elliott, 1994). The faculty of the future will not only visit high schools to recruit potential students, but also visit middle and elementary students to create close ties with students early in their educational careers.

Faculty Diversity

The faculty of the future will be a diverse body representing a variety of cultures, ethnic groups, backgrounds, experiences, philosophies, and ideas. Among the unifying elements of the group will be a strong commitment to students, to community, and to learning. In addition, community college faculty members will become leaders both in and out of the classroom (Future Faculty Task Force, 1995). As facilitators of learning, they will guide student learning activities to ensure that desired outcomes are achieved or surpassed. Educators will also lead their students in team building, collaboration, and cooperative activities. As leaders, they add "motivational, intellectual, and interpersonal dimensions to their teaching goals" and "[teach] the learner how to learn" (Baker, Roueche, & Gillett-Karam, 1990, pp. 10-11). Faculty members must "assume leadership roles and become active participants in classroom research" (Hudgins & Williams, 1997, p. 65) if student success is to be achieved. Outside the classroom, faculty members will serve as team or cluster leaders and committee meeting facilitators. They will also develop strong relationships within the community, both as a service and as a vehicle for further partnering with various groups in the college district (Future Faculty Task Force, 1995).

Sources of Funding

As traditional funding sources become increasingly limited, future faculty members will help find alternate sources of program funding. Faculty members will seek grants from government as well as private sources, and they will forge partnerships with business and industry to develop and support mutually beneficial programs. Among these are recruitment efforts that include business, industry, and community service organizations (Roueche & Roueche, 1998). As faculty members develop close ties with business and industry, they will become involved in programs that place educators in the work environment. Serving as loaned employees, faculty members will learn

on site how industry works while discovering the skills its employees need. With such information, learning facilitators can better develop relevant curriculum and tie content to the workplace. At Valencia Community College, the Focus on the Workplace program allows faculty members up to 210 hours of release time to spend in a discipline-related workplace. The experience is designed to allow faculty members to:

- identify the skills and knowledge required for entry-level position success

- communicate up-to-date workforce needs and expectations to students and co-workers

- keep up with trends related to... discipline and field

- develop teaching methods that connect the workplace to...classroom applications

- absorb corporate culture (Focus, n.d.)

After participating in the program, faculty members are better prepared to design learning activities relevant to student and employer needs (Focus, n.d.).

Faculty Effectiveness

Future faculty members will participate in systematic assessment of their effectiveness and will create professional development plans to improve their skills. As educators, faculty members will direct their own professional growth and will be responsible for reporting progress to appropriate college administrators (Jenrette & Napoli, 1994). Measuring faculty effectiveness will include analysis based on "knowledge of student needs and expectations; evidence of student growth and development; satisfaction ratings of 'external and internal customers' (employers and college instructors); student feedback; insights into organizational culture; and rewards associated with teaching" (Alfred, 1994, p. 265). At Baltimore City Community College, each faculty member's evaluation includes student and peer assessment as well as classroom observation and a general rating by the department chair (Tschechtelin, 1997).

Conclusion

The faculty role in community colleges of the future will differ dramatically from the traditional faculty role. Community colleges face challenges from proprietary schools, legislatures, tax payers, constituents, employers, and students. By guiding students through the educational process and providing opportunities for students to be active participants in their own learning, professional educators become true facilitators of learning rather than proverbial "talking heads" who are not heard by a passive, disengaged audience. For many members of society, the community college is the most important tool they can use to better their economic situation. Replacement by proprietary and corporate colleges may compromise those whose futures depend on inexpensive, open-access, postsecondary education.

The challenge to community college administrators is to create environments in which faculty members are supported, nurtured, and rewarded; the challenge is to develop a faculty that makes the choice to transform.

References

Alfred, R. L. (1994). Measuring Teaching Effectiveness. In T. O'Banion, *Teaching and Learning in the Community College* (pp. 263-284). Washington, DC: Community College Press.

Baker III, G. A. (1998). Keeping All Generations Happy: The Xers, Boomers, and Beyond. *Community College Journal, 65*(5), 10-16.

Baker III, G. A., Roueche, J. E., & Gillett-Karam, R. (1990). *Teaching as Leading: Profiles of Excellence in the Open-door College.* Washington, DC: Community College Press.

Barr, R. B. & Tagg, J. (1995). From Teaching to Learning—A New Paradigm for Undergraduate Education. *Change, 27*(6),13-25.

Boggs, G. R. (1995-1996). The Learning Paradigm. *Community College Journal,* 66(3), 24-27.

Boggs, G. R. & Michael, D. G. (1997). The Palomar College Experience. In T. O'Banion, *A Learning College for the 21st century* (pp. 189-210). Phoenix: Oryx Press.

Bumphus, W. (1997). Developing an Institutional Effectiveness Model: Continuous Quality Improvement at Work. In J. E. Roueche, L. F. Johnson, & S. D. Roueche, *Embracing the Tiger: The Effectiveness Debate and the Community College* (pp. 101-115). Washington, DC: Community College Press.

Commission on the Future of Community Colleges (1988). *Building Communities: A Vision for a New Century.* Washington, DC: American Association of Community Colleges.

Cross, K. P. (1994). Involving Faculty in TQM Through Classroom Assessment. In T. O'Banion, *Teaching and Learning in the Community College* (pp. 143-160). Washington, DC: Community College Press.

Eaton, J. (1998, April). Focus Session—Teaching & Learning. Presentation at the meeting of the American Association of Community Colleges, Miami Beach, FL.

Elsner, P. A. (1997). Becoming a Learner-centered College System at Maricopa. In T. O'Banion, *A Learning College for the 21st Century* (pp. 167-188). Phoenix: Oryx Press.

Ewell, P. T. (1994). The Assessment Movement: Implications for Teaching and Learning. In T. O'Banion, *Teaching and Learning in the Community College* (pp. 73-96). Washington, DC: Community College Press.

Focus on the Workplace. (n.d.). Orlando, FL: Valencia Community College, Office of Workforce Development.

Future Faculty Task Force (Fall 1995). Future Faculty Task Force Report. Lane Community College, Oregon.

Hudgins, J. L. & Williams, S. K. (1997). Seizing the Opportunity of Institutional Effectiveness. In J. E. Roueche, L. F. Johnson, & S. D. Roueche, *Embracing the Tiger: The Effectiveness Debate and the Community College* (pp. 53-65). Washington, DC: Community College Press.

Institute for Future Studies (1994). Critical Issues Facing America's Community Colleges (1994-1995). Warren, MI: Macomb Press.

Jenrette, M. & Napoli, V. (1994). The Miami-Dade Community College Teaching/Learning Project. In T. O'Banion, *Teaching and Learning in the Community College* (pp. 245-259). Washington, DC: Community College Press.

Lauridsen, K. (1994). A Contemporary View of Teaching and Learning Centers for Faculty. In T. O'Banion, *Teaching and Learning in the Community College* (pp. 229-244). Washington, DC: Community College Press.

learning@maricopa (1997, October). Phoenix: Maricopa Community College District.

Matthews, R. S. (1994). Enriching Teaching and Learning Through Learning Communities. In T. O'Banion, *Teaching and Learning in the Community College* (pp. 179-200). Washington, DC: Community College Press.

McClenney, B. (1997a). The Community College of Denver Creates a Climate for Learning. In T. O'Banion, *A Learning College for the 21st Century* (pp. 211-224). Phoenix: Oryx Press.

McClenney, B. (1997b). Productivity and Effectiveness at the Community College of Denver. In J. E. Roueche, L. F. Johnson, & S. D. Roueche, *Embracing the Tiger: The Effectiveness Debate and the Community College* (pp. 71-79). Washington, DC: Community College Press.

O'Banion, T. (1997). *A Learning College for the 21st Century.* Phoenix: Oryx Press.

O'Banion, T. & Associates (1994). *Teaching and Learning in the Community College.* Washington, DC: Community College Press.

Parnell, D. (1990). *Dateline 2000: The New Higher Education Agenda.* Washington, DC: Community College Press.

Ponitz, D. H. (1997). The Journey of Transformation for Sinclair Community College. In T. O'Banion, *A Learning College for the 21st Century* (pp. 104-126). Phoenix: Oryx Press.

Richardson, R. C. & Elliott, D. B. (1994). Improving Opportunities for Underprepared Students. In T. O'Banion, *Teaching and Learning in the Community College* (pp. 97-114). Washington, DC: Community College Press.

Roueche, J. E. (1998, April). Focus Session—Institutional Development: Dancing as Fast as They Can. Presentation at the meeting of the American Association of Community Colleges, Miami Beach, FL.

Roueche, J. E., Johnson, L. F., Roueche, S. D., & Associates (1997). *Embracing the Tiger: The Effectiveness Debate and the Community College.* Washington, DC: Community College Press.

Roueche, J. E. & Roueche, S. D. (1998). Dancing as Fast as They Can: Community Colleges Facing Tomorrow's Challenges Today. *Community College Journal,* 65(5), 30-35.

School 2 Work: Connecting What You Learn to What You Earn. (n.d.). Orlando, FL: Valencia Community College, School 2 Work.

Tschechtelin, J. (1997). The Baltimore Phoenix. In J. E. Roueche, L. F. Johnson, & S. D. Roueche, *Embracing the Tiger: The Effectiveness Debate and the Community College* (pp. 119-133). Washington, DC: Community College Press.

Turning Students Into Employees: Valencia's Internship Program. (n.d.). Orlando, FL: Valencia Community College, Workplace Learning & Placement Office.

Wingspread Group on Higher Education (1993). *An American Imperative: Higher Expectations for Higher Education.* Johnson Foundation, Inc.

Part II.

Leading and Implementing the Learning College

As interest in the Learning College grew, community colleges were strongly represented in the first wave of institutions to put this new theory into practice. Fifteen years ago, when the Learning Paradigm and Learning College concepts were in their infancy, implementation was a trailblazing effort, a series of untried routes, stops and starts, and dynamic adventures for college administrators, faculty, and staff who embarked on the journey. No detailed maps existed, but Terry O'Banion's 1999 monograph, *Launching a Learning-Centered College*, was designed as a practical tool to help leaders get started (pages 65-88). It includes a succinct overview of the background, definition, and principles of the concept, followed by four strategies to "jump start an institutionwide learning initiative." These include "capitalizing on a natural trigger event, identifying needs through an assessment, building on existing innovations, and initiating conversations on learning." Moving beyond initial adoption of the Learning College concept, O'Banion also includes the next phase of launching the journey, "key elements or strategies that must be designed and followed to steer the Learning College project through institutional waters toward landmark islands where successes can be declared."

> **The variety of approaches community** colleges have taken in this work is reflected in their stories, but all have learning as the true north on their compass.

The year after O'Banion's monograph was published, the League for Innovation received a $1.14 million grant to support the Learning College Project, with a goal of creating a network of 12 community colleges focused on becoming more learning-centered institutions. Kay McClenney served as the project evaluator, and her 2002 article, "Becoming a Learning College: Milestones on the Journey," summarizes the early themes that emerged from the work of these "Vanguard Learning Colleges" (pages 89-92).

Colleges involved in the Learning College Project were required to create cross-college teams that would be deeply engaged leaders and champions of this work at their institutions. Selection of some members of the team was left to the college's discretion, but certain institutional representatives—the president, chief academic officer, and chief student services officer, for example—were required participants. To help ensure support at all levels of the college, a member of the board of trustees was also a required participant on the cross-college team. This strategy was an effective one, and in "Bringing Teaching and Learning to the Board Room: A Professional Development Framework for Community College Governing Boards," Christine Johnson McPhail examines other ways of involving boards of trustees in the Learning College journey (pages 93-100). She recommends developing boards that model the philosophy of learning-centered institutions through unity of purpose, through structure and cultural context, and through accountability, advocacy, assessment, and evaluation. Two brief articles by Cynthia D. Wilson, "The Community College as a Learning-Centered Organization" and "Leadership for Learning," offer insights based on her work with the League's Learning College Project and closely related 21st Century Learning Outcomes Project (pages 101-104).

The Learning College journey has often been described (by numerous authors and speakers, including both editors of this volume) as one on which each college can learn from other institutions but ultimately must find its own path. The variety of approaches community colleges have taken in this work is reflected in their stories, but all have learning as the true north on their compass. In "Institutionalizing the Commitment to Learning: Evolution, not Revolution," Martha A. Smith and Andrew L. Meyer outline Anne Arundel Community College's "learning is learning is learning" philosophy in practice, from a pioneering organizational realignment to a "flexible job description" for faculty and other innovative approaches for learning (pages 105-107). Irving Pressley McPhail, in "Academic Strategy and the Management of the Learning College," describes the strategic LearningFIRST journey at The Community College of Baltimore County, one of the Vanguard Learning Colleges of the League's Learning College Project (pages 108-117). Isothermal Community College's "A Learning College Primer" is an introduction to its Learning

College philosophy and approach, designed for students and employees as well as community members (pages 118-122).

The final two articles in Part II also feature Vanguard Learning Colleges from the League's Learning College Project. "Valencia's Big Ideas: Sustaining Authentic Organizational Change Through Shared Purpose and Culture," by Sanford C. Shugart, Ann Puyana, Joyce Romano, Julie Phelps, and Kaye Walter, is an overarching view of the philosophical and practical approach

Valencia takes to institutionalizing the college's commitment to learning (pages 123-125). In "The Student Experience: First-Year Experience Program," Sylvia Jenkins and Joann Wright offer a case study of Moraine Valley Community College's impressively effective first-year experience program (pages 126-128). Moraine Valley's inclusive approach to designing, implementing, evaluating, and refining this learning-centered program is representative of the institution's Learning College philosophy in practice.

Launching a Learning-Centered College

— Terry O'Banion

O'Banion, Terry. (1999). *Launching a Learning-Centered College.* Mission Viejo, CA: League for Innovation in the Community College.

The Learning Revolution*

In the last decade of the twentieth century a revolution in learning swept through all sectors of education and began to have a profound impact on the educational enterprise. Some leaders (Dolence, 1998) began to refer to the 1990s as the Learning Age instead of the Information Age or Knowledge Age, in recognition of the impact of the Learning Revolution. The renewed interest in learning has been swift and far reaching:

- 1994–*Business Week* magazine declared a Learning Revolution in Progress.

- 1995–*Time* magazine featured a special section on the Learning Revolution.

- 1996–The first national conference on "The Learning Paradigm" was held in San Diego.

- 1997–The American Council on Education and the American Association of Community Colleges published *A Learning College for the 21st Century.*

- 1998–PBS and the League for Innovation in the Community College sponsored the third national teleconference on "The Learning College: A Progress Report."

- 1999–The Pew Charitable Trusts and the League for Innovation in the Community College initiated a national project to assess student learning outcomes.

These are only a few of the milestones in the rapidly spreading Learning Revolution. For the remaining year of this century, and for many years into the twenty-first century, the Learning Revolution will continue to be a leading theme of articles, books, conferences, commissions, and studies.

The Learning Revolution is not just an American phenomenon. In 1995 the Council of Presidents of the Province of Ontario in Canada released a commissioned paper, "Learning-Centered Education in Ontario Colleges," that said:

> This paper is about significant change involving the nature of college programs. It is about a shift in educational design toward what has been termed "learning-centered" education. Many have begun this shift, but it remains difficult, in part because it goes to the root of our understanding of education, and, equally, to the root of our roles as students, staff, and administrators (Council of Presidents, 1995, p. 1).

In the United Kingdom the Learning Revolution is also beginning to emerge as evident in the language used for a number of recently issued reports:

- *Learning Works*–June 1997

- *Higher Education in the Learning Society*–July 1997

- *Learning for the 21st Century*–November 1997

- *The Learning Age: A Renaissance for a New Britain*–February 1998

This current revolution in education is part of a larger social transformation. Peter Drucker, in *Managing for the Future*, succinctly captures this special period of change: "Every few hundred years throughout Western history, a sharp transformation has occurred. In a matter of decades, society all together rearranges itself—its world view, its basic values, its social and political structures, its arts, its key institutions. Fifty years later a new world order exists.... Our age is such a period of transformation" (1992, p. 95). The Learning Revolution, "in a matter of decades," will fundamentally change the education enterprise.

A Revolution With a Purpose. In a nutshell, the purpose of the Learning Revolution is to place learning first in every policy, program, and practice in higher education by overhauling the traditional architecture of education (O'Banion, 1997, p. 1). In the 1993 book, *An American Imperative*, the Wingspread Group on Higher Education said, "We must redesign all our learning systems to align our entire education enterprise for the personal, civic, and workplace needs of the twenty-first century" (Wingspread Group on Higher Education, 1993, p. 19). The Wingspread Group went a step further and indicated the challenge institutions of higher education will face if they are to implement the Learning Revolution: "Putting learning at the heart of the academic enterprise will mean overhauling the conceptual, procedural, curricular, and other architecture of postsecondary education on most campuses" (1993, p. 14).

> **These are** only a few of the milestones in the rapidly spreading Learning Revolution.

While there seems to be a revolution or reform movement about every decade in education, the Learning Revolution is quite different from reform efforts of the past, as illustrated by its two distinct goals: (1) to place learning first in every policy, program, and practice in higher education, and (2) to overhaul the traditional architecture of education.

*For a more extensive review of the Learning Revolution and the Learning College, see the author's book, *A Learning College for the 21st Century*, Oryx Press, 1997.

Placing Learning First. The current reform effort calls for institutions of higher education to make learning their highest priority. Many educators are offended by this recommendation because they believe they have always placed learning first. Of course educators at all levels place great value on learning, but institutional statements and reward systems often reflect other priorities.

Any student of education can cite the three primary missions most often articulated by universities: teaching, research, and service. However, in many universities, the reward system places higher value on research than on teaching and service. "Learning" is seldom, if ever, included as one of the primary missions, although its relationship to teaching, research, and service is clearly implied by most educators.

Our model of education reflects in

great part the adjustment to an agricultural and industrial economy of an earlier era.

Teaching is probably the most universally acclaimed mission, for all levels of higher education. In the community college such strong value is placed on teaching that the institution is often referred to as "the teaching college." One of the most significant documents ever written on the community college, *Building Communities* (Commission on the Future of Community Colleges, 1998), highlighted over and over the central value placed on teaching in the community college: "Building communities through dedicated teaching is the vision and the inspiration of this report" (p. 8). "Quality instruction should be the hallmark of the movement" (p. 25). "The community college should be the nation's premier teaching institution" (p. 25).

The current reform effort does not ask institutions to place less value on teaching or other missions, but to review their statements and reward systems to ensure that learning is valued as visibly as teaching and other missions. In Barr's 1994 study of California community college mission statements, he noted, "It is revealing that virtually every mission statement contained in the catalogs in California's 107 community colleges fails to use the word 'learning' in a statement of purpose" (p. 2).

For community colleges that want to become more learning centered, it will make a difference in policies, programs, and practices if learning is embedded in the institutional culture as the highest priority. Community colleges that wish to make this perspective an integral part of their culture can ask two basic questions that will keep faculty, staff, trustees, and administrators focused on the major goal: (1) Does this action improve and expand learning? and (2) How do we know this action improves and expands learning? These two questions can be applied to any area of activity in an institution to help its members become more aware of the importance of learning in everyday practice.

Precise answers to these questions about every institutional action will be hard to come by, but the very voicing of these questions will keep the transcendent goal of becoming a more learning-centered institution clear and visible for all to see.

Overhauling the Traditional Architecture. Every faculty member and administrator in education has been frustrated at some time with the traditional architecture of education that limits how they teach or manage and how students learn. Roger Moe, former majority leader of the Minnesota State Senate, has said, "Higher education is a thousand years of tradition wrapped in a hundred years of bureaucracy" (as cited in Armajani et al, 1994, p. 1). The current system is time-bound, place-bound, efficiency-bound, and role-bound.

The system is *time-bound* by credit hours and semester courses. College students are learning in blocks of time that are artificial. Excellent teachers know that learning is not limited to one-hour meetings held on Monday, Wednesday, and Friday, and they have been frustrated in teaching within these prescribed boundaries.

The system is *place-bound*. Learning is initiated, nurtured, monitored, and certified primarily by teachers in classrooms on a campus. We have experimented with distance education that takes courses off campus, but while it has increased student access, it retains the old model of education. Distance education, for the most part, is a nontraditional delivery system for traditional education. Work-based learning was supposed to break up that model, but it does not. It extends the model but is controlled by it because work-based learning is built around the current structure of the school. It still binds the student to a place.

The system is *efficiency-bound*. Our model of education reflects in great part the adjustment to an agricultural and industrial economy of an earlier era. Public school students are still dismissed early in the afternoon and in the summers so they can work on farms that no longer exist. When the economy became industrialized, education responded by creating a lock-step, factory model, which is the basis of American education today. Academic credit, based on time in class, makes learning appear orderly. This model creates an efficiency system to award credentials. Grades are collected and turned into credits, and these compilations are supposed to represent profound learning.

Finally the system is *role-bound*, which may be its greatest weakness. In education, we make the assumption that one human being, the teacher, can ensure that thirty very different human beings, in one hour a day, three days a week for sixteen weeks, can learn enough to become enlightened citizens, productive workers, and joyful, lifelong learners. Then we assume that this one human being can repeat this miracle three more times in the same sixteen-week period for ninety additional individuals. We provide little comfort and support when teachers fail to live up to this role-bound myth.

If we are to make any progress toward implementing the Learning Revolution, we need to replace the current educational system with a system designed for the kind of society in which we live, designed for the kinds of students who attend college, and designed to take advantage of new research on learning and new applications of information technology.

The Learning College

A number of community colleges have responded to the Learning Revolution by becoming more learning centered. The experiences of some of these pioneering community colleges, combined with the 38 years of community college experience of the author, have led to the creation of a new concept, the Learning College. This concept is in no way intended as the final answer for what community colleges should become, but it does provide a frame of reference institutional leaders can use to chart their own journey in becoming more learning centered. Each institution launching an initiative to become more learning centered should develop principles that represent the core values and commitments basic to that institution. Many of the principles that follow can be applied to most community colleges, but they will need to be tailored to the specific needs and resources of an institution. The list of principles will also need to be expanded to address the creativity exhibited by most community colleges.

The Learning College places learning first and provides educational experiences for learners any way, any place, any time (O'Banion, 1995-1996, p. 22). The model is based on the assumption that educational experiences are designed for the convenience of learners rather than for the convenience of institutions and their staffs. The Learning College is based on six key principles:

- The Learning College creates substantive change in individual learners.

- The Learning College engages learners in the learning process as full partners who must assume primary responsibility for their own choices.

- The Learning College creates and offers as many options for learning as possible.

- The Learning College assists learners to form and participate in collaborative learning activities.

- The Learning College defines the roles of learning facilitators in response to the needs of the learners.

- The Learning College and its learning facilitators succeed only when improved and expanded learning can be documented for learners.

Principle I. The Learning College creates substantive change in individual learners. If the current reform efforts are worth the energy and time they will require, then community colleges should settle for nothing less than substantive change in individual learners. This is a goal highly desired from educational experiences for our own children and all those in our care. No faculty member, administrator, support staff, or trustee argues with this principle, but it is not used to guide action. Stated up front and stated often, it can become embedded in the institutional culture, undergirding all other principles.

Institutional priorities, however, usually focus on the more obvious outcomes of learning, and are most often reported for groups: rates of graduation, persistence, or employment for selected cohorts. This is important information and must be collected by all institutions to satisfy external constituencies and to gauge average institutionwide success.

This general information provides only a rudimentary measure of institutional effectiveness, however. At some point in their efforts to become more learning-centered institutions, community college staff members should engage in a series of rich conversations about definitions of learning that go beyond institutional effectiveness data.

There should be discussions regarding the differences among training, education, and learning. Complex constructs regarding surface learning, basic learning, hardy learning, and more powerful learning may emerge from the discussion of personal values and experience in education.

In my definition, learning kindles new ways of seeing, thinking, and doing that lead to changed behavior. If that definition is even partially correct, then the institutional participants engaged in a conversation about learning may encounter new ways of seeing, thinking, and doing that will lead to changes in their behavior. In the Learning College, substantive change can occur in administrators, faculty, support staff, and trustees, as well as in students. Making learning a central topic of institutional conversation, and agreeing that substantive change in individual learners is a basic institutional principle, ensure that the current reform effort is a great deal more than business as usual.

Principle II. The Learning College engages learners in the learning process as full partners who must assume primary responsibility for their own choices. At the point a learner chooses to engage the Learning College, a series of services are initiated to prepare the learner for the experiences and opportunities to come. However, until there is a seamless system of education for lifelong learning based on principles similar to those of the Learning College, these services will be heavily focused on orienting the learner to new experiences and expectations that are not

> # There should be
> discussions regarding
> the differences among training,
> education, and learning.

usually found in traditional schools. Two key expectations need to be communicated to new learners at the first stage of engagement: (1) learners are full partners in the creation and implementation of their learning experiences, and (2) learners must assume primary responsibility for making their own choices about goals and options.

The services include assessing the learner's abilities, achievements, values, needs, goals, expectations, resources, and environmental or situational limitations. A personal profile is constructed by the learner in consultation with an expert assessor to illustrate what this learner knows, wants to know, and needs to know. The learner's self-assessment is a key component. A personal learning plan is constructed from this personal profile, and the learner negotiates a contract that outlines the responsibilities of both the learner and the Learning College.

As part of the contract, the learner takes responsibility for selecting from among the learning options provided by the Learning College. The assessment information, the terms of the contract, historical records from previous learning experiences, work experience, external evaluations, and all other pertinent information are recorded on the learner's "smart card" which serves as a portfolio of information, a lifelong record of educational experiences. The "smart card," similar to an Automated Teller Machine (ATM) card widely used by banks, belongs to the learner, who is responsible for keeping it current with assistance from specialists in the Learning College. In addition to the "smart card," other educational institutions and employers can develop their own systems to verify what they need to know about the learner.

If one option does not work, the learner should be able to navigate a new path to an alternative learning option at any point.

The Learning College also provides orientation and experimentation for learners who are unfamiliar with the learning environment of the Learning College. Some learners may need training in using technology, in developing collaboration skills, in locating resources, and in navigating learning systems. Specialists monitor these services carefully and are responsible for approving a learner's readiness to fully engage the learning opportunities provided.

In the Learning College, the orientation and experimentation process take as much time as is necessary to meet the needs of each learner. Some learners seeking minimal learning experiences about which they are very clear can begin their activities immediately following their first point of engagement. Some learners may wish to participate in the orientation and experimentation process for a few days or a few weeks. Some learners may be engaged in the process for several months. Since there are no restrictions on time and place for the engagement, there are no limitations governing the activities except the needs of the learner. There are many options for learners to engage the Learning College, including self-guided print and video modules, live and Internet-based activities, classes and laboratories on campus, and individual consultations with a variety of specialists. Continuing learners soon learn to navigate the Learning College system and use it to their full advantage.

The student does not, however, drive all the choices regarding learning. Colleges are collections of wise educators who know a great deal about the larger values associated with a college education. Faculty may want to require selected liberating experiences for students. A college might, for example, require all students to provide volunteer service to the community, examine their views on diversity, develop special skills such as how to access the Internet, express their creativity through some art form, or understand some special feature of their culture. A college has the right, perhaps even the responsibility, to provide the fullest education possible for its students. Its goal is not always best achieved if the collegiate experience is reduced to a shopping spree in which the customers select only the items with which they are already familiar.

Community colleges attempt to provide experiences that broaden and deepen the thinking of their students through programs such as critical thinking across the curriculum or required general education courses. Community college faculty should also continue to struggle to define what constitutes a common core of learning for all their students. However, in a more learning-centered college the options for how individuals learn the common core are greatly increased. The goal is to provide liberating experiences agreed upon by the faculty that are free of the constraints of the historical educational architecture.

Principle III. The Learning College creates and offers as many options for learning as possible. In the Learning College there are many options for the learner during the initial engagement and throughout the continuing educational activities—options regarding time, place, structure, staff support, and methods of delivery. The learner reviews these options and experiments with some that are unfamiliar.

Each learning option defines specific goals and competency levels needed for entry, as well as specific outcome measures of competency levels needed for exit. Learning Colleges are constantly creating additional learning options for learners, many of them suggested by learners based on their own experiences. A major goal of the Learning College is to create as many learning options as possible in order to provide successful learning experiences for all learners. If one option does not work, the learner should be able to navigate a new path to an alternative learning option at any point.

If a Learning College had to develop a full array of options from scratch, the task would be overwhelming and too costly. Fortunately, there are numerous resources available, many of them field-tested and free. Thousands of individual faculty members have designed better or alternative learning materials as part of their sabbaticals, on summer projects, with innovation grants from various institutions, and with support from federal and foundation grants. Individual colleges have initiated programs to design and to develop new learning opportunities for students, sometimes with a considerable commitment of college resources. Colleges have initiated consortia to work in collaboration with each other and with agencies and companies to produce new learning programs. State and federal agencies, especially the military, have created hundreds of learning options that are available at no cost. Business and industry have spent billions on training materials. Educational entrepreneurs such as book publishers, testing agencies, information networks, training organizations, and computer corporations, develop training materials that are often available to educational institutions for a fee paid by the students.

To manage the activities and progress of thousands of learners engaged in hundreds of learning options at many different times, at many different levels, in many different locations, the Learning College must rely on expert systems based on advancements in technology. Without complex, technological systems, the Learning College cannot function. Learning management systems are the breakthroughs that will free education and educators from the time-bound, place-bound, and role-bound systems that currently manage the educational enterprise.

Principle IV. The Learning College assists learners to form and participate in collaborative learning activities. In the Learning College, the university ideal of a "community of scholars" is transformed into a "community of learners." The focus on creating communities among participants in the learning process, on creating student cohorts, and on developing social structures that support individual learning, is a requirement of a Learning College, not just for students but also for the faculty, administrators, and support staff.

A number of learning theorists have noted the key role collaboration plays in learning. Learning is a social enterprise. Through social interactions, as well as through action on objects, learners make sense of the world (Abel, Cennamo, and Chung, 1996). Lane and Wenger (1990) suggest that knowledge needs to be presented in an authentic context (i.e., real-world settings and applications that would normally involve that knowledge) and that learning requires social interaction and collaboration. There are examples of effective collaborative learning models at all levels of education.

We also know from experience that programs designed to build cohorts of students and engage them in a common experience or curriculum greatly increase retention and, ultimately, program completion. Nursing programs in community colleges have some of the highest graduation rates in all of education, in part because they are often highly selective, but also because a cohort is guided together through a rigorous competency-based curriculum. Nursing students study together and support each other, and there is no disincentive for all to succeed at high levels because students are not graded relative to each other (as on a Bell curve) but relative to a fixed performance standard, the state certification exam.

The most widespread form of collaborative learning in the community college takes place in "learning communities," a specific term for a curricular intervention to enhance collaboration and expand learning. "Learning communities...purposefully restructure the curriculum to link together courses or course work so that students find greater coherence in what they are learning, as well as increased intellectual interaction with faculty and fellow students" (Gablenick et al., 1990, p. 5). These collaborations are also referred to as learning clusters, triads, federated learning communities, coordinated studies, and integrated studies; but "learning communities" has emerged as the favorite descriptor. When the same 30 students enroll for nine credit hours in a sequence of courses under the rubric of "Reading, Writing, and Rats," they have enrolled in a learning community.

In the Learning College, some learning communities and collaborative learning activities do not look very much like classrooms, and many will have dynamics defined by characteristics of pace, distance, membership, and means of communication. For instance, as the number of adult workers returning to college for education and training continues to grow, the workplace becomes a likely venue for establishing learning communities. Workplaces that value and encourage lifelong learning—whether driven by altruism or enlightened self-interest—make ideal sites for communities of learners, as common interests may be readily determined and the level of resources available to support the community may be very high. In such models, video-on-demand can distribute information, including interactive training modules, directly to the desktop of employees; information resources can be concentrated at a common work location; and assessment services or learning specialists can be housed at the work site.

Powerful networking technology can also help nurture a learning community by assisting its members in communicating with each other in both synchronous and asynchronous modes. Certainly if courtship can be accomplished in cyberspace, then learning communities can be formed there. The electronic forums established in the Maricopa Community Colleges are pioneering efforts to create communities of learners through technology networks.

The roles that college educators play in forming and supporting learning communities are yet to be thoroughly defined. However, in a Learning College, staff members recruit students into cohorts of common interests or circumstances. Process facilitators orient individuals and help them form groups or communities of learners. Resource specialists attend to the needs of both individuals and groups of learners. Learning facilitators design experiences that build upon group strengths and other dynamics. Assessment specialists design and implement valid assessments that can occur both individually and in the context of the learning community. The Learning College is designed not only around the unique needs of individual learners, but also around their needs for association. The Learning College fosters and nourishes communities of learners as an integral part of its design and as a key process for creating substantive change in individual learners.

Principle V. The Learning College defines the roles of learning facilitators in response to the needs of the learners. Everyone employed in the Learning College is a learning facilitator, including categories formerly designated administration and support staff. Trustees are also considered learning facilitators as they exercise their responsibilities for governance and policy development in creating a more learning-centered institution. Every employee is linked to learners in the exercise of his or her duties, although some activities such as accounting may be less directly related. The goal is to have every employee thinking about how his or her work facilitates the learning process.

If the current members of the staff do not have the skills to meet the needs of the learners, the Learning College contracts with specialists to provide the needed services. Specialists are employed on a contract basis to produce specific products or deliver specific services; some may work full time, but many work part time, often from their homes, linked to the institution and to learners through technology. A number of specialists may be scattered around the world, providing unique services and special expertise.

The groundwork is already being prepared for these new roles to emerge. A 1996 report by the Ohio Technology in Education Steering Committee recommended the term "learning consultant" to best describe the educator of the future. The report stated:

As learning consultants, educators will play many roles:

- Learning consultants will be mentors—guiding each learner to his or her own chosen goals.

- Learning consultants will be facilitators of inquiry—coaching learners and helping them remove barriers as they move toward discovery.

- Learning consultants will be architects of connection—observing the needs of individual learners and joining them to information, experiences, resources, experts, and teams.

- Learning consultants will be managers of collaboration and integration— combining the needs and abilities of *their* learning communities with the needs and abilities of other learning communities (1996, p. 13).

Learners also participate as learning facilitators, and this role could be made part of the options negotiated in the orientation process. Many do not have time, but others welcome the opportunity to offer their experience and knowledge to assist other learners. Colleges already use students as lab assistants and tutors to facilitate learning. In the Learning College, these roles and opportunities are expanded to capitalize on the resources students bring to the educational enterprise.

Most educators are familiar with the

concept of "the teachable moment."

The goal of Principle V is to use the resources of the institution to better meet the needs of students. It is also designed to free faculty from the restrictions placed on them by the historical role-bound architecture of education. In actual practice, colleges try to implement this principle by employing specialists (counselors, librarians, instructional designers, staff development trainers, etc.) and releasing selected teaching faculty from a class or two to conduct special projects. Still, the common denominator of the traditional role-bound model—one full-time faculty member teaching four or five courses each term—continues to dominate most of the thinking and most of the activities of the institution. An audit of the great variety of skills and expertise residing in the current faculty would be mind-boggling in its richness and complexity. Changing the historical architecture of education to allow the skills and expertise of the faculty to be better matched to the needs of learners would be an overwhelmingly complex task, but a task that could lead to more satisfied and successful faculty and students.

Principle VI. The Learning College and its learning facilitators succeed only when improved and expanded learning can be documented for learners. "What does this learner know?" and "What can this learner do?" are questions that provide the framework for documenting outcomes, both for the learner and the learning facilitators.

If the ultimate goal of the Learning College is to promote and to expand learning, then these questions are the yardstick by which the Learning College and staff are measured. Conventional information may be assembled for students (retention rates and achievement scores) and for faculty (ratings by students, peers, and supervisors; and community service), but the goal is to document what students know and what they can do, and to use this information as the primary measure of success for the learning facilitators and the Learning College.

All learning options in the Learning College utilize competency requirements for entrance and for exit. These competencies reflect national and state standards when available, or they are developed by specialists on staff or on special contract. Assessing a learner's readiness for a particular learning option is a key part of the initial engagement process and, thereafter, a continuing process embedded in the culture of the institution.

Learners negotiate and sign contracts for overall programs (e.g., general education core, basic skills, workplace skills) and may need to negotiate specific contracts for some learning options. Moreover, learners are encouraged to add competencies and goals beyond those established in the standards.

Portfolio assessment is one of the primary means by which learning is documented. A portfolio is a systematic, organized collection of evidence of what the learner knows and what the learner can do. It builds on prior information, is constantly revised and updated, and provides continuity for future learning activities. Specific benchmarks of achievement may be applied to determine credits earned, if credits continue to be the hallmarks for moving learners along the path of education.

Guiding the portfolio assessment process is one of the primary functions of learning facilitators. Since many of the learning options will be student-led collaborations, contract sessions with specialists, or experiences facilitated by tutors and coaches, learning facilitators will have more time for portfolio assessment. It may be possible to codify some of the assessment process for easier management, and technology advances will provide some assistance.

These six principles form the core of the Learning College. They refer primarily to process and structure and are built on the basic philosophy that the student's learning is central to all activities of the educational enterprise. There are certainly other principles that must be considered in creating this new paradigm of learning. Course content, funding, and governance are examples of pertinent issues that must be addressed and for which principles must be designed. Still, these six principles provide a starting point for those who wish to create a more learning-centered college, a college that places learning first and provides educational experiences for learners any way, any place, any time.

How to Jump Start an Institutionwide Learning Initiative

Many colleges are well into their journey to become more learning centered and do not need to be concerned about how to get started. For colleges that have not yet taken the first steps, however, there are a number of options worth exploring. The leaders who will initiate these first steps need to make sure that the action is appropriate for the climate and culture of the college. The options for launching an institutionwide learning initiative that are reviewed here include capitalizing on a natural trigger event, identifying needs through an assessment, building on existing innovations, and initiating conversations on learning.

Capitalize on a Natural Trigger Event. Most educators are familiar with the concept of "the teachable moment." That moment is a specific point in time when everything comes together for a teacher and a student, and learning occurs in an extraordinary way. There is a confluence of forces, an "alignment of the planets," that prepares the way for the teachable moment. The outcome for the learner is an aha moment—an insight or an understanding that transcends everyday learning. The moment is a powerful experience and serves as a powerful motivator for searching out more such experiences.

For leaders thinking about launching a Learning College, it will be important to take advantage of "the teachable moment" in the life of the college. A more accurate reference for "the teachable moment" in organizations is a "trigger event," an event that launches energy and creates opportunity, an event that leaders can use to focus thought and rally troops to action.

There are a number of natural activities constantly unfolding in the life of a college that can serve as a "trigger event." Most often these are not dramatic events. Usually some project or process has been under way for months when a leader begins to see that the activity can provide leverage for channeling a vision that is much larger than was originally intended. Natural trigger events are usually chaotic until a leader transforms the event or events into a call for action. In retrospect, leaders create an anecdotal history of the event that makes it appear to be a planned process thoughtfully connected to the newly focused energy. In reality, most trigger events are not planned steps of action, but an awareness of the key role trigger events play in the change process may assist leaders in creating such events or at least increase their ability to recognize them when they do occur.

External forces often create situations that can be turned into trigger events by visionary leaders. When The Pew Charitable Trusts invited the Maricopa Community Colleges to join the Pew Higher Education Roundtables to "establish a foundation for action and exchange among leaders of institutions committed to fulfilling their education missions more effectively," the trigger was in place. A number of natural activities converged at Maricopa to create a propitious moment for expanded action. College staff had been engaged for several years in a major quality initiative to create more effective operations and more collaborative communication. For over a decade, Maricopa had been experimenting with applications of technology to improve teaching and learning and institutional management that made it the leading-edge community college in the nation in the use of technology. Furthermore, Maricopa had created an institutional culture in which innovation and creativity were championed and supported. When members of the roundtable began their conversations, they came with a history that had prepared them for substantive change. Given the opportunity to examine the kind of future Maricopa needed to prepare for, the Roundtable participants chose to launch a long-range project to create a learning-centered institution. The Roundtable became the trigger event that would change Maricopa's future forever.

Along with Maricopa, many community colleges in the United States and Canada are currently engaged in exploring applications of total quality management or continuing quality improvement. Some of these colleges are also experimenting with a process adapted from Peter Senge's (1994) concept of the "learning organization" that complements quality processes. Experimentation with these processes helps create a mind-set for change that can serve as a triggering event to launch a Learning College. Most colleges begin experimenting with quality processes at fairly low and safe levels, a wise move given the propensity of educators to be suspicious of major change efforts, especially those borrowed from business and industry. Early success is directed toward improving services, such as mail delivery, and may eventually lead to improving communication and even decentralizing decision making. At some point, often identified in retrospect, a leader or group of key stakeholders gives voice to an opportunity to move quality processes to a new level and a new dimension: "What we are really about here is inventing our future, creating a whole new kind of institution that places the learner at the center of everything we do." Thus a vision is born from processes and activities already in place, processes and activities that can serve as a triggering event.

External forces
often create situations
that can be turned into trigger events by visionary leaders.

That is exactly what happened at Jackson Community College in Michigan. Jackson had been applying continuous quality improvement processes since 1990 and had found them to be quite useful. In fact the president of the college at that time played a key role in creating the Continuous Quality Improvement Network, a coalition of approximately a dozen community colleges committed to quality processes. In 1994, staff members at Jackson were still applying continuous quality improvement processes but with no intention to redesign the college to become a Learning College. On March 16, 1994, a triggering event occurred that dramatically changed the focus of the college's quality efforts. Staff at a training session were involved in exercises about systems design when a staff member leaned over to the president and asked, "Wouldn't it be great if we could design the college for real, rather than as an exercise?" In this case the triggering event was fairly dramatic and specific, but it took place within the context of ongoing processes. A visionary president seized the opportunity, and in a few weeks the college had launched a major initiative to become a Learning College.

For the leaders who want to make their institutions more learning centered, there are a number of natural and ongoing activities that can be molded into a trigger event. Every community college is struggling with how and how much technology to bring into the institution. Technology is a natural boundary breaker, a natural change agent, and it can lead to a triggering event. In developing the college's long-range technology plan, someone has to raise questions about the purpose of the technology. The first conversations are likely to focus on how technology will impact teachers and teaching. At some point, it must be asked how technology will be used to improve and expand learning, and this is the propitious moment for the leader or leaders to capitalize on the opportunity to launch a larger vision.

Deciding whether or not to construct a new building also provides an opportunity to raise key questions that can trigger new directions for the college. Although few colleges have the resources to construct new buildings these days, those that do must consider the advisability of building in the context of the opportunities created by distance learning technologies. Few institutions of higher education have examined the long-range impact of distance learning on their programs and practices. Such an examination, triggered by plans to construct new buildings, could in turn, lead to an examination of the college's overall philosophy and mission. Leaders can use information about national reform efforts and the examples of those colleges that have been transformed into Learning Colleges to broaden and to expand the college conversation about buildings into a conversation about change.

Institutional crises have always provided opportunities for initiating change efforts. A number of colleges have launched their initiatives to become Learning Colleges in response to sharp enrollment declines or dramatic reductions in resources. When a new president replaces a fired president, the potential and expectation for change may reach its highest point. Less dramatic, but longer-range crises such as the "graying" of the faculty or the changing nature of the students and surrounding communities can also serve as triggers for action when these changes are orchestrated by effective leaders who see the big picture.

In summary, major initiatives to transform community colleges into Learning Colleges do not suddenly appear full blown on the agendas of educational institutions. Institutional history, culture, and ongoing activities provide the bedrock from which a new vision must be chiseled. The vision that will guide the college into the future will often be connected to a triggering event embedded in the institution's daily life. The leader or leaders who want the college to move toward a new model of learning will be sensitive to the opportunities for change that already exist, and they will capitalize on these trigger events to move the college in new directions.

Identify Needs Through an Assessment. In those colleges where natural processes and activities do not readily suggest triggering events, leaders may have to be more proactive in creating a climate that encourages change. One way to create such a climate is to involve all college constituents in an assessment of institutional values, missions, programs, needs, processes, or structures. If Socrates was right that the unexamined life is not worth living, there may be some built-in motivation on the part of faculty and staff to examine college life, especially if there has not been such an examination in recent years or if there is some rationale for an examination, such as a

changing student population, graying faculty, declining resources, or increasing technology. In unhealthy colleges where tensions between administration and faculty, or among other groups of stakeholders, focus all activity on faculty and staff concerns rather than on learner needs, such assessments will not work. In healthy colleges, however, an institutionwide assessment of some key issue tailored to the specific needs of the college may assist in triggering action that can lead toward an expanded model of learning.

In *An American Imperative*, the 1993 reform report that urged institutions of higher education to become more learning centered, there is a self-assessment instrument specifically designed to raise awareness about the college's commitment to placing learning first. The assessment is based on core questions from Howard Bowen's 1982 book, *The State of the Nation and the Agenda for Higher Education*. The questions are designed to help faculty and staff transcend the contentious issues that are present in the cultures of all colleges and universities. The process suggests that all college staff and faculty, including trustees, begin with the following "First Questions":

- What kind of people do we want our children and grandchildren to be?

- What kind of society do we want them to live in?

- How can we best shape our institutions to nurture those kinds of people and that kind of society?

A college that allows sufficient time for a serious and substantive examination of these questions by a great majority of its members is preparing the way for major initiatives leading to significant change. These core questions are followed by a series of questions under the headings "Taking Values Seriously," "Putting Student Learning First," and "Creating a Nation of Learners." This assessment, introduced into the institution in an appropriate way (a strategy that will be different for each college), can unleash pent-up concerns and commitments that can translate into action toward becoming a Learning College.

Another assessment designed specifically for the community college can be found in the author's 1994 book, *Teaching and Learning in the Community College*. The final chapter is a set of "Guidelines for Auditing the Effectiveness of Teaching and Learning." The author makes the following case:

The teaching and learning climate is the visible product of a particular institution's invisible values. What faculty, administrators, board members, and staff truly believe about students and their abilities to learn, and about teachers and their abilities to teach, is reflected in the climate of teaching and learning. It is a case of yin and yang in which values influence climate, and climate, in turn, influences values. The values and climate are made most visible in the written policies and statements, practices, and related behaviors of the stakeholders in the institution. An audit of the policies and statements, practices, and related behaviors is an important first step for leaders who wish to make teaching and learning the highest priority of the community college. (O'Banion, 1994, pp. 304-305)

A series of questions about institutional values and practices related to teaching and learning are clustered under each of the following general areas:

- Institutional Policies and Statements

- Student Success Policies

- Curriculum Review and Development

- Instructional Innovation

- Information Technology

- Faculty Selection and Development

- Institutional Effectiveness

This teaching and learning audit, tailored to the specific needs and history of the institution, can serve as a trigger to elicit core values from an institution's policies and practices. In the hands of effective leaders, this information can be used to launch initiatives that place learning first.

The assessment instruments from *The American Imperative and Teaching and Learning in the Community College* are specifically designed to measure the extent to which a college places learning first. As such, these approaches may be too direct for some colleges that are still unsure about leaping wholeheartedly into explorations of new models of learning. For colleges that desire to move more slowly but want to use an assessment approach to stimulate action, there are numerous instruments on institutional climate and institutional effectiveness that may better serve their purposes. A checklist (Armes and McClenney, 1990) derived from the report, *Building Communities*, encourages evaluation and discussion of a number of issues that surfaced in the key report from the Commission on the Future of the Community College. This report has been widely circulated in community colleges, and the checklist raises important issues that can lead to discussions regarding new approaches to learning.

All community colleges are periodically accredited, and the accrediting process is an ideal opportunity to examine a college's commitment to placing learning first. In the past, accreditation processes did not directly address learning as the key mission and value of an institution, but more recent emphasis on student outcomes helps to redress this oversight. For a college that wishes to become more learning centered, however, leaders will need to expand and enhance the accreditation process to tailor it to their own purposes. The accreditation process can be designed to focus more directly on learning by incorporating some of the questions from the first two instruments described above. In this way, a scheduled college activity such as accreditation can be used to trigger increased activity to move the institution toward becoming a Learning College.

Build on Existing Innovations. Since their beginning almost 100 years ago, community colleges have been institutions given to innovative practices and programs. In fact, the community college as an institution is one of the most important innovations in the history of higher education.

The 1960s was the "Golden Age of Innovation" for community colleges. Driven by the demand for access, the community college of the 1960s grew rapidly and experimented constantly in response to new roles, new needs, and new students. The League for Innovation in the Community College was born during this period as a reflection of the innovative spirit of this rapidly expanding sector of higher education. However, during the middle 1970s and into the early 1980s, interest in innovation declined as complex social and economic forces altered the environment in which innovation had flourished. Cross observed at the time, "the late 1970s and early 1980s represent a plateau between two periods of high energy and a sense of mission in the community colleges" (1981, p. 113).

That plateau was not to last for long. "As the 1980s passed into the 1990s, innovation is returning to center stage. At every level of education, in all parts of the country, and for a variety of reasons, there is a renaissance of innovation" (O'Banion, 1989, p. 10). The resurgence of innovation in the community college began in the middle 1980s, reflecting the energy generated by the reform movement initiated by the 1983 report, A *Nation at Risk*.

> Shocked out of the doldrums of the 1970s by dozens of national reports on the decline in the quality of education, community colleges, along with other institutions of higher education, are committed to overcoming the problems of the past decade. College leaders and faculty are beginning to recognize, on the one hand, the lack of quality in their programs, and, on the other hand, the need for increased quality if the very nation is to flourish. These factors are driving forces for innovation. (O'Banion, 1989, pp. 10-11)

So while reform was being advocated, community colleges were going about their business "reforming" practices by introducing a variety of innovations, including classroom assessment, learning communities, distance learning, tech-prep, business and industry services, distinguished teaching chairs, and a host of others. These innovations, however, were not cast in a framework of major reform. They emerged in isolation, each with its champions, and were implemented as stand-alone innovations disconnected from the emerging reform efforts to place learning at the center of the educational enterprise.

At this point no leader has attempted to mobilize the range of independent innovations that currently grace the education landscape and use these to support and guide the development of a Learning College. Such action could be a trigger event leading to substantive change.

The following innovations could provide the building blocks for a Learning College:

- active and contextual learning used in tech-prep, school-to-work, and service learning;

- collaborative learning as expressed in learning communities, electronic forums, and in study groups such as those pioneered by Uri Triesman;

- improved and expanded approaches to assessment and outcome measures as demonstrated by personal portfolios, experiential learning, and skills standards;

- increased focus on the customer as implemented in customized programs, service kiosks, and learner-centered advising;

- expanded and more flexible structures as seen in open-entry/open-exit programs, distance learning, information networks, and differentiated staffing;

- improved teaching as expressed in classroom assessment, distinguished teaching chairs, and teacher formation as championed by Parker Palmer;

- continuous quality improvement processes to flatten organizations, increase collaboration, and empower participants;

- application of technology to expand knowledge bases, data collection and analysis, communications networks, and time and information management;

- experimentation with the allocation of resources around concepts of performance-based funding and learning-outcomes funding; and

- new models of decision making such as shared governance and the Carver governance model championed by the Association of Community College Trustees.

The challenge for leaders is to create a new framework from existing innovations by cobbling these innovative practices and programs into a newly assembled *gestalt* moving toward the Learning College. This approach has the advantage of building on what many key faculty and staff in the college are already doing. It is nonthreatening and avoids the defensiveness that comes with approaches based on rejecting old paradigms and pledging allegiance to new paradigms. Rounding up the innovations that already exist in many colleges and aligning them with concepts and values expressed in learning-centered paradigms has great potential for triggering a major reform initiative.

Initiate Conversations on Learning. The Learning Revolution has been in process for over five years, and a number of community college faculty, administrators, and trustees have been reading articles and books and attending conferences on issues related to learning. *The Learning Revolution: A Guide for Community College Trustees* was distributed to all community college trustees by the Association of Community College Trustees in the spring of 1997. As of the summer of 1998, over 12,000 copies of *Creating More Learning-Centered Community Colleges* had been distributed by the League for Innovation. In January of 1999 Palomar College sponsored the third annual conference on the "New Learning Paradigm." In addition, PBS and the League for Innovation cosponsored three national teleconferences in 1997-98 and a series of monthly articles in *Community College Week* anchored by an Internet bulletin board, all on issues related to the Learning Revolution and the Learning College. As a result of these activities, and many others, an increasing number of community college faculty, staff, and trustees are well aware of the issues related to the Learning Revolution and are eager to address these issues on their campuses.

When the League for Innovation surveyed the presidents of its 600-plus Alliance for Community College Innovation member colleges, they indicated strong interest in the Learning College concept. In a 1997 survey, 84 percent of the presidents strongly or very strongly agreed that their institutions would "move to become more learning centered." In a survey a year later, 73 percent of the colleges had launched an initiative to become a more learning-centered institution. Most had already reworked their mission or vision statements to reflect an emphasis on learning.

Leaders who wish to begin an institutional journey to help their colleges become more learning centered can capitalize on this state of interest and readiness by creating "conversations on learning" across the college. A conversation on learning is a focused discussion, involving 10-12 participants and led by an experienced facilitator, that has as its goal increased and expanded learning on the part of participants. The conversation is usually scheduled for two-hour periods weekly or biweekly over a semester or a year. Participants are provided brief reading materials to stimulate discussion, may participate in structured exercises, and work toward specific goals. All topics relate to learning. While the author knows of no written guidelines for designing and conducting these conversations on learning, there are highly competent instructional design specialists and staff development officers working in community colleges today who could synthesize the existing disparate efforts to create the processes and materials required to conduct such conversations. Carefully planned, perhaps as a series of staff development programs throughout the year, this approach would allow the interests and concerns of faculty and staff to surface in an open system rather than within the context of a predetermined strategic plan. The conversations would create awareness, expand knowledge and understanding, and possibly motivate action.

Depending on the culture of the institution, conversations may work best when they are cross-functional, with representatives from a variety of areas within the college. In other cases conversations could be limited to representatives from specific disciplines or programs. Some conversations would thrive if students, trustees, secretaries, or community representatives were included. All conversations should be offered on a voluntary basis or as one of the options for scheduled activities in which faculty and staff are expected to participate. The overall goal is to create as much interest as possible in issues related to the Learning Revolution and to identify those in the institution who can provide leadership and support for an institutionwide learning initiative.

The following questions suggest the richness of the topics that can be included in conversations on learning:

- What kinds of learning do we value most?

- What conditions do we need to create to best support the kinds of learning we value most?

- How do we measure the kinds of learning we agree to produce?

- What are the primary learning styles of our students, and which of these can we best accommodate?

- How can we provide more learning experience options for our students to respond to their diverse learning styles?

- How do we distinguish between learner-centered education and learning-centered education?

- How can we use technology to help our students extend and expand their learning?

- What criteria do we need to apply in selecting new faculty, administrators, and staff to help ensure we are becoming a more learning-centered institution?

These are some of the basic questions to help planners begin, but more questions and issues can be identified from an institution's history, and many more will emerge when the serious conversations begin. It is important to keep the conversations on a positive note as much as possible and to create a framework so that participants are working toward visible goals. Faculty, administrators, and staff should welcome the opportunity to participate in conversations that have intellectual substance on issues about which they care deeply, but the process needs to be carefully designed, and the purpose needs to be made clear. The overarching purpose of these conversations on learning is to create the conditions that lead to a commitment to launch an institutionwide initiative to become more learning centered.

Key Steps in Launching a Learning College

Once a Learning College has been launched—by capitalizing on a trigger event, by identifying needs through an assessment, by building on existing innovations, by holding conversations on learning, or by whatever means leaders may choose from their store of creativity—there are key elements or strategies that must be designed and followed to steer the Learning College project through institutional waters toward landmark islands where successes can be declared.

The strategies are idiosyncratic to the culture of the institution and the character and abilities of its leaders. The strategies are not linear or formulaic, as they often appear in written descriptions, including the steps that follow. Some are more important than others, but all may be of value. Institutions need to choose and experiment with strategies that appear appropriate to their needs; strategies that do not work need to be revised or discarded. In the final analysis, institutions must create their own set of strategies for becoming a more learning-centered institution. The following strategies are gleaned from the literature and from the experiences of a number of pioneering community colleges to serve as suggestions for those in charge of steering the Learning College initiative.*

Build a Critical Coalition. Major new reform and renewal efforts usually begin with a handful of people. In the case of the Learning College, several staff members might have heard a speaker at a conference or read an article that trigged their interest. The dialogue begins and more staff members join in. The CEO may have initiated the first discussion or, at least, is soon drawn into the ever-widening circle.

At some point in these early discussions, a leader, usually the community college president or an academic officer, or a key group such as a task force or a special committee, creates opportunities for next steps. The leader or leaders might articulate the broader theme(s) embedded in these early discussions and encourage continuing discussion, or, if they are more aware and committed to change, may apply one of the ideas reviewed in the previous section to jump-start the action. In any case, once it is clear that the elements of a renewal effort are beginning to emerge, a critical coalition of other key players must be created to achieve a critical mass that will sustain further action. The coalition must include the institution's senior administrators. "All the quality experts agree that if any quality program is going to succeed, it must involve the top. Without the commitment of senior management, nothing gets better" (Dobyns and Crawford-Mason, 1991, p. 8).

John Kotter of the Harvard Business School describes how the coalition works in business:

> In successful transformations, the chairman or president or division general manager, plus another 5 or 15 or 50 people, come together and develop a shared commitment to excellent performance through renewal. In my experience, this group never includes all of the company's most senior executives because some people just won't buy in, at least not at first. But in the most successful cases, the coalition is always pretty powerful—in terms of titles, information and expertise, reputations and relationships. (1995, p. 62)

In the community college the coalition is most often convened by the president or chancellor and will likely include vice presidents; key staff in technology and staff development; key leaders from the faculty, trustees, and students; and perhaps key representatives from the community. In very small community colleges the coalition may include four to six staff in the first year; in large community colleges the coalition may include 20 to 30 key representatives.

President Paul Gianini at Valenica Community College (Florida) describes the process: "In 1995 we decided to deliberately craft a transformation effort to institutionalize effective innovations and to focus on improving measurable learning outcomes. An institutional leadership team comprised of faculty, staff, and administrators took charge of designing and implementing processes to enable

* Many of the quotes in this section on key steps are from statements provided by the leaders acknowledged in the preface in response to a request from the author for examples. Citations have been avoided for easier reading. [Editors' note: The preface is not included in this volume. The referenced acknowledgement reads: "Brian Desbiens, President, and Paul Smith, Facilitator of Organizational Transformation— Sir Sandford Fleming College, Peterborough, Ontario, Canada; Byron McClenney, President—Community College of Denver, Denver, Colorado; Jerry Moskus, President—Lane Community College, Eugene, Oregon; and Ned Sifferlen, President—Sinclair Community College, Dayton, Ohio."]

Valencia to transform itself. We felt it was essential that an independent, collaborative group guide the process, one that has no other mission and whose meetings would not be consumed with the daily operational issues at a college. Under the guidance of this Leadership Team, we have undertaken a range of activities focused on collaborative approaches to becoming more learning centered."

In most institutions, coalition teams seldom emerge in orderly fashion as part of a carefully designed plan as they did at Valencia. In actual practice, coalitions emerge from the ongoing work of leaders who are trying to make a difference. Ned Sifferlen, president of Sinclair Community College (Ohio), remembers when the first critical coalition at Sinclair was formed in response to quality questions raised during the development of an academic assessment plan. Subsequently, the Quality Council was formed which produced an Institutional Effectiveness Model that incorporated vision, mission, core indicators of effectiveness, and key performance indicators that measured progress toward continuous improvement targets.

The vision
statement for the Learning College is the guiding star by which leaders will steer their activities.

In 1998, a Strategic Planning Task Force was created to ensure a smooth transition from the foundation established by the Quality Council to a strategic plan for the institution. In January 1999, the trustees participated in a process learning activity focused on the principles of the Learning College, the results of which were integrated into college strategy. Finally, a new Center for Interactive Learning (CIL) opened Fall Quarter 1998 to serve as a test bed for innovation related to the Learning College. One function of the CIL is to serve as an incubator where faculty members redesign curricula, investigate new learning methods, develop interactive instructional materials, and work out implementation plans to replicate and disseminate successful pilot projects. The success of the various coalitions that emerged from the ongoing work of the college is evidenced in innovative projects that are highly visible in the CIL.

Leaders at Sir Sandford Fleming College (Ontario, Canada) indicate that it is hard to pinpoint when, where, or how they decided to become a learning-centered college. College leaders had been involved in a series of change processes for some time and had developed a Master Academic Framework that served to guide many of their efforts. Paul Smith, facilitator of organizational transformation at Fleming, said, "We actually have a variety of coalitions, both formal and informal, each of which is championing change related to an aspect of the new vision. Importantly, these coalitions, made up of influential leaders and staff who are action oriented, span all levels of the organization, including the board, students, faculty, college council, and increasingly, cross-functional task groups. We gain momentum and synergy from this multifaceted approach to change through the ripple effect." Fleming has created a College Leaders Team which consists of the members of its senior leaders team, academic leaders team, two union presidents, two student presidents, and the chair of the college council. The College Leaders Team oversees the reallocation of resources and the revision of the college

vision. There is clear recognition and commitment, however, to making sure that many coalitions of interested and committed staff members emerge across the institution.

Jerry Moskus, president of Lane Community College (Oregon), indicates that "the culture of Lane Community College is averse to grand plans launched from on high." A major factor in the success of the learning-centered college movement at Lane is its origins in a visioning retreat of the college council, a broadly representative group of faculty, classified staff, students, managers, and the president. A vision that emerged from this retreat—*quality learning experiences in a caring environment*—represented a consensus among many campus leaders, and thus it generated commitment from all campus groups. The visioning retreat might have had much less impact at Lane without the support of the faculty and classified employee unions. Union leadership was represented on the college council and participated in creating the new vision. It soon became apparent that union leaders were deeply committed to the learning-centered vision and wanted to actively support its implementation. The classified union has played a major role in the success of the Students First! project, a total redesign of student services; and the faculty union has partnered with management to lead a project to redesign instruction. The college council, broadly representing all key groups in the institution, including two key unions, serves as a critical coalition and a sounding board to guide the work of Lane's efforts to become more learning centered.

The critical coalition(s) becomes the first laboratory for testing out processes that will be used later in institutionwide efforts. Care must be taken to build a sense of trust and community among the members of the coalition, and special attention must be given to ensuring that each member understands the need for the project and the concepts involved in a Learning College. A great deal of reading is required. Retreats of two to three days are helpful in building a sense of community and in planning strategies. The coalition that is to guide the Learning College project must be powerful enough in its representation, and in its understanding and commitment, to withstand the forces resistant to change that will soon emerge. The membership of this early coalition may change at a later time when other structures and processes have emerged, perhaps taking on an oversight role, but in the beginning its formation is critical to success.

Create an Emerging Vision. Early in the project a written statement of the institutional vision for becoming a Learning College emerges. The vision statement for the Learning College is the guiding star by which leaders will steer their activities. The vision statement is brief—sometimes no more than a paragraph—and is a clear and vivid account of what participants want the Learning College to become. "The power of vision derives from its ability to capture the hearts and minds of an organization's members by setting forth a goal that is both feasible and uplifting" (Wilson, 1996, p. 5). Answers to "First Questions" suggested in *An American Imperative* such as, "What kind of people do we want our children and grandchildren to be?" can help provide responses for framing the vision statement.

Wilson (1996) defines vision as a "coherent and powerful statement of what the organization can and should be some set number of years hence" (p. 3). He notes that vision differs from, but complements, mission and philosophy.

> Mission states the basic purpose of the organization, defines its relationships to other organizations and constituencies, and sets general objectives. Philosophy articulates the values that should guide organizational behavior, defines the character of relations with stakeholders, and sets the style and culture of the organization. Vision builds on these statements to describe the future size, shape, and texture of the organization (that is, one should be able to get a good feel for the future organization from the vision statement); it sets specific goals and, more important, drives and guides action to achieve those goals. (p. 3)

The critical coalition often drafts the first vision statement, relying on one or two wordsmiths who are always present in educational groupings. The first draft is often murky and has an unfinished quality, but it begins to rally support and commitment from the coalition team. Over a period of months the vision evolves with more stakeholders contributing their views until key ideas hold up through each iteration.

The process should not be hurried, for this is the stage in which individuals are examining their own values and exploring the outer limits of positions others will tolerate and support. The process must address the criticisms of cynics and the dreams of visionaries. A balance must be struck between the ideal and the practical. Eventually, perhaps a year or more later, the vision statement is formed and agreed upon by the stakeholders.

The nature of vision statements and the process by which they are created reflect the rich diversity of ways community colleges approach change at their institutions. At Sinclair the vision statement of the institution is reflected in the vision statement of the Center for Interactive Learning: "a place where people of diverse backgrounds can see and experience the future of learning and work. The CIL is a place where everyone is a student. In the Center, we can fearlessly try out new ways of learning and teaching, evaluate our experiments, and ponder their implications."

At Lane, the president and his assistant prepared an idea paper as a first draft for the college's new vision statement. Influenced by their reading about "high performance work organizations," the authors envisioned a new Lane that would be values driven, team based, and collaborative, and characterized by open communication. They developed the idea that everyone on campus was to be a learner and that "learning" would become the collegewide, unifying value. The vision paper was revised a number of times with a great deal of feedback from campus constituents. The final paper has been distributed to every employee of the college.

In the late 1980s the president of the Community College of Denver (CCD), Byron McClenney, opened a convocation followed by a day-long activity in which faculty members and other staff contributed ideas that would lead CCD to a new commitment to accountability, assessment, and student success. In subsequent years, the vision statement has been revised several times to maintain continued staff involvement and to ensure that the vision statement reflects new challenges and opportunities.

At Fleming College, President Brian Desbiens notes, "We would emphasize that the real challenge is to develop a vision that reflects and is grounded in the future and thus pulls the organization toward it. Once the vision is created, the college can identify the steps required to lose the gap between the present and future." Although Fleming has been guided by a vision statement for a number of years, leaders indicate that it is time to revisit the process to make sure they are addressing current problems and future challenges that may have emerged in the last several years. The revision process will start with a small task group of about 10 people who will draft a paper which (1) identifies key trends; (2) identifies critical questions to be answered; and (3) develops some scenarios or range of responses to these questions. The 10 people will include members of the college staff, a board member, and a student leader. The paper will be circulated widely, and a variety of mechanisms will be used to obtain feedback and generate discussion. Leaders expect the project to take approximately six months, perhaps longer, since the goal is to create a vision all staff understand and support. Leaders indicate, "We will try to develop a *revolutionary* vision which represents some quantum leaps for us over the next five to ten years, but which will be implemented in an evolutionary manner consistent with our culture and resources. In our experience, once we develop and adopt a vision, the hard work begins, specifically, helping all staff to 'paint themselves into this picture' in behavioral terms."

The creation of a vision statement with buy-in from the great majority of college members is a significant step for institutions committed to change.

Create Action Plans. The creation of a vision statement with buy-in from the great majority of college members is a significant step for institutions committed to change. In some instances this task is so challenging that leaders are reluctant to initiate the next, more challenging step, which is to create action plans that will bring the vision to life. Unless college leaders move quickly, however, to create action plans with clear directions for steps to be taken and milestones by which to gauge progress, the initiative to become more learning centered will flounder at this critical juncture. The action plans place in clear relief the key policies, programs, and practices that will translate the elegant phrases of the vision statement into reality.

The action plan does not need to be spelled out in great detail at this point, but there must be a clearly articulated pathway for change, a framework for next steps, to make sure that momentum is not lost. College leaders at Fleming said, "We identified the tasks and processes we would be engaged with during the major restructuring process and provided timelines so the staff could gauge our progress. We provided frequent and regular communications about our progress, and these communications provided factual information, progress toward timelines, and also acknowledged and addressed the affective dimensions of the change process. We paid special attention to stress, depression, grief, and loss among our many college members which often results from major institutional change. When we met our timelines, staff had more confidence in the change process. We were also able to announce with some confidence when the 'worst' part of the change was over and that we could now focus on consolidating the changes, making the new model work, and most importantly, reinvesting our resources to move us forward."

At Valencia four action teams were created, and more than 180 college members volunteered to participate in team activities. Members of each team selected a facilitator and began their work by reading and discussing selected literature relevant to their charge. Each team developed a charter, and members committed to attend meetings over a six-month period to create plans. College staff who did not participate on teams agreed to review and comment on draft products developed by the teams. This helped to facilitate collegewide consensus as actions unfolded.

Valencia's Short Term Action Team identified actions that would not take a great deal of work to help the college become more learning centered and recommended these for immediate implementation. The Vision and Organizational Character Action Team continued to work on a draft vision statement to make sure that it reflected the college's core values, purpose, and mission. The other action teams referenced the draft statement of core values to help guide their work. The Core Process Action Team focused on assessing the college's central operations. This team developed a set of guidelines for realigning core processes of the college, which included designing and revising job descriptions and evaluating results achieved through new uses of technology. The Core Competencies Action Team set as its goal the identification of key competencies for students that embody the heart of the Learning College. Not only will the team identify key competencies, it will also recommend processes to nourish them. The goals of this team strike to the heart of the initiative to become a more learning-centered institution, and its work is ongoing.

As part of the fall opening conference in 1997, Valencia sponsored an institutionwide forum for interested faculty to review reports from each of the four action teams and to consider their recommendations. More than 300 faculty members attended these sessions and met in small groups to review recommendations and to provide feedback on next steps.

As both these examples illustrate, the action steps provided opportunities for members of the college community not only to help establish directions, but also to respond and react to directions recommended by groups of their colleagues. The need to involve all stakeholders in the institution in the transformation process is important at all points but especially when the major action steps are determined.

Involve All Stakeholders. In a community college the key stakeholders include administrators, full-time faculty, support staff, students, and trustees. Depending on the culture of the institution and its capacity to manage

complexity, part-time faculty and community representatives may be included as stakeholders.

The new "science" of management and leadership that prescribes flattened organizations, open communication, and empowered participation makes a strong case for involving all stakeholders in major reform efforts. Margaret Wheatley, an organizational change consultant, says, "Any change program that insists on defining how things ought to be done, that tries to impose a structure on everyone— without their involvement—works against our natural tendencies" (Brown, 1994, p. 24).

Wheatley believes:

> Change is a capacity built into nature and, I would add, a capacity built into human nature…. People are not inert, resistant lumps. We have had years and years of believing that without our efforts people will do nothing; without our plans and designs, our organizations will fall apart. But this is not the world we live in. Organizational leaders need to realize that complex systems can emerge, not from their designs, but when individuals interact with one another around some simple, straightforward principles of interaction and purpose. (p. 24)

Wheatley goes on to say:

> You need deep and meaningful involvement of the whole organization. This seems like an insurmountable barrier, to involve the whole organization, but I believe the starting point for real change is to focus energy and direction on this one key question: "Can we involve the expertise and experience of everyone in the organization?" We can't ignore that question. We've got to figure out how we can avoid the temptation to design things for people instead of engaging them in creating their own responses to change. (p. 26)

Few community college presidents will argue against the importance of involving all stakeholders in the process of creating a Learning College, but many will be unsure of how to manage this process. It is more practical to set a goal of involving all stakeholders who want to participate, and providing numerous opportunities for their participation. Stakeholders can participate in institutionwide convocations, workshops and seminars, and special training sessions. The staff development program can be reeengineered to focus on activities related to the Learning College, perhaps in the form of conversations on learning. In-house newsletters can provide important information regarding the Learning College project. In some cases, a special publication will need to be created to carry the message, as was the case with Miami-Dade's Teaching and Learning Project, a major reform effort initiated in the 1980s. Copies of key documents that evolve from project activities, such as the vision statement, and later documents, such as new policies for assessing students or selecting faculty or rewarding and promoting support staff, will need to be sent to every stakeholder for review and response. Universal opportunity to participate, not universal agreement, is the goal. Some proposed changes may need to be put to a vote.

At Valencia, leaders believe that transformation in higher education is made possible by collaboration. "If we have found one lesson to be more important than any other, it is this: higher education rests on a shared governance model. We have found that for such a change to be made, agreement on the changes must be reached collaboratively. In addition, what we have agreed upon has become conceptually stronger as a result of this collaboration. We find most useful a process of collaborative decision making that actively engages all those who want to participate in informed dialogue about the college's present and future. Still, this process has its challenges. Some college members feel that we are holding ourselves back when we allow time for full participation in the consideration of ideas and actions. Others caution that too fast a pace will derail the change process. Through our mistakes as well as our successes, we have come to see that faculty and administrative leaders must be as committed to the collaborative process as they are to the change agenda itself. They must be willing to trust their colleagues as professionals and to rely on one another's judgment."

Following the visioning retreat at Lane Community College that effectively launched Lane's learning initiative, the president and vice presidents met with every department on campus to explain the new vision and to secure feedback. Still, the Learning College concept did not really begin to gain a foothold on campus until two projects were initiated. The redesign of student services was based on advice from many staff and groups of students. The Strategic Learning Initiative, a project to redesign the instructional program, attracted large numbers of faculty. President Jerry Moskus said, "We began to see the ideas take hold the more we involved the members of our college."

At Lane, much of the current momentum of the learning movement results from a number of cross-functional, vertically integrated, permanent teams that address key issues on campus, such as technology planning, student and staff diversity, strategic planning, facilities planning and management, and enrollment management. "We involve all the stakeholders in these very important teams that move Lane's action forward."

At Fleming, "Consultation is our middle name and is deeply embedded in our culture." Fleming also uses cross-functional teams to solve problems that cut across areas and functions. In addition, the college council at Fleming is composed of elected representatives from all stakeholder groups and meets monthly to advise the president and monitor and recommend action on collegewide issues that can enhance the college environment.

Ensure Appropriate Support

Appoint a Project Manager. In addition to the continuing overall involvement and support of the college's CEO, a project manager should be appointed to coordinate the various activities of the Learning College initiative. Such an appointment signals the value the institution places on the project. The project manager should be a well-respected member of the college community. The staff development officer or the TQM coordinator might be considered, or a faculty leader who could be released from teaching duties for a period of several years. The project manager needs time to catch up on the related literature including educational reform, organizational change, leadership development, brain-based learning, information technology, continuous quality improvement, and assessment. If the project manager is already trained in skills to facilitate groups, that is a great asset. The project manager must work closely with the CEO and the coalition team to keep the Learning College project on target.

At Fleming, a special position was created called "Facilitator of Organizational Transformation," which functions as a project manager for the institution's initiative to become more learning centered. The individual reports to the president and is a member of the Senior Leaders Team. The person in the position is responsible for facilitating, planning, developing, and implementing organizational transformation initiatives across the college and is expected to provide leadership in all areas of change management. Part of the rationale for creating the role is to assist the college in developing and maintaining the momentum for change and in resisting the tendency to regress to the old ways of doing business. The role is intended to be a temporary one, since it is assumed that over time the functions will be performed by the Human and Organizational Development Division or other leaders as part of their regular leadership roles. The position is reviewed periodically to refocus the role on the next stage of transformation and to assess continuing need for the position. Fleming chose specifically to staff the position with a member of the college community who had credibility with staff because of a long history with the college and a thorough understanding of Fleming's culture. At various times the incumbent has served as a faculty member, a dean, director of staff development, and director of planning and special projects. A number of colleges have attempted major reforms, including efforts to become more learning centered, through faculty committees and task forces. Some CEOs take pride in the fact that their initiatives are faculty driven and created from the bottom up. Such approaches can be very successful because they are faculty led, but they can be even more successful if a project coordinator is assigned to the faculty committee. Faculty committees do not have time to follow through on the details of a major initiative.

Provide Support for the Project. As difficult as it is in these times to allocate resources for new projects, a modest budget should be created for project activities. In most colleges, this budget can be created by reallocating funds from current budgets in staff development, travel, and internal communications. The president's "discretionary fund" can also be tapped.

Support will need to be provided to train facilitators. A change effort of the magnitude envisioned here will work only if many staff members participate in carefully designed sessions to increase their understanding of the issues and to elicit their participation. Building a new set of shared values

Building a new set of shared values across a campus community, by involving more representatives of more stakeholder groups than has probably ever occurred, is a monumental effort.

across a campus community, by involving more representatives of more stakeholder groups than has probably ever occurred, is a monumental effort. Helping representatives from various groups learn how to operate in newly formed teams is a significant undertaking. Colleges cannot achieve these goals unless they become learning organizations with all stakeholders participating as learners.

In Lane Community College's initiative, many teams, clusters, and groups were created to carry out the business of developing a more learning-centered organization. Cross-functional strategic teams and vertically integrated project teams did much of the basic work. These teams and groups became more effective through training. An Organizational Development Action Team (ODAT) was responsible for ensuring that training in communication skills, team effectiveness, meeting effectiveness, conflict resolution, and customer service was offered. To provide this training, ODAT identified 50 "movers and shakers," or informal campus leaders, who could be trained to train others. By 1996, over 300 Lane staff had participated in communication training.

As Jerry Moskus, president of Lane, said, "Working in teams does not come naturally to educators socialized to be strong individualists, suspicious of movements and groups." Fortunately, educational institutions have the internal resources to provide education and training for their own members, and this formidable resource can be used to prepare stakeholders for the new behaviors required in a Learning College.

A number of colleges have created very visible signs of their support for the learning initiative by offering special grants to encourage faculty to focus their expertise on related projects. For example, Sinclair sets aside $200,000 a year for The Learning Challenge Awards. The awards are designed to support projects that will improve and expand student learning, and are made only to teams to encourage collaboration. The proposals from faculty teams must include activities related to student learning outcomes that can be measured. Fleming College provides similar incentives with a $100,000-a-year special budget to encourage innovative grants in curriculum development and instructional processes that will improve and expand student learning.

Ensure Trustee Support and Involvement. Since creating a Learning College is a major change for an institution, the governing board must be fully involved from the beginning. The trustees will need to participate in training sessions and begin to prepare for policy and resource changes that will be the result of philosophical and structural changes. If the entire architecture of education needs to be changed, as has been called for by a number of national task forces and commissions, this is serious business that cannot occur without the full support of the trustees.

Throughout 1994 and 1995, the governing board of Maricopa Community Colleges held a series of strategic conversations on such topics as chaos theory, new learning paradigms, leadership and the new science, system unity, diversity, and continuous quality improvement. These conversations were facilitated by faculty, classified staff, students, and administrators, and served to illustrate Maricopa's commitment to involving all stakeholders. Through the strategic conversations many ideas emerged,

networks were formed, and new structures evolved. The governing board members grew in their understanding of the issues, and in their commitment to the goals of the comprehensive and complex project designed to help Maricopa become a learning-centered institution.

At Fleming, the board chair and other board members are very involved in providing leadership for the transformation. Board members and the president collaborate and provide mutual support on contentious issues, when they arise, particularly when these issues attract public attention. The monthly board agenda includes items related to the transformation process, and a number of change issues are addressed by standing committees of the board. The board holds an annual retreat to review and help anticipate strategies related to the transformation, and board members are actively engaged in a variety of college meetings and activities. In addition, business leaders on the board and in the community facilitate the transformation proces by sharing their own experiences of changes taking place in their organizations, and by advocating on behalf of the college.

More and more trustees in community colleges are becoming aware of concepts associated with the Learning College. As one example, community college leaders in Michigan have launched a statewide learning initiative in collaboration with Michigan State University. Guidelines for the initiative, titled *Becoming a Learning College*, published in 1998, spell out specific responsibilities of trustees in creating a Learning College:

> The Board of Trustees must work together to promote commitment and development opportunities for each of its members.
>
> Commitment
>
> - Establish board commitment to a Learning College.
> - Become change agents for the Learning College by
>   - o Setting the pace for the college community;
>   - o Empowering the president to address change issues;
>   - o Developing external links consistent with changing community needs; and
>   - o Maintaining accountability to the larger community for serving its diverse needs.
>
> Development Opportunities
>
> - Encourage all trustees to become continual learners.
> - Provide opportunities for the trustees to become more knowledgeable of the Learning College concept. (Michigan State University, 1998 p. 6)

Create an Open System of Communication. If convening a single meeting and distributing one key paper about the Learning College are the only efforts to bring about change, an intended initiative is doomed to an early death. This is not a project that can succeed by tossing one stone in the pond and following up on all the ripples. Creating a Learning College means tossing hundreds of stones into the pond, dumping boulders into the pond, and even filling in the pond and digging a new one. This kind of change will not occur unless the community of stakeholders is kept fully informed on a regular basis about what is happening, and unless there are mechanisms provided whereby they can communicate across the entire community of participants. Fortunately, technological innovations now exist, and are being installed in many community colleges, that allow for a rich exchange of information and opportunities for intimate connectivity.

Wilson says, "If a vision is to shape the future and drive action, then the leader—and others in executive positions—must communicate it broadly, consistently, and continuously, until it becomes an integral part of the organization's culture" (1996, p. 5).

The message must be driven home again and again through speeches, newsletters, meetings, articles, interviews, surveys, and actions. Kotter suggests that business executives who communicate well incorporate the message in their hour-by-hour activities:

> In a routine discussion about a business problem, they talk about how proposed solutions fit (or don't fit) into the bigger picture. In a regular performance appraisal, they talk about how the employee's behavior helps or undermines the vision. In a review of the division's quarterly performance, they talk not only about the numbers but also about how the division's executives are contributing to the transformation. In a routine Q & A with employees at a company facility, they tie their answers back to renewal goals. (1995, p. 64)

The project manager has major responsibility for ensuring that the mechanisms are in place for the communication that is needed. The CEO of the college needs to take responsibility for many "official" roles in communicating about project activities, as well as many unofficial ones. If the initiative is led by a faculty task force, its members must participate actively and often to ensure continuing communication. As the project emerges and matures, more and more participants will take responsibility for communicating their needs and their ideas.

The colleges cited in this monograph as examples of institutions committed to becoming more learning centered are healthy institutions that do not always have to build new processes to get their work done. For example, many of these colleges already rely on open systems of communication.

Jerry Moskus says that "Lane's efforts to create an open system of communication predate its efforts to become a learning-centered college. In the late 1980s, the college embraced shared decision making, a system that enabled all stakeholders to contribute to the institution's process of decision making. A new governance system was established to support shared decision making, and this structure provided a means for involving many stakeholders in implementing the new learning-centered vision."

Lane capitalized on its existing open system of communication to launch the new learning-centered vision by disseminating a paper on the new direction to all staff. Then the president and vice presidents met with each department to discuss the paper. The vision statement was included in many college publications and referenced on the college letterhead. The campus newsletter, *The Daily*, which is distributed to all staff members, frequently includes articles and attachments related to the new vision.

At Fleming, *The Transformation* newsletter is issued periodically to keep staff updated on the restructuring and transformation process. As with Lane, open communication and consultation are fundamental values ingrained in the culture of Fleming. In many ways they are not acting differently than they have in the past, although the content of the message has changed to support the transformation of the culture to become more learning centered. Fleming uses a variety of communication methods including meetings, email, hard copy memos and documents, and the Internet. Sinclair takes advantage of groupware systems to involve its constituents in an open system of communication.

At the Community College of Denver, a partnership of faculty members, classified staff, and administrators has been in place since 1986 to help the college move from a deficiency model of student achievement to a success model in which each person and unit seeks to support student learning. From holding philosophical discussions to undertaking practical problem solving, the faculty and staff at CCD have been building a culture focused on student success that has as its cornerstone collaborative decision making. A professor in the arts department at St. Louis Community College at Florissant Valley (Missouri) remarked on the team effort and good communication at the Community College of Denver on a recent visit: "I am very impressed with the team effort at CCD. Everyone seems to work together on common themes. Energy does not seem to be wasted on politics. The staff seems aligned on common goals and processes. It was absolutely awe inspiring to hear and see all of the fine things you were doing."

Consider Consultants and Established Processes. Several of the colleges engaged in creating Learning Colleges have made effective use of external consultants. In some cases, consultants can provide an overall perspective on educational reform and the growing emphasis on learning, and these consultants are useful in addressing the entire faculty and staff or in making presentations to the board of trustees and key community groups. Other consultants are specialists in some key area such as chaos theory, portfolio assessment, brain-based research, or technological networks; they are useful in meetings with groups working on specific projects. Process consultants can be brought in to train facilitators or can be used on a continuing basis to facilitate group meetings.

Consultants are educational resources and should be used wisely. They can escalate learning for stakeholders, challenge

Creating a
Learning College

means tossing hundreds of stones into the pond, dumping boulders into the pond, and even filling in the pond and digging a new one.

reluctant participants, help identify other resources, and provide information on what other institutions are doing across the country. But consultants do not make the same commitments to the project as do college leaders, they do not have to suffer the same consequences, and they are not in the project for the long haul. Consultants should be used for what they can offer, but they should not be expected to shoulder primary responsibility. College leaders and staff must own the project. Responsibility for the kind of change involved in creating a Learning College cannot be handed off to others, no matter how competent or highly recommended they come.

Faculty are
fully aware of leaders

who trot out new language

that is not fortified with new

beliefs and new behaviors.

Consultants have enabled the staff at Lane to learn new skills in support of the new learning-centered vision. A husband-and-wife team of communication consultants trained large numbers of staff in workplace communication skills needed for teamwork. The redesign of student services was undertaken with the day-to-day assistance of outside experts in process reengineering. The faculty effort to redesign instruction has occasionally involved invited speakers on instructional topics. When implementation of the new vision produced conflicts within campus departments and teams, an expert on mediation was hired to teach mediation skills and to help particular groups resolve existing conflicts. The development of new values statements to define future work roles and relationships among staff was guided by an expert on labor relations. A management consultant helped the executive leadership group move from the traditional president's cabinet structure to a leadership team.

At Fleming, consultants are used sparingly and in a very focused way. Staff members at Fleming often ask consultants for a range of options to be considered, but the staff themselves actually select the option that fits best with the culture of Fleming. Consultants are usually sought who have content expertise and facilitation skills not readily available on campus. However, Fleming values and recognizes the consulting skills of its own staff and has created several formal consultant roles in the college, including the Human and Organizational Development Consultants and the Training and Development Services Consultants.

Colleges may also want to consider borrowing some of the specialized processes that have been designed for other settings. The total quality management and continuous quality improvement movements, for example, have designed a number of detailed processes for identifying problems, designing alternative solutions, making decisions, improving communication, assessing skills, and building community that will prove useful in changing the organizational culture of a college. These processes are updated versions of techniques that have been around for some time, but they have been improved through refinement and through application and testing in varied settings. Many of the TQM processes are refined versions of techniques described in Alex F. Osborne's *Creative Imagination*, issued decades ago. Current processes also reflect a great deal of experimentation with "T" groups and encounter groups that dominated educational processes in the 1960s.

Processes in current use have their own language, their own special names, and special champions. Many are outlined in step-by-step detail and accompanied by training manuals. These processes are not magic solutions, however, and they are seldom based on scientific experimentation. In the right hands they can usually achieve their purpose. College leaders and the project manager should review these processes carefully and select the ones that will work best in the established culture of the college. Every consultant will champion his or her favorite process, and faculty will recommend the process they have most recently experienced.

While some colleges may hire consultants who bring their own specialized processes to bear on activities at the college, other institutions adapt these special processes to their own culture. Leaders at Fleming, for example, say, "We have not adopted any particular large-scale, established process such as TQM in any major way; these tend to be viewed as 'gimmicky' at our place. We tend to create our own by adapting aspects of established processes to our own culture. However, we do use a variety of established tools, including brainstorming, force-field analysis, process design, Delphi techniques, and focus groups."

Pay Attention to Language. Colleges that want to become Learning Colleges should examine their official documents and their daily language to ascertain what priorities are being conveyed. At Palomar College (California) leaders reviewed official documents and incorporated the language of their newly developed learning paradigm in all their documents. Student learning is now a clear purpose in the mission statement of the college. Student learning is everyone's job, as indicated in revised job descriptions. Recruitment brochures now indicate the college's commitment to student learning and its interest in receiving applications from individuals who share that commitment. College goals now include student learning outcomes as key elements. The president of Palomar College, George Boggs, says, "College educators need to be sure they are saying what they intend to say."

It is possible, of course, to create new language but retain old beliefs and behaviors. Seasoned community college educators can spot with ease those who do not "walk the talk." Faculty are fully aware of leaders who trot out new language that is not fortified with new beliefs and new behaviors. Such action is a vacuous exercise that serves only to harden existing layers of cynicism.

President Jerry Moskus at Lane believes that renaming phenomena can actually lead to change in behavior. "More and more," he says, "the word 'learning' is being used in place of 'education' and 'learner' is replacing 'student.' The word 'learner' has proven useful to describe the large group of people served by Lane who are not enrolled in formal classes and thus are not really students in the formal sense. The campus radio station takes on a different meaning when its mission is viewed as producing learning rather than merely informing or entertaining its listeners. The Retired Senior Volunteer Program has changed its emphasis from providing services to helping seniors and volunteers learn."

In addition to the Learning Challenge Grants at Sinclair, noted earlier, a number of strategic task forces have adopted the language of learning. Everyone at Sinclair has participated in the development of a mission model that has "learning" as its central focus and that identifies how each employee's work group contributes to and measures its contribution to learning.

Leaders at Fleming are deeply aware of the importance of language, and they have made sure they retain the old language that reinforces the culture and make connections to Fleming's history, tradition, and strengths. The terms "quality," "caring," and "future orientation" are key words from an early vision statement at Fleming, and leaders continue to use these key words to express core institutional values.

Fleming has also introduced new language into the institutional culture to signal the changes that are occurring. The word "learning" has been added to the mission statement; leaders are referred to as "leaders" rather than as managers or supervisors; alternative delivery systems are now referred to as "distributed learning"; independent study has become "guided learning"; and although teachers are still referred to as teachers, the term "facilitators of learning" is openly discussed. In their job postings for new staff, the new language is demonstrated in such phrases as "demonstrated participatory leadership skills," "effective team member," "facilitation and teambuilding skills," and ability to "establish an appropriate learning environment for students."

As community colleges explore and experiment with Learning College models, there is an opportunity to create a new language about learning, a language specific to community colleges. In the past, community colleges have borrowed a great deal of the language used by universities and four-year colleges to describe their own values and their practices. Currently community colleges are busy adapting language from business and industry. Surely there is a special language of learning embedded in the idiosyncratic experiences of community college faculty as they continue decade after decade to provide learning opportunities for the most challenging learners in all of higher education.

Reallocate Resources. Very few community colleges, if any, operating in the current economic climate of reengineering and downsizing, have the resources to support new projects, especially projects of the magnitude and duration associated with creating a Learning College. In almost all cases, current resources will have to be reallocated to support project efforts, and there is not a great deal of experience from which to derive guidelines.

Some creative college leaders have actually used the financial depressions in their institutions as leverage to launch a Learning College. At Jackson Community College in Michigan the picture was particularly bleak. The college had lost 12 tax elections in a row; equipment was obsolete; enrollment was dropping; collective bargaining agreements left no room for negotiation; and the district had lost hundreds of base manufacturing jobs over the last few years. This situation, along with the appointment of a new president, was used as a precipitating condition—a trigger event—to initiate a very successful transformation toward becoming a Learning College.

There may be lessons to be learned regarding the reallocation of resources from a restructuring project supported by The Pew Charitable Trusts. A number of institutions of higher education, including community colleges, held round-table discussions and designed projects to restructure their institutions for the future. Recognizing that "the need for academic restructuring owes much of its urgency to tough financial times" (*Policy Perspectives*, April, 1994, p. 8a), college participants addressed the issue of declining resources, and a number of recommendations emerged in the project's newsletter, *Policy Perspectives*. The core recommendation relates to reducing the high, labor-intensive cost of higher education by reducing the number of faculty and administrators. The following summary of these recommendations comes from the February 1993 and April 1994 issues of *Policy Perspectives*.

- Higher education remains an enterprise too often prone to define progress in terms of addition rather than substitution or subtraction (1994, p. 8a).

- A variety of institutions over the past 12 months have confirmed our sense that where institutions have succeeded most they have done so principally by imposing budget discipline in response to changes in their circumstances. Such discipline is a necessary first step in reshaping the culture of an institution (1993, p. 6a).

- The institution must establish the "priority" changes it needs to make and then set goals for substantial and lasting changes in each of these areas, sending the message that marginal changes will not be sufficient (1993, p. 6a).

- The kinds of saving and reductions in current expenditures that are required both to offset diminished revenues and to provide sufficient capital for investment in new programs cannot be achieved without setting aside the principle that personnel reductions will only be made if all else fails (1994, p. 8a).

- In times of transition the first instinct of most institutions is to protect the faculty. We believe, however, that this transition is different. Changes in how faculty regard themselves and their institutions lie at the heart of the restructuring process (1993, p. 9a).

- A substantial portion of the administrative growth of the past decade. . . has resulted from the entrepreneurial instincts of administrative staff and the sense on the part of senior administrators that it is easier to solve a problem by creating a new administrative unit than by making an established unit take on a task not of its own choosing. Accordingly, restructuring needs to begin on the administrative side of the house (1993, p. 9a).

- Given strong leadership and a sustained commitment to the retraining of current staff, we believe that a five to seven year process designed to re-engineer operations can yield a 25 percent reduction in the number of full time employees an institution requires (1993, p. 7a).

- Fundamentally, restructuring will strengthen institutions precisely because the process itself will force a sustained reexamination of functions and procedures that have grown haphazardly over the last three decades (1993, p. 7a).

This is pretty brutal stuff for most educators. This is the kind of discussion that weakens the resolve of community college leaders to lead change and strengthens the resolve of faculty unions and administrators to resist change. Open discussion about changing the rules of the labor-intensive formula in higher education creates faculty concern that the call for transformation and change is actually an attempt to get rid of faculty. That may be the motivation of some community college administrators—allegiance to movements is used for all kinds of purposes—*but it is not the position advocated here.* Healthy institutions will be able to deal with this issue openly and honestly; unhealthy institutions will use the issue to feed their neuroses.

Community colleges have not

traditionally paid much attention to evaluating their activities or assessing student outcomes, but in recent years that situation has begun to change.

There are responsible administrators, however, operating in healthy institutions today who will address this issue head-on, and these are the leaders and the institutions that will create the models of the Learning College of the future. Chancellor William Wenrich of the Dallas County Community College District has linked the faculty productivity role with the need for a new model of learning.

> Increasing "educational productivity" relates to one of two alternatives: 1) increasing the quality or quantity of learning by students without increasing cost proportionately, or 2) maintaining the quality and quantity of student learning while reducing the proportional cost. The key element is to make more effective use of the most critical learning resource, the full-time faculty members. (1994, p. 1)

He goes on to define a new role for faculty as "masters of the learning environment" and notes that "some faculty will be unwilling or unable to adapt to this new paradigm. To the extent financially feasible, they should continue to teach in a traditional mode, but upon their departure, their replacements should be expected to exhibit the professional skills to be masters of the learning environment" (p. 1). This humane but clear approach is one example of how community college leaders can implement new structures to reallocate resources to ensure support for the creation of Learning Colleges.

Healthy colleges do not shy away from reallocating resources to make internal changes in their organizations that address new realities and new opportunities to become more learning-centered institutions. Fleming College provides a dramatic example of how the reallocation of resources can lead to a more creative and workable organizational structure that supports efforts to become more learning centered. In 1995, Fleming had to face a 20 percent reduction in its overall budget because of reduced support from the federal and provincial governments in Canada. Based on some of the recommendations made by The Pew Charitable Trusts, Fleming's organizational design team recommended a one-third reduction in administrative ranks to model the scope of the changes that would be required of the front-line services and academic programs. Deans and chairs were replaced by academic team leaders, who were drawn primarily from faculty ranks and were selected by faculty members with agreement from the faculty bargaining unit. A comprehensive memorandum of understanding was developed with the faculty union, and both management and the union agree that, to date, the new model is working extremely well.

In essence, the college broke up the old administrative structure common to most colleges and established six centers of specialization in such areas as natural resources, community development and health, law and justice, management and business studies, interdisciplinary studies, and applied computing and information technology. Academic team leaders selected by faculty members and their team members are fully responsible for the daily operation of each center including such responsibilities as staff hiring, formative faculty evaluation, professional development, budget development and monitoring, program development, evaluation of team performance and leadership, and marketing and promotion of the center's programs. This new organizational structure eliminated an entire layer of managers and brought the work of the faculty closer to those responsible for making learning happen. The college also terminated four programs, modified eight, and gave sixteen others two years to make improvements.

The Community College of Denver has also taken steps to reallocate resources in a very dramatic way. It has become a leader in actually implementing, with faculty support, a faculty pay-for-performance schedule. Using an evaluation scheme that was developed by the faculty, based on a collective set of teaching and learning values, faculty receive differentiated pay based on their performance and their contributions to helping the institution meet its overall core indicators of effectiveness focused on student success.

Evaluate, Evaluate, Evaluate. Community colleges have not traditionally paid much attention to evaluating their activities or assessing student outcomes, but in recent years that situation has begun to change. Along with the rest of higher education, community colleges have been strongly influenced by the assessment movement, particularly in response to new standards set by the regional accrediting associations, and calls for accountability and mandates of performance-based funding by state legislators. Assisted by improved assessment tools and new technologies, such as computer-assisted assessment, community colleges are beginning to undertake the systematic assessment and evaluation of all their activities.

At Sinclair Community College, interest in student assessment actually prepared the way for Sinclair's journey to become a Learning College. In 1985 college staff began discussing the need to develop learning outcomes for each of the college's programs. A number of major initiatives emerged as a result of this discussion, and, by 1990, Sinclair had a comprehensive and exemplary institutionwide assessment program in place. Sinclair's president in 1990, David Ponitz, noted that "the goal for an institutionwide assessment effort was to improve student learning and the processes that contribute to effective and efficient learning." Without using the language of "the Learning College," Sinclair had taken a major step in that direction when it established as a priority the commitment to develop "processes that contribute to effective and efficient learning."

In 1991 the pace of the Sinclair journey picked up when the college embraced Total Quality Management. In developing a new vision statement, each department wrote mission statements that specified the departmental roles in contributing to learning as the central mission of the college. Because Sinclair had spent time in developing an effective system of assessment to measure student learning, it was natural for college staff to want to assess the effectiveness of their mission statements. Six core indicators of institutional effectiveness have since been adopted, and critical success factors have been identified for each core indicator. Sinclair is well on its way to creating a Learning College within the framework of a detailed and effective system of evaluation.

Fleming has had a teacher and course evaluation process in place for about four years. Each course and teacher is evaluated by students twice a year. The results are shared with individual faculty members and their leaders, and the aggregate results are shared with center teams in the college community, especially student associations interested in how the college is responding to student feedback. Fleming has also had a system of annual evaluation of administrators for many years. Two years ago the college introduced a multirater, multilevel, leader evaluation, which, in part, is intended to reinforce the new roles expected of leaders in a team-based organization.

In addition to evaluating personnel, Fleming has also developed a fairly comprehensive plan to evaluate programs and priorities. Annual priorities, indicators, and benchmarks are developed for each of the college's six basic goals. Performance indicators are used by the teams to identify areas which need improvement, as well as to identify the strategies that can make improvement possible. This information has been used in the restructuring process as a basis for determining which programs to terminate, modify, or place on notice.

The new team-based model has been evaluated annually to determine how staff members feel about their roles in the new structure. In addition, Fleming has identified nine characteristics of effective teams which the teams use as a basis for evaluating their progress. As the college changes its historical architecture to a team-based model, the leaders at Fleming want to know if the new architecture works better than the old.

Leaders at Fleming have raised the critical question: Do these changes in architecture actually enhance student learning? In the Applied Computing and Information Technology Center, the team has redesigned the curriculum to enhance student learning. Employers had been reporting that graduates from Fleming obtained the vocational technical skills required for employment, but they also indicated that graduates needed more skills

associated with problem solving, working in teams, self-direction, and interactions with others. As a result of this feedback from employers, the team in the Applied Computing and Information Technology Center developed a new curriculum model that includes a final semester focused on these team-based problem-solving skills that is untimed, student led, faculty mentored, and project based. The chief academic officer at Fleming, Terry Dance-Bennink, said, "We believe that this level of innovation was encouraged and supported by the team-based model which expects teams to be more accountable for the success of their area, and which concomitantly has empowered teams to make decisions about what innovation and strategies to pursue, develop, and implement."

At the Community College of Denver there has been a strong emphasis on evaluation for over a decade. Cited by the North Central Association of Schools and Colleges for its exemplary evaluation and accountability models, the college prepares annual reports on student success and prints student evaluations of the college and its faculty in its class schedules. President Byron McClenney reports, "This open process of sharing the outcome measures has created a climate in which every staff member at the Community College of Denver wants to perform well and is proud of the performance of the institution."

The 1993 report from the North Central Association of Schools and Colleges highlights many of the characteristics of the college that illustrate its commitment to Learning College practices. The report is worth citing in some detail as illustration:

> The planning initiatives of CCD that the team in 1987 cited as exemplary have been extended and elaborated to address the spirit of accountability and planning as well as its intention. The entire college community collaborated in shaping the plans for the future and in deciding on the allocation of funds for each of the initiatives. The accountability measures were equally discussed, determined, and activated by those most involved as well as those who provided an outside vision. Administrators, classified staff, advisory groups, and faculty participated fully. To the credit of the college, they endeavored mightily to secure full student input, but as is often the case in a community college, the students' input was often limited due to other commitments students constantly faced.

> However, the input from the college faculty was sought, analyzed, utilized, and the resulting measures for accountability and effectiveness were accepted by all involved. Then the results arrived. The college shared the results with everyone, discussed the ramifications of the surveys, of the tests, of the assessment scores, of the telephone interviews, and of the follow-ups to decide just what the results indicated. Then the college instituted new programs, new policies, new measures, and undertook the entire process once again. As a result, the accountability and effectiveness measurements are part of the college fabric, and the results are seen as starting points for next year's efforts.

As the number of students tested has increased, so has the sophistication with which the college has examined the data. With larger numbers participating, more complex analysis by student groups has been undertaken, and specific needs have been noted. Once a need has been determined, the college sought to build its student and academic support models to address the need and then evaluated the results of this service.

As a result, the process is, in theory and in practice, a complete cycle. Data are not accumulated to fill reports that remain on shelves. This college uses the data to improve retention, to ask itself just what it is looking for in teaching, how it can assist students who enter with lower academic skills, and what assistance teachers need to do a better job. Frankly the team was pleased to evaluate a college that undertook the planning/accountability/assessment activities in the spirit in which they were meant. The college decided to take a look at itself and to improve what it was doing and then to present this information to the community and ultimately to the state.

The Community College of Denver has developed a cycle of evaluation and assessment that is probably one of the best in a community college in North America. As a result of this attention to evaluating their policies, programs, and practices and of using the evaluations to improve, the college has assembled some powerful data on institutional effectiveness:

- Increase in number of graduates 1987 to 1997—82 percent

- Number of people of color as percent of total number of graduates, 1987—22 percent; 1997—44 percent

- 1997 graduates employed or engaged in further study—97 percent

- Employer satisfaction with skills of graduates—100 percent

- Transfer student GPA—3.0

Creating a Learning College is, in part, a journey into the unknown. Evaluating activities along the way is necessary to gauge progress and make corrections. Only by evaluating what is happening and what has been achieved will community colleges be able to develop models of the Learning College that others will want to emulate.

Commit to the Long Haul. In 1986, Miami-Dade Community College initiated its well-known Teaching and Learning Project that resulted in, among other things, the creation of 100 distinguished teaching chairs. Not anticipating that the project would become so large or take so long, former president Robert McCabe began referring to the initiative as "The Project That Ate Miami-Dade" (Jenrette and Napoli, 1994, p. 258).

Time is the enemy of all projects designed to initiate major change. Linda Thor, president of Rio Salado Community College in Phoenix, notes this fact in reference to her college's total quality initiative. "If there is one simple

process required to implement quality leadership in an organization…It is, simply put, TIME. It will not—it cannot—happen quickly…" (Thor, 1996, p. 114).

In their efforts to create a Learning College at Jackson Community College, Lee Howser and Carol Schwinn also note the importance of planning for the long haul. "Making cultural changes in an organization takes an extraordinary amount of time. Whatever the original time line, double it! …[F]undamental change requires conflict resolution and substitution of old behaviors. The process just takes time."

Jerry Young, president of Chaffey College in California, has indicated that he worked for five years as a new president at Chaffey to open up the system to the point faculty could say, "This isn't working." Just building an awareness of the problems will be a long process for some colleges, and this stage must precede any meaningful action toward becoming a Learning College.

At Fleming College, leaders have been concerned about the pace of change and recognize that a college and its culture can become "unglued" if the change is overwhelming and not managed. With a 20 percent reduction in its overall budget in 1995, the college was placed in crisis mode, but the leaders had already established an overall framework for change and had created a culture of trust in which they could operate to make this situation work for the benefit of the college. President Brian Desbiens developed a metaphor for the change process that would prove very effective. The first period of change lasted for about 18 months and was very intensive and traumatic. Desbiens referred to this period of the college's life as operating in white-water rapids. He communicated to faculty and staff that the period of white-water rapids would eventually flow into a bay in which they could slow down the pace, examine their progress, and set new goals for the future. The metaphor worked exceedingly well in describing the reality of the change efforts at Fleming, and the college designed many of its actions around the timeline provided by the metaphor. The really difficult, major changes were implemented in a specified period of time, and the college was able to announce with some confidence when the "worst" part of the change was over. Recognition of these peak periods of change has helped the college steer its course over the long haul on its journey to become a more learning-centered college.

Jerry Moskus at Lane Community College notes, "While it is certainly true that implementing the Learning College concept takes a long time, it is also true that we in community colleges must learn to take less time to implement new initiatives. Part of the appeal of the Learning College is that it promises to make community colleges more flexible and responsive." The community college does face a challenging dilemma trying to operate between the traditional culture of higher education, which takes its time in making changes, and the culture of the business community, where change is often immediate and dramatic.

Leaders planning to launch a Learning College should be realistic about the time it will take to create this new educational enterprise. Changing the historical architecture designed in earlier agricultural and industrial periods will require years of destruction and construction, not to mention the time it will take to change the behaviors of those who represent "1,000 years of tradition wrapped in 100 years of bureaucracy," a description of higher education, cited earlier, offered by Roger Moe, Majority Leader of the Minnesota State Senate.

Celebrate Changes and Accomplishments

In an effort as comprehensive and complex as creating a Learning College, it is a good idea to develop a culture of celebration that recognizes milestones of special achievement. Real transformation of the educational culture takes a very long time, and celebrating short-term wins can keep the momentum going. Most staff will not join the long journey unless they can see results along the way, preferably during the early stages.

Some early achievements might include a general awareness of problems and issues and a general consensus of the need for change—no mean achievement for many institutions. Institutionwide agreement on new values and mission statements is an achievement to be noted and appropriately celebrated. The creation of a new student assessment system or a new organizational structure, or the addition of new information technologies may be worth celebrating. Leaders should orchestrate celebrations and opportunities for recognition around each of these milestones and use each one to vault to the next.

It is important, however, not to celebrate a short-term achievement as final victory. The premature victory celebration stops momentum and provides opportunity for traditional forces to regain territory. Each celebration should be planned as an opportunity to leverage new plans. Kotter advises business leaders to capitalize on every achievement as a passage to the next:

> Instead of declaring victory, leaders of successful efforts use the credibility afforded by short-term wins to tackle even bigger problems. They go after systems and instructors that are not consistent with the transformation vision and have not been confronted before. They pay great attention to who is promoted, who is hired, and how people are developed. They include new re-engineering projects that are even bigger in scope than the initial ones. (1995, p. 66)

Several of the colleges cited here, as good examples of institutions becoming more learning centered, celebrate their achievements in very concrete and visible ways with ceremonies to recognize new facilities and new programs. The Learning Resource Center at Fleming College and its Learning Commons provided a very concrete example of how college teams were developing a new model based upon learning principles. As staff members at Fleming said, "During our restructuring period, we kept the vision, and the emerging reality, of the LRC front and center as a symbol of our future directions and to help boost morale through concretely investing in our future." Fleming also organized a successful celebration when it opened its new student center and used the occasion as an opportunity to recognize the effective leadership demonstrated by students.

The opening of Sinclair's Center for Interactive Learning in late 1998 was a great cause for state and national celebration. The Center for Interactive Learning is a major new structure on Sinclair's campus, but it is also the embodiment of a new spirit committed to translating policies, programs, and practices into more learning-centered activities.

Sinclair also celebrated its success in revising the traditional architecture with a fall 1998 conference for all employees, with a theme that included "Disappearance of Traditional Boundaries." Over 50 initiatives developed by various college teams were nominated by peers to be featured in a special fair honoring college heroes who had made changes that are eliminating traditional boundaries at Sinclair Community College.

Lane Community College has celebrated the achievements of milestones for years. At the beginning of its journey to become a more learning-centered college, Lane held a restructuring ceremony complete with refreshments and entertainment. Two vice presidents came dressed as the Blues Brothers, the Research and Planning Choir performed, and the president and others spoke about why change was needed and what changes were envisioned.

Once each month Lane staff gather at a scheduled celebration hour to recognize special employees with awards. Ice cream, cake, and entertainment are provided, and managers are encouraged to allow as many staff as possible to attend. The event always concludes with opening the microphone to anyone who wants to recognize a staff member or group for special service. The monthly celebrations have provided a pleasant and memorable way to recognize college milestones and individual staff achievements.

One of the reasons for developing systematic approaches to evaluation is to be able to document institutional achievements. When learning begins to saturate the culture, and when structures and programs have been designed to increase and to expand learning, then the evaluation and assessment systems will document the success as a sound basis for celebration.

Colleges that refocus their basic systems on learning by expanding learning options for students, engaging students as full partners in the learning process, designing educational structures to meet learner needs, defining the roles of learning facilitators based on the needs of learners, and measuring their success based on increased and expanded learning for students, will create an educational enterprise that can help students make passionate connections to learning. These accomplishments will be worth great celebration in the institution and throughout society. The Learning College that places learning first and provides educational experiences for learners any way, any place, and any time, has great potential for fulfilling this dream.

Epilogue

As community colleges embrace the Learning Revolution, they will begin to launch journeys to become more learning-centered institutions. In this brief monograph, key steps of that journey have been outlined and illustrated with examples from a small group of pioneering community colleges. The steps outlined here are relevant to most efforts to bring about institutional change, with one major difference. This journey will take a college and its leaders into unknown territory from which they are not likely to return. This is not a journey that tinkers around the edges of change, and that reaches its destination when a new program is tacked onto the crumbling architecture of the past. This journey calls for radical change: (1) to place learning first in every policy, program, and practice, and (2) to overhaul the traditional architecture of higher education.

In the early flat maps of the world, cartographers warned "Beyond this place be dragons and monsters." For those brave leaders willing to launch institutionwide initiatives to become more learning centered, there may be dragons and monsters ahead; there will surely be major battles. A key battle will take place in efforts to change the traditional architecture that most of us in education have learned to navigate successfully. Why would we want to change an educational system that has rewarded us and in which we prosper? George Washington is reported to have said:

> One of the difficulties in bringing about change in an organization is that you must do so through the persons who have been successful in that organization, no matter how faulty the system or organization is. To such persons, you see, it is the best of all possible organizations, because look who was selected by it and look who succeeded most within it. Yet, these are the very people through whom we must bring about improvements.

If we are to bring about the changes recommended in this monograph, we must struggle with our own demons that would keep us mired in the past. That struggle can lead us to move beyond the edge of chaos to discover a new world of education, a bright, new world in which the learning of our students guides our practice, sets our policies, and determines our programs. It is a journey well worth launching.

References

Abel, S. K., Cennamo, K. S., & Chung, M. (1996). A "Layers of Negotiation" Model for Designing Constructivist Learning Material. *Educational Technology*, (36(4), 39-48.

Armajani, B., Heydinger, R, & Hutchinson, P. A Model for the Reinvented Higher Education System: State Policy and College Learning. Denver, CO: Education Commission of the States. (ERIC Document Reproduction Service No. ED 370 492).

Armes, N. and McClenney, K. (1990). Building Communities: A Checklist for Evaluation and Discussion. *Leadership Abstracts*, 3 (3), 1-2.

Barr, R. B. (1994, February). A New Paradigm for the Community Colleges. *The News*.

Brown, T. (1994, April 18). An Interview with Margaret Wheatley. *Industry Week*, 243, 18.

Commission on the Future of Community Colleges. (1988). *Building Communities: A Vision for a New Century*. Washington, DC: American Association of Community Colleges.

Council of Presidents. (1995). Learning-centered Education in Ontario's Colleges. Manuscript in preparation.

Cross, K. P. (1981) Community Colleges on the Plateau. *Journal of Higher Education, 52,* (2), 113-123.

Dobyns, L. & Crawford-Mason, C. (1991) *Quality or Else: The Revolution in World Business*. Boston: Houghton Mifflin Company.

Dolence, M. (1998, July). Transformation of the Community College. Speech given at the Innovations 1998 conference, Dallas, TX.

Drucker, P. T. (1992). *Managing for the Future: The 1990s and Beyond*. New York: Penguin Books.

Gabelnick, F., MacGregor, J., Matthews, R. & Smith, B. (1990). *Learning Communities: Creating Connections Among Students, Faculty, and Disciplines*. New Directions for Teaching and Learning, 41.

Institute for Research on Higher Education (1993, February). Policy Perspectives. (Report volume 4, no. 4). Philadelphia, PA: University of Pennsylvania.

Institute for Research on Higher Education (1994, April). Policy Perspectives. (Report Volume 5, No. 3). Philadelphia, PA: University of Pennsylvania.

Jenrette, M. and Napoli, V. (1994). The Miami-Dade Teaching/Learning Project. In T. O'Banion (Ed.), *Teaching and Learning in the Community College*, pp. 245-259, Washington DC: American Association of Community Colleges.

Kotter, J. P. (1995) *Leading Change: Why Transformation Efforts Fail. Harvard Business Review*, 73 (2), 59-67.

Lave, J. and Wenger, E. (1990) *Situated Learning: Legitimate Peripheral Participation*. Cambridge, UK: Cambridge University Press.

Michigan State University. (1998, January). Becoming a Learning College: The Building Blocks of Change. A report of the Strategic Thinking Task Force, Lansing, MI.

O'Banion, T. (1989). *Innovation in the Community College*. New York: Macmillan Publishing Company.

O'Banion, T. (1995-1996). A Learning College for the 21st Century. *Community College Journal*, 66 (3), 18-23.

O'Banion, T. (1997a). *Creating More Learning-centered Community Colleges*. Mission Viejo, CA: League for Innovation in the Community College.

O'Banion, T. (1997b). *A Learning College for the 21st Century*. Phoenix, AZ: Oryx Press.

O'Banion, T. (1997c). The Learning Revolution: A Guide for Community College Trustees. [Special Issue]. *Trustee Quarterly*, 1.

O'Banion, T. (1997d). The Purpose, Process, and Product of the Learning Revolution in the Community College. *Leadership Abstracts*, 10 (7), 1-2.

O'Banion, T. and Associates. (1994). *Teaching and Learning in the Community College*. Washington, DC: American Association of Community Colleges.

Ohio Technology in Education Steering Committee. (1996, March). Technology in the Learning Communities of Tomorrow: Beginning the Transformation. Ohio Board of Regents.

Senge, P. (1990). The Fifth Discipline: The Art and Practice of the Learning Organization. New York: Doubleday/Currency.

Thor, L. (1996). Leadership: The Driver of the System. In D. Seymour (Ed.), *High Performing Colleges: Volume I: Theory and Concepts*. Maryville, MO: Prescott Publishing Company.

Wenrich, W. (1994). Masters of the Learning Environment. Unpublished manuscript, Dallas County Community College District, Dallas.

Wilson, I. (1996). The Practical Power of Vision. *On the Horizon*, 4 (2), 3-5.

Wingspread Group on Higher Education (1993). *An American Imperative: Higher Expectations for Higher Education*. Racine, WI: The Johnson Foundation, Inc.

Becoming a Learning College: Milestones on the Journey

— Kay M. McClenney

McClenney, Kay M. (2002). "Becoming a Learning College: Milestones on the Journey." Learning Abstracts 6(3).

Three years ago, the League for Innovation in the Community College identified through a competitive process 12 Vanguard Learning Colleges. These colleges, committed to collaborative work on developing in their institutions an ever more powerful and effective focus on student learning, are Cascadia Community College, The Community College of Baltimore County, Community College of Denver, Humber College, Kirkwood Community College, Lane Community College, Madison Area Technical College, Moraine Valley Community College, Palomar College, Richland College, Sinclair Community College, and Valencia Community College.

Throughout the three-year project, the League and the colleges addressed five strategic objectives that focused work in these areas: organizational culture, staff recruitment and development, technology, learning outcomes, and programs for underprepared students. Near the end of the grant-funded period, each of the colleges hosted a final evaluation visit by League staff and the project's external evaluator. The agenda included sessions with the president and the college's Vanguard project team, an exhibition of results related to the five major objectives, a special session on evidence of learning, and focus groups with faculty and with students.

The prevailing metaphor for the Learning College Project has been "the journey," emphasizing the conviction that becoming a learning college involves a long-term and continuing commitment—a journey, not a destination. From materials reviewed and from interviews, presentations, and focus groups conducted, the project evaluation yields five important milestones on that journey.

Milestone #1. The College as Its Own Critic

An initially surprising theme emerged as a significant milestone on the journey toward becoming a learning college. Many, many people pointed to a new level of honesty and rigor in institutional self-examination as an important result of the Learning College Project.

This is a big deal. Higher education generally is highly skilled at critiquing other social institutions and very slow to criticize itself. And community colleges in particular have been reluctant to engage in tough-minded self-critique, in part because the institutions have suffered too long from inappropriate evaluation (or even disdain) from the outside and inferiority complexes on the inside; in part because their resources and capacities for institutional research have been limited; in part because they have until recently gotten by with anecdotes as a substitute for evidence; and in part because they often are too busy doing the work to have time to assess how well they're doing it. So affirming and acting on the value of rigorous self-assessment is a major step forward.

Data emerged as an important force in the Vanguard colleges as project leaders, the evaluator, and people on the campuses continuously pressed the question, "How do you know...how good you are? ...how well you are doing? ...what students are learning?" As one team member reported, "We had to learn not to be fearful of displaying our warts, our deficiencies. And then data became a tool that promotes change. This more honest self-assessment actually produces more significant progress and accelerated improvement in our work."

> **As one team** member reported,
> "We had to learn not to be fearful of displaying our warts, our deficiencies."

The emphasis on the difference between looking good and being good was a common theme. As one college team member said, "We developed the courage to have substance supersede our need to market ourselves." A faculty member from the same college embellished the thought: "I look at it as polishing chrome versus fixing the engine. For too long, we've been really busy polishing the chrome."

Another aspect of integrity, frequently observed, was captured in this question: "Do our resource allocations match our rhetoric about learning? Are we facing up to the places where the match is not good?" One testimony went like this: "We're putting everything—effort, time, money—where we say the priority should be. That is integrity, and people recognize it."

Bringing the discussion together, an administrator attested to a new standard at her institution. People there understand, she said, that as they monitor college progress and performance, their charge is "to be brutally honest, but with hope."

Milestone #2. Assuming Collective Responsibility for Student Learning

By and large, the business of teaching and learning in American colleges and universities has traditionally been a dramatically isolated and individualistic enterprise. The faculty member designs his own course, develops her own tests, sets his own standards, gives her own grades, all the while declaring, "My classroom is my kingdom." Collective responsibility for student learning is not something most faculty members learned to value in graduate school.

But it is precisely that sense of collective responsibility, cutting across classrooms, disciplines, departments, and divisions, that is requisite to development of a learning college; and in the Vanguard Learning Colleges, it has emerged in powerful ways. As one team member proclaimed, "The big answer to 'what's new here?' is that people are taking more collective responsibility for student learning." Said another, "Our need and intent is to make the work much more systematic, more public, more transparent. It's not just our private work any more." And a dean of developmental education celebrated, as well: "Finally, we're taking the focus off of divisions and departments and putting the focus on students. I don't own the underprepared student. We all do."

Breaking Down Institutional Silos. It turns out, unsurprisingly, that "knowing people as people" still makes a difference. A remarkable number of interviewees commented on the value of the cross-functional mix of people on the Vanguard teams and in other work groups organized on campus to carry out related tasks and initiatives. One person said, "The mix of people required for the Vanguard team was unprecedented at our college. It promoted honest exchange and addressed disconnects across work areas and roles." A support staff member observed, "The cross-functional team has helped more than anything to break down silos."

> **There is a** continuing need for rigorous studies of educational practices to yield models and strategies that are proven effective.

People at Cascadia Community College cited the importance of "fuzzy edges"—avoiding silos of people, programs, and ideas. Examples include their work to integrate technology into the instructional program; create skills standards for arts and sciences faculty that are analogous to state-defined skills standards for professional and technical faculty; and incorporate shared responsibilities into job descriptions. At Moraine Valley, people have not limited their targets to "breaking down the invisible walls." They started with the visible ones, physically reorganizing some areas of the campus.

Several colleges are continuing the cross-functional team approach and expanding it more generally across the college in planning, implementation of strategic goals, and monitoring implementation and continuous improvement.

Extending Collaboration to the Learning Process. Happily, the emphasis on collective endeavor extends also to the classroom. Vanguard faculty pointed to the strengths of collaborative learning, citing research that shows results including higher achievement, increased retention, deeper understanding and critical thinking, and greater social competency. Stating what has become a core value at his college, a faculty member asserted, "We're not through here until everyone in this class has learned this material. Everybody's learning is everybody's responsibility."

Milestone #3. Benchmarking Best Practices

As the colleges have embraced rigorous self-assessment and assumed more collective responsibility for student learning, they have also enthusiastically affirmed the power of benchmarking as a tool for spurring initiative and improvement. Participants hailed the availability of best practice models among the Vanguard Learning Colleges as hugely beneficial; and many noted that intercollege observations and collaboration raised the bar for performance. As one faculty member said, "When Toyota built Lexus, they bought BMWs and Mercedes, stripped them down, and used the best of the best. We're building a Lexus here."

For benchmarking to be meaningful, the community college field must insist on a rigorous definition of the term "best practice." That phrase should refer to educational practices for which there exists compelling evidence that they work in promoting student learning and persistence. Too often, the term has been cheapened by describing programs and practices as "best" without such evidence, based instead on PR, politics, personal preference, good looks, hunch, or ideology. There is a continuing need for rigorous studies of educational practices to yield models and strategies that are proven effective.

Milestone #4. Building a Culture of Evidence

Having previously lived comfortably (like most community colleges) in a culture of anecdote, the Vanguard Learning Colleges have made significant progress on the task of building a culture of evidence within their institutions, and the impact has been substantial. "The most compelling thing," says a chemistry professor, "is that question I'm now asking myself: 'How do I know that I'm doing what I think I'm doing? How do I know that students are learning what I think I'm teaching?'" Another respondent asserted, "The concept of documenting evidence that an initiative or activity has improved student learning is perhaps the most dramatic change that has occurred at the college through the work on the Vanguard Project."

The Vanguard Learning Colleges provided numerous examples of important lessons learned from their data—and what they had done in response. At the Community College of Denver, for example, a one-credit-hour seminar required of all entrants to health sciences programs has produced marked improvements in the rate at which students successfully complete their first semester (i.e., from a 60-to-70 percent semester completion rate prior to implementation of the seminar to 90 percent or higher after implementation). Moraine Valley Community College's new College 101 orientation course also has produced significant positive results. On average, new full-time freshmen who successfully completed COL 101 ended the fall semester with a significantly higher percent of credit hours earned, significantly higher GPAs, and strikingly higher retention rates, compared with students who did not take the course and students who registered but did not successfully complete it. At Richland College, data about in-course retention prompted faculty to redesign a particular biology course that showed a retention rate of only 30 percent. Sinclair Community College faculty and staff, unhappy with dismal student success rates in distance learning (DL) courses, identified several retention strategies: reduce late registration, increase interaction with students enrolled in DL classes, expand information on the DL website, and develop a web-based student orientation course called Passport to Learning.

What Kind of Evidence? Most of these colleges describe themselves as much more data-oriented than a few years ago. They collect more data, make more data-driven decisions, and demonstrate more commitment to a philosophy of continuous improvement. The available data shed light in multiple directions. For example, the colleges have data to support enrollment management; data describing the college's students; data about institutional effectiveness, including information about student and employer satisfaction; and some useful and promising models for student cohort tracking, such as those at Humber College and Denver. Colleges also have some useful data pertaining to the quality of instructional programs. Often these are special studies (of student success in developmental education, for example), many of them initiated or requested by faculty members. Generally they are episodic rather than regular and isolated rather than generalized. Finally, as some people pointed out, we also have grades. Said one Vanguard team member, "We think our strongest evidence of learning is at the course level. We just don't know what exactly it is."

Still, there is much work ahead in creating credible cultures of evidence. One challenge is virtually a community college hallmark; that is, when push comes to shove, the people are generally more interested in doing the work than in examining its efficacy. This phenomenon was illustrated repeatedly. Asked about how well a particular intervention was working, an enthusiastic student services director stopped flat, looked quizzical for a moment, and then said, "We don't know. We're so busy trying to help students that we don't have time to find out whether we actually are."

There are many interesting activities going on, to be sure. For example, people talked about transcript analysis at Valencia—"getting acquainted with students one at a time;" flashlight survey tools and classroom assessment techniques at several colleges; and faculty projects (at The Community College of Baltimore County and Kirkwood, for example) on assessment of student learning.

Not surprisingly, every college has its examples of good assessment. In general, programs with specialized accreditation or external certification and licensure exams are far more likely to be systematic in assessment and in their uses of assessment results. Still, assessment has not found its way to systematic and collegewide implementation. As one faculty member commented, "We have a lot of trees, but still not a very good view of the forest."

What the Colleges Still Don't Know. Despite the amount of data community colleges collect and report, we still don't know much—especially not in any systematic way, in any way that is public and transparent—about what, how well, or at what level students are learning.

Milestone #5. Defining and Assessing Student Learning Outcomes

The work of defining and assessing student learning outcomes is some of the hardest and also some of the most important work in undergraduate education. Given the powerful focus of the Learning College Project on, well, learning, a sort of litmus test for the project evaluation was in pointed discussions about the extent to which each college has moved forward on that centrally important agenda. The 12 Vanguard Learning Colleges reported on their progress, both in writing and in a discussion session during the campus evaluation visit. With a few notable exceptions, the overall status of this work might be characterized as Random Acts of Progress.

Nonetheless, there is considerable activity in the arena of learning outcomes assessment, and there are some laudable initiatives. A couple of the colleges qualify as exemplars; others are at various points along the road. Some are being particularly thoughtful about how they proceed. But all seem to understand the inevitable necessity of following through with the work and are anticipating next steps.

Promising initiatives include the work at The Community College of Baltimore County, where Learning Outcomes Assessment Projects are the primary vehicles for measuring progress toward students' achievement of defined learning outcomes. These include individual course projects (30+ to date) and high-impact course projects (five to date and an additional five during the current year, impacting 13,700 students over two years). Through GeneRal Education Assessment Team (GREAT) projects, CCBC is gathering data to ascertain the degree to which students are achieving the college's general education program goals. With incremental expansion, the projects eventually will include every general education course. CCBC's general education assessment also involves use of the ETS Academic Profile, which provides national norms for community college students.

At Cascadia Community College, the entire college is organized around four major learning outcomes. Faculty members are working to articulate levels of learning within those outcomes and within courses, seeking a developmental approach. They are focusing also on key "literacies" such as cultural literacy,

Still, assessment has not found its way to systematic and collegewide implementation.

media literacy, and communication literacy as they attempt to "break out of the curriculum" to promote students' development of crosscutting competencies. Cascadia stands out as a place where the "how-do-we-know?" question is characteristically answered through examination of student work. Products include projects, video, web pages, and electronic portfolios—an innovation also pioneered at Palomar College.

Kirkwood Community College is promoting assessment through a faculty grant program conducted through an RFP process. In department and division meetings, significant time is devoted to faculty discussing their assessment projects, and participants report that the work engenders thoughtful conversation and applause from colleagues. Projects may be proposed at three levels: a single course section, multiple courses or multiple sections of a single course, or a cluster of courses or a program.

The challenge of the work on learning outcomes assessment in many community colleges is captured in an exclamation from a faculty member at one of the Vanguard Learning Colleges: "We're babies at this! I even have the startle reflex." Another explained, "It takes time for faculty to come to agreement about outcomes." It takes even longer, it might be observed, for some (or maybe most) higher education institutions to arrive at agreement that they even want to come to agreement about the important outcomes of student learning. Slowly, but slowly, that is changing.

The status of the work varies, of course, across the Vanguard colleges and across community colleges nationally; but the significant challenges appear to be these:

- to move from definition of learning outcomes to design and implementation of assessments;

- to improve the quality of assessments (e.g., moving from faculty checklists to authentic student performances);

- to upgrade reporting and information systems so that assessment results can be more readily reviewed and used in decision making;

- to examine the educational processes behind the outcomes and target areas of needed improvement;

- to link learning assessments to grades and degrees;

- to ensure that assessment itself promotes learning; and

- to bring disparate efforts to scale, so that assessment is systematic and collegewide.

The Journey Continues

At a relatively early milestone on the journey to become truly learning-centered institutions, the Vanguard Learning Colleges recognized that continuing progress will require a commitment to question everything—fundamental assumptions and longstanding traditions included. In 1993, the Wingspread Group on Higher Education articulated the scope of the challenge with these words: "Putting learning at the heart of the academic enterprise will mean overhauling the conceptual, procedural, curricular, and other architecture of postsecondary education on most campuses." While not everything will need changing, some of the changes that clearly are needed are also clearly difficult—what the Vanguard Learning Colleges came to call "the hard stuff." And as one college leader quite accurately observed, "The trouble is, the 'hard stuff' is really hard." Still, there is among these colleges, as at increasing numbers of others across the country, a determination to press on down the road. Their spirit is revealed in statements like these: "We've come very far and have a powerful obligation to move ahead. We cannot turn back." "However good we are today, it's not good enough, and it's not as good as we're going to be."

Bringing Teaching and Learning to the Board Room: A Professional Development Framework for Community College Governing Boards

— Christine Johnson McPhail

The community college has been stereotyped as the misunderstood sibling among higher education institutions. Critics of the community college have argued that it may have deviated too far from its original mission in its efforts to respond to the challenging and competing needs of its students. Despite this criticism, community colleges continue to identify new and different ways to address the learning needs of their students. In recent years, the Learning Revolution evolved on the scene to enhance student success by challenging community colleges to shift their focus (paradigm) from teaching to learning (Barr and Tagg, 1995; Obanion, 1997; McPhail and McPhail, 1999).

Almost two decades have passed since the advocates of the learning-centered college told us about the malaise caused by the teaching focus of the community college. Some viewed the shift from teaching to learning as a means to recapture the drive that founded the community college movement, reinforced its multiple missions, and now finds expression in the success of the learner. To others, the learning-centered college movement offered many community colleges a renewed context to reaffirm their commitment to educate large populations of students underserved by other segments of higher education and to make substantial changes in their delivery of programs and services. The velocity of the learning-centered community college was fueled by intense and sometimes conflicting scenarios: major strides in the use of technology, declining fiscal resources, increasingly diverse student populations, and impending retirements of faculty and leaders. My observation is that these scenarios increased the capacity for community colleges to move beyond simple open-door policies and practices to a new evolution of learning focusing on the success of students.

Educational research reveals that new knowledge grows out of the process of relating new ideas to what we already know and exploring the interrelationships among ideas. Strategically connecting the work of the governing board to the core missions of the college—teaching and learning—can bridge teaching and learning to the board room. For a number of years, I have paid special attention to the transformative works of the 12 Vanguard Learning Colleges that served as incubators and catalysts for the learning college concept by working to build on values that place learning first throughout their institutions. According to the League for Innovation in the Community College (2009), these colleges developed and strengthened policies, programs, and practices across their institutions with a focus on five project objectives: organizational culture, staff recruitment and development, technology, learning outcomes, and underprepared students.

After conducting a close review of the activities, programs, and services of the Vanguard Learning Colleges as well as other learning-centered colleges, I am convinced that most learning-centered colleges have not operationalized the involvement of trustees in their learning college initiatives. I'm not talking about a few isolated cases, but the majority of the learning colleges show little or no visible evidence that the role of trustees has been identified or that they were involved in the learning college initiatives at their institutions (McKay, 2004). In trying to understand community colleges' passage from teaching to learning institutions, we need to ask pointed questions: Where are the trustees in this transformation? How are they being trained to make decisions and adopt policies that support teaching and learning?

In community colleges, it is generally understood that a trustee is a party who is given legal responsibility to hold property in the best interest of or for the benefit of the institution. I'm of the opinion that the term trustee is not broad enough to describe the responsibilities the community college trustee must assume. To be certain, community college trustees hold an inescapable duty to keep and protect the funds and property of their respective institutions. Further, in recent years, community college trustees, similar to other education leaders, have been held increasingly accountable for the actions and decisions they make about the institutions they serve. While there might be some disagreement about the role of trustees in the governance of institutions, ultimately most educators concur that trustees should

> ...most learning-centered colleges have not operationalized the involvement of trustees in their learning college initiatives.

play a role in rethinking, redefining, and restructuring their institutions. Although I am impressed with the enormous role of community college trustees, I question some of the dysfunctional distinctions some educators place on the leadership role of trustees.

Many trustees, when they assume their roles, are relatively inexperienced in issues confronting community colleges, though they themselves may be college graduates. Consequently, many new trustees are initially uncertain about their duties and responsibilities. From the start of their job, community college trustees must attend new trustee orientation training and trustee meetings. An untrained or absent board member lends little help to the institution. Trustees should know the origin, purpose, and programs of community colleges. They must also understand how the quality of teaching and learning is connected to the overall historical mission of the community college.

But, where is the professional development training for trustees? To effectively meet the challenges of public community colleges, governing boards must function as a leadership team. Given the increased scrutiny community colleges find themselves facing, the issue of professional development for trustees is no longer optional. The professional development needs of trustees are a topic worthy of deeper consideration in today's community college. Yet, few community colleges have allocated funds to support professional development of trustees beyond attendance at one or two conferences, training for new board members, and or an occasional board retreat.

A compelling perspective for the professional development of trustees is a fine topic for exploration, but here it is accompanied by practical strategies for implementing a professional development program for trustees that allows them to examine their own beliefs, question traditional governance practices, and understand more deeply how the principles of the learning college have the potential to transform the way they govern community colleges. What does change really mean for trustees to develop a professional framework for board development, to shift from traditional governance to a learning-centered approach? The professional development framework provides a vehicle for trustees to focus on the most important issue facing community colleges—student learning. Much of the discussion about teaching and learning is focused on experiences within the organization or in the classroom: teaching and learning, curriculum, organizational culture, staff recruitment and development, underprepared students, technology, and student outcomes. To date, few voices have proclaimed the importance of understanding the role of the trustees within the context of teaching and learning. In addition, little has been done to involve community college trustees in the learning college movement (McKay, 2004). Using my personal observations and study of governing boards, I have identified six principles designed to develop a professional development framework for community college governing boards.

The learning-centered college is a strategic

mechanism that provides a focus for trustees to place learning at the forefront of their decisions.

A Professional Development Framework for Board Development

1. Create unity through mission and vision. Effective community college trustees need to understand the historical mission of the community college in order to understand the contemporary calls for change and reorganization. And nowhere is this need any greater than in trustees' involvement in the facilitation of teaching and learning initiatives in the community colleges. I believe that community college trustees are interested in educating themselves about the learning college. The paradigm shift suggested by Barr and Tagg (1995) and O'Banion (1997)

is connected to issues related to governance. Just as the learning college creates substantial change in the learner, it should also create change in the way the college is governed. The success of the learning college is intricately interwoven with the vision and leadership of its board of trustees.

Governing boards must have both the vision and capacity to forego their individual interests for the needs of the institution on behalf of the learner. I suggest that community college governing boards work with administrators to create a learning-centered governance vision statement. A learning-centered vision statement would serve as the driving force behind the decisions made by the board of trustees. The statement could be placed in prominent positions on the campus, on business cards, and so on.

Despite the growing interest in the learning college movement among community colleges, boards of trustees across the United States are not involved in significant numbers, and some are asking questions about its relevance to their roles. The learning college has been heralded as an answer to many of the problems plaguing contemporary community colleges—accountability, institutional effectiveness, student outcomes, and so on. Indeed, the learning college movement has created a new environment for many American community colleges. While many community colleges may have made significant changes in the delivery systems of their academic and support programs in an effort to become learning-centered environments, only minor shifts appear to be taking place within the governance structures of these institutions.

Carver and Mayhew (1994) suggested that boards must explicitly design their own products and processes. They observed that boards rarely enunciate and hold fast to the principles guiding their own operation, making them appear directionless and even at times capricious. The learning-centered college is a strategic mechanism that provides a focus for trustees to place learning at the forefront of their decisions. In other words, learning-centered governance provides a sense of unity for governance that could crystallize a uniform vision for community college trustees to govern community colleges.

A few years ago, I spoke with a community college president about professional development training for his governing board. He told me that there was no need for professional development for the board. He said, "I have one of the best boards in the community college system; they do what I tell them to do." I was impressed and intrigued by the response of the president and started to study the work of this perfect board. I learned that the board did, in fact, have several prestigious members, and I soon learned that it was one of the most dysfunctional boards I have ever observed! This situation taught me two things: some presidents do not know what a good board is, and some board members do not know how to be good board members. To effectively meet the needs of the contemporary community college, presidents and governing boards must function together as a leadership team. Further, board members must be knowledgeable about what it takes to promote and support teaching and learning in community colleges.

I believe that this notion might be by far one of the most challenging aspects of institutional governance for the next several decades. However, making the shift to focus governance on teaching and learning is not a one-size-fits-all proposition. Each trustee in each system will need to interpret the learning college principles in a form that is applicable to his or her own institution and the overall mission of the college. The beauty of the learning college movement is that the implementation of the principles continues to be defined as they unfold in situ. The learning college (O'Banion, 1997) is based on six key principles:

- The learning college creates substantive change in individual learners.

- The learning college engages learners as full partners in the learning process, with learners assuming primary responsibility for their own choices.

- The learning college creates and offers as many options for learning as possible.

- The learning college assists learners to form and participate in collaborative learning activities.

- The learning college defines the roles of learning facilitators by the needs of the learners.

- The learning college and its learning facilitators succeed only when improved and expanded learning can be documented for its learners.

The evolutionary process allows for a certain amount of creativity on the part of the institutions implementing the principles. Everyone agrees that the focus of the learning-centered college is positive educational outcomes for the learner. What is less obvious is the role of trustees in the learning college movement. The role assigned to trustees at any particular community college depends, of course, on the principles and protocols accepted for community college

---

Key Implementation Strategies for Learning-Centered Vision and Mission

- The board understands the historical mission and evolution of community colleges.

- The board works with administration to create a vision and mission statement that focuses on learning and student success.

- The board demonstrates a commitment to the mission of the college by making mission-driven decisions and related polices.

- The board understands the learning college principles and makes the connections to the governance process.

- The board designates a specific time on the board agenda for the president or designee to provide a brief description or explanation of the learning-centered agenda items. The description would explain how this action improves and expands learning at the college. The data and performance indicators will link the board action to the implementation of the learning-centered functions at the college.

---

trustees in general. A stable and democratic board of trustees is impossible without widespread acceptance of some common set of values and without a minimum degree of literacy and knowledge on the part of the trustees.

In a learning-centered college, the governing board, as educational leaders charged with the responsibility of the institution, will rely on the learning college principles to frame their policy adoptions and decisions will evolve from this foundation. Yes, we will still have the multiple mission focus of the community college, but viewed through a focused lens, success for all learners, and a uniform set of values.

2. Re-examine the structure and cultural context of the board. Trustees have different backgrounds (Smith, 2000), face issues differently, and need to learn different concepts. I'm not interested in making drastic changes in the fundamental way that community colleges are governed. I do want trustees to change structures, and maybe their minds, about what is important and enhance governance on behalf of the learner. Specifically, I would like to identify and close the gap between "current board practices" and "learning-centered practices." An examination of colleges that have made the shift from teaching to learning suggests that the commonalities of what trustees must do to be in step with the process and move toward what I call learning-centered governance are strikingly similar. In an article titled, "The Learning Revolution: A Guide for Community College Trustees," Terry O'Banion (1999) observed that community colleges that begin the journey to become more learner-centered will almost always reorganize their current structure to ensure more collaboration and teamwork among institutional members. O'Banion called for a deep and meaningful involvement of the whole organization. However, trustees have their own culture, structure, and politics, and many of these cultural attributes make it difficult for trustees to change the way they govern the nation's community colleges.

I have noticed that some trustees think in a way that limits their vision and impedes their ability to understand and respond to the transformation potential of the learning college. In the December 12, 2000, issue of *Community College Times* (p. 3), I posed a couple of key questions about trustee involvement in the learning college movement: "What transformation is taking place in the way trustees govern learning-centered institutions? Are trustees committed to and knowledgeable about the changes necessary to governing learning colleges in the 21st century?" In the same article, I suggested that governance of the learning-centered college cannot be business as usual and that change must take place in the manner in which decisions and policies are made. Some trustees took offense to a statement I made about their responsibilities: "Yet many trustees understand neither the concept of the learning college nor their responsibilities to ensure that policies are made to provide adequate resources for learning to take place." This lack of understanding creates a huge gap in the governance process and impedes the long term sustainability of the teaching and learning environment.

I readily acknowledge that what I am advocating about professional development for trustee involvement with

Table 1. Professional Development Framework for Governing Boards

Current Governance Practices	Learning-Centered Governance
Trustees have limited knowledge of the mission and teaching and learning process.	Trustees are trained to understand the mission of the college. This facilitates a range of options to institutionalize learning-centered governance. Establish a curriculum for on-going board education.
Personal interests sometimes interfere with effectiveness.	Trustees are trained to understand that they act and speak as a board and execute a uniform learning-centered vision for the college.
Trustees have been taught to value and hold on to past political processes.	The mission of the college drives decisions of the board. The focus is on teaching and learning outcomes and other measures of accountability.
Bylaws and numerous standing committees stagnate and restrict the involvement of board members.	Trustees appoint temporary committees to deal with special issues/problems as they arise. Establish a professional development committee for board training.
Trustees are often criticized for micromanagement so they sometimes become disengaged from the learning process.	Trustees must take risks, become more inquiring, and actively monitor how their decisions impact the operations of the college.
The education or board training process is sometimes limited to one or two training sessions per year.	Trustees must develop and execute ongoing curriculum for trustee training programs and become full partners in the learning process. A segment of each board meeting is devoted to board education. Develop a line item budget for professional development of board members.
Administration sometimes exclusively defines the vision for the board.	Trustees must participate with the administration in the design of the vision and evaluation processes. Teaching and learning is in the forefront.
CEO leadership teams create and monitor the organizational culture.	Trustees create climate and work with leadership team to keep it positive and focused on learning outcomes and other measures of accountability.

teaching and learning does not lend itself to an immediate change in the governance patterns of trustees, but with carefully crafted trustee orientation, training, and education (including seminars, conferences, retreats, presentations), trustees could learn a great deal about the learning college principles and teaching and learning in a short period of time.

There are opportunities for trustees to learn about the community college from several perspectives. The transition from teaching to learning calls for a transformation of the entire college culture; it affects all stakeholders at the institution. It is time to bring teaching and learning to the board room. Table 1 describes two specific ways of approaching governance in the learning-centered environment; the first approach, current practices—"the way we do things around here"—emphasizes the fact that trustees make decisions based on past procedures, rules, and rituals. The second, a learning-centered design, is an approach that is responsive to the changing and diverse needs of the learners. The first approach allows trustees to see their role in a vacuum, separate and apart from the college and the learner; the second approach provides trustees with information that helps them see how their role as trustees engages them as full partners in the learning process at the institution.

Inside the learning-centered college, trustees are encouraged to evaluate the current situation and search for ways to make the transition from traditional governance practices to ongoing professional development. Just as some instructors in learning-centered colleges reached the decision to end old ways of teaching, trustees can work together to define new ways of governing. In the learning

college, trustees will be willing to change the rules and the rituals so they more directly relate to the learner and make policies that support substantial change in the learner. With this type of decision making, trustees evolve to become full partners in the learning process.

3. Imbed Accountability into Governance Practices. A community college trustee is much more than a person entrusted with property or the fiscal resources of the college. Community college trustees have responsibility for building an institution that, with increasing accountability, can serve contemporary students and the students of tomorrow. It is precisely this key function that makes the role of the community college trustee so vital to sustaining and facilitating the continued evolution of teaching and learning in community colleges. In general, knowledge about certain problems has not always led to right action. For example, the commonly accepted dichotomy in educational leadership—administration versus governance—takes governance for granted. Community college educators talk so much about the importance of administration in community colleges that the role governance plays in the leadership equation is too often overlooked. A deeper understanding of the role of trustees requires more attention to the education and development of the trustee.

All trustee organizations have goals, boundaries, and levels of authority, communications systems, coordinating mechanisms, and distinctive procedures (Bolman and Deal, 1991). The traditional paradigm of governance has, at best, resulted in compliance with rules, regulations, and policies. In many cases, it has produced mediocre to competent governance. It often leads to boards with narrow thinking, board dependency on the CEO, and board focus on processes and procedures rather than outcomes and results. On the other hand, learning-centered governance requires the board to transcend the boundaries of the traditional governance model. In the learning-centered college, the board measures and communicates how well the vision and mission of the college is being accomplished by connecting it to student outcomes.

Learning-centered trustees look for ways to integrate learning-centered principles into all aspects of the governance process. They conduct learning-centered board meetings, and their connections with the college become opportunities to learn more about the learning college's impact on the learner. A focus on learning-centered governance has two major benefits:

1. Trustees are liberated from roles that no longer serve any meaningful function and that may have outlived their purpose.

2. The outcomes of the learning college are clear and direct—it places learning first. No other education reform initiative has offered governing boards such a strong vehicle for unity.

The notion that the learning college movement will reform governance in community colleges may be far-fetched for some, but I see it as a strategic approach to integrating and applying the learning college principles into the art of policy making activities of the college. It enables the board to provide trusteeship at a much deeper level than is presently realized under the current structure of institutional governance. If indeed the learning college places learning first and provides educational experiences for learners, anyplace, anyway, and anytime (O'Banion, 1997), boards of trustees must redefine their roles and accept responsibility for changing policies and practices that are consistent with the principles undergirding the learning college.

In the learning college, trustees must understand that the colleges can no longer be tied down to outdated practices and procedures. In order to place learning first, trustees will need to make expedient decisions that support new programs and delivery systems. When the board makes it clear that learning is the foundation for its policy making, stakeholders will see that the learning revolution is taking place at the college. A professional development or ongoing education program will ensure that board members know what they are accountable for, whom the board is accountable to, and more significantly, the board member's role in being accountable.

4. Empower trustees to serve as advocates for the college.
Leaders of the learning college movement speak with tremendous pride about the transformative power of the learning college in many areas of the institution. Some have suggested that the integration of the learning college principles does, in fact, change the culture of the institution. How can you change the culture of the institution when key stakeholders such as trustees are not actively engaged in the change process? How can you establish and sustain the idea of professional development for trustees when so few trustees appear to be involved in board education and development on a routine and consistent basis? I believe that with appropriate information, trustees can become

strong supporters of the learning-centered college. Armed with accurate information, they will be able to see that professional development for the board is also at the core of the shift from teaching to learning and a transformation that can fundamentally change community college education.

Without board commitment, the gains will not be sustained over time. For example, in 2006, Board Chair Lenore Croudy and President M. Richard Shaink from Mott Community College determined that they wanted the college to embrace a more learning-centered focus. All members of the board became engaged in the learning-centered-college conversation. As a part of the board education process, each board member was asked to read a specific chapter in McPhail's (2005) *Establishing & Sustaining Learning-Centered Community Colleges* book. A designated time was set aside at board meetings for board members to discuss the book. Mott's board also took the conversation outside of the board room and launched collegewide learning-centered conversations (facilitated by Christine McPhail) with faculty, community agencies, and representatives of the K-12 system. The information that was collected from the conversations helped to advance the integration of the learning college principles into the culture of the college. Further, learning-centered principles were integrated into the college's strategic planning and accreditation processes. Finally, Mott's team—president, board chair, and faculty members—made presentations about their learning-centered work at conferences such as those sponsored by the Association for Community College Trustees and the Higher Learning Commission.

We learned from our experiences at Mott Community College that transitioning from the old way of governing to a learning-centered focus of governance can be accomplished when the leadership role of the board is respected and supported by the administration. The learning-centered college affects every aspect of the college, including governance; the so-called "stable understanding about how things work around here" is being challenged and reformed. The transition at Mott Community College was possible due to the commitment of the board and the president. The board chair took on a leadership

---

Key Implementation Strategies for Accountability

- The board makes decisions and adopts policies that support teaching and learning.

- The board provides guidance and direction for accomplishing the mission of the college.

- The board ensures that the college's planning and decision-making processes are informed by data.

- The board recognizes the respective roles of internal and external constituencies.

- The board adopts goals and policies that promote improved student learning.

- The board establishes a professional development plan for board members. A budget allocation is assigned to fund the trustee professional development plan.

role that was supported by the college president, and there was no evidence of role conflict because the chair and the president were members of the same team.

In order for trustees to govern in a manner consistent with the forces converging on the board room, they must change or risk being ineffective. Just as the students and structures of the colleges are changing, the ways trustees govern must change. The culture of governance is changing and the definition of effective governance is changing. Learning-centered governance presents a logical framework for trustees to change the way they govern community colleges.

Implementation Strategies for Promoting Advocacy

- The board understands, supports, and promotes the mission and vision of the college.

- Board members are actively engaged in the community and articulate the mission and vision of the college.

- The governing board establishes communication channels with internal and external stakeholders.

- The board establishes and maintains partnerships with business, legislators, and community organizations to advance the mission of the college.

- The governing board routinely and consistently engages in professional development.

---

5. Conduct a learning style assessment: How do board members want to learn? Since, the board's major responsibility is to assist, guide, and evaluate the progress of the institution, it is critical for trustees to know the college—its purpose, its constituencies, its programs, and its physical and financial conditions (Chait, Holland, & Taylor, 1993). Many difficulties are avoided when this takes place. But, how do trustees acquire information to govern the college? Chait, Holland, and Taylor (1993) suggested that governance information has four essential properties:

1. **Strategic.** The data and performance indicators provided to the board are directly related to issues of corporate strategy.

2. **Normative.** Performance data are displayed for the board against norms, targets, and anticipated results so that trustees can readily compare actual performance to historical trends and "industry" standards, and to prompt board action.

3. **Selective.** Trustees routinely receive only that information necessary to exercise proper oversight, to monitor institutional and management performance, and to prompt board action.

4. **Graphic.** Whenever possible, data are displayed in graphic formats that communicate directly and succinctly.

Just as students learn differently, there is no single best way to access and acquire the skills necessary to govern community colleges. Thus, some boards may prefer to acquire knowledge about teaching and learning through strategic, normative, selective, or graphic modes. Community college leaders in charge of board training are encouraged to assess board members' preferred ways of learning. This assessment will provide information to develop meaningful professional development for board members. It is time for community colleges to take board training and professional development to a serious level.

At a recent board retreat, I listened to a board chair describe how unhappy she was with the big box of information that was delivered to her home by courier before each board meeting. She said, "I dread to come home to that big box of documents. Why can't I have a simple summary of a couple of pages? And, the week-end memo needs to be called a week-end magazine. I wish my president understood how be brief and to the point. What happened to technology?" At the same meeting, I listened with interest as the president from this board member's college told other presidents about his wonderful week-end memo. He described how hard he worked on that memo and how impressed he was with how it looked. He did not know that his board did not like the week-end memo and the board chair definitely did not like the pre-board meeting delivery of binders of material. If this president had conducted a learning-assessment of board members, he would have known how board members preferred to acquire information. The information must be presented in a way that it is likely to be welcomed. A professional development program for trustees includes delivery mode, instructional style, and an assessment of ways trustees prefer to receive information.

6. Evaluate Board Performance. Finally, it is time to turn our attention to the effects and outcomes of board performance and professional development for trustees. I recommend summative types of evaluations because they address outcomes. In other words, look at questions such as:

- To what extent did policies and decisions do what was intended?

- What happened as a result of the decisions?

- Did the action improve and expand learning, and how do we know?

- How will board decisions be communicated to all stakeholders?

- Did professional development and board education enhance board performance?

For trustees, this evaluation means discovering if major decisions and policies actually facilitated and fostered meaningful learning options for all students. I believe this is the ultimate test of the effectiveness of governance as leadership. When all is said and done, it will more than likely be concluded that there is no standardized way to

---
Implementation Strategies for Board Learning and Ongoing Education Program

- Develop learning-centered policies. Trustees could empower the president and the leadership team to provide a written learning-centered preface to each major policy issue related to learning-centered action items. The preface would explain why this issue now comes to the board and how it improves and expands learning at the college.

- Add board education to the board meeting agenda. The board's commitment to teaching and learning could be reinforced in a number of ways. The agenda and work plans could be prominently displayed in graphic formats at each meeting and in the board room.

- The board's website could display information about its learning-centered governance and decisions. This would serve as an ongoing reminder of the board's commitment to teaching and learning. Important information could be archived for the board to access instead of burdensome books and binders of information.

- Integrate learning-centered governance practices into local and national learning college initiatives. Trustees can conduct focus groups and presentations as ways to promote and elevate trustee involvement in the learning college movement. Trustees and constituent groups can engage in regular conversations about the significance of board involvement in the teaching and learning taking place at the college.

- Provide laptops and necessary technology for board members to access information on a consistent basis.

- Develop and implement a communication plan for the business of the board. Communicate results widely and whenever possible. Share data about board decisions in graphic formats that communicate board actions directly and succinctly. Share board decisions with all stakeholders and encourage community engagement on a routine and consistent basis.

- Conduct strategic focus groups with board members when appropriate.
---

assess effectiveness of governance. Thus, strategies to assess that effectiveness may be as diverse as the community colleges and the communities served. The decisions and policies of the governing board are the propelling forces to institutionalize learning college principles.

Learning-centered governance requires trustees to see the learning college as a way to strengthen the mission of the community college, a system that creates a kaleidoscope of learning options for a diverse population of learners. A key purpose for bringing teaching and learning information to the board room is to create a common ground for stimulating, improving, and expanding learning options for the community college learner. The concept of learning-centered governance should affirm what is centrally important to community colleges—the success of the learner. It also strengthens the overall governance process.

In many contexts, the transition to providing professional development and ongoing education for the board may be imperceptible, simply a move from traditional rituals, rules, and roles to learning-centered decision making and policy adoption. The challenge here is that the results of trustees' governance activities are often confined to the board room. While a board may take actions that influence learning outcomes for students, these results are rarely articulated to show the larger college community how trustees view the governance and decision relationship to outcomes for the learner.

Governing boards embarking on a more focused board development journey will face a transitioning paradox: how to maintain traditional fiduciary accountability functions without stifling the potential and benefits of the new focus on learning and advocacy. I believe that it is a struggle to change to the new and different and a struggle to explain why the change must occur. Thus, the good and bad news for community colleges is the same—change. However, the president and campus administrators are not excluded from the professional development for trustees; instead, they need to understand and support trustee professional development. There is an interconnection between teaching and learning and governance decisions that cannot be overlooked.

Developing a professional development framework for trustees to bring teaching and learning to the board room is an important component of the learning-centered college. I believe that this is an educational reform that may fundamentally change the way community colleges function. However, it is clear that while including teaching and learning on the governance agenda offers a uniform sense of direction for governing boards, governing board members will need to demonstrate their capacity and versatility to implement this concept in ways that enhance learning that is unique to their environments. Indeed, the important players in the articulation of professional development for trustees are the trustees themselves.

References

Association of Governing Boards of Universities and Colleges (1996). *Renewing the Academic Presidency: Stronger Leadership for Tougher Times*. Washington, DC: Commission on the Academic Presidency.

Barr, R. & Tagg, J. (1995, November/December). From Teaching to Learning: A New Paradigm for Undergraduate Education. *Change 27*, 13-25.

Bolman, L.G, & Deal, T.E. (1991). *Reframing Organizations: Artistry, Choice, and Leadership*. San Francisco: Jossey-Bass.

Carver, J. & Mayhew, M. (1994). *A New Vision of Board Leadership: Governing the Community College*. Washington, DC: Association of Community College Trustees.

Chait, R., Holland, T., & Taylor, B. (1991). *The Effective Board of Trustees*. New York: MacMillan.

Cohen, A. & Brawer, F.B. (1999). *Managing Community Colleges: A Handbook for Effective Practice*. San Francisco: Jossey Bass.

Cooper, T. L. (1998). *The Responsible Administrator: An Approach to Ethics for the Administrative Role*. San Francisco: Jossey-Bass.

League for Innovation in the Community College. (2009). Website, www.league.org

Moore, M. H. (1995). *Creating Public Value: Strategic Management in Government*. Cambridge, Massachusetts: Harvard University Press.

McKay, S. L. (2004). *Chief Executive Officers' and Board of Trustees' Perceptions and Preferences of Their Levels of Involvement in Institutional Governance Activities*. Unpublished doctoral Dissertation, Morgan State University.

McPhail, C. J. (Ed.). (2005). Learning-centered Governance in Community Colleges. In C. J. McPhail (Ed.), *Establishing & Sustaining Learning-centered Community Colleges*, pp.139-153. Washington, DC: Community College Press.College Press.

McPhail, C. J. (2000, December 12). Reframing Governance: At a True Learning College, Trustees Have a Lot to Learn, Too. *Community College Times*, pp 3, 6.

McPhail, I.P., & McPhail, C.J. (1999). Transforming Classroom Practice for African-American Learners: Implication for the Learning Paradigm. *Removing Vestiges*, 25-35. Washington, DC: Community College Press.

O'Banion, T. (1997). *A Learning College for the 21st Century*. Phoenix: Oryx Press.

Roueche, J.E., Taber, L.S., & Roueche, S.D. (1995). *The Company We Keep: Collaboration in the American Community College*. Washington, DC: Community College Press.

Smith, C. (2000). *Trustees in Community Colleges: A Guide to Effective Governance*. Washington, DC: Association of Community College Trustees.

Vaughn, G.B. & Weisman, I.M. *Community College Trustees: Leading on Behalf of Their Communitie*s. Phoenix: Oryx Press.

The Community College as a Learning-Centered Organization

— Cynthia D. Wilson

Wilson, Cynthia D. (2002). "The Community College as a Learning-Centered Organization." In N. Thomas, Ed., *Perspectives on the Community College: A Journey of Discovery*. A joint publication of Macomb Community College Institute for Future Studies and League for Innovation in the Community College. Phoenix: League for Innovation in the Community College.

Responding to pressures for improved accountability in undergraduate education during the 1990s, a handful of community college scholars and practitioners started a conversation that examined the focus of two-year institutions. Barr and Tagg (1995) began the discussion by suggesting that the longstanding designation of community colleges as teaching institutions be replaced by an organizational focus on learning. Reaction ranged from hasty defense—"We've always been focused on learning!"—to thoughtful examination of institutional policies and practices. In many cases, colleges that took an honest look at themselves found that, although their ultimate purpose was education, their policies and practices were not always best designed to promote learning.

Continuing the learning conversation, O'Banion (1995-96) presented the learning college as an institution that "places learning first and provides learning opportunities anyway, anyplace, anytime" (p. 22). He offered six principles on which such a college would be based, including the creation of "substantive change in individual learners" by providing multiple options for learning, enabling students to take responsibility for their own learning choices, and using learner needs to determine personnel roles (O'Banion, 1997, p. 47). Evidence of substantive change in learners would be gathered through authentic assessment of individual student learning and documented in clear statements of student achievement and samples of student work; this evidence would indicate the success of the learning-centered institution (O'Banion, 1997).

Concurrent with, and in some cases as a result of, this learning conversation, community colleges across the country initiated or enhanced "anyway, anyplace, anytime" programs such as weekend college, off-campus courses, online offerings, and learning communities. However, providing multiple options for learning is only part—and arguably the easier part—of the learning college concept. The fundamental element is "placing learning first," the focus on learning that extends throughout the organization. Community colleges that have embarked on the journey to become more learning centered are finding that placing learning first presents challenges of organizational transformation that extend far beyond variety in course scheduling. Indeed, these challenges impact every aspect of the college (McClenney, 2001).

Why Bother?

Despite the difficulties of making learning central to the college, the need for collegewide concentration on learning is real. The forces that prompted community college leaders to develop and promote the ideas of the learning-centered college are still demanding that colleges be accountable for individual student learning, and few community colleges are able to provide adequate evidence that learning has taken place (Wilson et al., 2000). Funding agents, accrediting bodies, employers, and constituents want to ensure that the institutions they endorse are producing graduates who are capable not only of living and working in today's environment but also of adapting to meet the needs of tomorrow's world. The learning-centered education movement provides an answer for colleges seeking ways to meet requirements levied by internal and external forces: the systematic collection of evidence that provides an increased capacity for the college, and for individual students within the college, to demonstrate that specifically defined learning has occurred.

Developing a Culture of Learning

Chickering and Gamson (1987) list "encouraging active learning" as one of the seven principles for good practice in undergraduate education, holding that students engaged in active learning "talk about what they are learning, write about it, relate it to past experiences….apply it to their daily lives….[and] make what they learn part of themselves." The learning college moves this idea beyond student activity associated with coursework, embedding learning at the very heart of the organization. In the learning-centered organization, all members of the college talk and write about learning as well as relate and apply it to their work.

Support. To ensure that learning is the primary focus throughout the college, support for learning-centered education occurs at all levels. Fundamental support is achieved by building learning college principles into strategic plans and developing budgets that sustain the implementation of those plans across the college. Since many community college educators have acquired expertise in an academic discipline, vocational art, or administrative skill but have received little pedagogical training, professional development is a primary element in the strategic plan and the budget. And since all college employees are engaged in efforts to improve and expand learning, all employees are involved in professional development programs that help them define and enact their roles as learning facilitators.

Outcome-Based Learning. To document substantive change, faculty and staff first develop clear statements of learning outcomes, the knowledge, skills, and abilities a successful student will acquire in a course or program. Once outcomes are clearly stated, learning environments and experiences are designed to help students acquire the necessary knowledge, skills, and abilities to demonstrate achievement of those outcomes (Baker, 2001).

Learning outcomes are developed for various levels: college, program, course, and student. Members of the college identify a set of overarching learning outcomes that are grounded in institutional values and embedded in program, course, and individual student learning outcomes. At the course level, faculty and staff define specific learning outcomes and develop learning experiences designed to ensure that all students who take a particular course are correctly placed, are appropriately challenged, are able to achieve the outcomes at acceptable levels, and are prepared for future learning experiences. (Baker, 2001; Stiehl & Lewchuck, 2000) Assisted by an advisor, the individual student identifies a set of personal learning outcomes and a plan for achieving those outcomes. The student and advisor monitor student outcomes and plans, revise them as needed, and document progress.

The learning college moves this idea beyond student activity associated with coursework, embedding learning at the very heart of the organization. In the learning-centered college, faculty, staff, and students become leaders of learning, shaping and shifting the leadership responsibility as appropriate. The learning environment serves as a rich research venue for students and faculty as they continuously assess and revise learning experiences to ensure their effectiveness.

As an individual student achieves outcomes, the level of achievement is documented in clear statements of individual student accomplishments. Annotated transcripts include lists of acquired knowledge, skills, and abilities as well as portfolio-style demonstrations of student capabilities. Grades are not necessarily obsolete; however, with the outcomes necessary to achieve a grade or level clearly stated, they become more meaningful than a broadly defined A, B, or C.

Leadership. In the learning-centered college, faculty, staff, and students become leaders of learning, shaping and shifting the leadership responsibility as appropriate. Faculty and staff lead the development of learning environments and experiences, acting as resource coordinators, monitors, and supporters of learners and learning, and assessors and evaluators of student learning. The learning environments extend beyond physical and virtual classrooms to on-site and online resources such as libraries, tutoring centers, and mentor programs. Learning experiences include a variety of activities ranging from traditional lectures and exams to collaborative and service learning. (Wilson, 1999)

Within well-defined parameters, students also have leadership opportunities as they take responsibility for and control of their own learning. In these environments, the student growth experience includes learning to define personal learning goals and becoming true partners in developing and implementing learning activities. This does not absolve faculty and staff of their responsibilities in supporting individual student learning; rather, it expands the scope of responsibility for learning by engaging the learner more fully in the learning process.

Research. Authentically assessed and appropriately documented individual student learning provides data for accountability requirements, but learning college research is not limited to the institutional research office. The learning environment serves as a rich research venue for students and faculty as they continuously assess and revise learning experiences to ensure their effectiveness. Similarly, faculty and staff routinely monitor and evaluate courses and support services across terms, using their findings to improve courses and programs.

Making the Journey

Those involved in the learning college movement often refer to the process of becoming more learning centered as a journey. Making this journey is one way community colleges are responding to pressures to ensure student learning and to provide meaningful evidence of that learning. Colleges that embark on the journey can certainly learn from those that have gone before; however, the distinctive features of each college's culture often require that individual institutions create their own paths. Members of a college community can begin by engaging in conversations on learning (O'Banion & Milliron, 2001) and by taking an honest, thorough, and perhaps difficult look at the work they are doing and the ways they are doing it. Through these discussions, they can determine where they are on the learning journey and begin to map a course that will take them where they want to be.

At Your Institution: Discussion Points

- Identify elements of your college culture that reflect a focus on learning and those elements that do not.

- Identify strategies that your college's planning and budgeting processes can employ to support a culture of learning within current funding parameters.

- In what specific and realistic ways can your college be structured to promote and ensure learning at all levels of the organization?

- How is learning defined in your institution, and in what ways is the documentation of student learning a thorough and meaningful representation of individual student learning?

References and Resources

Baker, R. L. (2001, Spring). Educational Cartography: Mapping the Learning Outcomes Frontier. *Michigan Community College Journal 7*(1), 79-87.

Barr, R. B., & Tagg, J. (1995). From Teaching to Learning: A New Paradigm for Undergraduate Education. *Change, 27*(6),13-25.

Chickering, A. W., & Gamson, Z. F. (1987). Seven Principles for Good Practice in Undergraduate Education. *AAHE Bulletin 39*(7), 3-7.

McClenney, K. (2001). Learning From the Learning Colleges: Observations Along the Journey. *Learning Abstracts 4*(2).

O'Banion, T. (1997). *A Learning College for the 21st Century.* Phoenix: Oryx Press.

O'Banion, T. (1995-96, December/January). A Learning College for the 21st Century. *Community College Journal.*

O'Banion, T., & Milliron, M. D. (2001). College Conversations on Learning. *Learning Abstracts 14*(4).

Stiehl, R., & Lewchuck, L. (2000). *The Outcomes Primer.* Corvallis, OR: The Learning Organization.

Wilson, C. D. (1999). *Faculty in the Learning College: An Examination of Theorist and Practitioner Perceptions.* Dissertation: The University of Texas at Austin.

Wilson, C. D., Miles, C. L., Baker, R. L., & Schoenberger, R. L. (2000). *Learning Outcomes for the 21st Century: Report of a Community College Study.* Mission Viejo, CA: League for Innovation in the Community College.

Leadership for Learning

— Cynthia D. Wilson

Wilson, C. D. (2002). "Leadership for Learning." *Learning Abstracts* 5(7).

The community college is entering its second century in the sweep of a learning-centered movement that reaches beyond the classroom to encompass the entire institution. In the midst of this reform effort, administrators and faculty who joined the community college movement during its 1960s boom are fulfilling predictions of turnover waves at their institutions. This exodus of pioneers committed to the principles of open access and community service leads to challenges for today's community colleges. However, it can also be an opportunity to hire a new group of professional educators who are dedicated to learning and to responding adequately and enthusiastically to the learning-centered movement. Indeed, as learning college theory is informed and honed by emerging practice, the need for leadership for learning is becoming increasingly apparent.

An Integrated, Inclusive Approach to Leadership

Leadership for learning involves making decisions, defining values, setting goals, and determining strategies designed to facilitate the core work—learning—of the educational institution. In so doing, it moves beyond traditional notions of leadership as an administrative or management function. It is, instead, an integrated process that involves administrators, faculty, and other college employees in a shared effort to ensure that learning occurs and is documented in meaningful formats for the institution and the individual members of the institution. Both the institution and the people within it then use this evidence to assess performance and implement strategies for improving courses, policies, programs, and practices on individual as well as organizational levels.

Leadership for learning also includes a broad range of activities across the college: defining all functions by their particular contributions to learning; evaluating these functions based on the effectiveness of the contributions to learning; determining methods and strategies for assessing the effectiveness of the contributions; developing job descriptions based on expected contributions; hiring personnel who meet the criteria; and basing performance review, retention, promotion, and tenure on the assessed effectiveness of defined contributions to learning.

Leadership for learning involves leaders across the college taking a holistic, systems view of the organization. As Terry O'Banion advises, it means asking—and answering—two fundamental questions of every decision: (1) Does this decision improve and expand learning? (2) How do we know? Leadership for learning focuses the minds of education professionals on these questions, causing them to look thoroughly and consistently at the ways policies, programs, practices, and decisions impact learning.

Identifying Leaders for Learning

Leadership programs are often designed to train administrators to perform managerial tasks and to understand and work within the various organizational, cultural, and political environments of the institution; the more senior the position, the more focus is placed on taking a holistic view of the organization. And while administrators are traditionally trained to take a global perspective of the organization, faculty are trained to focus on their disciplines. The faculty make up a large, well-educated, and at times strongly independent segment of the college community, and they are routinely cited by administrators as among the greatest obstacles to change. Leadership for learning dismisses the *us versus them* dichotomy of faculty and administrators; it adopts instead what Cindy Miles calls "the power of *and*." It embraces the *us and them* of all employee groups, or the *power of we*, resting with (a) administrators and staff who ensure that physical, organizational, and fiscal structures are in place to support learning and (b) faculty who ensure that appropriate and effective learning environments and experiences are available for learners.

Leadership for learning recognizes that the work of the organization is so interconnected that it includes all members of the college. Indeed, at times traditional roles will shift. For example, a nonfaculty employee may become involved in activities traditionally performed solely by instructional staff: a food services team member assesses the achievement of workplace skills by a work-study student under his supervision. As traditional roles are jumbled and lines blurred, all members of the college have a place in the leadership for learning.

With leadership incorporating the "we" of the community college, supporting the organizational whole becomes the purview of all members of the institution. And, arguably, when an educational institution is rightly focused on learning, every member of the organization should be supporting it. As leadership teams become increasingly inclusive, all areas of the institution are engaged in ensuring that improved and expanded learning is occurring. To bring all members of the college together as leaders for learning—leaders across the college who take a holistic view of the organization, who share the vision, live the values, support the mission, and pursue the goals of the institution, and who lead the organization and its members toward improved and expanded learning—seems a practical approach to developing a successful learning institution.

As leaders for learning, all employees view the whole as well as their own specific parts, noting the connected, systemic ways in which the organization-as-organism functions, falters, survives, and thrives. In leadership for learning, all members of the college define and take on new roles as they share the obligation and responsibility for ensuring that the core work of the college is done.

Faculty. The faculty leadership for learning becomes an explicit expectation rather than a vague assumption. As leaders for learning, faculty consider their changing roles in the context of the entire organization and its fundamental purpose. These changing roles include a faculty focus on collaborating with colleagues across the college to identify learning outcomes, develop learning environments and experiences that engage students in achieving those outcomes, design assessment strategies for determining levels of student achievement of outcomes, and document student achievement of outcomes in meaningful ways that move beyond traditional grades and course credits.

Staff Members. Leadership for learning also includes employees who are not administrators or faculty. Among these employees, each group examines its role in light of the core work of the institution—learning—and determines from both organizational and individual perspectives the best ways to use that role to improve and expand learning. This could involve collaborating with students, faculty, administrators, community members, business and industry representatives, and others to locate and use all available resources to promote and ensure student learning.

Students. As leaders for learning, students take responsibility for their own learning. Assisted by faculty and staff, they develop learning goals as well as strategies for achieving those goals. They participate in developing learning environments and experiences that will facilitate achievement of their learning goals. Waukesha County Technical College (WI) has developed a Student Growth and Development Plan in which students, assisted by advisors, assess their progress toward achieving the college's Critical Life Skills and identify activities that will help strengthen areas in which additional work is needed. Students who complete Valencia Community College's (FL) LifeMap set education and career goals and develop plans for achieving those goals, beginning with the work they do at Valencia. In programs like these, students are exercising and experiencing leadership for learning.

Administrators. Leadership for learning does not absolve administrators from their leadership roles in fulfilling the college vision and mission; instead, it extends responsibility for achieving the vision and mission throughout the college. Presidents and executive cabinet members continue to be premier leaders, encouraging and empowering all members of the college to support improved and expanded learning not only in their specific departments or areas, but also across the institution. Using inclusive, integrated strategies, administrators ensure that the organization is supported by all its members.

The ideas of the Learning College are compelling, and an increasing number of colleges are embarking on the journey toward becoming more learning centered. Leadership for learning solicits the contributions of all members of the college on the journey and provides support to sustain them along the way.

References

Miles, C. L. (2002). Organizational Readiness: Middle Age and the Middle Way. In Thomas, N. (Ed.), *Perspectives on the Community College: A Journey of Discovery* (pp. 19-22). Phoenix: League for Innovation in the Community College.

O'Banion, T. (1997). *A Learning College for the 21st Century*. Phoenix: Oryx Press.

Institutionalizing the Commitment to Learning: Evolution, not Revolution

— Martha A. Smith and Andrew L. Meyer

Smith, Martha A. and Meyer, Andrew L. (2003 June). "Institutionalizing the Commitment to Learning: Evolution, not Revolution." *Learning Abstracts, 6*(6).

"It is not the strongest of the species that survive, nor the most intelligent, but the one most responsive to change."
Charles Darwin

Conducting an environmental scan of contemporary challenges faced by community colleges can be depressing. Declining state funding is just the latest in a series of clear indicators that a business-as-usual approach is not a viable or wise option in leading an educational institution into the brave and daunting new world of the 21st century. Adopting new strategies, predicting the trends and needs of the future, and organizing and staffing to maximize flexibility and effectiveness are necessary components of a successful organization in these difficult times. Yet above these characteristics, being an organization that can learn and adapt is essential.

Fortunately, through a strategic visioning process, Anne Arundel Community College (AACC) has developed its own approach to not just surviving, but thriving. The Learning College concept of putting learning first in all decisions was a movement long overdue in higher education. Becoming learning centered requires pervasive, strategic, and intentional intervention, design, and initiative. In these challenging times, developing the ability and the courage to question the status quo, to focus on core values, to have a clear and penetrating mission and vision that truly drive decision making, and to have an institutional value system that places learning first in all operations, decisions, and programs, provides a college with the essential tools and flexibility to function effectively.

Our college conducts strategic planning, as other colleges do. But we emphasize that it is really a strategic learning process as much as a strategic planning process. It is essential for us to know what is happening in our service area, our state, our nation, and the world. We need to know who our learners are and what types of learning experiences they need to be fulfilled as citizens and workers in our society. We try to be strategic planners, thinkers, and learners.

What We Have Learned

In conducting our environmental scanning in recent years, it became clear that in order to meet an increasing demand for lifelong learning opportunities not tied to traditional, credit-driven modalities, we needed to use every instructional weapon in our arsenal. We needed to value equally all instructional programs and services. With the creation of a level playing field for all instruction, the artificial and self-imposed barriers that had formerly created a caste system that valued credit over noncredit instruction and transfer over training functions would begin to erode, true internal collaboration would increase, and an organizational culture grounded in a true one-college model would emerge. To do this, we began to embrace a simple phrase, Zen-like in its simplicity but powerful in its impact: "*Learning is learning is learning.*"

Anne Arundel Community College is the largest single-campus community college in Maryland. It has seen exponential growth in recent years. During the period of FY97-FY02, when growth in state-funded credit and continuing education enrollments among the 16 Maryland community colleges averaged slightly less than 17 percent, enrollments at AACC grew over 24 percent. In FY02, the college served over 60,000 students. The increase in the percentage of enrollments between FY97 and FY05 is projected to be almost 30 percent.

In this period of unprecedented growth, the college was driven by its strategic plan. The plan identifies planning priorities driven by mission mandates. Planning priorities include (a) meeting community needs; (b) student success; (c) community outreach, impact, and presence; and (d) institutional integrity. The strategic plan seeks to amplify the institution's mission mandates: quality, access, affordability, responsiveness, and accountability.

As a college priority, *meeting community needs* is in many ways the major driver of the strategic plan. The complex and diverse needs of our community effectively caused the college to re-examine its priorities, ultimately placing equal importance on transfer programs, occupational programs, continuing education activities, and workforce development initiatives. The resulting growth in enrollments has led to discarding the old organizational paradigm, where units of the college (e.g., transfer, career, continuing education, developmental) operated in silos that were defined, predictable, and contained. The emerging model for the college is more dynamic, reflecting a variety of delivery modes, formats, and timeframes; entry and exit points; measurements of knowledge, skills, and abilities; and credentialing methodologies to meet community needs. Faced with creating internal systems to support the exponential growth in enrollments while dealing with the external pressures that all community colleges currently face, we chose to reinvent ourselves to meet new challenges and new opportunities.

Perhaps the most important step was creating the new and still emerging paradigm—a continuum of lifelong learning—as the framework for the learning college at AACC. This required blurring the lines between credit and noncredit instruction, not as the goal, but to foster the growing realization that the college was in the business of producing learning in students regardless of their age, educational plan, or mode of instruction. The key to this evolution was a series of organizational initiatives designed to accelerate the transformative process.

Organizational Realignments

In 1996, the college president realigned the organization to position the institution to be more responsive to internal and external forces. Back then, college senior administrators held traditional titles: Vice Presidents for Academic Affairs, Student Services, and Finance. The president created a new position of Vice President for

Continuing Education and Workforce Development in order to demonstrate the college's commitment to the business community and the concept of lifelong learning, while combining the Student Affairs and Academic Affairs positions to reinforce commitment to student success. Consequently, the functions of continuing education and workforce development were given parity with traditional academic units of the college. Over the next four years, this new division worked with the college's academic departments on new program development while sharing resources, both human and physical, to deliver quality instructional programs, thus strengthening the college's overall linkages to the business community while fostering a culture of internal cooperation and collaboration.

Driven by the strategic plan, and responding to the growing respect earned by new continuing education and workforce development initiatives, the president moved the organizational structure to the next iteration. In 2000, the college returned to three vice presidents, but their titles and responsibilities reflected an increased commitment to the central mission and vision: Vice President for Learning, Vice President for Learner Support Services, and Vice President for Learner Resources Management. The notion that learning was everyone's responsibility was further reinforced through the merger of two instructional vice presidents into one position responsible for the totality of the college's learning offerings. The Vice President for Learner Support Services' position consolidated student support services with instructional and administrative information technology responsibilities. The concept of Learning Resources Management emphasized that offices and services previously viewed as being peripheral to instruction now played a critical role in assuring that learning was fully supported and maximized at all levels of the college. These realignment initiatives sent a clear message to all stakeholders that the college was serious about learning and meeting the needs of all learners.

Having reorganized to emphasize the commitment to learning, the next step was to implement an accelerated approach to new initiatives, aimed at meeting community needs. Several specific approaches were developed.

Learning Response Team (LRT)

The president created the Learning Response Team to replace the traditional President's Cabinet as the senior leadership team. The LRT places focus on administrative and management structures and systems that enable the college to meet the new and emerging learning needs in a timely and effective manner. Furthermore, the new structures and systems had to ensure maximum continual improvement of all instructional programs, initiatives, and services.

With weekly meetings chaired by the president, the LRT is comprised of the vice presidents, all deans, and other key administrators. Appointing members beyond the traditional academic leadership set the tone that everyone is responsible for the success of our learners.

The LRT takes a systems approach to its work. The group routinely examines issues, problems, and opportunities that are brought forward by faculty and staff. Each topic is viewed within the context of the college's mission and strategic plan. If action needs to be taken, the scope of the project is carefully defined and a learning design team

is identified to develop an implementation plan. Underlying assumptions and limitations such as fiscal, physical, and human resources are identified.

Initiatives advanced by the LRT have included the establishment of the college's coordinating council for developmental education, integration of service learning into the curriculum, expansion of the honors program, and implementation of a prior learning assessment system. Additionally, the LRT reviewed and endorsed proposals for the creation of several now successful programs, including the Hospitality, Culinary Arts, and Tourism Institute; the Center for Teacher Preparation and Professional Development; and the Institute of Criminal Justice, Legal Studies, and Public Services.

Learning Design Team

When the LRT approves a new project, a Learning Design Team is generally formed to move the initiative forward. The members of the LRT identify who should be part of the Learning Design Team and the respective roles of its members. Faculty, administrators, professional staff, and individuals from the community may be asked to participate in the process. Members of a Learning Design Team are asked to develop a plan that will implement new structures and systems to support the initiative. Members of the team select an approach, develop detailed project requirements, create a timeline, and analyze budget implications.

One of the outcomes of the Learning Design Team has been close collaboration between credit and continuing education and workforce development units of the college. Colleagues across the institution have worked together to focus on delivering instructional programs in new educational arenas. In many cases, the groups have seen the need to create new entities, such as institutes or centers, in which both credit and continuing education learning opportunities are provided to meet the diverse needs of all populations served in the community.

For example, the plan to implement the Hospitality, Culinary Arts, and Tourism (HCAT) Institute included vision and mission statements, staffing and facility requirements, external partnerships, and an annual budget. The HCAT implementation plan took into account all of the learning opportunities related to the industry, ranging from associate degrees and certificates to avocational classes and international internships. The driving force behind the HCAT Institute is the realization that regardless of the way components of the program are delivered, there is one educational bottom line: learning is learning is learning.

New Ways of Doing Faculty Business

Because of increasing enrollments and new delivery methods, formats, and time frames, instructional staff were faced with increasing demands. The college examined how best to use its own workforce to meet these demands, and implemented several nontraditional approaches to provide learning opportunities.

Since 1998, AACC has been recruiting and hiring new faculty under a new *flexible job description*, which allows the teacher to meet contractual obligations in a variety of ways other than teaching the standard five three-credit courses per semester. Faculty with these contracts are encouraged to accept assignments to support business and industry contract training efforts, teach continuing education courses, serve as mentors to other faculty, and work in teams to develop outreach to the community. The college recently converted 10-month faculty positions to 12-month positions in order to ensure that a consistent level of teaching and instructional support takes place all year.

Instructional Specialists. The college also began to hire full-time instructional specialists to support a variety of delivery modes, formats, and time frames in certain disciplines. This enables the college to assign specialists to a variety of differing environments and locations. For example, instructional specialists in reading can be assigned to facilitate instruction to Adult Basic Education students in Anne Arundel County as well as developmental students enrolled at the college.

Trainers. In support of its business and industry training programs, AACC has created an instructional category of full-time trainers, hired to support individual training contracts with a local organization. Each trainer is required to work a 40-hour week that typically includes a combination of training and instructional design duties. The length of the trainer contract generally coincides with the duration of the training contract with the organization.

Helping Faculty Focus on Learning

Designs for Learning. Driven by the college's strategic plan and implemented in 1997, the Designs for Learning Project funds faculty, both individually and in teams, to design innovative instructional strategies and alternative pedagogies appropriate to the college's learners and its instructional programs. Preference for funding is given to teams because this approach gives a project a broader base of expertise, creates a synergy diffused across programs, and maximizes the possibilities for duplication among a range of discipline faculties. All proposals include a plan for learning assessment that projects a potential for increased learning and increased student success through application of specific technologies or alternative pedagogies.

Online Academy. Created in 1998, the Online Academy creates a collegewide structure for developing online courses that fosters creativity and focuses on instruction within the context of a team approach. Developed by faculty and staff, the academy helps teachers develop asynchronous learning opportunities through a six-step process from conceptualization of the course to its delivery. The Academy targets the development of credit courses that meet general education requirements or are part of a certificate or degree program identified for online delivery. The Academy also supports the development of noncredit courses and training modules. To date, over 75 credit courses have been developed through the Online Academy.

Learning College Orientation. Beginning in fall 2000, the college embarked on a deliberate and concerted effort to give all new instructional employees, both credit and noncredit faculty, the necessary support to produce increased learning in all encounters with students. New faculty members hired under the flexible faculty job description are given a supplemental development contract for a week in the summer before their first year's teaching contract begins. During that week, they go through an intensive orientation to our college and the concepts of the learning college. Additionally, as part of their first-semester

course load, they are assigned 45 hours of professional development activities founded on the learning college concept. Workshops, seminars, and round tables are presented throughout the first year of teaching to introduce this freshman class of faculty and instructional staff to Anne Arundel Community College's philosophy, mission, and learning goals.

In addition, all activities are designed to create a learning network in which the college's many development and support mechanisms are made user-friendly to the new faculty and instructional staff. The intent is to help faculty master areas such as classroom assessment, applied learning and research, use of competency-based strategies in instruction, and managing a classroom of multigenerational learners. By giving new faculty an intensive orientation to contemporary pedagogical practices and a shared understanding of the learning college concept, we view this program as a solid investment in our future and our organizational culture.

Advancing Consensus

During the past year, further steps were taken to accelerate the evolution. Our Strategic Planning Council participated in a retreat with a consultant who took them through an evaluative process where they benchmarked the college against the Krakauer Criteria for a Learning College. Almost 100 criteria were examined and evaluated, with responses ranging from "no evidence this item has been implemented" through "this item has been fully implemented across the entire college." This exercise was helpful in identifying, through a gap analysis, areas where the current strategic plan was not fully aligned with identified and prioritized criteria for a true learning college. Subsequently, the entire college community was asked to respond to an extensive survey in which strategic priorities, collegewide goals, and highly rated learning college criteria were identified. Faculty and staff responses to the relative importance of each item indicated the college community felt that the goals and strategic priorities were highly aligned with the identified learning college criteria. Faculty and staff were also given an opportunity to comment on each area of the process and to recommend multiyear strategic objectives that should be considered for subsequent implementation.

The Journey Continues

During the past seven years, faculty and staff at AACC have undergone a tremendous shift in their approach to the work of their community college. The focus on learning has generated increased respect for the various areas of the college and has led to equity among academic, continuing education, and workforce training programs. As we have made this shift, we have also increased our ability to respond quickly and effectively to new initiatives that meet community needs. Our faculty continues to evolve as we invest in their continuing professional development and expand their potential through diverse teaching opportunities.

We have come a long way, and there is much more to accomplish. We continue to take Darwin's caution about change to heart. The evolutionary journey to become a true learning college continues at AACC, with all faculty and staff increasingly focused on a common goal: to help those in our community reach their full potential as citizens, workers, and learners.

Academic Strategy and the Management of the Learning College
— Irving Pressley McPhail

George Keller (1983) defines strategy as "agreeing on some aims and having a plan to defeat one's enemies, or to arrive at a destination, through the effective use of resources" (p. 75). Between 1998 and 2003, The Community College of Baltimore County (CCBC) put that definition to the test by embarking on a journey to advance the learning college paradigm as academic strategy. Through the college's *LearningFIRST 1.0, 1998-2003, Strategic Plan (LearningFIRST)*, we managed the institution with a firm and disciplined commitment to aligning strategic planning, budgeting, and resource allocation. *LearningFIRST* defined the strategic management of the institution and is discussed here in the context of the unique relationship between planning, budgeting, and resource allocation in higher education, and through analysis of some of the impediments to linking planning and budgeting successfully in the academy. The keys to effective resource allocation, reviewing resource allocation problems in higher education, and the critical elements of the CCBC approach to linking planning, budgeting, and resource allocation implemented during this period are also explored.

In practice, The Community College of Baltimore County (CCBC) made a firm commitment to a *culture of planning* as the primary catalyst for leading the organizational transformation toward a more learning-centered institution (McPhail, 1999; McPhail & Heacock, 1999; McPhail, Heacock, & Linck, 2000). CCBC's *LearningFIRST* presented the college's vision as a single college, multicampus, learning-centered institution, and contained the college's vision statement, mission statement, statement of beliefs, and strategic directions (Table 1 and Figure 1).

CCBC made a deliberate effort to link planning, budgeting, and resource allocation. The college's operating budget was developed by explicitly incorporating the *LearningFIRST* vision statement, mission statement, statement of beliefs, and strategic directions. The fiscal year 2004 operating

Figure 1. LearningFIRST 1.0: Core and Supporting Strategic Directions

budget was the fourth year that all requests for additional funding above the maintenance of effort level were specifically linked to *LearningFIRST*.

The Planning and Budgeting Paradox

We know that linking planning, budgeting, and resource allocation has proven difficult in higher education. "Those in higher education who are seeking the perfect relationship between planning and budgeting are like the physicists who are searching for the unified theory of forces. Both sides draw closer and closer to eloquent solutions, but are confounded by unexpected complexities

Table 1. LearningFIRST 1.0. Vision, Mission, and Statement of Beliefs

Vision: The Community College of Baltimore County (CCBC) is a premier, learning-centered, single college, multicampus institution. **Mission:** The Community College of Baltimore County is a learning-centered public college that anticipates and responds to the educational, training, and employment needs of the community by offering a broad array of general education, transfer and career programs, student support services, and economic and community development activities. The College serves its diverse community as a center for lifelong learning to improve the quality of life in Baltimore County and the region in a time of rapid societal and technological change. The Community College of Baltimore County commits to the optimal use of available resources in a responsive and responsible manner.	**Statement of Beliefs:** The Community College of Baltimore County acquires its direction through adherence to its Vision and Mission Statements. The implementation of the college's strategic and operational plans is the primary means for focusing the entire organization to this end. The college will achieve institutional excellence from its strategic planning process in concert with a persistently positive attitude on the part of faculty, administration, and staff. As a learning-centered community college, CCBC will • make learning its central focus; • make students active partners in the learning process; • assume final responsibility for producing student learning; • focus on learning outcomes to assess student learning and success; • create a holistic environment that supports student learning; • ensure that every member of the college community is a learner; and • evaluate all areas of the College by the ways they support student learning.[1] [1] The statement of beliefs was drawn from a number of authors who have defined learning-centered education. The outline and the beliefs stated were drawn most heavily from principles articulated in the following publication: Terry O'Banion, *Creating More Learning-Centered Community Colleges* (see page 38).

in the physical world and the world of organized individuals" (Meisinger, 1990, p. 1).

Meisinger (1990) concluded that, in higher education, the theorists call for clearly delineated goals and a set of objectives for which priorities have been established (the strategic plan), an implementation framework that estimates the cost of achieving these goals and objectives (the budget plan), an allocation of funds for these goals and objectives (resource allocation plan), and a scheme for measuring the success in achieving the goals and objectives (evaluation plan).

He argued that few people would disagree with these prescriptions for linking planning, resource allocation, and budgeting more effectively, but like the Wall Street maxim to "buy low and sell high" or the real estate maxim, "location, location, location," the complexities of the real world make this advice too simple to be helpful.

Schmidtlein (1990) viewed the situation with similar skepticism. He noted that, "Within the field of public administration, the belief that budgets should be derived from well-conceived plans appears to be an unquestioned article of faith. Like the search for the Holy Grail, theorists and practitioners for many years have maintained a quest for the secret to a successful linkage. Some theorists have claimed success, but, like claims for cold hydrogen fusion, the results of their formulations have been inconclusive and controversial" (p. 9).

Types of Planning and Their Relationship to Budgeting

The observations shared here draw principally upon the seminal work of Frank Schmidtlein (1990), who identified many of the impediments to successful planning and budgeting. Schmidtlein is the former director of the Institutional Planning Project at the National Center for Postsecondary Governance and Finance, University of Maryland, College Park. His work is suitable for this discussion because it draws upon information obtained from a three-year national study of higher education institutional planning that presents planning and budgeting typologies and the linkages between them.

Planning usually includes several levels and may vary from comprehensive to issue specific. When examining this connection between planning and budgeting, it is important to be clear about the type of planning, or which combination of types, is reviewed. Each type of planning has different implications for achieving such a connection. Schmidtlein identified six principal planning types:

1. *Strategic Planning.* Determining the nature of the environment in which an institution operates, assessing its internal strengths and weaknesses, and developing a "vision" of its future character, given these assumptions

2. *Program Planning.* Determining the nature of the programs needed to implement the college's vision and the types of structures and processes required to support these programs

3. *Operational Planning.* Establishing short-range objectives, determining their relative priorities, and deciding the kinds and levels or resources to be devoted to each objective

4. *Issue-specific Planning.* Determining the policies and actions required to resolve issues affecting a specific campus function or limited set of functions

5. *Budget Planning.* Determining the goods and services needed to implement desired programs, estimating their costs, determining potential sources of revenue, and reconciling competing claims for resources, given assumptions about revenue limitations

6. *Facility Planning.* Determining the character of physical facilities needed to effectively implement an institution's programs.

Strategic Planning's Links to Budgeting. Planning is a complex process and it was important to establish clear operational definitions when launching the *LearningFIRST* process at CCBC. Schmidtlein defines strategic planning to include determining the nature of the environment in which an institution operates, assessing its internal strengths and weaknesses, and developing a "vision" of its future character given these assumptions. According to Schmidtlein, strategic planning does not provide program, operational, or budget guidance for decisions on specific priorities or on goods and services a unit should request in budget documents. It does, however, provide a context for a college's vision for a market niche and an institutional mission appropriate to exploit that niche. Consensus on a mission creates a set of shared values and assumptions that in turn create a context for program planning, operational planning, and budget decisions. In practice, strategic planning provides the context but rarely provides explicit guidance for budget decisions. Schmidtlein (1990) advanced the notion that under optional conditions, strategic planning leads to agreement on a college's mission and provides a broad "vision" of its future directions.

Program Planning's Links to Budgeting. It is generally understood that program planning, by its very nature, provides somewhat more specific guidance for budgeting than strategic planning. Program planning determines the nature of the programs needed to implement the college's vision and the types of structures and processes required to support these programs. In most institutions, the relative priority of programs fluctuates from year to year. While operational agreement on programs provides a greater degree of guidance for budget decisions than does strategic planning, a large area remains for discretionary budget decisions.

Operational Planning's Link to Budgeting. Schmidtlein (1990) stated, "The primary function of operational planning is to develop consensus on specific items to be included in a budget, or at least the new items, since most of the items in a budget represent continuing commitments" (p. 12). He observed that operational planning rests on the hope that, through an early planning cycle, analysis can take place and political struggles can be settled, avoiding interference with the technical work involved in costing out elements in the budget, identifying fund sources or accounts, and preparing budget justifications. At many institutions, operational planning often takes place as budgetary decisions are being made.

In practice, organizational units nearly always view planning as an opportunity to enlarge their budgets. As a result, unit plans frequently contain "laundry" or "wish" lists of new items for which they seek resources. The politics of reconciling financially unrealistic unit requests with districtwide priorities complicates the development of planners' explicit strategic plans.

Many community colleges will readily admit that plans are often not an adequate guide for budget decisions because units typically are reluctant to document their significant problems. Some may fear that media, governing boards, and the general public will make inaccurate assessments of a problem's magnitude. In addition, adversaries may be able to use such negative information against them in budgetary allocations or other aspects of resource acquisition. As a consequence, plans appear to be a better guide for new initiatives than they are for reductions or reallocations of funds. My observation is that, even in the best of times, departments or divisions tend to view their budget base as an inheritance and seek to limit budget discussions to requests for increases, turning reducing or reallocating of funds into a highly contested political process.

Keys to Effective Resource Allocation

There is no one-size-fits-all approach when it comes to resource allocation. William Massey (1996), in his critical work, *Resource Allocation in Higher Education*, suggested that institutions are in a battle against a well-established educational institution maxim known as Bowen's Law: "Universities will raise all the money they can and spend all the money they raise" (p. 5). Bowen's Law sends a sound message to community colleges, and is all the more reason educational institutions must identify and understand the keys to effective resource allocation in higher education.

Understanding the System of Incentives. The first major key identified by Massey (1996) focused on the system of incentives that guides spending in colleges and universities. According to Massey, incentives are based partly on intrinsic values and partly on instrumental ones. A good example is the view that college academic, vocational, and contract education programs with strong job and market values serve to cross-subsidize academic programs with low intrinsic values. Low intrinsic value programs are ones that have high traditional liberal education value but low job and market value. Massey maintains that an effective resource allocation process will allow the college to achieve an appropriate balance between its identified intrinsic values, and those of the marketplace.

Recognizing and Managing Complexity. Higher education institutions generally use incremental or formula concepts to develop their budgets. This process drives the need to be aware of the diversity of intrinsic values of the institution. The diversity springs partly from differences in technical and professional background, partly from

differences in educational purposes, and partly from political self-interest. Each group argues for its view in terms of high principles, often reinforced by the fact that success also furthers political self-interest.

The third key to resource allocation reform is the ability and capacity to manage complexity. In higher education institutions, resource allocation reform usually involves decentralizing detailed budgeting responsibility away from central organizational units where it traditionally has been held. According to Massey (1996), and based on my own observations as a CEO, centralization can disempower those who represent the institution's core competencies, undermining the incentives for productivity improvement and making accountability for such improvement impossible. To minimize distraction to resource allocation, it is logical that effective resource allocation in colleges and universities include appropriate decentralizion of power.

Resource Allocation Problems

In studying the resource allocation pattern of higher education institutions, we discover that efforts to balance values and market forces, cope with value diversity, and manage complexity tend to lead chief executive and business officers to insist upon central control over resources. As I mentioned earlier, the most common control method is incremental line-item budgeting. At many institutions, the need to manage complexity drives the allocation process. Attention is focused on additions and deletions because the base budget is too hard to analyze. After using incremental budgeting over a period of time, the incremental character emerges. Various budget centers tend to assert ownership of base funding levels and come to view most of their costs as fixed. While many institutional leaders may not like the process, they often are drawn into the politics of the situation.

Massey (1996) proposes that the antidote lies in resource allocation reform at several levels. The first priority is to dissolve the operating units' sense of base budget ownership and their belief that cost and quality are synonymous. Unit management needs to understand that resources will flow in relation to market demand and assessed performance. I believe that as the rate of change within the institution increases and external demands increase, the willingness and ability to change also increases.

Today's increasingly changing economic environment highlights the importance of the change process and its value to institutional effectiveness, a concept that was demonstrated at CCBC during this period. Another key priority in resolving resource allocation problems is dialogue. Maintaining dialogue about program relevance, quality, and productivity, and implementing the processes and data needed to make the dialogue meaningful are critical to addressing the problem. Resources should be invested according to the so-called high-assay principle. According to this principle, if one owned several gold mines, it would make sense to invest in the one with the highest assay or opportunity for growth and values. In colleges and universities, high-assay means quality relative to institutional values, vision, mission, and goals delivered as productively as possible.

Five Year — Strategic Plan ↔ Long-Range Plan

One Year — Operational Plan ↔ Budget

Quarterly — Results Management

Figure 2. The Integrated Planning Process

Massey (1996) described the final priority as the capacity to relax restrictions on how operating units manage resource trade-offs. Cost centers should be free to determine for themselves how to meet the agreed upon objectives within the available budget allocation.

The Integrated Planning Process

The Integrated Planning Process (IPP), as developed by Patrick Below (Below, Morrisey, & Acomb, 1987), presents a total framework for depicting an organization's planning and control system. The IPP has been modified over time by the author to fit the academic planning context. Figure 2 presents the three-tiered model in use at CCBC from 1998-2005.

Annual Operational Planning Process. The planning process at CCBC was continuous and intended to achieve real results. It was designed to provide the overall vision, mission, and strategic directions for the college and each of the three campuses. It welcomed and encouraged planning at all levels and assumed that planning behavior was a fundamental responsibility of all managers, administrators, and other college leaders.

CCBC was involved in three major types of planning: strategic, operational and long-range. The operational plan consisted of annual objectives for each of the strategic directions in the *LearningFIRST*: Student Learning, Learning Support, Learning College, Infusing Technology, Management Excellence, Embracing Diversity, Building Community and Enrollment Management. CCBC assured

Table 2. Action Planning Worksheet KRA: Student Learning ADMINISTRATOR: Henry Linck

OBJECTIVE 1.2.1: To conduct five high impact learning outcomes assessment projects.

Actions Steps	Accountability		Schedule		Resources*	Feedback Mechanisms
	Primary	Others	Start	Complete		
1. Select courses for inclusion.	Academic Division Deans	R. Mince H. Linck D. McKusick A. MacLellan Faculty	2/02	5/02	6 hours of reassigned time for Ann MacLellan; $90,000 (approved 03 Operational budget for LOA projects.)	Notice to faculty of selected courses.
2. Identification of team leaders.	Academic Division Deans	A. MacLellan R. Mince	3/02	6/02		Faculty volunteer to serve as project team leaders.
3. Budget decisions made by teams (distribution of stipend).	LOA Teams	A. MacLellan R. Mince	5/02 / 6/02	8/02	IR staff hours for data analysis: 60-80	Budget approved by Henry Linck.
4. Project design (instrument, external validation, data collection and analysis, timeline, etc.) approved by Outcomes Associate, Deans, and VCLSD.	LOA Teams A. MacLellan	Academic Division Deans R. Mince H. Linck	6/02	9/02	Staff/faculty hours for conducting LOAs: 120-200	Approval of proposals.
5. Collection of data.	LOA Teams A. MacLellan G. Fink T. Hirsch	Faculty Deans	Fall 2002	Spring 2002		Data collected for all 5 projects and submitted to Planning, Research, and Evaluation for analysis.
6. Analysis of data.	LOA Teams A. MacLellan G. Fink T. Hirsch	Faculty Deans R. Mince H. Linck, D. McConochie	Spring 2002	Fall 2002		Data analysis completed and returned to LOA Teams.
7. Curriculum revision. (based on data analysis)	LOA Teams A. MacLellan R. Mince	Faculty Deans H. Linck	Fall 2002	Spring 2003		Curriculum revisions approved and implemented (?)
8. Ongoing updates and revisions, as necessary.	LOA Teams A. MacLellan	Faculty Deans R. Mince H. Linck	Spring 2003	Ongoing		Post data collection— to compare pre and post-results.
9. Collection of data.	LOA Teams A. MacLellan G. Fink T. Hirsch	Faculty Deans	Fall 2003 and beyond	Spring 2004 and beyond		Post data collection— to compare pre and post-results.

*Resources: Resource column should include estimated cost, time commitment (in staff FTE or hours), budget area (base, tier, capital) and budget organization.

that the strategic plan was carried out consistently in all parts of the college on an annual basis. Table 2 is an example of the Action Planning Worksheet (APW). The APW ensured that the operational plan was implemented. Implementation revolved around making the translation from the specific Strategic Direction in *LearningFIRST 1.0* to annual objectives linked to that specific Strategic Direction, and to specific actions and results. The goal was to make change happen.

The construction of the annual operational plan began with the articulation of primary issues related to each of the strategic directions. The chancellor's cabinet reviewed data to focus discussion on each of the strategic directions and identified results to address the issues. Next, the cabinet developed a concluding statement, which, along with the results, defined the direction for the operational objectives. The operational plan then took shape over several months.

Each spring, the chancellor's cabinet participated in a planning retreat devoted to operational planning. During this retreat, the participants developed the operational objectives based on the following:

- A comprehensive analysis of results of the quarterly and annual cabinet-level review of the college's success in achieving the prior year's operational plan;

- A review of new and/or different data related to current objectives that required changes; and

- The development of new objectives and desired results in accordance with performance indicators.

The chancellor's cabinet formulated tentative annual objectives and finalized the operational plan by July 1.

The cabinet then moved to approve the operational plan for the fiscal year just beginning. In September, the operational plan was submitted to the board of trustees and to the college community. Upon presentation, all cabinet-level administrators received the operational plan for use in their respective areas of responsibility. Each campus president also received the plan for use in campus-level planning implementation. CCBC determined its budget and spending on the basis of its strategic plan and allocated its resources in order to achieve the objectives determined in its operational plan.

For example, in the FY 2003 planning year, the college identified 27 objectives in the operational plan, which were addressed by one or more member of the chancellor's cabinet. A comprehensive review of the 27 operational plan objectives indicated that 26 (96 percent) were completed as originally formulated and one (4 percent) was completed as revised.

Annual Budget Development Process. The annual budget is the basic budgetary constraint intended to ensure that a government unit, in this case, The Community College of Baltimore County, does not spend beyond its means. The college operated within a balanced budget. At a minimum, balance should be defined to ensure that a government's

Table 3. Operating and Capital Budget Process

	Timeline - Operating and Capital Budget Processes	
	Operating Budget (Annual)	Capital Budget (Biennial)
August	Budget parameters determined	
September	Revenue and expenditure requests formulated	Formulation of Capital Improvement Plan (CIP)
October	Chancellor's cabinet review, prioritization, and transition of working budget into Administration's Proposed Operating Budget. Presentation to the Board of Trustees.	
November		
December	Presentation to and approval by Board of Trustees	Review CIP with County Office of Budget and Finance
January		
February	Forward Board of Trustees Operating Budget to Baltimore County Office of Budget and Finance for review and revision	County Planning Board review and recommended CIP
March		
April		County Executive review and development of proposed CIP
May	County Executive's recommended Operating Budget	
June	County Council review and adoption of Operating Budget	County Council review and adoption
July	New fiscal year begins	New fiscal year begins

use of resources for operating purposes does not exceed available resources over a defined budget period.

Budgeting is the process of translating the college's plans into an itemized, authorized, and systematic plan of operation, expressed in appropriated dollars, for a given period. The result of this process is a document that serves as a financial blueprint to monitor and control ongoing operations. Budgeting provides an opportunity to examine the composition and viability of the college's resources and current or anticipated program activities. This examination allows for the most efficient allocation of available resources to the college's priorities.

The mission of the budget process is to help decision-makers make informed choices about the provision of services and assets and to promote stakeholder participation in the process. The budgeting process is far more than the preparation of a legal document that appropriates funds for a series of line items. Budgeting is a broadly defined process that has political, managerial, planning, communication, and financial dimensions (see Wildavsky, 1979). The CCBC's operating budget had many essential features. The budget process:

- Incorporated a long-term perspective (prior, actual, and adopted budgets);

- Established linkage to organizational goals (*LearningFIRST*);

- Focused budget decisions on results and outcomes (allocation to new or expanding programs);

- Involved and promoted effective communication with stakeholders (cost center managers, campus governance, chancellor's cabinet, county government and constituents); and

- Provided flexibility to cost center managers (budget transfers).

The formulation of the CCBC's operating budget was the responsibility of the director of budgeting, who reported to the assistant vice chancellor for finance and administration. The director of budgeting was also responsible for assuring that the budget was subject to the controls established within the accounting system, and that expenditures by organizational managers remained within appropriation balances by category and by function.

The formulation process began with the setting of budget parameters by the chancellor's cabinet. During an August retreat, my cabinet members and I reviewed and approved the budget parameters. The approved parameters were incorporated into an operating budget development instruction letter and sent to all organization managers. During September, the organization managers developed their operating budgets based on these parameters and forwarded their budget requests, along with detailed line-item justifications, to the director of budgeting.

All organization requests were consolidated into a working operating budget by program and category. October was dedicated to the cabinet's review, prioritization, and transition of a working operating budget into the administration's proposed operating budget. The administration's proposed operating budget was presented to the board of trustees in

November for review and was approved by the board in December. The board of trustees' operating budget was forwarded to the Baltimore County Office of Budget and Finance (executive branch) in January, which reviewed, verified, and revised the operating budget during February and March. The office was authorized to increase, decrease, or delete any items in the budget.

The final product of this process, presented in April, was the county executive's recommended operating budget along with a budget message to the county council (legislative branch). During May, the county council reviewed the budget and decreased or deleted any items in the budget, except the following: those required by the public general laws of the State of Maryland and any provision for debt service on obligations then outstanding or for estimated cash deficits. The county council had no power to

Table 4. Highlights of the Adopted Fiscal Year 2004 Budget

Revenue	
County Appropriation	$35,632,254
Tuition and Fees	45,529,226
State Aid	32,130,873
Other Revenue	20,409,094
Total Revenue	**$133,701,447**

FTE Data	
Credit	11,349
Non-credit	6,390
Total	17,739
Cost per Student	**$7,537**

LearningFirst Strategic Plan Expenditure Allocation	
Student Learning	$53,905,600
Learning Support	21,241,761
Learning College	21,586,800
Infusing Technology	12,725,080
Management Excellence	16,671,296
Embracing Diversity	2,348,822
Building Community	2,239,050
Enrollment Management	2,983,038
Total Expenditures	**$133,701,447**

Expenditures by Category	
Salaries and Fringes	$92,387,186
Contracted Services	10,388,058
Supplies & Materials	3,314,256
Communications	1,582,160
Conferences & Meetings	935,510
Mandatory Transfers	21,379,063
Utilities	2,552,622
Fixed Charges	576,318
Furniture & Equipment	586,274
Total Expenditures	**$133,701,447**

Expenditures by Function	
Instruction	$54,470,487
Public Service	451,520
Academic Support	11,841,624
Student Services	9,256,819
Institutional Support	24,799,928
Operation & Maint. of Plant	11,502,006
Mandatory Transfers	21,379,063
Total Expenditures	**$133,701,447**

(1) - Includes Debt Service of $2,534,040.
(2) - FTE equals Full-Time Equivalent students. Thirty credit hours equals one credit FTE. 375 clock hours equals one non-credit FTE.

change the form of the budget as submitted by the county executive, to alter the revenue estimates, or to increase any expenditure recommended by the county executive. The budget was adopted into law by the affirmative vote of the county council in May. In June, the college component of the county's adopted operating budget was presented to the board of trustees of the college, for its information. (Table 3, p. 112) presents the time line for the annual operating and capital budget process used at CCBC.

Expenditures by Strategic Direction

The key strategy in linking planning, budgeting, and resource allocation was the documentation of expenditures by strategic direction (Table 4, p. 113). Figure 3 also demonstrates how expenditures were apportioned by use of a matrix to the eight *LearningFIRST* strategic directions

Note that expenditures are primarily monitored by function and by category within each function. Note also that direct percentage allocations to Student Learning (40.3 percent) and Learning Support (15.9 percent) total 56.2 percent. In *LearningFIRST*, the integration of learning and student services under a single vice chancellor for learning and student development created a holistic environment that supported making learning the central focus of the college. This holistic paradigm for learning and student

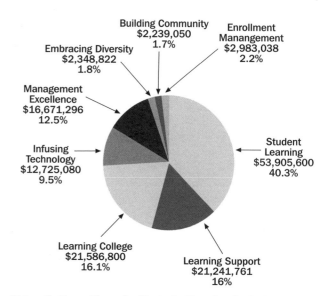

Figure 3. Expenditures by Strategic Direction (Including Grants)

development was also supported by a dual role for the three campus presidents as chief learning officers and chief administrative officers for the campuses.

Table 5. Operational Objectives Form

Fund #:	6000
Organization # / Name:	61195-PA Collaborative Program
Program #:	10
Cost Center Manager:	Carol D. Eustis

Project:	Physician Assistant Program
Objective:	To serve the educational needs for the licensing of Physician Assistants
Description:	This program, in collaboration with Towson University, prepares students for licensure by engaging in a 57-credit certificate program offered by CCBC and a 33 credit Master's in Physician Assistant Studies.

Strategic Direction:	Student Learning, Learning Support, Learning College, Infusing Technology.
Strategic Plan Objectives:	Create a learning centered environment that enables students to develop and achieve the professional skills they will need for practice. To prepare students for licensure.
	To provide students with state of the art technology to further enhance their skills.
	To better prepare students to move into the clinical setting.
Funding	
(Base/Tier/Technology Fee):	Tier
Technology Plan Link:	
Timeline for Completion:	August 15, 2004

Category/Description	Account #	$ Request
Instructional Equipment	7030	$75,000

Justification

The clinical simulation model, Sim-Man, is a state of the art patient that can be programmed to provide medical scenarios covering a broad range illnesses and systemic malfunctions. The model serves to replicate situations that students may or may not see in clinical rotations. Therefore it serves not only as a "without harm" patient for students to perfect skills but also provides a vehicle to further expand their training prior to licensure and practice. Students are provided immediate feedback as to the appropriateness of their plan of care and the consequences of their critical thinking in dealing with symptoms, illness etc. as programmed and demonstrated by Sim-Man. This learning tool serves to enhance students preparation and training. Sim-Man includes not only the full form patient able to accommodate the insertion of IV's, injections, detection of heart and breathing sounds, coughing to mention a few and can also be programmed to respond verbally to the students. The associated computer and hardware provides for a real patient in the laboratory setting.

A further methodology for linking budget requests to strategic directions was the operational objectives form. Table 5 demonstrates how *every budget request* must be linked to a specific strategic direction in the *LearningFIRST* strategic plan. I believe that this requirement was the driving force behind our effectiveness.

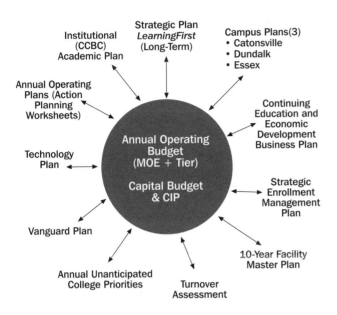

This graphic represents the primary planning and operational resources affecting the development of the annual operating budget, the capital budget, and the capital improvement program.

Figure 4. Primary Planning and Operational Resources

Finally, Figure 4 illustrates how multiple institutional planning processes influenced the annual operating budget, the capital budget, and the capital improvement program.

Monitoring, Evaluating, and Renewal

Our commitment to the culture of planning at CCBC was matched with an equally compelling commitment to a culture of evidence. As a Vanguard Learning College, we were focused on the implementation and integration of all programs and services that enhanced the success and performance of CCBC's learners. In the midst of a perfect storm—increasing student enrollment, declining state funding, and steady state local county funding—we were determined to maintain our momentum and to continue our focus on student learning as our central institutional commitment.

Monitoring the implementation of *LearningFIRST* was critical to maintaining the focus on vision. We were attuned to the pragmatic challenges of actually implementing creative ideas. Guthrie, Garns, and Pierce (1988) warn that it is imperative to allocate resources in accord with agreed upon priorities based on the plan. This became a collaborative function of the chancellor's cabinet.

The principal tools for monitoring, evaluating, and renewing the strategic plan were the quarterly review process and the broad-based distribution of mid-year and end-of-year accountability reports. Again, the emphasis was on creativity and change.

Table 6. Operational Plan Accountability Form

CHANCELLOR'S CABINET

2002-2003 OPERATIONAL PLAN

OPERATIONAL PLAN ACCOUNTABILITY FORM

NAME: Henry Linck

TITLE: Vice Chancellor for Learning and Student Development

QUARTER: I _____ II _____ III _____ IV _____ X _____

KRA: Student Learning

OBJECTIVE: 1.2.1 To conduct five high impact learning outcomes assessment projects.

STATUS: COMPLETED _____ X _____

ON SCHEDULE _____

BEHIND SCHEDULE _____

SIGNIFICANT ACCOMPLISHMENTS:

The CCBC *Guide for Learning Outcomes Assessment and Classroom Learning Assessment* (enclosed) has been distributed to all full-time faculty and will soon be available via the CCBC web page. A number of other colleges have requested a copy of our Guide and continue to "borrow" the excellent work that we have done at CCBC to develop their own LOA policies and procedures. CCBC has been recognized as a national leader in the area of Learning Outcomes Assessment-most recently in an article entitled "Benchmarking Best Practices in the Learning College" by the Vanguard Learning College Project Evaluator, Kay McClenney.

All five high impact LOA projects for FY'03 have completed the first phase of their assessment. Baseline data has been collected for HLTH 101, PEFT 101, CINS 101, and SDEV 101. The ENGL 101 project included a pilot phase to test the writing prompts and scoring rubric that will be used to assess the data. More than 400 writing prompts have been collected. The prompts will be scored during summer '03. The first round of data from the other four projects will also be analyzed during the summer and faculty will begin developing curricular changes in fall '03.

Another significant accomplishment is the approval of the Learning Outcomes Assessment Advisory Board's (LOAAB) Core Competencies Learning Outcomes Assessment Initiative by the Learning/Academic Affairs Council (see attached). LOAAB has done tremendous work this year to get the Assessment Initiative written and approved. CCBC now has an approved definition of assessment, an assessment mission statement, and four core competencies that will be addressed (and eventually assessed) in every CCBC course. The four core competencies are: Communication, Critical and Analytical Thinking, Global Perspective and Social Responsibility, and Independent Learning and Personal Management.

ATTACH APPROPRIATE DOCUMENTATION:

Each quarter, the chancellor met with every member of the chancellor's cabinet to review progress on assigned areas of responsibility in the annual operational plan. The focused discussion centered on the operational plan accountability form (Table 6, p. 115) that was completed by each cabinet member and backed up with appropriate documentation.

Each February, a mid-year report was issued to internal and external constituencies. This document served as a catalyst for communications throughout the community and helped keep everyone focused on the primary institutional commitment to student learning. A comprehensive end-of-year report was prepared each August and widely distributed throughout the institution.

Leadership's Role in Linking Strategic Planning, Budgeting, and Resource Allocation

The literature suggests that organizational leaders cannot rely solely on strategic planning to create linkages between the many components of the organization. Bryson (1995), for example, argues that strategic planning is not a substitute for effective leadership; instead, strategic planning is simply a set of concepts, procedures, and tools designed to help leaders think and act strategically on behalf of their organizations and their stakeholders.

Leaders are called upon to perform political, spiritual, and intellectual functions as well as managerial and group maintenance tasks. These range from providing vision and strategies for change and mobilizing a constituency to facilitating group decisions or creating coalitions. Unless the organization is very small, no single person or group can perform them all. Effective linking of strategic planning, budgeting, and resource allocation functions is a collective phenomenon, typically involving sponsors, champions, facilitators, teams, task forces, and others in various ways at different times.

Linking strategic planning, budgeting, and resource allocation at CCBC occurred amidst the onslaught of bad financial news, stagnant or shrinking revenue, and growing public pessimism. The expectation was that we would do more with less. The following leadership strategies enabled the chancellor's cabinet to work collaboratively with all key constituent groups in managing through gloomy financial times (McPhail, 2003).

Tie the Numbers to Your Vision. I believe that the college's vision and mission must drive college operations. Budgeting is no exception. Quite frankly, it may be the college function most critically linked to vision and mission since no activity can take place without appropriate funding. At CCBC, we evaluated every budget request in terms of whether or not it advanced our learning-centered priorities. How well it stood up to the litmus test of student learning determined its fate.

Build It From the "Bottom Up." With the college's vision and mission emanating from the top and flowing down and out, a "bottom-up" approach to budget building is crucial. First, it makes individuals and departments accountable. More importantly, it enhances buy-in for the vision and

mission throughout the organization. Everyone grows accustomed to thinking strategically and "for the good of the college." A sense of unity and a commonality of purpose evolve. The resulting budget clearly demonstrated that the whole is greater than the sum of its parts.

Avoid Taking a "Pie-in-the-Sky" Approach. There's no room for wishful thinking in today's economy. Realistic expenditure and revenue projections should become second nature. Revenue projections, in particular, require a strong partnership between the finance, enrollment management and planning, and research arms of the college. Rely on their joint expertise for scientific projections. But don't stop there. Adopt a holistic approach to budgeting. View projections in light of past performance of peer colleges and up-to-date environmental scanning. It's about more than the numbers.

Give Finance a Real Seat at the Table. Make your chief financial officer (CFO) a leader at the table in terms of college decisions, not just the financial ones. See budgeting as more than pure fund appropriation. Funding is pervasive to every decision, every action. That's why it's important to appoint a member of the college's finance team to standing college committees, such as strategic enrollment management. Such front-line and executive-level financial guidance goes a long way toward ensuring sound financial decisions.

Drive Carefully, But Be Ready to Shift Gears. Virtually every speaker on the motivational circuit today promotes the concept of "balance." This principle applies to budgeting as well. You need to balance control with flexibility. While you want to be on top of spending, you don't want to miss the forest for the trees. Work with your CFO and other college leaders throughout the year to identify and fund those "unanticipated college priorities." Otherwise, you won't be as fluid and responsive as you need to be.

Make Friends With Technology. If vision is the vehicle that drives all college operations, then technology is the engine. To be at the forefront of the information revolution, we must integrate technology into all that we do, including budget management. At CCBC, we used our online information system, BANNER, to make up-to-date budget information immediately accessible to all budget managers. There was no need for CCBC's managers to wait for monthly budget office reports when they could more easily monitor spending on a daily basis. It generated goodwill, gave them direct oversight and led to better management decisions.

Don't Rush a Good Thing. Detail requires time. You simply shouldn't force the budget planning and approval process. We allowed ourselves a solid four months from the onset of budget planning to the final adoption by our board of trustees. Along the way, we provided training via workshops for all budget managers throughout the organization, which coached them, among other things, on writing clear, detailed, line-item justifications. As a result, we had the answers ready when we got questions from a trustee or the county executive. We could respond quickly and appropriately. This built credibility and trust.

Be Open Year-Round. Regular and honest communication is important with all stakeholders. It's not enough to work with budget managers during the planning phase, with trustees during the adoption phase, and so on. Assign a finance representative to each major area of the college organization. Make sure each manager has a trusted contact to call on for help with budget decisions or transactions. Invite representatives of the college's funding agencies to your board of trustee meetings. Keep the lines of communication open and avoid surprises. You'll be thankful you did when tough decisions need to be made and you need their support.

Raise the Bar. Encourage excellence and seek third-party validation to acknowledge it. You'll not only build internal confidence for a job well done, you'll also enhance your credibility with trustees and funding agents. As a college that sought to attain "premier," learning-centered status in teaching and learning as well as organizational excellence, we were committed to the highest principles of governmental budgeting. Earning the 2003 Bellwether Award for the *LearningFIRST*, in addition to consecutive Government Finance Officers Association (GFOA) Distinguished Budget Awards, affirmed this commitment.

Be Willing to Take a Stand. You can't be all things to all people at a time when funding is dwindling and resources are stretched to the limit. In the end, to try to do so will lead to poor quality, which is counter to the college's vision of excellence. At CCBC, we made structural changes that, although difficult, identified about $1.5 million over a two year period to help fuel our priorities and preserve our core programs and services. Ultimately, this may have been one of the best ways to safeguard the college's mission.

A Final Thought

My mentor and friend, the late George Keller, observed that "the heart of strategic thinking is the creation of a set of initiatives…to maintain stability or win a new position amid a blizzard of discontinuities, unprecedented threats, and surprising changes" (Keller, 1997). Our efforts to implement *LearningFIRST* defined a new paradigm for linking strategic planning, budgeting, and resource allocation to meet the challenge of sustaining organizational transformation and becoming more learning-centered during a period of fiscal decline and retrenchment. Our efforts, further, proved counter to the conventional wisdom and evidence regarding integrating planning with budgeting and resource allocations. A pioneering study by James E. Williams (1999) is a case in point. Williams surveyed all 107 California community colleges to determine, among other things, the extent to which the planning, budgeting, and financial resource allocation processes were integrated. Williams concluded that such integration did not exist or was very weak. This is the general conclusion reached in the planning and budgeting literature.

The success of the *LearningFIRST* journey suggested much in the way of assembling the elements of strategic planning, budgeting, and resource allocation such that the *LearningFIRST 2.0, 2003-2008, Strategic Plan* was enhanced by these integrative processes.

References

Below, P.J., Morrisey, G.L., & Acomb, B.L. (1987). *The Executive Guide to Strategic Planning*. San Francisco: Jossey-Bass Publishers.

Bryson, J.M. (1995). *Strategic Planning for Public and Nonprofit Organizations: A Guide to Strengthening and Sustaining Organizational Achievement*. San Francisco: Jossey-Bass.

Guthrie, J.W., Garns, W.L., & Pierce, L.C. (1988). *School Finance and Educational Policy: Enhancing Educational Efficiency, Equality, and Choice*. Englewood Cliffs, NJ: Prentice-Hall.

Keller, G. (1983). *Academic Strategy: The Management Revolution in American Higher Education*. Baltimore, MD: Johns Hopkins University Press.

Keller, G. (1997). Examining What Works in Strategic Planning. In M.W. Peterson, D.D. Dill, L.A. Mets, & Associates (Eds.), *Planning and Management for a Changing Environment*. San Francisco: Jossey-Bass.

Massey, W.F. (1996). *Resource Allocation in Higher Education*. Ann Arbor: University of Michigan Press.

McPhail, I.P. (1999, September). Launching LearningFIRST at The Community College of Baltimore County. *Learning Abstracts, 2*(6).

McPhail, I.P. (2003, March 18). 10 Steps to Better Budgeting in "Blue" Budget Days. *Community College Times*, p. 2.

McPhail, I.P., & Heacock, R.C. (1999). Baltimore County: A College and Community in Transition. In R.C. Bowen & G.H. Muller (Eds.), *Gateway to Democracy: Six Urban Community College Systems* (pp. 75-83). San Francisco: Jossey-Bass.

McPhail, I.P., Heacock, R.C., & Linck, H.F. (2000). LearningFIRST: Creating and Leading the Learning College. *Community College Journal of Research and Practice*, 25, 17-28.

Meisinger, R.J. (1990). Introduction to Special Issue on the Relationship Between Planning and Budgeting. *Planning for Higher Education, 18*(2), 1-8.

Schmidtlein, F.A. (1990). Why Linking Budgets to Plans Has Proven Difficult in Higher Education. *Planning for Higher Education, 18*(2), 9-24.

Wildavsky, A. (1979). *The Politics of the Budgetary Process*. 3rd ed. Boston: Little, Brown.

Williams, J.E. (1999). *Linking Strategic Planning, Budgeting, and Resource Allocation in California Community Colleges*. Unpublished doctoral dissertation, University of LaVerne.

A Learning College Primer

— Isothermal Community College

Isothermal Community College. *A Learning College Primer.* (2008). Spindale, NC; Author.

Greetings from the President

Welcome to Isothermal Community College…a community of individuals committed to "improving life through learning." Learning is the central focus for Isothermal and charts our continuing journey to become a preeminent "Learning College." Faculty, staff, and students are all challenged and encouraged to demonstrate a commitment to our Learning College philosophy, and we rise to the challenge. Our collaborative efforts demonstrate how we have and continue to create a climate that nurtures and supports each learner. We are delighted that you have decided to join us on our journey and look forward to an exciting and mutually beneficial learning experience.

Dr. Myra B. Johnson
President

Mission

Isothermal Community College exists to improve life through learning. It is a simple statement, but when one tries to get to the essence of what the college is all about, it says it all. This is our mission. This is the driving force behind our focus on becoming a learning college.

Vision

Our vision is *to transform Isothermal Community College into a pre-eminent center recognized nationally for excellence in learning and services.*

Values

In improving life through learning, we embrace the following values:

- A commitment to excellence
- Nurturing an organizational climate of integrity, care, and respect for individuals
- Innovation, evaluation, and informed change
- Elimination of barriers to learning
- Self-directed learning and critical thinking
- The preservation and perpetuation of our diverse cultural heritage
- Serving as a catalyst for positive community growth

Learning College

Terry O'Banion, author of the book, *A Learning College for the 21st Century* (1997), first used this phrase to describe a paradigm shift from a focus on teaching to a focus on learning in higher education. O'Banion's work makes the following statements about the role of a Learning College:

- Creates substantive change in individual learners
- Engages learners as full partners in the learning process
- Creates and offers as many options for learning as possible
- Assists learners to form and participate in collaborative learning activities
- Defines the roles of instructors by the needs of learners
- Identifies the roles of all college employees in supporting learning
- Succeeds only when improved and expanded learning can be documented for its learners

Lifelong Learning

Isothermal Community College provides a broad range of educational experiences to serve the unique learning styles, schedules, and academic aspirations of a diverse student population throughout their adult lives. The range includes literacy classes and high school completion programs; certificate, diploma, and associate degree programs; training in specialized skills; and courses that are just for fun.

The college responds to needs of our students through a variety of learning options. For the convenience of our learners, educational experiences are offered

- Mornings, afternoons, and evenings
- On our Polk and Spindale campuses
- At community sites and high schools
- At business sites
- In traditional classroom settings
- Online, through distance learning, and in hybrid courses
- In partnerships with community organizations
- Through cultural events and arts programming
- Through Rutherford Early College High School (REaCH)

Team for the Advancement of a Learning College (TALC)

In the spring of 1996, Isothermal Community College made a commitment to become a learning-centered college. An early initiative was the empowerment of a committee on learning, which evolved into the Team for the Advancement of a Learning College (TALC) Leadership group. This Leadership Team seeks input from the college community to guide its efforts to keep learning at the forefront of our mission. All college employees (faculty and staff) who have the desire to be active in our quest to become a learning college are encouraged to do so. The TALC leadership group includes chairs and co-chairs from each of the learning task forces, plus additional representation from the college at large.

All task forces were developed to respond to institutional barriers identified by faculty and staff. Original task forces included Professional Development—Faculty, Professional Development—Staff, Technology, and Cooperative Learning (an active learning technique for which all faculty receive training). Since the implementation of the TALC learning initiative, task forces have been added, merged, or dissolved as needed to accomplish our mission. The Technology Task Force was dissolved as a result of its becoming incorporated into a department. The Institutional Effectiveness Task Force was created and then dissolved once it had served its purpose in the SACS renewal of accreditation process. The Cooperative Learning Task Force merged with the Learning Communities Task Force to form the Learning Strategies Task Force. Five additional task forces have been added to facilitate TALC efforts: Assessment, Enhancing Systems and Processes (ESP), Campus Life, Business and Industry, and Academic Advising. A brief description of each current task force's charge follows.

Academic Advising Task Force. The function of the Academic Advising Task Force is to review and support the academic advising system of the college. This includes:

- Determining areas where professional development is needed for advisors

- Developing a training program and professional development opportunities for advisors that go beyond the mechanics of registration

- Promoting "Developmental Advising" practices on campus (see http://www.nacada.ksu.edu/ Clearinghouse/AdvisingIssues/dev_ adv.htm for more information)

- Seeking ways to better educate students about their role in the advising process

- Working to ensure that advisors are informed about the advising system on our campus

- Looking for ways to improve our advising system so that the needs of all parties involved will be effectively met

Assessment Task Force. This task force researches methods of assessment and explores ways to effectively assess what we do. The college's comprehensive assessment plans include both academic and service area assessment. A major undertaking of this task force has been the development of a campuswide assessment plan that focuses on the college's stated learning outcomes and general education competencies.

Business and Industry Task Force. This task force seeks to improve the lines of communication between college faculty/staff and employers in the service area. This partnership informs curriculum planning as faculty integrate real-world concepts into the curriculum.

Campus Life Task Force. The Campus Life Task Force explores activities and programs that cultivate a sense of community and promote morale among Isothermal employees. The goals of the Campus Life Task Force include:

- Serving as a planning partner for social activities and celebrations

- Encouraging and supporting employee wellness

- Providing resources to promote personal safety, e.g. seminars, workshops

- Exploring ways to work with student organizations to promote campus life

Enhancing Systems and Processes (ESP) Task Force. In support of the College's Learning Initiative, the ESP Task Force strives to identify and remove barriers to student success as well as to foster the independence of students. This task force reviews institutional practices to identify barriers or impediments that reduce staff effectiveness or that have a direct negative impact on student learning. The task force not only initiates improvements in college policies, processes, systems, and services, but also makes recommendations to guide institutional priorities through informed change.

Learning Strategies Task Force. In October 2001, the Learning Communities and Cooperative Learning Task Forces merged to form the Learning Strategies Task Force in order to broaden the focus to a greater variety of learning strategies. This task force explores strategies for improving learning through the following:

- Steering efforts to train new faculty in learning strategies

- Sharing cooperative learning techniques

- Serving as planning partners for newly trained faculty and staff

- Serving as a resource by demonstrating the techniques

- Meeting regularly to discuss ways to support learning efforts

- Acknowledging contributions to the learning college (viz. the Golden Apple Award)

- Supporting the implementation of "Learning Communities"

- Contributing to the enhancement of global learning

Professional Development—Faculty Task Force. This task force explores and researches areas for faculty development. Specifically this includes identifying perceived faculty needs, determining how best to address those needs, and then planning, implementing, and evaluating the professional development activities.

Professional Development—Staff Task Force. This task force explores, determines, plans, implements, and evaluates professional development activities for staff. The two Professional Development Task Forces work together to plan professional development activities for all college employees.

Outcomes Assessment

In October, 1998, Isothermal embarked on a comprehensive assessment initiative. Under the umbrella of the Assessment Task Force, the college has selected six general education competencies for curriculum assessment institutionwide. Assessment teams, made up of representatives from across campus, have developed rubrics for measuring these outcomes. These outcomes are as follows:

- Communicate effectively through writing, reading, speaking, and listening, and through demonstration of information literacy

- Analyze problems and make logical conclusions

- Demonstrate positive interpersonal skills through cooperative learning and group interaction

- Demonstrate quantitative competencies

- Demonstrate basic computer skills

- Understand diverse historical and cultural perspectives

Other components of the college's assessment plan include program assessment, classroom assessment, individual student assessment, faculty and staff assessment, and service-area assessment. All of these are ongoing aspects of the learning college at work.

Active Learning

The most basic philosophy that human beings learn best by doing is the underlying concept of active learning (O'Banion, 1997). In the paradigm shift to a learning college, student roles change from passive to active, and students become fully responsible for their own choices and activities. In other words, they become more responsible for their own learning. Teachers become learning facilitators who establish environments conducive to learning and who guide students toward expected outcomes, but it is the active involvement of the student that makes the difference. At Isothermal Community College, this paradigm shift has

- Encouraged new ways of teaching and learning;

- Stimulated creativity;

- Helped remove barriers to learning;

- Promoted teamwork;

- Created new methods for assessing outcomes.

Cooperative Learning

"Cooperative learning is a teaching/learning strategy that creates a learning climate where understanding, caring, and stimulation allow students to respond with an avid interest in learning while growing in self-confidence, independence, and creative energy" (Rogers, 1969, cited in O'Banion, 1997). Since the fall of 1998, Isothermal Community College has engaged in an active partnership with The Center for Cooperative Learning at the University of Minnesota under the direction of David Johnson and Roger Johnson. The Johnsons have conducted specialized training on our campus for faculty and selected support personnel. All full-time faculty and several adjunct faculty members have completed the foundations course in Cooperative Learning; many have also completed courses in Advanced Cooperative Learning, Structured Controversy, and Leading the Cooperative School. A number of Isothermal personnel are now certified as Cooperative Learning trainers for the foundations course. This commitment to cooperative learning continues to impact the way students, faculty, and staff engage in the learning process.

Learning Styles

Research on multiple intelligences, as well as gender and culture related learning styles, clearly indicates that traditional education and standard lecture formats may not work for a majority of students. At Isothermal, all learning styles are valued. Isothermal faculty are informed about different learning styles, which is significant in two ways. First, it allows faculty to recognize, value, and provide opportunities for all students. Second, as faculty develop an awareness of their own learning styles, which has a significant influence on preferred teaching styles, they can expand their repertoire of teaching strategies.

Students are given the means, usually in ACA classes, to assess their learning styles so they can be aware of the methods of learning that work the best for them. While they may begin activities with the style most comfortable to them, they are also encouraged to broaden their skills by exploring and using styles not so familiar and comfortable.

Learning Communities

O'Banion cites research indicating that learning is significantly improved in learning communities that have been shown to increase critical thinking skills, student motivation, writing skills, and retention.

Isothermal's Learning Strategies Task Force directs the implementation of learning communities. An initial community was piloted in fall 2000 with developmental students. An Arts and Sciences curriculum learning community was developed for fall 2001. In a learning community students take a block of courses which, for example, may include biology, composition, basic computer skills, and study skills. Content in each of the courses is reinforced by the other instructors. For example, biology may provide content which is used in essays. The study skills course provides information on effective reading and research, and the computer skills course teaches students effective technical methods of presenting researched information. Students are also given ample opportunity in all of the learning community classes to develop teamwork and leadership skills. The college plans to increase the number of learning communities in the future.

Learning Technology

Technology permeates every facet of our society. To be competitive in the marketplace and to function effectively in our knowledge-based society, our students should be equipped to utilize information and technology. In addition, they should be able to exploit technologies to enhance communications and expand their learning experience. Technology is a tool that can enhance awareness, enrich learning resources, and extend the learning experience beyond traditional boundaries. Learners, not technologies, should be the focus of our efforts, and the following is what Isothermal believes should be considered before applying technologies in the learning environment:

- Technologies should serve a clearly identifiable need.

- Faculty, staff, and students should have adequate access, training, facilities, and support.

- Technology should supplement but not supplant effective pedagogy.

- Innovative learners should be allowed to experiment in a secure environment.

- Effective innovations should be acknowledged and rewarded.

Learning Support Services

At Isothermal Community College all students are offered a variety of opportunities to grow as learners and to have access to services that support that growth. Our learning-centered support services include the following:

- Academic Advising

- Financial Aid

- Success and Study Skills Class (ACA 115)

- Supplemental Instruction

- Career Services

- Disability Services

- Computer Labs

- Online Writing Tutorial Service (Smarthinking)

- Library Services (Including Online Services)

- Student Activities

- Student Government, Clubs, and Organizations

- Counseling Services

- Placement Testing

- Veterans Benefits

Developmental Education

The mission of the Developmental Education Program is to increase the likelihood that students will improve their academic performance and will persist in college. Developmental students have diverse learning styles, abilities, and expectations that require different levels of instructional support. A variety of teaching strategies such as cooperative learning, computer-assisted learning, one-on-one interactions, and lecture improves student learning. Developmental personnel encourage students to become independent learners and then give them the tools to do so.

Developmental Education offers courses in composition, reading, and mathematics. All Developmental Education classes place instructional emphasis on building student self-confidence and developing effective study skills, along with developing content skills necessary for success in curriculum courses. Critical thinking and problem solving skills are of primary importance in all Developmental Education courses.

Economic Development

Isothermal Community College plays a proactive role in shaping the readiness of both employers and the workforce for current demands and future opportunities. The college works directly with groups such as Rutherford County Economic Development Commission, Isothermal Planning and Development, and the Employment Security Commission to identify needs and solutions. Anyone seeking to upgrade skills may participate in open enrollment classes while other sessions are developed by the Office of Customized Training to meet the needs of individual employers.

Diversity

Isothermal Community College is committed to diversity enhancement and to the development of a climate that is conducive to the inclusion and participation of both students and professional associates without regard to veteran status, race, color, religion, age, gender, national origin, or disability. The college is further committed to providing opportunities and activities that promote the advancement of minorities and women to positions of leadership at our institution.

We believe that all members of the Isothermal Community College staff, faculty, and student body must be dedicated to personal and academic excellence and must practice personal and academic integrity.

We believe that we should respect the dignity of all persons, their rights and property, and that we should demonstrate concern for others, their feelings, and their need for conditions that support their work and development.

We believe that prejudice and bigotry are unacceptable, that we should always strive to learn from differences in people, cultures, ideas, and opinions and that we must refrain from and discourage any behavior, actions, or deeds which threaten the freedom and respect every individual deserves.

We believe that learning is central to the college's mission, that diversity in learning styles requires diversity in teaching styles, and that an environment which fosters and celebrates learning is the responsibility of the entire college.

We believe that allegiance to these beliefs will promote the concept of diversity, that the Isothermal Community College concept of diversity encompasses a spirit of inclusion that is reflected in its curriculum programs and in its recognition of the many variations in teaching, learning, and management styles represented by its faculty, staff, and students.

We believe that diversity is based on one principle: that there should be respect for the dignity and for the rights of every individual.

In times of change, learners inherit the earth, while the learned find themselves equipped to deal with a world that no longer exists. Eric Hoffer

Acknowledgement. Isothermal Community College is greatly indebted to the Community College of Baltimore for the concept, format, and selected content of this publication. Cover design by Brent Heflin, Advertising & Graphic Design student of Isothermal Community College.

Selected References

Angelo, T. and Cross, K. P. (1993). *Classroom Assessment Techniques: A Handbook for College Teachers*. San Francisco, CA: Jossey-Bass.

Banta, Trudy W. (1996) *Assessment in Practice: Putting Principles to Work on College Campuses. San Francisco*, CA: Jossey-Bass.

Barr, R. B. and Tagg, J. (1995). A New Paradigm for Undergraduate Education. *Change*. 27.6

Johnson, D. W., Johnson, R. T., and Smith, K. (1998). *Active Learning: Cooperation in the College Classroom*. Edina, MN: Interaction Book Co.

Johnson, D. W., Johnson, R.T., and Holubec, E. J. (1998a). *Advanced Cooperative Learning* (3rd edition). Edina, MN: Interaction Book Co.

Johnson, D. W., Johnson, R. T., and Holubec, E. J. (1998b). *Cooperation in the Classroom* (revised). Edina, MN: Interaction Book Co.

Johnson, D. W., and Johnson, R. T. (1995). *Creative Controversy: Intellectual Challenge in the Classroom*. Edina, MN: Interaction Book Co.

Johnson, D. W. and Johnson, R. T. (1994). *Leading the Cooperative School*. Edina, MN: Interaction Book Co.

O'Banion, T. (1997). *A Learning College for the 21st Century*. Phoenix: Oryx Press.

Valencia's Big Ideas: Sustaining Authentic Organizational Change Through Shared Purpose and Culture

— Sanford C. Shugart, Ann Puyana, Joyce Romano, Julie Phelps, Kaye Walter

An important part of the sustained efforts toward improving student learning at Valencia Community College has been the development of several key ideas that serve as fulcrums for change, signifiers for emerging organizational culture, and rallying points for action. The process of moving from promising innovation to large-scale pilot, to sustained solution, that is, the process of institutionalizing the work, depends heavily on a community of practice shaped by powerful common ideas. While these ideas aren't unique to Valencia, they are authentically ours in the sense that they are organic to our work, having rooted themselves in the discourse of campus conversations, planning, development, and day-to-day activity. A few of these follow.

1. Anyone Can Learn Anything Under the Right Conditions.

This idea marks a change in belief about our students. Most of the culture of education is built on a long-standing myth that talent for learning is relatively scarce and that many, perhaps the majority of our population, just aren't "college material." Despite the fact that the scientific evidence offers no support to this position, most people believe they themselves are mathematics disabled. Most believe that only certain people can learn to play the piano and that if they haven't learned a foreign language by a certain age, it is nearly impossible for most people to do so. This erroneous belief is comfortable for us because it gives us a ready means to ration educational opportunity rather than fulfill the promise of access we regularly make in our rhetoric. Further, it offers cover for methods of teaching that are known to be less effective for producing good learning results. And it reinforces framing our challenges in terms of students who are "underprepared" for college while ignoring whether the college is prepared for our students.

The fact is nearly anyone can learn nearly anything, under the right conditions. This is a matter of scientific truth. While genius in selected fields seems to be relatively rare, the capacity for competence is almost universal. Our students, with extremely rare exceptions, have all of the biological gifts, the inherent capacities to learn everything we teach.

We often remind ourselves of this truth with an anecdote. After a speech when this point was emphatically made, the speaker was approached by a teacher who said she agreed that this was true in most disciplines. The speaker asked, "What is it you teach?" The teacher replied, "German, a language that is very difficult and nonintuitive. In fact, after twenty years of teaching, I can tell you there are some people who just can't learn German." The speaker thoughtfully replied, "Well, how fortunate for them they weren't born in Germany." You see, virtually all Germans learn to speak German. This isn't a genetic endowment, a sort of "Deutsche gene." Rather, the conditions for learning to speak German just happen to be rather good in Germany and so nearly everyone learns the language. This should be no different for the language of mathematics or music or physics, or any other discipline we teach.

This idea shifts the focus from the deficiencies of the learner to the conditions of learning. Our task as a college is to partner with the learner, who controls many but not all of these conditions, to create the very best conditions for him or her to succeed. This has been a powerful idea for our work.

2. Start Right

A practical review of the evidence of student progress in nearly any community college makes this point, which has come to mean a number of related things at Valencia. This evidence reveals that the college, in spite of being the largest producer of graduates among community colleges in the country, still churns hundreds of students at the front door. Some fifteen courses, all of them available to first-semester students and about a third of which are developmental, account for nearly forty percent of the college's total enrollment. With success rates in each of these courses at most colleges hovering around 50 percent, the chances of students being successful in their first five courses on first attempt—a powerful predictor of future success and graduation—is often below 10 percent. So Start Right is a reminder that the greatest challenge and opportunity for improvement in results is at the beginning of a student's experience with us. Developing a deep and detailed understanding of the early experiences of our students has enabled the college to focus resources intensively on the pre-curricular, curricular, and co-curricular experiences of our students at the front door of the college to measurable effect. And this strategic allocation

> While genius in selected fields seems to be relatively rare, the capacity for competence is almost universal.

of resources is sustained with the support even of faculty and staff whose departments might have taken a more competitive view in advocating for their own resource priorities. They understand the importance of early success and persistence to later opportunities to engage their students in more advanced studies.

As the Start Right principle has taken root at the college, it also has come to refer to the details of each student's beginning. We know that student success is enhanced by proper assessment, placement, advising, orientation, and readiness to learn, before the first day of class. Re-engineering our schedule, admissions, registration, orientation, and other processes to make this possible for all first-time students has been a major effort driven by the Start Right principle.

Finally, Start Right also refers to the way every semester and class begins. Most colleges experience great chaos at the beginning of every term. Much of this is self-inflicted: inefficient scheduling, extended late registration, drop/add, and other poor management habits often condemn the first week of every semester to housekeeping. Beleaguered faculty often resort to what is known as "syllabus day," the tradition of handing out a syllabus, going over a few procedural matters, and dismissing class early on the first day. This is rational behavior when one can't be sure who will be in the class by the second or third meeting.

We believe
students need a

clear direction—a plan to graduate—as soon as possible in their college careers.

So we have worked to create a Start Right experience for every semester, using precision scheduling, dramatically reducing any late adds to classes, and enforcing an application deadline for new students to give time for all these processes, to reduce the chaos of the beginning of term, and to reclaim the first week for learning. Our rallying cry is, "Make the first minute of the first meeting of the first class a learning minute!"

For various stakeholders, these choices involve risks such as potential loss of enrollment, tougher and earlier requirements for planning, and more demanding conversations with late-arriving students who have expectations that they will be served as customers rather than learners. Our innovations related to Start Right are able first to be tried and measured, and later sustained and institutionalized, because of the broad commitment to the underlying idea. And when our results aren't as good as we might have hoped, we can return to the innovation and refine it or try something else with less resistance because the big idea continues to fuel our consensus on goals.

3. Connection and Direction

Valencia's model of student services, the way we engage students to be ready for learning, is based on this principle. We believe that students must make a real connection very early in their experience at the college with staff, with faculty, and with other students. Without this connection, commitment is weak and hard to sustain, often leading to attrition or half-hearted engagement. Many students find the college culture intimidating, strange, and overwhelming. Our students and many staff and faculty remind us that the students with whom we wish to close the achievement gap are also most likely to require relationships with persons they trust in the college in order to be ready to learn and willing to persist. Developing both face-to-face and virtual options for these connections to occur for all students is an ongoing focus in our work.

But students don't come to college just to make a connection. They are here for a purpose, sometimes barely understood even by the student. We believe students need a clear direction—a plan to graduate—as soon as possible in their college careers. Most community colleges have a planning tool for this; oddly, it is generally required in the

final semester and is called an Application for Graduation. A plan developed early in one's college experience can change, but to have no plan at all, a common experience for community college students, is far worse than having a plan that may need revision. So the college has built complex systems of student support around the importance of developing and following a plan as early as possible. Using a geographic metaphor and designing processes around a model of student development, we call these systems LifeMap. "Life's a trip. You'll need directions…" is a refrain throughout the college, including significant marketing efforts to existing students to become more engaged. The Connection and Direction idea has become shorthand for years of deep thought and discussion of the value we bring to students when student and academic services partner effectively. It serves as a touchstone in the active conversation about what is working or not working in the college, while also providing a framework for inquiry into the student experience of our offerings and environments.

4. The College Is How the Students Experience Us, Not How We Experience Them

This notion seems obvious, but the deep culture of nearly every college and university in the country tends toward marginalizing students, who after all are temporary members of the college community. Our basic unit of analysis in most of our conversations about the college is a group of students—a section, a class, a cohort, a demographic. None of these classifications speaks to the way students experience the college. They are persons, unique individuals, and they experience college in a powerfully personal way. This came home to us in a student focus group led by a renowned researcher on student persistence. When he asked five very different students who had succeeded against the odds at a community college what had made the difference for them, each gave essentially the same answer—a person's name. No one named the college's great technology, the programs of instruction, the learning resources, or the tutoring programs, where in fact they had met the persons they named. They all named people who had taken a strong interest in their learning and supported them in some way. We learned from seeing the college as the students experience it that our programs are merely vessels; the persons who work in them are the wine. This principle seems true for all students, but especially true for students of color, of alternate language, and of other conditions that may make the college seem a foreign and unwelcoming place. (See Connection and Direction, above.)

It is easy to plan for what is best for the college—what programs, what buildings, what staffing and salary structures, what partnerships will benefit the institution or one of its interest groups the most. But the more important question in all of these decisions and many others is, "What do we want our students to experience?"

For Valencia, this principle has powerfully shaped our program strategy, our scheduling of classes, our technology decisions, the way we deploy staff and faculty, our admissions and registration systems, our campus environmental planning, our building designs, our approaches to institutional research and analysis, and many other college systems. But it is the nature of this work that it is never really finished.

5. The Purpose of Assessment Is to Improve Learning

No college will significantly improve its results in student learning until it steps up meaningfully to the assessment challenge. The difficulty here is that most colleges in the U.S. have a mixed history with learning assessment. Beginning in the 1960s with Management by Objective models brought over from industry, to the institutional accountability models developed and deployed throughout the 1980s and 1990s, mostly to limited effect, assessment has been used to describe many things that are far removed from the actual learning process. And they were perceived, perhaps justly, as a means of addressing distrust of faculty or institutions. Therefore, it is no wonder many faculty are, at first, anxious over this conversation. This situation has been no less true or important to our work at Valencia than at any other college, and we may have further to go in this area than any other in our journey toward learning-centeredness. Rightly understood, establishing clear learning expectations and identifying the methods of assessment are essential steps to partnering with an adult learner. Only when equipped with this information can the learner effectively adjust his or her own conditions of learning for improved results. Therefore, the most important user of authentic assessment is the learner. And next to the learner, the most important user is the facilitator of learning, or professor. Everyone else—the department, institution, state office, the USDOE—is a footnote.

This is not to say that others in the college shouldn't be using assessment of learning for purposes such as creating better conditions or testing the effectiveness of various methods and innovations. But they need to be kept properly in the secondary role or they will inevitably undermine the most important work: to equip students and faculty with the information they need to make a difference in learning.

Because of these dangers, Valencia began its deep work in learning assessment with years of collegial development of assessment techniques directly with faculty. Long before initiatives like Achieving the Dream came along, hundreds of faculty had been exposed to the value and practical methods of assessment for the classroom—formal and informal, formative and summative. While the goal of creating a community of professional practice around norms of effective teaching and learning hasn't been fully realized at the college, our progress in this work has made the more difficult and intrusive conversation about assessment much easier and more productive.

Furthermore, when someone has a great idea about something else we should be asking our faculty, staff, or students to measure and report, we have a test that keeps us from wandering too far from best practice: How will this assessment improve learning? This frees faculty and academic leaders to collaborate on a common assessment agenda and defuse the traditional sources of anxiety that often surround placing a serious emphasis on assessment. It also gives a basis for making decisions to use such tools as the Community College Survey of Student Engagement and a reason and template for engaging a deeper and broader conversation about what the data may say and mean.

6. Collaboration

These ideas, and others, are deeply influential in our work because they have become a part of our culture, our way of thinking about and representing our work, a vocabulary for our discourse about the things that matter most to us in our work. They represent more than strategy, the way we choose to focus our efforts to get things done. These ideas help us decide what is worth doing and enable us to agree on purposes. When agreement on purposes, on ends, is strong, disagreements on means are less likely to become obstacles. In fact, dissent on means becomes vital in our work to get the results we all seek. And these ideas don't come from the top down or the bottom up. Because they are a part of culture, they emerge from an ongoing dialogue in the organization over the reality we are facing, what the data say and mean, what we believe, what might make a difference in our students' learning. This is collaboration. It is different from buy-in, which implies someone selling an idea. In fact, advocacy—the habit of selling one's ideas—actually hinders our work more often than not. Inquiry is the better habit. And to cultivate this habit in such a large organization, we have had to invent new technologies of collaboration. Committees alone certainly don't work. We use a variety of high-bandwidth meetings, online polling tools, processes for making meaning from data, redesigned governance structures, and, most of all, the habit of dialogue to reach conclusions, especially on big issues. Everyone has voice and if the group struggles to reach a clear conclusion, the dialogue continues. In this cauldron of work, our best ideas are formed and shared in a way that makes it impossible to identify whose idea it originally was. This is collaboration at Valencia, and all the other big ideas depend on this value, process, and commitment for their legitimacy.

These ideas
help us decide what is worth doing and enable us to agree on purposes.

Making a Difference

These are a few among a number of big ideas that have made and continue to make a difference in the efforts at Valencia to make dramatic and sustained progress in student learning. We should emphasize that these ideas have emerged from reading together, deep discourse, important stories, long reflection, iterative and inclusive planning, and, most importantly, deep collaboration within our organization. The ideas themselves may have some value, but their power to engage, change, sustain, redirect, unify, and encourage our work is rooted in the authenticity of their origins in our ongoing conversation. It is to this conversation and the big ideas they may yet produce that we commend our colleagues.

The Student Experience: First-Year Experience Program

— Sylvia Jenkins and Joann Wright

Jenkins, Sylvia, and Wright, Joann. (2008). "First-Year Experience Program." In R. T. Flynn and G. E. de los Santos, eds., *Student Services Dialogues: Community College Case Studies to Consider*. Phoenix: League for Innovation in the Community College.

Context

The learners who enter higher education through the doors of community colleges represent many levels of academic preparedness and a variety of interests, ages, career objectives, and circumstances. Students identify the college environment and learning engagement among challenges they face in college (Astin, 1993). For students to persist and succeed both academically and socially, there needs to be a level of integration to the extent that students share the attitudes and values of peers, faculty, and communities within the college (Tinto, 1993). Helping students achieve learning and success during their early college enrollment improves their chances for success all along the way. To address these issues and to help our students be successful, Moraine Valley Community College implemented a comprehensive first-year student support program we call the First-Year Experience (FYE).

Through self-exploration and group interaction, the course facilitates students' academic and social integration into the college environment and helps students build the skills necessary for success.

FYE is an excellent example of a collegewide collaborative effort that has improved and expanded the college's learning-centered environment. The program enhances the learning of students, faculty, and staff across the college community. Through their participation in FYE, students develop a better understanding of their responsibilities for learning and develop critical skills to become more self-directed learners. The program provides opportunities for students to develop collaborative, supportive learning relationships with other students and with instructors. Through FYE, faculty and staff have a special opportunity to learn about students and foster supportive relationships outside of their traditional disciplines of instruction or administrative roles.

Summary of the Case

The First-Year Experience was fully implemented for the first time in fall 2000. Development of the different components of FYE occurred over several years and included numerous faculty, administrators, and staff across campus. Components that had previously existed—placement testing and new student orientation—were revised and updated, and new components—an introduction to college and student success course called COL101 and a master academic plan—were added following several years of pilot testing and review. All components were designed to create a comprehensive, integrated experience for students.

The college created a new position of assistant dean, New Student Retention, to direct implementation of the program. The assistant dean is officially a member of the student development administration; however, she works closely with her peers in the division of academic affairs as she directs the coordination of all department, faculty, and staff involved in FYE.

Since its initial implementation, FYE has undergone continuous review and improvement. The mandatory training program for faculty has been expanded to include ongoing faculty forums as well as a mentoring program for new COL101 instructors to receive continuous support and guidance from more experienced instructors. A student needs assessment component has been piloted using the Noel-Levitz College Student Inventory to gain specific insights about the needs of first-time students. Beginning in fall 2004, all educational planning sessions taught by academic advisors are conducted in computer labs so students can take full advantage of the many online resources that have been built into the program.

FYE is designed to help students make a successful transition to the college environment and develop and strengthen skills and strategies required for college-level learning. FYE includes four intentional and intrusive support components: (1) placement testing and enrollment in appropriate entry-level courses including developmental education; (2) student orientation and registration; (3) the COL101 course; and (4) completion of an individualized master academic plan. All first-time, full-time students are required to participate in all four components to gain access to the college's registration system.

All applicants who indicate intention of attending the college full time receive communications from the office of New Student Retention about the college's placement requirements. Full-time students are required to complete assessment of reading, writing, and math skills. COMPASS computerized placement is offered on a walk-in basis throughout the year, with extended hours during registration periods. Students with acceptable ACT test scores or previous successful college credit may use them instead of COMPASS as official proficiency-level qualifiers. Students register for classes, including any needed developmental education classes, based on assessment and placement results.

Once students complete basic assessment, they are formally invited to attend a mandatory half-day small-group Student Orientation and Registration (SOAR) program. SOAR, facilitated by a team of counselors and academic advisors, focuses on preparing students for their first semester of college. The SOAR curriculum includes informational sessions and small-group discussions introducing the academic and social environments of higher education; review of placement test scores; educational planning processes; an introduction to the online SOAR website, including online registration tools; and individual assistance with course selection and registration. Students participating in SOAR complete an online inventory that assesses what they have learned through the SOAR process. As part of the inventory, students may review any of the SOAR topics about which they remain uncertain. Students are encouraged to return to the SOAR website for additional information regarding policies, procedures, and academic programs throughout their enrollment at the college.

The cornerstone of FYE is the one semester-hour student success and transition course, COL101, "College: Changes, Challenges, Choices." A campuswide task force involving faculty and administrators developed the COL101 curriculum and continues its involvement to ensure the ongoing success of the course. COL101 is designed to enhance student development and student learning and to improve student retention and academic success. The course has a maximum enrollment of 22 students in each section, focuses on issues that individuals face as new college students, and provides ongoing peer and instructor support during the critical first semester of college. Through self-exploration and group interaction, the course facilitates students' academic and social integration into the college environment and helps students build the skills necessary for success. Students assess their own learning styles and identify strategies to use their skills according to different types of teaching styles.

Collegewide Commitment and Collaboration. The COL101 course introduces college resources available to students throughout their enrollment. For example, college librarians teach one session in each section of COL101 in which they focus on information literacy and assist students in accessing and evaluating print and online resources. In addition, the counseling faculty members provide a comprehensive curriculum of workshops and seminars that expand on the topics introduced in the COL101 course. To enhance the diversity unit in the COL101 course, the staff in multicultural student affairs and the campuswide diversity committee sponsor multicultural awareness events and welcome new student participation each semester. COL101 not only helps students learn skills needed for success in college, but also helps them apply these skills in their lives beyond the college environment.

As part of the seamless integration within the curriculum of COL101, each student develops an individualized master academic plan. All students participate in an educational planning session taught by academic advisors to support the development of the plan. In these sessions, students learn about academic programs and matriculation resources available online and in print, and are provided assistance in determining educational requirements for their intended college major and career. Each student must submit a completed plan as part of the COL101 course. Students also learn about registration for the second semester as part of the COL101 experience.

Faculty and administrators across the college teach COL101. All instructors are required to have an earned master's degree, and prior to teaching the course for the

first time, each instructor must complete a five-hour training session led by the assistant dean, New Student Retention, with support from the counselors, librarian faculty, and other members of the COL101 task force. The training is offered several times each semester.

Questions to Consider

1. What elements of the FYE program are designed to help ensure student success?

2. In what ways does FYE integrate various areas and departments that might otherwise tend to exist in silos? How does this integration help secure collegewide support for and commitment to this program?

3. One of O'Banion's principles of the learning college states that employee roles are based on learner needs. How does FYE demonstrate this principle of a learning-centered college?

4. What evidence would support claims that the FYE program is effectively introducing students to the college and helping ensure student success at the college?

Thoughts and Analysis

During the first seven years of implementation, approximately 23,000 students participated in the First-Year Experience, and over 550 faculty and administrators have participated in the required instructor training session. To accommodate increasing student enrollment, the number of COL101 sections offered each semester has continued to grow. During fall 2007, 158 sections of the course were taught, with approximately 2,856 students enrolled.

COL101 completers also

earned higher cumulative grade point averages at the end of their first year than those who did not enroll and those who did not successful complete the course.

The Office of Institutional Research has conducted follow-up research on each cohort of new full-time students since fall 2000. The research consistently shows that students who successfully complete COL101 during their first semester perform better than their peers who do not enroll in COL101 or who enroll but do not successfully complete the course. Specifically, the research shows, at a statistically significant level, that COL101 completers earned higher first-semester grade point averages than those who did not enroll and those who did not successfully complete the course. COL101 completers also earned higher cumulative grade point averages at the end of their first year than those who did not enroll and those who did not successfully complete the course. Successful COL101 students completed a higher percentage of their first-semester credit hours and were also more likely to continue their enrollment to the second semester and second year.

Students complete evaluations of their experiences at the end of different components of the FYE program. Evaluations are collected at the end of the SOAR program and at the end of the COL101 course. The evaluations allow students to report their level of satisfaction with FYE and to indicate what they have learned along the way. During fall 2005, a pilot program in assessing specific learning outcomes of COL101 was implemented in all sections of the course. Through FYE, the college is able to continuously assess student needs and revise our programs to ensure their intended positive impact on student learning, student development, and student success.

Outcomes

The success of the First-Year Experience program on student academic achievement and retention has been acknowledged through receipt of several local and national awards, including the 2004 Teaching and Learning Excellence Award, Illinois Community College Board; the 2003 First Place Terry O'Banion Shared Journey Award,

National Council on Student Development and League for Innovation in the Community College; the 2003 Best Practice Award, National Council on Student Development; the 2003 Exemplary Program Award, National Association of Student Personnel Administrators; the 2003 Innovation of the Year Award, Moraine Valley Community College.

For more information about the First-Year Experience at Moraine Valley Community College, contact Joann Wright, Dean of Counseling and Advising, at wright@morainevalley.edu.

References

Astin, A. W. (1993). *What Matters in College: Four Critical Years Revisited.* San Francisco: Jossey-Bass.

Tinto, V. (1993). *Leaving College: Rethinking the Causes and Cures of Student Attrition* (2nd ed.). Chicago: The University of Chicago Press.

Part III.

Assessment and Evaluation in the Learning College

In 1999, a year before the Learning College Project and its dozen Vanguard Learning Colleges began building a network of learning-centered institutions, the League for Innovation, with support from The Pew Charitable Trusts, convened a group of college presidents for a conversation about establishing and assessing 21st century skills and to design a large-scale project to help community colleges struggling with this work. Part III of this volume begins with the report from the first two phases of that 21st century skills initiative. *Learning Outcomes for the 21st Century: Report of a Community College Study*, by Cynthia D. Wilson, Cindy L. Miles, Ronald L. Baker, and R. Laurence Schoenberger, includes findings from focus groups and results of a survey on the status of 21st century skills in U.S. and Canadian community colleges. It also includes, from Baker and Schoenberger, respectively, two approaches to the identification, implementation, and assessment of student learning outcomes (pages 131-147).

The third phase of this work was the League's two-year 21st Century Learning Outcomes Project, supported by a $1.4 million grant from The Pew Charitable Trusts. "Learning Outcomes for the 21st Century: Cultivating Student Success for College and the Knowledge Economy," by Cindy L. Miles and Cynthia Wilson, is a report on the progress colleges made toward defining student learning outcomes, developing and delivering curriculum focused on those outcomes, and assessing student achievement of the outcomes (pages 148-154). The 16 community and technical colleges engaged in this project were focused on the core work of the Learning College—learning outcomes and assessment—which all 28 colleges in the League's two learning-centered projects agreed was the most challenging aspect of the journey. In "Evaluating Individual Student Learning: Implications From Four Models of Assessment," Mary Hjelm and Ronald L. Baker, who served as facilitators in the

A few of the colleges had no qualms at all and went forward with the inventory; others, though, feared such a self-assessment would damage their efforts, if not derail them altogether.

League's 21st Century Learning Outcomes Project, present four approaches the 16 institutions involved in the project took in designing and implementing assessment at their colleges (pages 155-157).

The Learning College Project was also producing findings, and after its first year, project evaluator Kay McClenney reported on "a baker's dozen" of early themes in "Learning From the Learning Colleges: Observations Along the Journey" (pages 158-159). At the project's formal end, she also assembled a set of "promising practices" at the Vanguard Learning Colleges, which she records—making a strong case for evidence-based judgments in determining effectiveness—in "Benchmarking Best Practices in the Learning College" (pages 160-161).

In the Learning College Project, the League received additional funding to produce an institutional inventory of learning-centered practices based on an article Terry O'Banion had written for *Community College Journal*. The project staff—O'Banion, Cindy Miles, and Cynthia Wilson—designed the "Learning College Inventory" (pages 162-166) to be used, at the funding agent's request, to determine college status at the start of the project and again at the end of the project as a standard method for individual colleges to determine progress. The inventory was to be completed by all employees at each college; anonymity would be assured; the findings were to be used solely for each college's own self-assessment at the beginning and end of the project; and the findings would not be used for any kind of comparison or benchmarking among the colleges. For a project based on a concept that advocates assessment and evidence, this seemed to the project staff a reasonable plan, and the inventory was presented to the colleges at their first gathering. A few of the colleges had no qualms at all and went forward with the inventory; others, though, feared such a self-assessment would damage their efforts, if not derail them altogether. Their arguments were convincing, and other strategies for determining progress were used. Three years later, during the final evaluator site visits, all the colleges that had initial misgivings about administering the inventory reported that, if introduced at that point, it would be accepted as a useful tool in the institution's self-assessment repertoire. The great lesson from this experience was that one of the earliest steps, if not the first step, on the Learning College journey must be the college's cultural readiness for close, inclusive, deeply honest self-assessment; for the results of such self-assessment; and for the conversations and ensuing revisions of practice that legitimately follow meaningful self-assessment.

Ideas surrounding the Learning College were advanced by the movement among accrediting agencies toward quality enhancement and learning outcomes, with processes such as the Higher Learning Commission's AQIP and the Southern Association of Colleges and Schools' QEP. In "Accreditation and the Learning College: Parallel Purposes and Principles for Practice," Ronald L. Baker and Cynthia Wilson examine ways accreditation processes and the Learning College concept are aligned in promoting student learning, institutional effectiveness, and continuous improvement, and in endorsing the use of evidence when answering the how-do-we-know question (pages 167-168). John Tagg continues his exploration of how we know—and why we often don't know—in the final article in this section, "Double-Loop Learning in Higher Education" (pages 169-174).

Learning Outcomes for the 21ˢᵗ Century: Report of a Community College Study

— Cynthia D. Wilson, Cindy L. Miles,
Ronald L. Baker, R. Laurence Schoenberger

Wilson, C. D., Miles, C. L., Baker, R. L., and Schoenberger, R. L. (2000). *Learning Outcomes for the 21ˢᵗ Century: Report on a Community College Study*. Mission Viejo, CA: League for Innovation in the Community College.

Foreword

Every new generation of college leaders faces the same tough question: what is the common core of knowledge and skills that should be the hallmark of an educated person? For the first few hundred years in American higher education, the trivium and quadrivium—the seven liberal arts handed down from the Middle Ages—provided a clear answer. The answer became less clear as knowledge expanded in the 1800s and 1900s, and by 1950 the General Education Movement boldly suggested that "the common core of knowledge for the common man," as Earl McGrath referenced it, was the antithesis of the classical liberal arts core.

In the past fifty years, American education has been on a roller coaster in its continuing quest for a common core of knowledge and skills; each new decade reflects a different perspective and describes the core in a different language: general education core, basic skills, common core, critical life skills, and core competencies. This ever-changing perspective may be a reflection of the reality that we live in a rapidly changing world, and the most we can hope for is to keep up with the changes and try our best to define, teach, assess, and document the core du jour.

The authors of this report have done an excellent job capturing what community college leaders currently dub the common core. "21ˢᵗ Century Skills" resonates well across educational institutions, business and industry, foundations, and policy groups as a moniker for the common core of knowledge and skills required for college students beginning their careers at the start of this new century. Through a series of focus groups with key leaders and an international survey, conducted under the auspices of the League for Innovation in the Community College, these authors document the current status of 21ˢᵗ Century Skills, discover the preference for the language of "learning outcomes," and illustrate how two community colleges are trying to implement programs to help students acquire the skills. They also discover that the real challenge has not changed for hundreds of years: it is easier to talk and argue about what to call the common core and to teach it than it is to assess student acquisition of the skills and to document the acquisition in a useful and meaningful way. Their work, however, paves the way for substantive efforts planned by the League for Innovation that will address the difficult issues of assessment and documentation of 21ˢᵗ Century Skills.

Terry O'Banion
President Emeritus and Senior League Fellow
League for Innovation in the Community College

Learning Outcomes for the 21ˢᵗ Century: Report of a Community College Study

"We must design a new blueprint for education, a plan for the future that specifies what students need to know, when they need to learn it, and what we need to do to help them." **Edward M. Kennedy, 1994**

When Senator Kennedy called for a "new blueprint for education," he was promoting Goals 2000 legislation aimed at K-12 educational reform. Now that 2000 is upon us, his call seems to be echoing through the halls of community colleges across the U.S. and Canada. Community colleges are responding to the allegation against higher education made by legislators, policymakers, employers, and educators that we cannot readily demonstrate the specific learning achievements of our students. A consensus is emerging among these groups that the widespread reform efforts stimulated by publication of *A Nation at Risk* in 1983 have failed, and that this failure is largely because those efforts were centered on processes rather than outcomes.

Now, as the page turns on a new century, a number of community colleges have shifted their attention to outcomes, in particular the most important educational outcome—learning. They have committed to "placing learning first" in every policy, practice, and program in the institution and to employing or preparing personnel who can support that goal. Leaders in these pioneering institutions are providing impetus for a new reform movement focused on demonstrating and supporting student achievement by asking hard questions of all institutional decisions and actions: (1) Does this action (change in policy, practice, program, and personnel) improve and expand student learning? (2) How do we know this action improves and expands student learning?

> **Now, as the** page turns on a new century, a number of community colleges have shifted their attention to outcomes, in particular the most important educational outcome—learning.

The League for Innovation in the Community College (the League) has been leading the charge toward developing more learning-centered, outcomes-driven approaches in higher education. League President Emeritus Terry O'Banion has written more than a dozen books, monographs, and articles and has spoken extensively on the topic, and in 1997 the League adopted the Learning Initiative as one of its four central program areas under which all League research, publications, and programs are organized. In the same year, the League launched the Innovations conference to bring together educators from around the world who are interested in improving institutional and student learning. In 1998 the League began developing several large-scale projects to stimulate and support the work of two-year colleges in what has been variously called the Learning Revolution, the Outcomes Movement, and Learning-Centered Education. The study reported in this monograph is an early product of one of these projects aimed at helping community colleges better define and certify student learning.

This report traces the study through four stages: (1) an exploratory focus group involving presidents from ten U.S. community colleges recognized as leaders in the learning outcomes movement; (2) a follow-up focus group with representatives from 15 colleges, including two Canadian representatives, to achieve consensus on what constitutes 21st Century Skills; (3) a survey of the status of 21st Century learning outcomes practices in U.S. and Canadian community colleges; and (4) two institutional narratives describing model community college approaches to 21st Century student learning outcomes, one at Cascadia Community College (WA) and the other at Waukesha County Technical College (WI).

Defining the Project: An Exploratory Focus Group

On February 25-26, 1999, the League for Innovation, with support from The Pew Charitable Trusts, convened a focus group of presidents from ten community colleges identified as leading institutions in terms of their focus on learning and outcomes. The purpose of this meeting was twofold: (1) to begin a conversation on establishing competencies for and assessing outcomes of student learning in the community college, and (2) to create a framework for a national project to support community colleges in their efforts to better define and certify student learning. Institutions represented by their senior leaders in this exploratory meeting were Cascadia Community College (WA), Community College of Baltimore County (MD), Community College of Denver (CO), Cuyahoga Community College (OH), Johnson County Community College (KS), Lane Community College (OR), Midlands Technical College (SC), Richland College (TX), San Diego Community College (CA), and Sinclair Community College (OH). Joining the ten presidents in the meeting were representatives from The Pew Charitable Trusts (PA), the National Center for Higher Education Management Systems (CO), and Senior League Fellows K. Patricia Cross (CA) and Robert H. McCabe (FL). League staff members Terry O'Banion and Cindy L. Miles facilitated the meeting.

The consensus
of the group was that
the use of competencies or proficiencies would improve our present methods of documenting student learning.

Focus group participants discussed the growing pressures on community colleges to document that their students possess core competencies suited to the requirements of our current Knowledge Age and global economy. They agreed that traditional efforts to codify student learning through grades and credits alone are insufficient and that we need additional, more precise methods of illustrating and certifying student learning. The consensus of the group was that the use of competencies or proficiencies would improve our present methods of documenting student learning. During the meeting, Peter Ewell and Karen Paulson from the National Center for Higher Education Management Systems (NCHEMS) shared a white paper they prepared for this project, "21st Century Skills for Community College Education: The Critical Role of Competencies," in which they argue that "America's community colleges have a rare opportunity to take the lead in developing innovative approaches to meet the skills challenges of the new millennium." Ewell and Paulson explained the paper's premise that preparing students with the 21st Century Skills that "encompass levels of literacy, numeracy, and technical knowledge far above that possessed by the nation's current workforce and citizenry" will require collective cross-disciplinary approaches that call for "remaking the basic building blocks of community college programs around assessed competencies rather than traditional coursework."

In the NCHEMS paper, Paulson and Ewell argue that "community colleges are more experienced with the use of competencies than their four-year counterparts, often embracing them widely within particular vocational programs." However, they also note that "this use of competencies has not generally affected a college's more 'academic' offerings," and call for embedding competency-based concepts more fully into "every aspect of a community college's approach to learning." Paulson and Ewell recommend a comprehensive competency-based approach that fosters a common "language of proficiency" and offers benefits to both individual students and institutions. Students would benefit, the authors maintain, by being able to clearly show their achievement of specific levels of essential knowledge and skills in terms of transfer to other institutions, documentation for employment, recognition of prior achievement, and certification of lifelong learning. Institutions would benefit from greater internal alignment across programs, departments, and classrooms and from enhanced ability to meet external accountability pressures and to improve programs and services.

The presidents participating in the focus group responded with interest to the NCHEMS paper. Each described his or her college's efforts to use competencies or proficiencies to certify student learning, and most agreed that their institutions are at early stages in implementing full-scale programs to identify and certify student learning competencies. The great majority of these leading colleges are currently using competencies for the purposes of program review and institutional effectiveness, but most admitted they have far to go in the use of competency-based processes and programs to certify learning outcomes for all students.

The authors of the NCHEMS paper acknowledge that a competency-based approach to higher education is not without pitfalls, and focus group participants reinforced this perspective. The presidents articulated a number of challenges: defining, measuring, and codifying skills and knowledge for common acceptance and application; articulating learning outcomes across institutions and sectors of education; identifying and dealing with the effects of competency-based approaches on faculty roles; breaking down and accurately assessing complex skills and abilities; and finding the resources to support efforts to develop a more outcomes-based curriculum or become a more outcomes-based institution. Most agreed that the first hurdle to overcome would be achieving consensus about the skills, knowledge, and abilities that students, employers, and other institutions demand and recognize as important.

Focusing on 21st Century Skills

After much discussion and review of current efforts in the ten community colleges represented in the focus group, participants agreed that a national project centered on identifying competencies and assessment strategies for "21st Century Skills" would be the most effective avenue for leveraging the greatest amount of change regarding the certification of student learning in community colleges. They agreed that in the community college, 21st Century Skills incorporate the "hard" skills of literacy, numeracy, and information technology literacy, as well as the "soft" skills of teamwork, communication, problem solving, and the ability to work with diverse groups, and that success in the workforce or in further education depends on acquisition of these skills. The group reviewed the *New Basic Skills*—six core skills for secondary education identified by Murnane and Levy (1996)—that are a combination of these hard and soft skills. Focus group participants agreed that a version of these new basic skills appropriate for community colleges could help repair the skills of underprepared high school students, update the skills of returning workers, and certify the skills of graduates for entry into the workforce or transfer to further education.

The presidents agreed that the value of focusing on 21st Century Skills for a large-scale demonstration project is in the interdisciplinary impact of this approach: these skills cut across existing programs and involve faculty members from developmental education, workforce training, and academic transfer programs. They also noted that another powerful outcome of developing full-scale competency-based curriculum models would be helping to remove the stigma attached to remediation, since in a competency-based environment all students are involved in learning to fill their gaps in essential skill areas.

Although participants debated whether such a project should focus on a subset or take on the full range of 21st Century Skills, they agreed that the process should involve a team of faculty members across institutions to identify the skills and to benchmark levels of proficiency for each skill. Most agreed that academic leadership would be needed for any project and that such a project should be focused on instructional development. Focus group members also expressed great interest in the idea of documenting student learning of core skills in an electronic transcript or portfolio that would be useful to employers, other colleges, and to the students themselves. One president described his vision of such a "smart card," a technology-based transcript that would contain a student's assessment scores, competency levels, course credits, and grades, as well as nontraditional examples of achievement such as video clips, photos, or electronic documents of student projects or presentations to demonstrate learning beyond that measured by traditional tests. Most participants also saw value in establishing a project website to share project progress and other exemplary activities that would assist the greatest number of community colleges in creating competency-based programs. Several participants noted the importance of anchoring the project with the League because of its reputation in the community college world. Clearly, by the close of the meeting, participants were highly motivated by the ideas exchanged, and they all indicated interest in being involved in any further project developments.

The 21st Century Skills Project

Following the February 1999 meeting, the League developed a two-stage project designed with an overall goal to *increase the capacity of community colleges to define and certify the acquisition of 21st Century Skills for their students*. Stage One of this project, supported by The Pew Charitable Trusts, was a planning project with two research objectives, the findings of which are reported in the next two sections of this monograph:

1. Achieve consensus among leading colleges regarding what constitutes 21st Century Skills.

2. Determine the current status of activity regarding efforts of community colleges to define and certify competencies related to student learning.

Achieving Consensus on 21st Century Skills

The first step in defining a large-scale project to support community college efforts in certifying student learning was to better define the terminology surrounding our objectives. Findings from the initial focus group and a review of the literature of learning outcomes and competency-based education revealed a need for consensus about what constitutes "21st Century Skills" for community college students. Although the presidents participating in the exploratory focus group unanimously agreed that 21st Century Skills should be the program priority for this project, the colleges refer to these skill sets by names idiosyncratic to the culture of their respective institutions: *core competencies, learning outcomes, generic skills,* and *critical life skills,* for example. Agreement among these leading institutions on a common frame of reference for what constitutes 21st Century Skills was an important beginning for this project.

Expanding interest in the project led the League to invite representatives from 15 community colleges—the ten whose presidents participated in the February 1999 meeting and five others whose presidents expressed high interest in the project—to help accomplish the first project objective of achieving consensus on a definition of 21st Century Skills: Cascadia Community College (WA), Central Piedmont Community College (NC), Community College of Baltimore County (MD), Community College of Denver (CO), Cuyahoga Community College (OH), Humber College of Applied Arts and Technology (ON), Johnson County Community College (KS), Kirkwood Community College (IA), Lane Community College (OR), Midlands Technical College (SC), Richland College (TX), San Diego Community College (CA), Sinclair Community College (OH), Sir Sanford Fleming

College of Applied Arts and Technology (ON), and Waukesha County Technical College (WI).

To determine, prior to the convening of the group, a preliminary set of terms used among the colleges to describe 21ˢᵗ Century Skills, League researchers reviewed institutional documents outlining the colleges' definitions of key student learning outcomes or skills. Document analysis indicated that colleges were in various stages of definition, some having clearly delineated collegewide skills, with subsets, levels of achievement, and outcomes, while others were in the early stages of defining these skills. Although the colleges varied in the titles they gave to skill categories, the researchers identified similarities in skill sets. For example, all of the eleven colleges that provided documents included *communication*—written, oral, or both—as a critical skill category, and ten colleges had a category of *thinking skills*. *Teamwork* and *personal skills* were identified in more than half of the colleges. Other commonly identified skill categories were *technology, math, diversity, learning, arts, science, resource management, creativity,* and *SCANS*. The participating community colleges' skill sets were presented on a matrix to provide a starting point for the focus group's consensus building process.

On November 6-7, 1999, representatives from the 15 colleges met in Santa Ana (CA) to participate in the focus group. The group's objectives were (1) to develop a consensus on the 21ˢᵗ Century Skills to be addressed in the large-scale community college project and (2) to brainstorm the project framework. Eight of the 15 participants were the academic leaders for their institutions, two were college or campus presidents, and the remaining five were key leaders responsible for programs related to defining and assessing learning competencies at these colleges.

Focus group participants reviewed the matrix of comparative typologies of core student competencies or skills and shared their institutional experiences in developing and implementing processes to define and assess student learning in terms of these skills. Participants discussed challenges to developing a common set of skills in terms of institutional differences and bridging the gap between academic and technical or workforce terminology.

Although the colleges differed slightly from each other regarding identification and definition of 21ˢᵗ Century Skills, sufficient consensus was achieved to identify and loosely define a set of eight categories of core skills:

1. Communication skills (reading, writing, speaking, listening)

2. Computation skills (understanding and applying mathematical concepts and reasoning, analyzing and using numerical data)

3. Community skills (citizenship; diversity/pluralism; local, community, global, and environmental awareness)

4. Critical thinking and problem solving skills (analysis, synthesis, evaluation, decision making, creative thinking)

5. Information management skills (collecting, analyzing, and organizing information from a variety of sources)

6. Interpersonal skills (teamwork, relationship management, conflict resolution, workplace skills)

7. Personal skills (ability to understand and manage self, management of change, learning to learn, personal responsibility, aesthetic responsiveness, wellness)

8. Technology skills (computer literacy, Internet skills, retrieving and managing information via technology)

Participants pointed out that these skills are anchored in a set of four fundamental assumptions:

1. These skills are important for every adult to function successfully in society today.

2. Community colleges are well equipped and well positioned to prepare students with these skills.

3. These skills are equally valid for all students, whether they transfer to a four-year college or university or pursue a career path after leaving the community college.

4. These skills may be attained anywhere; many students will enter the community college having already achieved some or all of these skills, and community colleges must work to document and credential such prior learning.

Further discussion among focus group participants revealed general agreement regarding the trend among students toward a desire for marketable skills over general education. As one participant described it, "our students no longer want 'just-in-case' education, they want 'just-in-time' skills." Focus group members also underscored the potential implications that adopting a 21ˢᵗ Century Skills approach to student learning has on shifting the role of community colleges from delivery of learning to credentialing, assessing prior learning, and offering multiple learning options for students to attain their desired skills.

To better understand the selected colleges' efforts to establish competency-based programs for 21ˢᵗ Century Skills, League staff members made site visits to five institutions: Central Piedmont Community College, Community College of Denver, Midlands Technical College, Richland College, and Waukesha County Technical College. These visits validated the keen interest expressed by focus group representatives from these colleges in defining, developing, delivering, and documenting 21ˢᵗ Century Skills for their students. Researchers also discovered several common challenges that colleges face in pursuing these objectives, particularly in terms of insufficient resources and models for putting these ideas into practice. College staff involved in these efforts repeatedly underscored several needs they encounter in trying to institutionalize a student learning outcomes approach: the need for time to design and develop new policies and practices; the need for established models, particularly for assessing and documenting skills; and the need for appropriate training for faculty and staff. The site visits reinforced findings from the focus groups that suggest most community colleges are in the early stages of their journeys. Nevertheless, from these visits, document analysis, and focus groups, a set of 21st Century Skills and the challenges of implementing them on an institutional level began to emerge. The next step was to get a wide view of how community colleges in general are using competency-based models to support student learning.

Survey of the Status of 21st Century Student Learning Outcomes

Our second research objective was to determine the current status of activity regarding efforts of community colleges to define and certify competencies related to student learning. The projects of the League's Learning Initiative have made clear that hundreds of community colleges are committed to becoming more learning-centered institutions. In a July 1997 League study of the 523 presidents of the League's Alliance for Community College Innovation (Alliance) member colleges, 97% of the 324 respondents (a response rate of 62%) indicated their institutions will move toward becoming more learning centered in the next three to five years. In addition, 98% responded that the options for learning in terms of time, place, and methods offered by their colleges would increase. However, the extent to which the nation's community colleges are using competency-based models to achieve these broad goals was not known.

Using data gathered through a review of literature, document analysis, focus groups, site visits, and key consultants, a draft survey was developed. The draft was field tested in the 15 colleges and with the project consultants, and revisions were made. In November 1999, the survey was mailed to the chief academic officers of the 677 U.S. and Canadian Alliance member colleges. Respondents were given the options of submitting replies by mail or fax, or completing an online version of the survey. The online survey form was produced and hosted by League corporate partner E-Curriculum, a company pioneering evaluation and research for online learning (www.e-curriculum.com). Results from all forms were integrated into the online version, after which E-Curriculum calculated the results and presented them in graphic form.

The purpose of the survey was to conduct a baseline assessment of the extent of the efforts of U.S. and Canadian community colleges to establish and assess student achievement of 21st Century Skills. The survey incorporated items to determine community college interest in and level of implementation of 21st Century Skills initiatives. It was also designed to ascertain the terminology most often used to describe 21st Century Skills, the barriers to implementing 21st Century Skills initiatives, the resources needed for implementing such initiatives, and exemplary models of implementation. The descriptor 21st Century Skills was defined on the survey instrument:

> 21st Century Skills (often referred to as core skills, general education core, critical life skills, core competencies, basic skills, etc.) usually include 4 to 6 key areas deemed essential for student

success in the Knowledge Age that characterizes the new global economy. Throughout the survey, the language used to refer to these skills is "21st Century Skills."

The 677 U.S. and Canadian member colleges of the League's Alliance for Community College Innovation represent a wide cross section of North American community colleges, and we consider this representative of community colleges across the U.S. and Canada. With 259 responses—a response rate of 38%—the results of this survey provide a status report useful in defining the next steps of a continuing project that can benefit community colleges throughout the U.S. and Canada.

Survey Results. Generally, the results of the survey validated study findings from document analysis, focus groups, site visits, and review of the literature. Results of the eight survey items and brief discussion of these results in the context of other study findings follow.

More than 90% of the respondents indicated that their colleges are addressing the issue of 21st Century Skills.

1. Is your college currently addressing the issue of 21st Century Skills?

	NUMBER	PERCENT
Yes	238	92%
No	21	8%
Total	259	–

The high level of community college engagement in efforts to address this issue is consistent with the widespread interest among study participants in preparing students for the 21st Century.

2. Check one item in the following list that your faculty and staff use most often when referring to 21st Century Skills:

21st Century Skills	NUMBER	PERCENT
Basic Skills	8	3%
Core Competencies	21	9%
Core Skills	62	26%
General Education Core	10	4%
Generic Skills	81	34%
Life or Critical Life Skills	8	3%
Work Skills	8	3%
Other	14	6%
TOTAL	30	12%
	242	–

Early in the study, we observed that a great variety of terms were used to refer to what we were calling 21st Century Skills, and that few colleges we encountered were using this term. The survey results support this observation. Among respondents, the most commonly selected terms used for the key set of learning outcomes needed by students were *general education core* (34%) and *core competencies* (26%). Of the six other terms, none were reported in use by more than 9% of the colleges represented in this study.

We found that the term we used for this study, *21st Century Skills*, was used by only 3% of the respondents. Nine percent of the colleges indicated that they use the term *basic skills*, 6% use *work skills*, 4% use *core skills*, 3% use *life or critical life skills*, and 3% use *generic skills*. Approximately 12% of the respondents said they use terms other than those offered in the survey, and many of the 13 alternate terms were slight variations of the eight options on the survey. For example, *core abilities* and *general education and workplace competencies* were listed and are similar to *general education core* and *core competencies*. The only term that departed from the list was SCANS, reported by five colleges.

3. If your college has agreed on a set of 21st Century Skills, check all of the following skill areas that are included:

	NUMBER	PERCENT
Collaboration/teamwork	155	67%
Communication (written/oral)	209	91%
Creativity	98	43%
Critical thinking/problem solving	203	88%
Cultural/global studies/diversity	135	59%
Humanities	116	50%
Information management	159	69%
Learning skills	114	50%
Mathematics	181	79%
Personal responsibility/management	109	47%
Technology literacy	199	86%
TOTAL NUMBER OF COLLEGES RESPONDING	230	–

The 21st Century Skills listed in this survey item were derived from focus groups, site visits, and document analysis of curriculum material from the fifteen institutions that participated in the early phase of the study. All but two of the eleven skills were identified by at least 50% of the respondents; the two remaining skills were identified by over 40%.

Of the 230 institutions indicating that they have agreed on a set of 21st Century Skills, almost half include all eleven items listed on the survey. Most colleges represented in this study include *communication (written/oral)* (91%), *critical thinking/problem solving* (88%), *technology literacy* (86%), and *mathematics* (79%) in the set of 21st Century Skills. Many institutions also include *information management* (69%), *collaboration/team work* (67%), *culture/global studies/diversity* (59%), *humanities* (50%), *learning skills* (50%), *personal responsibility/management* (47%), and *creativity* (43%).

Approximately 10% of the respondents answered the open-ended prompt for "other" skill areas used at their colleges. As with the previous question, many of these are semantic variations of the categories listed in the survey; however, six additional areas were noted by at least three respondents: ethics (7), natural sciences (7), social responsibility/citizenship (5), aesthetics (4), workplace readiness (4), and health and wellness (3).

4. Indicate the level of implementation your college has achieved for each of the following items:

1=None 2=Discussion 3=Planning 4=Partial Implementation 5=Full Implementation

	1	2	3	4	5
A. We have agreed on a definition of 21st Century Skills.	12 / 5%	37 / 16%	39 / 16%	72 / 30%	79 / 33%
B. We have integrated 21st Century Skills into our curriculum.	6 / 2%	28 / 12%	30 / 13%	135 / 56%	41 / 17%
C. Faculty Teach 21st Century Skills in their courses.	6 / 2%	18 / 8%	24 / 10%	157 / 65%	35 / 15%
D. We have agreed on how to assess student achievement of 21st Century Skills.	13 / 6%	53 / 22%	69 / 29%	87 / 37%	14 / 6%
E. Faculty routinely assess student achievement of 21st Century Skills in their courses.	14 / 6%	40 / 17%	54 / 22%	118 / 50%	12 / 5%
F. We document student achievement of 21st Century Skills in ways other than grades and course credit.	40 / 17%	58 / 24%	47 / 20%	80 / 34%	13 / 5%

This survey item explores the progress institutions are making toward defining and certifying acquisition of 21st Century Skills. Chief academic officers indicated the level of implementation of their colleges in terms of defining, integrating, teaching, assessing, and documenting student achievement of these skills.

A. Definition. Only one-third of the colleges responding indicated that they have achieved full agreement on a definition of 21st Century Skills. Another 30% reported that they have achieved partial agreement on a definition. The remaining 37% of the colleges represented in this study noted that they are either in the discussion or planning stages or have no activities under way in defining 21st Century Skills.

B. Integration. Among respondents, 73% report that they are either partially or fully integrating 21st Century Skills into the curriculum. About a fourth of the respondents indicate they are in the discussion or planning stages of implementation. We note with interest that more colleges indicated they are integrating skills into the curriculum than reported having agreed on definitions of those skills. Findings from site visits and focus groups suggest that this discrepancy may be a result of colleges recognizing the importance of integrating 21st Century Skills into the curriculum and beginning work toward this implementation while not having complete systems in place for that integration. Half as many institutions indicate they have reached full integration (17%) as have reached full agreement on definition (33%) of 21st Century Skills.

C. Instruction. Eighty percent of colleges in the study reported that their faculty are teaching 21st Century Skills in at least some of their courses. About 18% said they are in the discussion and planning stages for instruction. Again, more colleges indicated that faculty are teaching the skills than reported having defined or integrated the skills into the curriculum.

D. Assessment Methods. Of the respondents, 43% noted that they have either partially or fully agreed on methods of assessing student achievement of 21st Century Skills. More than half of the colleges in the survey reported they have not moved beyond the discussion and planning stages of determining methods of assessment.

E. Assessment. More than half (55%) of colleges in the study indicated that faculty routinely assess student achievement of 21st Century Skills in their courses. Almost 40% reported that they are in the discussion and planning stages of faculty assessment of student achievement of these skills, and approximately 6% indicated that faculty do not routinely assess student achievement of these skills in their courses.

More colleges reported activity in assessment of student achievement of 21st Century Skills (55%) than reported having developed standard practices for this assessment (43%). This mirrors the relationship between agreement on definition of 21st Century Skills and the integration of these skills into the curriculum. In both sets of responses, the findings indicate that although colleges are actively engaged in student achievement of 21st Century Skills, many do not have formal institutional processes in place for curriculum development, instruction, and assessment of 21st Century Skills.

F. Documentation. Only about 5% of colleges reported having fully implemented documentation processes for student achievement of 21st Century Skills in ways other than grades and course credit. Another 34% indicated partial implementation of nontraditional documentation processes. Approximately 44% of respondents said they are in the discussion and planning stages, while 17% indicated they are not addressing documentation other than through grades and course credit.

Documenting student achievement of 21st Century Skills in ways other than grades and course credit can provide clear evidence of student learning, and findings from focus groups, site visits, and document analysis underscore the increasing importance of certifying student learning outcomes. Despite this emphasis, survey results reveal that college activity in documenting student achievement of 21st Century Skills is substantially lower than it is in defining, integrating, teaching, and assessing these skills.

5. Check the term in the following list that your faculty and staff use most often when they talk about assessing 21st Century Skills. Check only one.

	NUMBER	PERCENT
Abilities	7	3%
Competencies	92	37%
Grades	8	3%
Knowledge	5	2%
Performance standards	11	5%
Learning outcomes	93	38%
Proficiencies	7	3%
Skills	13	5%
Other	10	4%
TOTAL	246	–

We thought this item important because preliminary exploration of college activities with 21st Century Skills revealed differences in the use of language surrounding assessment. We created this item to discover the assessment terminology that is most widely used among U.S. and Canadian community colleges.

The chief academic officers of the colleges responding to the study reported that *learning outcomes* (38%) and *competencies* (37%) are the terms most often used by faculty and staff in discussing assessment of 21st Century Skills. The other assessment terms—*skills* (5%), *performance standards* (5%), *grades* (3%), *abilities* (3%), *proficiencies* (3%), and *knowledge* (2%)—listed on the survey are used by fewer than 6% of the colleges in the study. Those who selected *other* (4%) either listed variations of the term *outcomes* or indicated that no single assessment expression was used at their institutions.

6. Rate the following barriers to integrating the use of 21st Century Skills in your institution.

1=Not a Barrier 2=Minor Barrier 3=Major Barrier

	1	2	3
Lack of agreement on language and definitions for 21st Century Skills	100 40%	134 53%	17 7%
Lack of agreement on how to assess 21st Century Skills	33 13%	144 57%	75 30%
Lack of leadership from college administration	193 77%	52 20%	7 3%
Inadequate funds to support needed activities	85 33%	123 49%	45 18%
Inadequate time for needed activities	31 12%	118 47%	104 41%
Lack of useful models for successful integration of 21st Century Skills	73 29%	122 48%	57 23%
Lack of useful assessment tools for 21st Century Skills	47 19%	119 47%	86 34%
Articulating 21st Century Skills with K-12 systems	54 22%	116 48%	74 30%
Articulating 21st Century Skills with other community colleges	120 48%	108 44%	19 8%
Articulating 21st Century Skills with 4-year colleges and universities	59 24%	116 47%	73 29%
Articulating 21st Century Skills with employers	119 48%	113 45%	17 7%
Integrating the use and assessment of 21st Century Skills into liberal arts/transfer programs	74 30%	118 48%	53 22%
Limitations imposed by state agencies or legislators	137 55%	79 32%	31 13%

Of the 13 barriers listed on the survey, all but two were identified as major or minor barriers by more than half of the respondents. Respondents indicated that the greatest barriers to integrating 21st Century Skills in their institutions are *inadequate time for needed activities* (88%), *lack of agreement on how to assess 21st Century Skills* (87%), *lack of useful assessment tools* (81%), *articulating with K-12 systems* (78%), *articulating with 4-year colleges and universities* (76%), *lack of useful models for successful integration of 21st Century Skills* (71%), and *integrating the use and assessment of 21st Century Skills into liberal arts/transfer programs* (70%). Over half of the respondents also identified as major or minor barriers *inadequate funds to support needed activities* (67%), *lack of agreement on language and definitions* (60%), *articulating 21st Century Skills with employers* (52%), and *articulating 21st Century Skills with other community colleges* (52%). The least frequently noted barriers are *limitations imposed by state agencies or state legislators* (45%) and *lack of leadership from college administration* (23%).

The most frequently cited barriers—lack of time, lack of agreement on assessment, and lack of useful assessment tools—may help explain why many institutions are in early stages of 21st Century Skills activity. Although leadership from college administration was found to be the least frequently identified barrier to integrating 21st Century Skills in the institution, this survey was completed by college administrators and thus may reflect bias from that perspective.

7. To what extent does your college assess competencies in the following program areas:

1=None 2=Low 3=Moderate 4=Considerable 5=Complete

	1	2	3	4	5
Occupational/technical programs	1 <1%	14 5%	37 15%	139 55%	63 25%
Liberal arts/transfer programs	8 4%	59 24%	101 41%	59 24%	18 7%
Workforce training programs	5 2%	21 8%	50 20%	115 46%	59 24%
Remedial/developmental programs	2 1%	22 9%	67 26%	112 44%	51 20%

The survey findings verify that colleges most often assess competencies in their occupational/technical programs. Workforce training programs and remedial/developmental programs were also noted to have a high incidence of competency assessment. Less than a third of the respondents indicated that competencies are assessed to a considerable or complete extent in liberal arts/transfer programs. These findings validate our observations and experience as well as reports from focus group participants that outcomes assessment is more frequently associated with vocational than with academic programs.

The survey also included a final, optional item requesting that respondents identify exemplary college models of implementation of 21st Century Skills. More than 50 recommendations were submitted. Two of the community colleges cited—Cascadia Community College and Waukesha County Technical College—were asked to submit

institutional narratives to provide the study with a closer look at 21st Century Skills development at the college level. These colleges were selected in part because they provide contrasting approaches to 21st Century Learning Outcomes.

Waukesha County Technical College has been involved in outcomes-based education since the early 1980s, when a grassroots movement began among a few student services faculty; during the past two decades, that movement has grown to encompass the entire college. Cascadia, a new community college, started its institutional life by designing a complete curriculum through a holistic outcomes-based process. Both colleges were also identified as leaders in outcomes-based education, and representatives from these institutions participated in the focus groups for this study.

21st Century Learning Outcomes: An Integration of Context and Content
Ronald L. Baker

Preparing for its opening in the fall of 2000, Cascadia Community College is designed to create a culturally rich learning environment that employs best practices for teaching and learning, diverse pedagogies, and delivery methods designed to foster achievement of 21st Century learning outcomes. Cascadia, Washington's 33rd community college, will be co-located with the University of Washington-Bothell on a 125-acre campus that is currently under construction.

Because limited resources made impossible the hiring of a full complement of faculty to develop the curriculum, Cascadia employed creative and effective planning and development strategies to meet the required outcome of a comprehensive curriculum ready for delivery when the college opens. Key among these strategies was the selection of a Curriculum and Learning Design Team (CLDT) of individuals with faculty credentials and practical classroom teaching experience to research current trends and best practices. The results of this team's research form the foundation for Cascadia's curriculum.

Four faculty were selected for the CLDT: Sharon Buck, developmental mathematics and college success strategies; Pam Dusenberry, developmental English and college success strategies; Tris Samberg, chemistry and service learning; and Charles Sasaki, history and diversity education. Later, Peggy Moe was hired to direct the development of Cascadia's professional-technical programs. Individually, the team members contribute expertise and perspective for key elements of the curriculum. Collectively, they craft and design the culture and framework for the curriculum as a whole. In employing this team strategy, Cascadia faced an unusual paradox: creating a complete curriculum prior to the arrival of the college's teaching faculty while involving the same faculty in the Learning Outcomes for the 21st Century development of that curriculum. Cascadia met this challenge by creating a multilevel framework of learning outcomes that allows individual judgment and creativity in the implementation of strategies to foster and assess those outcomes. This principle is reflected in the development of Cascadia's 21st Century learning outcomes.

Guiding Principles and Processes

Each institution launching an initiative to become more learning centered should develop principles that represent the core values and commitments basic to that institution. Terry O'Banion, 1999

Many colleges are transforming their curricula from a teaching-centric model to a learning-centric model. Most commonly this transformation occurs course by course. As a new college, Cascadia has the rare advantage of creating its outcomes-based curriculum holistically rather than piecemeal. The college also has the opportunity to build on the learning theory research and outcomes development work of numerous educators. By designing the curricular outcomes first, the college is able to develop individual courses that fit with and contribute to the overall objectives of the curriculum. A critical first step for Cascadia was determining the strategic directions and learning outcomes that characterize the college's culture and manifest its mission. Lacking an institutional history and without a full complement of faculty and staff to guide the process, the college developed strategic directions and overarching learning outcomes by designing and implementing an outcomes-based planning process.

Curriculum Planning Process

Adapted from the work of Ruth Stiehl (Stiehl and Lewchuk, 2000), Cascadia's curriculum planning process created an operational framework for the development of programs and courses. Beginning with the creation of a common glossary of terms to aid in communication, curriculum planning proceeded through the following interdependent stages of implementation:

- Evaluate the context for learning.

- Define the intended learning outcomes.

- Design assessment methods and measures.

- Define content of courses, programs, and degrees.

- Identify best practices for delivery and support.

- Re-evaluate the context and refine the process.

To evaluate the context for learning, the CLDT turned to Cascadia's core values. Although a sense of those values existed informally, clarity and consensus on core values were essential if they were to form the foundation for the college curriculum, programs, and services. Following a series of discussions, consensus was reached on six *institutional core values*:

- **Diversity.** Diversity and affirmation of cultural differences are hallmarks of a true learning community. Pluralism, diversity, and equity are therefore at the core of Cascadia's mission. Individual difference is affirmed and celebrated in our community of learning.

- **Access.** Cascadia serves learners with a broad range of knowledge, skills, and experiences through open access to programs and services. We nurture new and expansive patterns of thinking, encourage

respect for self and others, and provide a safe, healthy, and barrier-free learning environment.

- **Success.** Student achievement is a hallmark of our mission and Cascadia places high value on the academic and personal success of all students. The Cascadia Learning Model approaches the learner holistically and integrates personalized support services into the academic experience to foster student success.

- **Learning.** Educational excellence characterizes our mission. We believe that learning is transformative and personal and that all members of the community are learners. We strive to make learning relevant and connected by tailoring programs and services to needs and goals. Supporting our principle that learning is integrated and interconnected, interdisciplinary connectivity, technological fluency, and Learning Outcomes for the 21st Century global understanding are embedded throughout the curriculum. We further support this principle by linking programs and services with the community, area enterprise, and other educational institutions.

- **Innovation.** As a learning organization, Cascadia values creative pathways to fulfill its vision and mission by constantly encouraging collaborative learning and growth. We continually expand our capacity to create high standards of performance through the acquisition of new knowledge and our commitment for constant responsiveness to the needs of our community of learners.

- **Environmental Stewardship.** We value the conservation of natural resources and embrace environmental sustainable practices. Cascadia is honored to protect and preserve the restored campus wetlands and to develop their intellectual, academic, and social value for the region and the nation.

Overarching Learning Outcomes

The curriculum design team researched current trends and practices and worked with community groups, students, and educators from other institutions to identify degree, program, and course learning outcomes. Affinity processes were used to gather and synthesize ideas generated by members of the various groups. The results of these activities were analyzed, refined, and triangulated both internally and externally for reliability and validity. Following in-depth review and analysis, four overarching collegewide learning outcomes were developed as goals for all members of the college community. These four collegewide learning outcomes, in turn, form the foundation for Cascadia's curriculum:

Learn Actively. Learning is a personal, interactive process that results in greater expertise and a more comprehensive understanding of the world.

- Develop expertise, broaden perspectives, and deepen understanding of the world by seeking information and engaging in meaningful practice.

- Construct meaning from expanding and conflicting information.

- Engage people in learning, both individually and with others, through reading, listening, observing, and doing.

- Take responsibility for learning.

Think Critically, Creatively, and Reflectively. Reason and imagination are fundamental to problem solving and critical examination of ideas.

- Create, integrate, and evaluate ideas across a range of contexts, cultures, and areas of knowledge.

- Recognize and solve problems using creativity, analysis, and intuition.

- Examine one's attitudes, values, and assumptions and consider their consequences.

Communicate With Clarity and Originality. The ability to exchange ideas and information is essential to personal growth, productive work, and societal vitality.

- Organize and articulate ideas for a range of audiences and purposes.

- Use written, spoken, and symbolic forms to convey concepts creatively.

- Use technology to gather, process, and communicate information.

Interact in Diverse and Complex Environments. Successful negotiation through our increasingly complex, interdependent, and global society requires knowledge and awareness of self and others, as well as enhanced interaction skills.

- Build interpersonal skills through knowledge of diverse ideas, values, and perspectives.

- Collaborate with others in complicated, dynamic, and ambiguous situations.

- Practice civility, empathy, honesty, and responsibility.

Transfer Degree Distribution Area Learning Outcomes

Washington community colleges have a direct block transfer agreement with four-year colleges and universities within the state. The oversight body for that agreement is the Inter-College Relations Commission (ICRC). The ICRC agreement establishes guidelines for minimum requirements regarding transferability of the Associate degree among participating institutions. These guidelines identify basic (foundation) requirements for communication and quantitative/symbolic reasoning as well as distribution requirements for the humanities, social sciences, and natural sciences. Like similar agreements in other states, these requirements are stated in course credits rather than learning outcomes.

To maintain internal consistency and integrity with college core values and overarching learning outcomes, focus groups were convened to develop learning outcomes for basic (foundation) requirements and each of the distribution requirements areas. The groups included carefully selected community and technical college faculty with expertise and experience in each of the ICRC required areas. The challenge for each group was to transform implied learning outcomes reflected as course requirements in the ICRC guidelines into articulated learning outcome statements that simultaneously fulfill ICRC requirements and support Cascadia's learning outcomes. As evidenced by the statements and learning outcomes that follow, that goal was achieved.

Basic (Foundation). Critical skills enable learners to access, process, construct, and express knowledge. These cross-curricular forms and abilities include argument, problem solving, analysis, and syntheses and are organized into three areas: communication, quantitative reasoning, and technology.

Communication

- *Content Analysis and Evaluation.* Learners will listen to, locate, choose, evaluate context, comprehend, paraphrase, summarize, analyze, synthesize, and evaluate texts—oral, written, and electronic.

- *Development of Evidence.* Learners will use supporting evidence to create, develop, and present arguments and reasoning.

- *Creative Expression.* Learners will create communications that reflect audience, cultural awareness of self and others, disciplinary awareness, and historical and political settings.

- *Representation.* Learners will use standardized symbol systems (language, visuals and graphics, numbers, etc.) to interpret, evaluate, create, and express knowledge.

Quantitative Reasoning

- *Nature and Practice of Logic.* Learners will articulate and make conscious the problem-solving process, honoring both logic and intuition.

- *Recognition of Patterns.* Learners will identify and make use of repeatable events in developing understanding and expression.

- *Evaluate Quantifiable Events.* Learners will use and evaluate descriptive statistics, quantify data, and use probability and other mathematical tools to assist in understanding and communication.

- *Expression of Concepts.* Learners will understand and apply a variety of quantitative perspectives using abstraction and modeling.

Technology

- *Evaluation of Effects.* Learners will understand the impact of different technologies on individuals and society.

- *Willingness to Change.* Learners will demonstrate an open attitude to relevant and significant technologies.

Humanities. Languages, literature, the arts, and philosophy are the essential cultural expressions of being human. Underlying these subjects are central ideas that vary across times and cultures. These ideas include aesthetics, ethics, symbolism, and creativity as well as core concepts and perspectives used to analyze and understand creative expression. Through the humanities, learners participate in others' subjective experience of reality and convey to others their own.

- *Content Analysis.* Learners will gain knowledge of the core content of at least two humanities disciplines and apply that knowledge through analysis, synthesis, and evaluation.

- *Personalization.* Learners will investigate the context and language of the human experience to examine and explore their everyday worlds and to expand their experience and understanding of other cultures and times.

- *Creative Expression.* Learners will discover and use a creative process for self-expression to communicate an understanding and/or interpretation of human experience through visual, musical, dramatic, oral, or written products.

Social Sciences. To enhance social responsibility, learners in the social sciences expand their understanding of the nature and behavior of individuals as well as their interaction and organization in multiple cultural contexts.

- *Individual and Societal Levels of Analysis.* Learners will analyze interrelationships between individual and sociohistorical forces.

- *Diversity.* Learners will evaluate how social structures impact diversity, inequality, and social change.

- *Evaluation of Evidence.* Learners will identify and evaluate qualitative and quantitative evidence to draw conclusions about human behavior consistent with social science theory.

- *Theory and Method.* Learners will demonstrate facility to move between frameworks, to use varieties of evidence, and to arrive at multiple conclusions.

Natural Sciences. Science literacy provides a foundation for informed citizenship in our increasingly technological society. Learners practice, communicate, and apply science in order to understand the natural and physical world and the consequences of human activity within it.

- *Nature of Science.* Learners will comprehend and describe science as a process of generating knowledge that relies on testable hypotheses, verifiable data, and evolving theories that explain natural phenomena.

- *Practice of Science.* Learners will conduct scientific investigations, i.e., design and modify experiments, make accurate observations, and apply quantitative and qualitative strategies to interpret numerical and graphical data.

- *Communication of Science.* Learners will read technical information with understanding and express technical information in written, verbal, and graphical forms for a variety of audiences, both within and outside science.

- *Application of Science.* Learners will know and apply fundamental concepts in the biological, chemical, and physical sciences to make informed decisions and engage meaningfully in ethical issues that involve science and technology.

Course Learning Outcomes

The final stage in developing the framework for Cascadia's curriculum was the identification of individual course learning outcomes. With the overarching college learning outcomes and distribution area learning outcomes as contextual guides, individual courses serve as vehicles to achieve not only discipline-specific learning outcomes, but broader cross-discipline learning outcomes as well. Course Outcomes Guides (COGs) disclose intended learning outcomes that support the achievement of subject content expertise as well as the development of context for that expertise. By considering individual disciplines at this stage of curriculum development, there is greater assurance that both discipline-specific learning outcomes and overarching college learning outcomes are addressed in each course.

A number of resources were consulted in the development of the curriculum. In particular, the considerable body of work developed by professional organizations and peers at other colleges and universities stimulated thinking and expanded perspectives. In many cases, that body of work helped Cascadia's curriculum developers establish directions and identify specific learning outcomes that were adapted and incorporated into course COGs.

In addition to the resources consulted in the design of the curriculum, a variety of strategies were employed to develop content for course COGs. For some courses, existing staff expertise was utilized. For areas outside the expertise of Cascadia staff, focus groups of discipline experts were convened to develop content for course COGs. In selective cases, individual faculty from other community and technical colleges were contracted to develop course COG content. Outcomes from these groups were used to develop individual course COGs. All COGs were reviewed internally, and in most cases externally, before receiving final college approval.

Summary

Beginning with a clear understanding of Cascadia Community College core values (diversity, access, success, learning, innovation, and environmental stewardship), the CLDT developed overarching learning outcomes for all members of the college community. The overarching learning outcomes—learn actively, think critically and reflectively, communicate with clarity and originality, and interact in diverse and complex environments—form the guiding principles for the curriculum as a whole. Consistent with college core values, block transfer distribution area learning outcomes support both discipline-specific learning outcomes and overarching college learning outcomes. Finally, course outcome guides for each course identify learning outcomes that support the development of subject area expertise as well as learning outcomes that cross subject areas. Expertise of peers and colleagues and research into current practices were reviewed, adapted, synthesized, and incorporated as appropriate into Cascadia's curriculum.

The outcome of this project is a set of institutional core values that guide overall college directions that, in turn, guide the curriculum. Based upon these values, learning outcomes are defined at the college, degree, distribution area, program, and course levels. The resulting infusion, coordination, and alignment of learning outcomes at course, program, and degree levels supports a relevant outcomes-based curriculum that is internally consistent with core values, reflective of best practices, and focused on student success in the 21st Century.

Waukesha County Technical College: A Student Learning Centered College
R. Laurence Schoenberger

Waukesha County Technical College (WCTC), a comprehensive technical college in southeastern Wisconsin, serves a population base of approximately 365,000. The college has embraced a student development philosophy since the 1970s and is currently functioning as a student learning centered organization. WCTC's current institutional focus is driven largely by grassroots support from champions committed to creating a collegewide learning environment serving all students and other customers.

The college's educational system is designed to help students develop life and work skills that enable them to demonstrate an independent role in society and the workplace. Five *Signature Abilities* result from a student's experiences in the system:

- The student will be able to function responsibly in the community.

- The student will be able to function productively in the workplace.

- The student will be able to apply learning.

- The student will be able to cope with change.

- The student will be able to build effective relationships.

To help ensure that students attain the Signature Abilities, WCTC has implemented several initiatives. Four of these initiatives serve as examples of WCTC's commitment to maintaining a focus on student learning and student success in the 21st Century: *Critical Life Skills, Student Outcomes Assessment,* the *College Matriculation Plan,* and the *Quality Value Process.*

Opportunities for students to attain WCTC's Critical Life Skills are delivered across the college, and student achievement of these skills is measured and documented through Student Outcomes Assessment and the College Matriculation Plan. The Quality Value Process facilitates a continuing organizational focus on providing appropriate opportunities for student learning and on measuring student acquisition of essential skills.

Critical Life Skills

WCTC embarked on a major shift in focus of instruction and delivery in 1986 when instructors and other employees identified a foundation of Critical Life Skills as essential for the occupational and personal success of every WCTC graduate. The foundation concepts of Critical Life Skills are taught directly in general education classes and are applied across the curriculum in occupational courses. Assessment criteria have been developed to evaluate each of the skills in general education courses as well as in occupational courses. The 23 distinct, measurable outcomes that comprise Critical Life Skills are clustered into four areas: communication skills, analytical skills, group effectiveness skills, and personal management skills, and have been adopted by the college's program advisory committees.

Communication Skills. Use reading, writing, and verbal skills to organize and communicate ideas and information in personal and group settings.

- *Grammar.* Use the basic mechanics of standard written English, such as spelling, punctuation, and grammar.

- *Writing.* Use written communication appropriate to the situation to express ideas, needs, and concerns clearly, concisely, and accurately.

- *Interpersonal Communication.* Communicate in interpersonal or small group settings, such as classes, meetings, etc.

- *Public Communication.* Communicate in a formal public setting.

- *Reading.* Read critically and analytically.

Analytical Skills. Use numerical and mathematical concepts, logical reasoning, principles of science/technology, information analysis, and ethical reasoning to make effective decisions and solve problems.

- *Problem Solving.* Demonstrate effective problem-solving skills.

- *Critical Thinking.* Apply the techniques of analytical thinking and effective decision making.

- *Science and Technology.* Apply principles of science and use technology appropriate to occupations.

- *Professional and Personal Ethics.* Apply a collection of generally accepted ethical standards for "right conduct" in both personal and professional areas.

- *Mathematics.* Demonstrate numerical and logical reasoning and apply mathematical concepts in occupational and personal settings.

- *Information Seeking.* Identify and fulfill information needs.

Group Effectiveness Skills. Apply social interaction skills to develop positive relationships and to work effectively with family, community groups, and co-workers.

- *Conflict Resolution.* Apply effective techniques to resolve interpersonal conflict.

- *Social Responsibility and Effective Citizenship.* Demonstrate awareness of the social and global environment by making informed decisions for effective participation in the community.

- *Teamwork.* Work effectively and cooperatively in a group setting.

- *Valuing Diversity.* Value differences among people.

- *Effective Relationships.* Develop positive relationships with family members, co-workers, friends, and others.

Personal Management Skills. Develop self-sufficiency and responsibility for effectiveness in personal and occupational life.

- *Career Development.* Make career choices appropriate to current personal needs and to the changing nature of the labor market.

- *Career Securing.* Demonstrate effective job search skills.

- *Study Skills.* Use effective study skills in order to master course content.

- *Stress Management.* Manage stress in appropriate ways.

- *Coping with Change.* Understand and manage change appropriately.

- *Time Management.* Organize activities to accomplish desired tasks in the time available.

- *Self-Concept.* Evaluate one's self-concept in regards to self-esteem, values, attitudes, interests, goals, strengths, and weaknesses.

Under the coordination of the Student Development Steering Committee, each instructional department completed a significant review of the role Critical Life Skills play in educating WCTC students. The review process involved (1) ranking the value of each Critical Life Skill in every occupational program, (2) including appropriate Critical Life Skills for each course in the Course Outcome Summary every student receives at the beginning of a course, and (3) completing a matrix in each occupational program illustrating which courses teach to and assess Critical Life Skills. As a result of this review, WCTC has a comprehensive system that identifies courses in which Critical Life Skills are delivered to students and in which student achievement of these skills is assessed.

To increase student awareness of Critical Life Skills, the Student Development Steering Committee has communicated with a wide range of college and community stakeholders. Major information sharing efforts include placing Critical Life Skills posters in buildings and classrooms and distributing Critical Life Skills brochures and folders throughout the college community.

Student Growth and Development Plan

Student success in attaining Critical Life Skills is heightened through the new *Student Growth and Development (SG&D) Plan* piloted during the 1999-2000 academic year. The SG&D Plan provides students with a self-assessment of their Critical Life Skills status and is a practical working document for students and advisors to use for planning and monitoring Critical Life Skills experiences throughout a student's time of study at WCTC.

Through the SD&G Plan, faculty and advisors receive information from students that helps in designing appropriate opportunities for student learning and for application of Critical Life Skills outside the classroom. In addition, the SD&G Plan provides the foundation for development of a future Critical Life Skills Transcript, envisioned to be a portable document certifying mastery of these skills that students will be able to take to employers or transfer institutions.

Student Outcomes Assessment and College Matriculation

WCTC believes that the primary reason to conduct assessment is to benefit students by strengthening their learning. Two complementary initiatives—the *Student Outcomes Assessment (SOA) Plan* and the *College Matriculation Plan*—are designed to help students succeed at WCTC. To assess student learning, including attainment of Critical Life Skills, the SOA Plan includes three major components: pre-enrollment assessment, during-enrollment assessment, and post-enrollment assessment. The SOA Plan encompasses the many assessment techniques currently in place, those under consideration for change, and those planned for future implementation.

Pre-Enrollment Assessment. Based on the premise that appropriate placement is a key to success, WCTC's admissions procedure includes pre-enrollment assessment activities for all associate degree programs and courses. Currently, all applicants to WCTC associate degree programs are required to complete either the ACT ASSET or COMPASS assessment. Prior to enrollment, students also may be assessed, as appropriate, in a variety of other ways. Examples of additional assessment include proficiency testing, transcript reviews, interviews with counselors, vocational assessment workshops, and standardized test instruments.

To support the Student Outcomes Assessment processes, WCTC's College Matriculation Plan incorporates pre-enrollment assessment, college preparedness/academic skill building, and academic advising as key components to ensure student success. The matriculation plan defines pre-assessment expectations for students and provides academic advisors to assist students in self-assessment. Advisors also help students understand the importance of assessment in monitoring their progress. Students who do not meet program readiness scores are required to attend an orientation at the WCTC Learning Place, where an individual educational plan is developed to remedy academic deficiencies in writing, reading, and math. During college preparedness, the student may register for a maximum of 12 credits and is placed in a conditional admissions status.

The college
strongly believes
that assessment must be led by faculty, who have always been involved in measuring learning.

During-Enrollment Assessment. During-enrollment assessment is course-embedded and may be summative or formative; it occurs while a student is enrolled in a course and includes assessment of student achievement of Critical Life Skills. Some of the effective during-enrollment assessment techniques used by faculty include classroom portfolios, projects, simulations, quizzes, and instructor evaluations. Not limited to gauging student achievement, the various assessments also provide an evaluation of instructional methods. As part of the SOA Plan, assessment activities are reviewed on a regular basis, and reports on assessment activities are shared among the college instructional divisions.

The College Matriculation Plan's new Academic Advising Program assigns an academic advisor to each program student. Within the past 18 months, the college has staffed, trained, and placed more than 100 academic advisors, including both faculty and administrators, and the advising program now serves over 1,800 students.

Post-Enrollment Assessment. Post-enrollment assessment occurs after the student has left WCTC. Examples of these assessment activities include graduate follow-up surveys, employer follow-up surveys, licensure exam results, and telephone surveys. Post-enrollment activities may be initiated by departments or divisions, or by the Research and Evaluation Services department. These activities are often part of the program review process.

SOA Organization. Central coordination and leadership of the SOA Plan is the responsibility of the SOA Steering Committee. This committee, co-chaired by the executive vice president and the SOA facilitator (a faculty member), consists of a 25-member team of instructional deans, associate deans, faculty, instructional managers, and the curriculum specialist. The committee monitors and maintains assessment activities, shares effective examples of assessment, facilitates pre/during/post-enrollment strategies, shares data on tracking and improving student learning, and interprets and evaluates the college's assessment progress.

The college strongly believes that assessment must be led by faculty, who have always been involved in measuring learning. Implementation of the SOA Plan is the responsibility of each instructional division through an SOA division implementation team, which usually meets monthly and includes the dean, associate deans, faculty, and staff. Approximately half of the division committee members are

faculty who are compensated for their efforts. Having one or two members of each division implementation team on the SOA Steering Committee ensures alignment among college divisions.

Quality Value Process. The implementation of Critical Life Skills and Student Outcomes Assessment throughout the curriculum and across college divisions began as a grassroots effort and continues to receive support through an inclusive organizational structure. WCTC's internal Quality Value (QV) process integrates the principles of continuous quality improvement, customer focus, and personal empowerment into the daily work processes and long-range planning activities of the college. As the foundation for the college's organizational structure, the QV process has become part of the culture of the institution as faculty, staff, administrators, board members, and union leaders and members work together to ensure student learning.

For more than a decade, the Quality Value Executive Committee (QVEC) and a small, dedicated QV staff have helped members of the college community work toward improving all processes that directly affect learning, teaching, and college administrative work methods. To date, 340 college staff members have completed Commitment to Quality, a two-credit college level introductory course in quality improvement principles and teamwork methods. More than 40 employees have also completed a Facilitator Training course to help develop the skills needed to guide teams in process improvement and problem solving projects.

In the same way the QV process assists faculty, staff, and administration in ensuring that students attain the Critical Life Skills, it also provides opportunities for these college employees to reinforce their own learning. Through their involvement in the four categories of QV processes—Learning for Organizational Growth/Organizational Leadership, Improvement of College Processes, Problem Solving and Creative Teams, and Links to the Wisconsin Technical College System—work clusters engage in their own learning while they support the college's focus on student learning and student achievement of the Signature Abilities and Critical Life Skills.

Learning for Organizational Growth/Organizational Leadership. Learning opportunities sponsored by the QV staff include formal seminars and workshops for staff and informal coaching about quality improvement methods. Major workshops have included nationally prominent guest speakers such as Peter Scholtes, Howard Gitlow, and Joe Colletti, as well as training in Franklin-Covey Leadership Center's programs, including 7 Habits of Highly Effective People, 4 Roles of Leadership, and What Matters Most. Informal coaching includes working with natural work groups to guide the development of unit mission and values documents, developing planning documents, developing and implementing curriculum improvements, and creating student feedback surveys. In addition, members of the QV staff provide significant support to the college by serving as planners and facilitators for annual strategic planning activities.

Improvement of College Processes. Major process improvements have been accomplished through the work of QV teams. One improvement team designed and created the Teaching Innovation Center, which provides daily support for faculty to improve teaching methodology and to integrate technology use into class activities. A team of nursing faculty designed and administered a student feedback survey to provide ongoing information to staff about improvements in curriculum and delivery strategies. Through the Teacher Improvement System, each faculty member uses continuous feedback from students, employers, self, and peers to select and implement four improvement ideas each academic year. The Support Staff Process for Development and Improvement has support personnel working with supervisors to plan and implement changes that benefit multiple stakeholders. These processes have refocused the thinking of college personnel toward student-focused improvements.

Problem Solving and Creative Teams. Teams are formed around a variety of issues to solve problems and create new methods under the guidance of the QV staff. Recently, a number of teams have been charged to develop balanced solutions to thorny problems. Following several years of unsuccessful collective bargaining attempts to address certain work-related issues, QV teams have taken the challenge to create new or to improve existing policies and work methods. One team, for example, addressed the policies and guidelines for providing distance learning opportunities for students. While some teams focus on a specific problem or group's concern, others tackle wide-ranging issues. One such team administers a collegewide climate.

Links to the Wisconsin Technical College System. QV staff from WCTC have contributed in-service and curriculum expertise to statewide educational development efforts involving their 15 sister colleges and the state board. They have made presentations in teamwork, benchmarking, becoming more student learning centered, and quality principles throughout the state. Over the past six years, QV staff from WCTC have also led an effort to develop a major statewide curriculum project. Working with colleagues from other technical colleges, WCTC staff members created a six-credit curriculum package that provides consistent training in quality-related topics to business clients throughout the state. Two WCTC staff members have served on the steering team for this project and have trained educators to use the materials.

Effects of QV Processes on Student Attainment of Critical Life Skills. WCTC's Quality Value activities support the college's initiative to champion student learning and acquisition of essential skills in direct as well as indirect ways. Faculty, staff, and administrator participation in QV processes has expanded the focus on Critical Life Skills and Student Outcomes Assessment throughout the institution. Developments such as the Teaching Innovation Center and the Teaching Improvement System support faculty in their growth and development. Faculty are applying QV processes and concepts such as continuous improvement and teamwork to improve their delivery of instruction and integrate Critical Life Skills into their courses.

At WCTC, the emphasis on Critical Life Skills extends beyond the traditional classroom. Student achievement of Critical Life Skills is assessed not only by teaching faculty,

but also by directors and sponsors of student activities, supervisors of interns and work-study students, and others in the college and community who are engaged in helping students attain these skills. By expanding the focus on student learning throughout the WCTC community, the QV process links, coordinates, and connects Critical Life Skills across the college.

Summary

WCTC's movement to identify essential skills began in 1986 as an effort by a concerned group of educators searching for a way to measure and document student learning. Since that time, it has become interlinked with the college's emerging student learning centered culture. With the identification of Critical Life Skills and the development of the Student Outcomes Assessment Plan, the college has institutionalized its pledge that students leave WCTC with the Signature Abilities, documented by student attainment of Critical Life Skills. The Quality Value process provides an inclusive environment in which faculty, administrators, and staff throughout the college are involved in the delivery, assessment, and documentation of student achievement of Critical Life Skills. The Student Growth and Development Plan and the movement toward documenting student achievement of Critical Life Skills further the college's central focus on learning and help equip students with a meaningful record of their accomplishments and abilities. Taken together, these initiatives help make Waukesha County Technical College a learning-centered organization that prepares its students to function productively and responsibly in the workplace and community of the 21st Century.

> **Teams are** formed around a variety of issues to solve problems and create new methods under the guidance of the QV staff.

Conclusions, Further Questions, and Next Steps

This study helped clarify the current status of community college efforts in defining and documenting student acquisition of 21st Century Skills and shed light on the language and issues surrounding the concepts of student learning outcomes and competency-based approaches to higher education. As a result of this preliminary foray into the realm of defining and assessing student learning for a new century, we have answered a few of our questions, refined those questions that are still unanswered, and verified that much work remains to be done. In this conclusion we offer a distillation of what we have learned and what work remains to best support community colleges in their efforts to foster student learning for the 21st Century.

Interest in the Topic. Although participants in this study are self-selected based on their interest in the topic of study or selected for their experience and success in learning-centered or outcomes-based education, and so are likely biased in this area, findings demonstrate great interest surrounding the issue of Learning Outcomes for the 21st Century. All our data sources, including direct observation, focus group reactions, literature review, and large-scale survey findings, point to widespread attention on improving the processes for determining what and how much students are learning in community colleges. No end is in sight for the movement toward outcomes assessment, accountability to external stakeholders, and demands of educational consumers for immediate, portable evidence of the outcomes of their investments in higher education. If anything, this aspect of the Learning Revolution seems to be accelerating.

Language of Outcomes. Survey findings also elucidate the use of language surrounding the topic. Although study participants reported that they understand our meaning when we use the phrase 21st Century Skills, very few actually use this term. Instead, community colleges are more likely to use general education core or core competencies to refer to the skill areas deemed essential for student success in the Knowledge Age. This study further indicates that when discussing assessment of student acquisition of these skills, respondents most often use the terms learning outcomes or competencies. Because learning outcomes was the most frequently cited term from our findings and the one most highly recommended by focus group participants, we advocate its use to reference the group of key student skills and abilities needed for success in the 21st Century. An interesting note on language that prompted discussion among study participants surrounds ways to describe the new job roles of faculty in a learning-centered, outcomes-based educational environment where they no longer act chiefly as disseminators of knowledge. Several study participants referenced the now familiar portrayal of moving from "sage on the stage" to "guide on the side." The president of Cascadia Community College offered a new designation that attracted considerable attention when she suggested addressing faculty in their new roles as "knowledge navigators."

Progressive Disorder. As we envisioned this survey, and indeed the project, we pictured the implementation of a 21st Century student outcomes model as progressing through the steps of building a consensus on a definition of 21st Century Learning Outcomes, integrating them into the curriculum, teaching them in courses, agreeing on assessment methods, routinely assessing student achievement of these skills, and, finally, documenting their achievement. The survey, however, validates what we found through site visits and focus groups: the stages of developing and institutionalizing processes to define student learning outcomes do not necessarily follow a linear progression. Survey findings indicate, for example, that more colleges are teaching the competencies than are defining, assessing, and documenting them. And, although an overwhelming majority of colleges reported that they are addressing 21st Century Learning Outcomes, those that are focusing on the competencies do not necessarily have an institutional initiative or plan for ensuring the definition, delivery, and documentation of these outcomes.

To some extent, the challenges colleges face in addressing 21st Century Learning Outcomes help explain their seemingly haphazard approaches to addressing these outcomes. Survey findings indicate that the greatest barriers to integrating the outcomes in the community college entail time and assessment issues. In site visits and focus groups, study participants repeatedly underscored the difficulty of developing uniform language, definitions, and assessment procedures for an institutional 21st Century Learning Outcomes initiative. Many said they need more resources and models, particularly for assessment and documentation of student achievement of the outcomes.

We conclude that community colleges committed to the goal of implementing a student learning outcomes initiative, but lacking one or more critical resources that allow linear progress toward this goal at the institutional level, may focus their energies in a certain division or on a single step in the system where they can make progress in the moment.

Questions That Remain. Given these difficulties, we are not surprised that community colleges are asking for help in answering questions about their involvement in student achievement of 21st Century Learning Outcomes:

- What are the 21st Century Learning Outcomes appropriate for community colleges?

- What competencies are appropriate for each of the 21st Century Learning Outcomes?

- What level or standard is appropriate for each of the competencies, and how are these best determined?

- How are these standards articulated with K-12 systems and four-year college and university systems?

- How are the competencies and the levels best taught?

- How are the competencies and the levels best assessed?

- How can community colleges transcript competencies and levels achieved for use by transfer institutions, employers, and students?

The final objective of this study is to define the parameters of a large-scale project to best support community college efforts toward defining and certifying student learning outcomes. Searching for answers to these questions begins that process, and to find the answers, global models are needed. These models could be generated by a group of pioneering institutions that would develop tools and serve as laboratories to support student achievement of 21st Century Learning Outcomes. These model community colleges could also serve as an advocacy group promoting an increase in the capacity of community colleges to prepare students to be successful participants in the new global economy.

Next Steps for the Community College. The community college is a particularly appropriate venue for leading and advocating outcomes-based learning in postsecondary education. With competency-based programs in place in vocational and developmental programs, community colleges are familiar with the process and may possess the fundamental knowledge and skill needed to advance the use of outcomes across the institution. The community college's well-established flexibility is evidenced by its history of moving rapidly to meet the changing and growing needs of students, community, business and industry, and other constituents. When competency requirements change, the community college has the adaptability to adjust quickly. As a bridge in the K-16 system, the community college is also well positioned to use learning outcomes to improve matriculation and articulation processes that assist entering students, transfer students, and returning students. During this study, we noted that at several institutions, including the two highlighted in this monograph, learning outcomes are not limited to student achievement. At Cascadia Community College, for example, learning outcomes are described as collegewide, emphasizing that the Cascadia community of learners includes all members of the college. The Quality Value process at Waukesha County Technical College supports the institution's learning-centered focus by providing learning opportunities for faculty, staff, administrators, trustees, and union leaders. This finding may indicate an emerging trend that provides additional support for the community college's appropriateness to lead postsecondary outcomes-based education: the commitment to learning extends through all areas of the institution.

Community colleges not only are well suited for leading outcomes-based education, but also are positioned to benefit from a focus on providing 21st Century Learning Outcomes for their students. In their white paper prepared to inform this project, Paulson and Ewell note the advantages of assessing and documenting competencies to both the student and the educational institution. As a student travels through the levels of traditional schooling and into the continuous training and development cycles that characterize the 21st Century workplace, and indeed the new century's society, documentation of outcomes accumulates into a valuable record of learning that has occurred throughout the student's life. For the student, this record is a comprehensive résumé, a true curriculum vitae. Similarly, for the educational institution, it is an accountability document that certifies individual student achievement.

The movement toward outcomes-based education is driven in large part by calls from community college constituents and funding agents to ensure that resources expended on education are used effectively. Legislators, taxpayers, employers, and students want assurance that those who complete publicly funded programs of study have been adequately prepared for work or further education, and they are no longer satisfied with grades posted on traditional college transcripts. The findings from this study indicate that of all the phases of implementing student learning outcomes, community colleges are least involved in documenting student achievement in ways other than grades or course credit. Documentation, however, is the only stage in the process that directly answers the increasing calls for accountability.

Despite the positive findings of this study, including the indications of overwhelming community college interest in addressing 21st Century Learning Outcomes, the central finding remains: Community colleges are not documenting student acquisition of 21st Century Learning Outcomes. As community college educators, we can say that we are focusing on these outcomes, that we are teaching them and assessing student acquisition of them; however, the findings of this study indicate that we are not completely addressing this aspect of student learning. Even among those colleges that seemingly are the furthest along, none have fully defined and implemented an institutionwide system that supports the delivery and documentation of student learning for the 21st Century. Still, community colleges are interested, often enthusiastically so, in 21st Century Learning Outcomes and the potential that documenting learning affords students, employers, the community, and the college. Community college educators around the world are sketching their customized version of Kennedy's blueprint as they engage in dialogue about how to define, develop, deliver, and document student learning in the new century. Further discussions, research, and development of models and best practices not only will help community colleges prepare students for the Knowledge Age, but also will help them create processes for certifying their achievement of learning.

References

Kennedy, E. M. (1995). "On the Common Core of Learning." In J.W. Noll (Ed.), *Taking Sides: Clashing Views on Controversial Educational Issues*, 8th ed. (pp 128-132). Guilford, CT: Dushkin Publishing Group. (Reprinted from The Educational Forum, Vol. 58, 1994).

Murnane, R. J., & Levy, F. (1996). *Teaching the New Basic Skills: Principles for Educating Children to Thrive in a Changing Economy*. New York: Martin Kessler Books.

O'Banion, T. (1999). *Launching a Learning-Centered College*. Mission Viejo, CA: League for Innovation in the Community College.

Paulson, K., & Ewell, P. (1999). "21st Century Skills for Community College Education: The Critical Role of Competencies." Paper prepared for the League for Innovation in the Community College, Mission Viejo, CA.

Stiehl, R., & Lewchuk, L. (2000). *OUTCOMES Primer: Reconstructing the College Curriculum*. Corvallis, OR: The Learning Organization.

Learning Outcomes for the Twenty-First Century: Cultivating Student Success for College and the Knowledge Economy

— Cindy L. Miles, Cynthia Wilson

Miles, C. L. and Wilson, C. (2004 Summer). "Learning Outcomes for the Twenty-First Century: Cultivating Student Success for College and the Knowledge Economy." In A. M. Serban & J. Friedlander, Eds., *Developing and Implementing Assessment of Student Learning Outcomes*. New Directions for Community Colleges, Number 126. San Francisco: Jossey-Bass.

During the 1990s, community colleges faced mounting external pressure to demonstrate results for what happens in college classrooms and to ensure that their graduates possessed core competencies for success in the burgeoning knowledge community. McClenney (1998) describes some causes underlying these demands for demonstration of learning outcomes: "The ugly truth about the current situation in American higher education, even in most community colleges, is that we do not have a clue what and how much students are learning—that is, whether they know and can do what their degree (or other credential) implies" (p.4).

> **Differences** notwithstanding, the project partnerships and interchanges led to similarities in outcomes sets and in assessment and documentation strategies.

In summer 2000, with funding from The Pew Charitable Trusts, the League for Innovation in the Community College (the League) developed a network of sixteen pioneering community and technical colleges in the 21st Century Learning Outcomes Project to design and test innovative, outcomes-based methods for defining, delivering, assessing, and documenting student learning. The colleges that participated in the project are Butler County community College (KS), Central Piedmont Community College (NC), Cuyahoga Community College (OH), Foothill College (CA), Hocking College (OH), Inver Hills Community College (MN), Johnson County Community College (KS), Kingsborough Community College (NY), Mesa Community College (AZ), Midlands Technical College (SC), Montgomery College (TX), San Diego Miramar College (CA), Santa Fe Community College (FL), Schoolcraft College (MI), Skagit Valley College (WA), and Waukesha County Technical College (WI).

The 21st Century Learning Outcomes Project described in this chapter was Stage Two (Implementation and Advocacy) of a larger-scale League effort to bring new outcomes-based standards for student learning to the community college field. In Stage One (Planning and Research), the League, supported by The Pew Charitable Trusts, researched the extent of U.S. and Canadian community college efforts to define, assess, and document student achievement of twenty-first century learning outcomes (Wilson and others, 2000). Stage Two was a three-year project funded for the first two years by The Pew Charitable Trusts and continued with support from the League and participating colleges through June 2003.

The sixteen participating colleges shared a commitment to the project's central goal to increase the capacity of community colleges to define and document the acquisition of the critical competencies that students need to succeed in the workplace, in transfer education, and in today's society. All sixteen colleges developed learning outcomes websites to share their project plans, reports, and activities as well as self-assessments, outcomes rubrics, and assessment or documentation models. Many of the colleges are maintaining these public websites, accessible through links from the 21st Century Learning Outcomes Project section of the League's website (see http://www/league/org/projects/pew).

Approaches to Implementing Learning Outcomes

Over the three years of the 21st Century Learning Outcomes Project, the sixteen participating colleges made individual progress toward the project's goal of enhancing the capacity of community colleges to define and document students' acquisition of critical learning outcomes. Each college worked independently, with feedback and support from partner colleges and project staff, toward the common project goal by focusing on five institutional objectives:

Define. Define a set of core competencies that encompass 21st Century learning outcomes.

Develop. Develop a set of curriculum components for 21st century learning outcomes with specific learning outcomes for each competency, levels of performance that students should meet, concrete indices of student work to demonstrate each level, and assessment strategies for measuring student achievement at each level.

Deliver. Identify and implement best practices and multiple models of delivery and assessment of 21st century learning outcomes.

Document. Develop nontraditional methods for documenting student achievement of 21st century learning outcomes beyond traditional grades, credits, and degrees.

Disseminate. Share model programs and practices with other institutions.

The sixteen project colleges came to this work with varying expertise, needs, resources, and constraints regarding student learning outcomes, and college progress toward project objectives varied accordingly. Preliminary focus groups with college leaders in Phase 1 of the project convinced the funding agency and project directors that community colleges varied too much in structure, governance, and culture to expect a single common solution to such a complex endeavor. Differences notwithstanding, the project partnerships and interchanges led to similarities in outcome sets and in assessment and documentation strategies. Notably, the colleges continue targeted institutional work in support of the project's goal more than a year after the end of the funded phase of the project. Universally, colleges reported achievements in their learning outcomes initiatives and many point to this project as a landmark in their work toward improving the quality and documentation of student learning in their institutions.

Definition of Learning Outcomes

All sixteen participating colleges successfully identified sets of 21st century learning outcomes for their institutions. The paths that project colleges took to reach these ends varied considerably, as did the resulting sets of learning outcomes, which range in number from four broad knowledge, skill, and ability domains to twenty-seven specific learning competencies. Although only the first step on the learning outcomes journey, reaching shared institutional agreement on the core competencies all those completing degrees or certificates should achieve was a significant undertaking for several colleges, marked by activities spanning a year or more. College approaches to defining student learning outcomes (or critical life skills, essential skills, or core competencies, as they are variously termed), fell into three categories: adoption of the set of "21st century skills," revalidation or amendment of existing sets of competencies associated with the general education core, and development of altogether new sets of core competencies.

Adoption of the Stage One Set of "21st Century Skills." In November 1999, the League convened academic leaders from fifteen colleges to develop consensus on a set of cross-curricular core competencies that two-year college graduates should possess to succeed in work, transfer education, and life. Drawing on results from a preliminary survey and document analysis conducted by the League staff, the focus group identified a set of eight broad categories of 21st century skills, encompassing the following so-called hard skills of literacy, numeracy, and technical ability, as well as soft skills such as teamwork, communication, problem solving, and the ability to interact with diverse groups:

- Communication skills (reading, writing, speaking, listening)

- Computation skills (understanding and applying mathematical concepts and reasoning, analyzing and using numerical data)

- Community Skills (citizenship; appreciation of diversity and pluralism; local, community, global, and environmental awareness)

- Critical thinking and problem-solving skills (analysis, synthesis, evaluation, decision making, creative thinking)

- Information management skills (collecting, analyzing, and organizing information from a variety of sources)

- Interpersonal skills (teamwork, relationship management, conflict resolution, workplace skills)

- Personal skills (ability to understand and manage self, management of change, learning to learn, personal responsibility, aesthetic responsiveness, wellness)

- Technology Skills (computer literacy, Internet skills, retrieving and managing information via technology)

Using these results, the League conducted five institutional site visits and a survey of U.S. and Canadian community colleges to test agreement on this set of 21st century skills and to assess the status of North American community colleges in establishing and assessing student achievement of such skills. Of the 259 institutions that responded to the survey, 92 percent indicated their colleges were addressing the issue of 21st century skills; more than two-thirds identified the 21st century skills from the focus group among their college's list of core competencies, with the exception of personal skills (47 percent) and community skills (59 percent). Two Learning Outcomes Project colleges (Central Piedmont Community College and Santa Fe Community College) adopted the Stage One set of 21st century skills for implementation in their college learning outcomes plan. (For complete Stage One study results see Wilson and others, 2000.)

Revalidation or Amendment of Existing Sets of Core Competencies. Most of the participating colleges (Cuyahoga Community College, Hocking College, Inver Hills Community College, Johnson County Community College, Mesa Community College, Midlands Technical College, Montgomery College, Schoolcraft College, Skagit Valley College, and Waukesha County Technical College) had previously identified sets of core competencies associated with their general education cores. Some of these colleges used project activities to refine their existing competencies, while others with recently developed sets of competencies or more mature learning outcomes approaches moved directly to other project objectives.

A variety of factors, including institutional culture, age of the existing competencies, and workforce demands, led colleges on different paths to revising their student learning outcomes. For example, Cuyahoga Community College revalidated its existing General Education and Life Competencies: communication, mathematics, sciences, arts and humanities, social and behavioral sciences, cultural diversity-interdependence-global awareness, computer and information literacy, critical thinking, and consumer awareness and health. As part of its ReVISIONing Learning Project, Hocking College revalidated its Institutional Core Competencies and renamed them Success Skills to reflect a stronger focus on employer and student learning needs.

Midlands Technical College revised its General Education Core, in place with modifications since 1990, to include an across-the-curriculum emphasis on information literacy, speaking, writing, and teamwork. Skagit Valley College built on general education principles formulated in the early 1990s to create an updated set of learning outcomes to reflect the skills and knowledge necessary for current academic and workplace success of its students.

Several colleges entered the project with well developed learning outcomes. Mesa Community College had a mature Student Outcomes Assessment Program, including learning outcomes for general education, the workplace, and developmental education (for a description of the program and assessment results see http://www.mc.maricopa.edu/organizations/emplotee/orp.assessment. Both Inver Hills Community College and Waukesha Couty Technical College had fully developed sets of 21st century learning outcomes with extensive rubrics or matrices illustrating levels of student achievement (see Inver Hill's Essential Skills and Rubrics at http://depts.inverhills.edu/LSPS/index.htm and Waukesha's Critical Life Skills Assessment Rubrics at http://www.waukesha.tec.wi.us/home/info/adm/skills.htm.)

Through the project, Johnson County Community College (JCCC) built on its nationally recognized Institutional Portfolio model of Institutional Effectiveness evaluation of General Education Learning Outcomes (writing, speaking, culture and ethics, mathematics, modes of inquiry, and problem solving). To review the validity of their general education outcomes, JCCC conducted a 2002 survey with follow-up focus groups of Kansas City business representatives to investigate what skills and abilities employers sought in hiring new workers. (Lindahl, 2002). Listening headed the list of sought after skills in the survey results, followed by personal responsibility and ethics; workplace responsibility, teamwork, and leadership; reading; decision making; observation; and ability to manage self. JCCC has used these findings to strengthen its Keeping Options Open high school career development and academic readiness program (Lindahl, 2002) and to guide development of an outcomes-based curriculum developed in collaboration with area employees and focused on core competencies employees need to be successful (Carlsen, 2002).

Such curriculum
components took
shape through the development of extensive learning outcomes rubrics and matrices.

Montgomery College demonstrated an unusual approach to building institutional commitment to a core competencies curriculum. Prior to this project, districtwide curriculum teams from the North Harris Montgomery Community College District identified nineteen core competencies to be addressed in all AA or AS degree programs. Still, the Montgomery College Learning Outcomes Team, directed by the college president, invited faculty, administrators, and staff to prepare white papers on each of the eight Stage One 21st century skills as a way of encouraging broader participation in curriculum reform efforts and to "discern the many nuances of classroom activities that address the core skills at Montgomery College" (Montgomery College, 2004). Volunteer authors included full- and part-time faculty members, associate and assistant deans, and a writing tutor. These papers became a springboard for collegewide electronic dialogues using the Daedalus software system, breakout sessions at the college's annual staff development day, and curriculum renewal efforts in the college's reaccreditation process.

Development of New Sets of Core Competencies. Four colleges (Butler County Community College, Foothill College, Kingsborough Community College, and San Diego Miramar College) developed new sets of learning outcomes, giving particular consideration to institutional history or culture that might influence the acceptance and successful implementation of an outcomes-based approach to student learning.

Butler County Community College (BCCC) took a comprehensive, institutional approach to involvement in the Learning Outcomes Project. BCCC's Learning Outcomes Project team included active involvement from the president; vice president of instruction; chief information officer; dean of business, technology, and workforce development; director of research and institutional effectiveness; director of academic assessment; and director of advising, as well as six faculty members. The team began meeting in November 2000 to make plans for a new, student-centered, faculty-driven program to address learning outcomes. In early 2001, the college determined that its current academic assessment outcomes were inadequate for a program of individualized student assessment and revamped the complex list of Lifetime Learning Abilities and Skills and Performance Characteristics from its earlier learning outcomes plan to a streamlined Learning PACT skills (personal development, analytical, critical thinking, and technological skills). The new Learning PACT outcomes, a set of learning outcomes deemed critical to a person's success in the twenty-first century workplace, were approved by the college's board of trustees, and an introduction to the Learning PACT was added to the college website and catalogue; distributed in a brochure given to faculty, staff, and students; and included in spring and fall semester college in-service activities (Butler, 2001).

Kingsborough Community College (KCC) also used a strategic institutional approach to identifying learning outcomes that began with a review of the college mission and development of a college values statement. From this foundation, the KCC project team drafted a set of core learning outcomes, shared these with faculty during an open forum and by e-mail for discussion and feedback, and integrated this feedback into a set of learning outcomes comprising seven skill areas: communication (written and oral); critical thinking and problem solving; computation, mathematics, and statistics; interpersonal (teamwork and team building); proficiency in computers and related areas; general education core (science, history, art, and music); and additional knowledge and skills in the major. In keeping with its institutional culture and governance marked by a strong faculty union, KCC reinforced the voluntary nature of participation in its learning outcomes program to encourage grassroots support.

Curriculum Development and Mapping. Participating colleges moved from identification of the critical outcomes to be achieved by students to development of comprehensive curriculum components for each outcome with the following elements: levels of performance, concrete indices of student achievement for each level, and assessment strategies for measuring student achievement at each level.

Such curriculum components took shape through the development of extensive learning outcomes rubrics and matrices. The most advanced among the project colleges in learning outcomes curriculum integration, Waukesha County Technical College, has worked since 1986 in a faculty-led grassroots approach to identify and integrate "critical life skills" throughout the curriculum. This integration of skills also extends beyond the classroom to include co-curricular areas such as financial aid, student life, and cooperative education. Waukesha's twenty-three critical life skills are grouped into the four broad areas of communication skills, analytical skills, group effectiveness skills, and personal management skills, with each individual skill defined by a rubric with six levels of indices of student achievement linked to recommended assessments for measuring the achievement of each skill at each level. In addition, each student has a Student Growth and Development Plan that includes a student self-assessment inventory for each of the twenty-three skills as well as a list of suggested services, activities, and programs available to enhance development of each skill. For example, a student assessed as needing development in problem solving is recommended, among other activities, to attend a District Board meeting and observe the decision-making process in action.

Several project colleges have engaged in extensive curriculum mapping using rubrics to determine what courses address which core learning outcomes at what level. As noted, many participating colleges have posted learning outcomes curriculum rubrics and resulting curriculum matrices developed during this project on their public project websites.

Implementation

The ultimate goal for *all* project colleges was to implement all learning curriculums for all students. Colleges decided on one of three areas for initially integrating the outcomes-based curriculum components they developed: in discrete courses, in some programs or academic areas, or across the curriculum. The approaches described below indicate differences only in starting points—that is, how colleges staged their learning outcomes implementation strategies. Within the three years of project activities, colleges moved from discrete course implementation to broader program area implementation for one or more of the learning outcomes. Several moved from pilot courses to programs to integration of one or more learning outcomes across the curriculum.

Implementation in Discrete Courses. A number of colleges began integrating learning outcomes with pilot implementation in a small number of courses. In this approach, a specific course is designed to address one or more learning outcomes (such as writing and critical thinking in a humanities course, computation and problem solving in a math course, diversity awareness in a sociology course), and individual student achievement of learning outcomes is assessed at the individual course level. At Butler County Community College, a speech class and an addictions counseling class pioneered implementing learning outcomes; two years later student learning outcomes are addressed in every course outline assessed in general education courses across the curriculum.

Implementation in Some Programs or Disciplines. Approaches to curriculum integration at the program level followed three general typologies:

- Some courses in some programs are designed to address some learning outcomes; student outcomes achievement is assessed at the course and program levels.

- Some programs are designed to address all learning outcomes; student achievement of learning outcomes is assessed at course and program levels.

- Certain broad academic areas (such as liberal arts, professional or technical studies) are designed to address all learning outcomes; student outcomes achievement is assessed at the course level.

Several colleges began integration of learning outcomes curriculum approaches across one or two divisions or program areas. At Foothill College, implementation began in fall 2001 in the Computers, Technology, and Information Systems division and the Language Arts division. Since then, the college has developed online course- and program-level matrices for evaluating core competencies across the curriculum. Skagit Valley College updated all its existing program level assessment plans to include 21st century learning outcomes.

Learning Outcomes Implementation Across the Curriculum. Learning outcomes integration across the curriculum followed three general approaches:

- One or more learning outcomes are piloted across the curriculum.

- Every course is designed to address some number of core competencies (but perhaps not all competencies in all courses); individual student achievement of learning outcomes is assessed and documented at the course level.

- Individual student achievement of learning outcomes is assessed and documented at the program or institutional level.

Hocking College developed a core competency map for each discipline to determine the integration of its success skills. Beginning with the success skill "communicates effectively," each academic program developed its own curriculum map and assessment strategies, such as capstone experiences and the use of internal as well as external evaluators. Similarly, Santa Fe Community College developed a system of curriculum mapping via a learning outcomes audit of all courses to determine the level and indices of each core competency delivered in each course across the curriculum.

At San Diego Miramar College, learning outcomes were integrated into the college's 2000 to 2005 strategic plan, reflecting a shift from broad institutional performance measures toward a focus on individual student learning.

Like Foothill College, Miramar developed and implemented online matrix forms to evaluate core competencies at the course and program levels. Through participation in this project, Miramar has developed a comprehensive three-stage approach, with associated instruments, to assess courses and programs for learning outcomes competencies:

- Evaluate individual courses (Comprehensive Core Competency Description, Levels of Competency Mastery, Course Assessment Sheet).

- Evaluate entire programs (Program Review Assessment Excel Worksheet).

- Make necessary changes to course or program content to achieve desired level of learning outcome competency integration.

For a number of years, Mesa Community College (MCC) has been a leader in the outcomes-based education movement and recognized nationally for its collegewide annual student outcomes assessment model. The program is overseen by the Student Outcomes Committee, a standing committee of the Faculty Senate, in collaboration with the dean of instruction. Through its student outcomes assessment program, MCC measures and documents the degree to which a focused sample of students attains specific learning outcomes valued and defined by faculty. MCC's program includes three targeted assessment areas: general education, career and technical education, and developmental education. During its Assessment Week, a sample of students participates in assessment of learning outcomes to help answer the question, "Are students learning as a result of their experience at the college?" Assessment results are aggregated and used to measure and compare learning among entering and exiting students. Assessment week results are not made available to individual students; however, results are reported to faculty to guide modification of curriculum and teaching practices. As a result of involvement in this project, Mesa had expanded its assessment pool tenfold to include more than three thousand students from nearly two hundred class selections each year.

A proven leader in implementation of individual student learning outcomes assessment, Waukesha County Technical College (WCTC) has integrated learning outcomes extensively throughout the college curriculum. WCTC has developed comprehensive curriculum rubrics and matrices for each learning outcome, with a plan to make them available electronically to all faculty members for all courses. Through the rubrics and matrices, each learning outcome is plotted throughout a program, indicating the level of its inclusion in a course and the level to which a student must achieve the outcome. Waukesha's Critical Life Skills Assessment Rubrics are available online at http://www.waukesha.tec.wi.us/home/info/ad./skills./htm.

Nontraditional Documentation of Student Learning Outcomes

Several colleges have made advances in nontraditional methods for documenting student achievement of learning outcomes that extend beyond traditional grades, credits, certificates, and degrees, such as electronic transcripts and portfolios (e-transcripts and e-portfolios). In November 2001, Learning Outcomes Project staff conducted an invitational E-transcript Summit to link project work on nontraditional learning outcomes documentation with similar work in other higher education organizations, including Alverno College, Florida State University, Johns Hopkins University, iLearningInc., and The Chauncey Group International. Five e-transcript or e-portfolio models were featured: Diagnostic Digital Portfolio, Alverno College; Skills Profile, Inver Hills Community College; Career Portfolio, Florida State University and Santa Fe Community College; Critical Life Skills Transcript, Waukesha County Technical College; and Career Transcript, Johns Hopkins University. Fifty-eight participants shared best practices and lessons learned from their approaches to electronic documentation, and linkages were made that bolstered documentation activities in project colleges.

Waukesha County Technical College remains involved in implementing its Critical Life Skills electronic transcript, which enables students to demonstrate their growth and development for technical skills and life skills. The transcript includes numerical ratings and descriptions that translate academic language into more commonly understood evidence of student learning. Waukesha also documents learning outcomes in extracurricular activities as well as in traditional courses.

Inver Hills Community College designed an Internet-deployed database to record and report student achievement. Faculty apply cross-disciplinary rubrics defining exemplary, acceptable, and unacceptable achievement levels to assignments, tests, and projects. (See http://depts.inverhills.edu/LSPS. rubrics.htm for the rubrics and a sample Skills Profile.) Students then receive a Skills Profile—a complement to the traditional transcript—that documents their skills, citing specific projects, tests, or assignments as evidence. In the early phases of the Internet system, a small group of volunteer faculty participated; however, faculty members now use the Internet to track levels of achievement for each competency, and the project is stimulating faculty involvement toward a goal of institutionalizing this approach to documentation of learning outcomes. Currently, e-transcripts and e-portfolios documenting student learning outcomes are under development or implementation at six of the project colleges: Waukesha County Technical College, Inver Hills Community College, Schoolcraft College, Johnson County Community College, Hocking College, and Midlands Technical College.

Unexpected Outcomes

Although the project began with the goal of cultivating a focus on learning outcomes, several college teams quickly found this work to be a catalyst for major institutional change. In some cases, it led to a complete shift in approach, particularly for colleges that had extensive institutional effectiveness and program review processes but no comprehensive processes for assessing and documenting learning at the individual student level. For others, the project served as a means of connecting a number of loosely related initiatives all aimed at improving the quality of undergraduate education.

Shifts in thinking occurred in curriculum design, with an emphasis on learning outcomes replacing a traditional focus on course objectives. Colleges also began exploring ways of ensuring that student learning outcomes would become the central success factors used in determining institutional effectiveness.

Why Is This So Hard?

Throughout the project, the recurring refrain was the same: "This is hard work!" McClenney (2001), the project's external evaluator, identified key reasons that colleges find this undertaking so difficult:

- Lack of collaboration among disciplines and other groups within the institution

- Lack of knowledge about assessment processes and tools

- Lack of awareness of the need for outcomes-based education

- Lack of appropriate, effective assessment tools and models

- A perception that some important learning outcomes are not measurable

- Traditional insulation from accountability for individual student learning at the classroom level

- Traditional resistance to self-assessment in higher education

- Lack of incentive for outcomes-based efforts resulting from past external requirements for accountability, funding, and policy that are rarely tied to individual student learning

- Increasing demands and constricting resources, which leave little time or incentive for educational reform efforts of this magnitude

Assessment Is the Really Hard Part

Throughout the project, participants universally identified assessment as the most difficult aspect of this work, and during seminars, focus groups, and site visits they explored the reasons for this determination. Team members from all areas of the colleges admitted that they do not know how to assess and that, as one participant put it, "the tools stink." One participant explained the difficulty with assessing learning outcomes by pointing out, "We are unaccustomed to being asked to gain consensus on what we're trying to achieve." Another acknowledged the bliss of ignorance as a complement to the fear of failure noting, "We don't really want to know how we measure up."

The lack of data also makes the work more difficult. As one member put it, "We don't know what we don't know." And still another pointed to the busy schedules of everyone in the college: "I'm already dancing as fast as I can." Despite these challenges, most college team members agreed that the hard work was worth it, citing such advantages as, "Faculty and students are completely transformed in their thinking about why they are here," and,

"For the first time we can begin to answer the how-do-we-know questions about learning."

Recommendations

Nearly all of the sixteen colleges that joined the 21st Century Learning Outcomes Project with the League in July 2000 remain engaged more than three years later in targeted institutional work toward implementing their learning outcomes agendas. Today many others have joined these colleges as the learning outcomes movement gains momentum in higher education, with accrediting commissions and other higher education associations advancing the cause. Other institutions embarking on a learning outcomes journey might take the following lessons from the pioneering experiences of these sixteen forerunners.

Learning outcomes implementation must be a continuous campus conversation. Such conversation allows for more natural emergence and implementation of ideas and integrates new employees into the ongoing conversation with veteran staff, through which they learn the history of the process, participate in the current analysis and implementation, and help shape the future though continued discussion.

The impetus for adopting an outcomes-based approach should be the institution's stated and lived value of student learning. Colleges may adopt an outcomes-based approach to learning as a means of pacifying external demands for accountability or securing sufficient funding; however, if the motivation for change does not stem from an explicit focus on student learning, the effort may fall short of its potential.

Since the accountability movement is not progressing in some colleges with the speed and urgency it might if the need were critical, other motivators can be effective. The movement to an outcomes-based educational approach can be adopted, for example, as a means of clearly distinguishing an institution in a crowded, competitive market. The movement may be prompted by the vision of a strong leader or the experience and prestige that come from joining a cutting-edge movement.

Faculty should be deeply engaged and supported from the onset in the leadership of any effort toward outcomes-based learning. Full support of faculty should include adequate professional development and reassigned work load for new curriculum development. Special assistance should be provided as needed particularly from experts in outcomes-based curriculum and assessment when redesigning curriculum. Taking the stance that this is work that faculty should be doing anyway is likely to be counterproductive; instead, acknowledging the outstanding work faculty are already doing and finding incentives to help them shift traditional teaching and curriculum methods to more outcomes-based approaches will be more successful.

A college should implement outcomes-based learning using a model that fits its culture and values. In no case should a college adopt another institution's program wholesale; however, a college can customize one or more approaches that resonate with its fundamental philosophy.

Learning outcomes approaches and assessment of student learning can strengthen academic quality and institutional effectiveness (Baker and Hjelm, 2001).

Clearly, one of the major lessons of this project is that this work is extremely difficult. Changing a college culture to a focus on learning outcomes requires long-term commitment and dedication of resources. Internal as well as external forces can cause the work to ebb and flow.

Although cuts in budget, changes in leadership, and temporary shifts in priorities pull colleges from this work, the underlying commitment to student learning remains. What matters most is that a learning outcomes approach can help a college demonstrate to its students that it offers them relevant curricula, meaningful information about their learning achievements, and more control over their learning to help them prepare for success in their professional and personal lives.

References

Baker, R. L. and Hjelm, M. (2001). "Evaluating Individual Student Learning: Implications from Four Models of Assessment." *Learning Abstracts, 4*(3).

Butler County Community College. (2001). Learning PACT Project: Quarterly Report, October 2001. http://www.butlercc.edu/league. Accessed Jan 31, 2004.

Carlsen, C. J. (2002). "Leading the Way to Connect Community to the College." *Leadership Abstracts, 15*(9).

Lindahl, S. (2002). "Learning Options and Readiness: High School Partnerships in the 21st Century." *Learning Abstracts, 5*(2).

McClenney, K. M. (1998). "Community Colleges Perched at the Millennium: Perspectives on Innovation, Transformation, and Tomorrow." *Leadership Abstracts, 11*(8).

McClenney, K. M. (2001). "Why Is This So Hard...And Why Bother?" 21st Century Learning Outcomes Project Seminar 2001. League for Innovation in the Community College. March 4, Atlanta.

Montgomery College. (n.d.). 21st Century Learning Outcomes Project: White Papers. http://www.woodstock.edu/students/academics/learningoutcomes/index.html. Accessed Jan. 31, 2004.

Wilson, C. D., Miles, C. L., Baker, R. L., and Schoenberger, R. L. (2000). *Learning Outcomes for the 21st Century: Report of a Community College Study*. Mission Viejo, Calif.: League for Innovation in the Community College.

Evaluating Individual Student Learning: Implications From Four Models of Assessment

— Mary Hjelm and Ronald L. Baker

Hjelm, M. and Baker, R. L. (2001). Evaluating Individual Student Learning: Implications From Four Models of Assessment. *Learning Abstracts* 4(3).

Historically, judging the achievement of institutional and student learning outcomes for higher education was the province of colleges and universities. More recently, however, higher education's role as sole adjudicator of institutional effectiveness and student learning achievement is eroding, due in part to a decrease in public confidence regarding the ability of colleges and universities to authenticate the achievement of explicit outcomes. One indicator of that decline is public skepticism regarding the meaning, relevance, and significance of traditional grades and degrees as effective measures of achievement of intended learning outcomes. Community and technical colleges, noted for their effectiveness in fulfilling public expectations, have not escaped the fallout from this trend. Along with other sectors of higher education, they are under pressure to augment implicit measures of institutional and student learning outcomes with authentic assessment and meaningful documentation of explicit achievements.

Graduated Scales

Authentic assessment and meaningful documentation of student learning outcomes is beneficial at a variety of levels within the institution: (1) at the institutional level, explicit documentation of student achievement provides evidence to demonstrate accountability to the institution's publics; (2) at the program level, program effectiveness and continuous quality improvement are enhanced through the measurement and evaluation of student achievement of expected educational outcomes; and (3) at the classroom level, an evaluation of student learning provides valuable information to both faculty and students. Such assessment and documentation benefits faculty by providing data that can be analyzed to inform and improve instructional strategies that enhance teaching effectiveness. Explicit assessment of learning outcomes benefits students by providing evidence of achievement levels for expected learning outcomes. Regardless of the assessment rationale, assessments of achievement of explicitly defined educational outcomes complement more general assessments of student learning such as course grades, program certificates, and institutional degrees.

Unfortunately, two obstacles hinder ready implementation of effective assessment and documentation strategies. The first obstacle is cultural, since many educators are grounded in a culture of subjective assessment that uses historical criteria of achievement. Consequently, they have little understanding of and place even less value in explicit assessment and documentation of student achievements. The second obstacle is a perceived lack of assessment models to review and consider for implementation.

Foundations of Assessment

Evaluation of the achievement of intended learning outcomes is no longer the sole domain of faculty. An expanding number of constituencies, including students, faculty, administrators, and board members, expect institutions to provide primary evidence of achievement of explicit student outcomes. Frequently that evidence takes the form of data derived from an assessment of student learning outcomes. Assessment of student learning is most effectively conducted when based upon meaningful and relevant criteria that authentically evaluate the achievement of knowledge, skills, and abilities. Its conduct should be authentic, continuous, systematic, and substantive in nature; give students more control over their learning; provide a positive, risk-free structure for reflection and feedback; and support improvement in both student learning and instructor effectiveness. Furthermore, the results of assessments should contribute to the documentation of levels of achievement and effectiveness and suggest directions for improvement of student learning.

> Given the spectrum of reasons for assessment, no single model can be applied universally to the broad range of intended higher education outcomes.

Taking Stock

A consideration for the adoption of a model of assessment should begin with thoughtful deliberation of two key questions: (1) Why do we want to assess student learning? (2) What should be assessed? While appearing obvious and simplistic, these questions have profound implications because they require a clear understanding and articulation of the purpose and expected outcomes resulting from assessment. Given the spectrum of reasons for assessment, no single model can be applied universally to the broad range of intended higher education outcomes. Consequently, colleges have adopted a variety of assessment models based upon the perceived needs for assessment. Many of these models have characteristics that influence an evaluation of individual student learning. A discussion of the characteristics and implications of four models of assessment may be beneficial to an analysis of the resulting implications for the assessment and documentation of student learning.

Outcomes Model

The Outcomes Model reflects a holistic approach to assessments of outcomes based upon the values and mission of the college. Planning begins with a broad consideration and subsequent refinement of the question:

What are the explicit outcomes and levels of achievement that a student must attain to receive credentials from this college? Although the Outcomes Model respects external interests, it is not determined by them. It may be influenced by factors such as SCANS or SKILLS standards, grants, or state requirements, but it is driven by values identified by the college as primary to its mission and vision. The first step in implementing this model is the identification of overarching institutional learning outcomes that provide a framework for development of more program-specific learning outcomes. Collectively, the institutional and programmatic learning outcomes inform decisions on learning outcomes at the individual course level. Assessment methods and tools are subsequently designed to measure achievement of these intended institutional, program, and course learning outcomes. Consequently, an assessment of student learning is a central and critical component of an overall assessment of institutional effectiveness.

Grassroots Model

The Grassroots Model emphasizes assessment of student achievement at the course and program levels. It is characterized by assessment efforts initiated and conducted by faculty, but assessment may be conducted and evaluated by anyone at the point of contact between the institution and its constituencies. This model is based upon a clear connection between the values held by faculty and the perceived benefit of measuring outcomes that reinforce faculty values and perceptions. Many faculty support the Grassroots Model because it enables them to integrate assessment with teaching and learning to improve the effectiveness of both. Faculty also support the Grassroots Model because it empowers them with the responsibility of defining the criteria and conditions by which learning is measured and evaluated rather than having those characteristics determined, imposed, and interpreted by others. Where the connection between values and perceived benefits to faculty is strong, faculty exhibit a high degree of buy-in and ownership of assessment, which in turn act as stimuli for inquiry and consideration by other faculty for implementation across the curriculum. An aggregation of class and program assessments of student achievement contribute to an overall assessment of learning outcomes at the institutional level that serves as an indicator of institutional effectiveness in one key area of the college's mission.

Mandate Model

The Mandate Model is based on the principle of accountability for resources invested in the college as a whole. It may be the model most fraught with anxiety within the education community because its agenda is externally motivated, if not externally controlled. It is designed to determine a "return on investment" to the institution's publics. Assessment criteria for this model frequently define short-term priorities for the institution, since funding support is commonly tied to the results of institutional assessments that are then evaluated by stakeholders outside the college community. It measures institutional performance directly, and student learning indirectly, based upon performance indicators such as years to degree completion that may, in some cases, be in misalignment with the spirit and mission of institutional mission. Since the focus for the Mandate Model is the institution as a whole, assessment criteria frequently lack a substantial academic foundation. Furthermore, criteria typically used for this model are simplistic and economic in nature and are defined by entities external to the college. Since the rationale and criteria for assessments are determined externally, assessment strategies tend to be narrow and reactive rather than broad and proactive. Consequently, assessment of individual student learning is often anecdotal and indirect rather than meaningful and direct. The Mandate Model does, however, provide a clear indicator to the college of what is valued and expected by external stakeholders.

Institutional Effectiveness Model

This model is designed primarily to evaluate the institution and its initiatives rather than to evaluate individual student learning achievement. Assessment criteria are drawn from the institution's mission statement–what it says it will do. The purpose of assessment in this context is to determine, on the whole, the institution's effectiveness in fulfilling its mission. In practice, this model assists in an evaluation of how well the institution is doing what it says it will do. Assessment results are returned to the college's stakeholders for an overarching evaluation of the institution rather than returned to individual students and faculty to inform and evaluate individual student achievement. Consequently, assessment results from this model apply to the institution as an entity and students as a whole with only indirect inferences to achievements by individual students. Therefore, these assessment results are of limited value in improving and certifying individual student learning.

Considerations

Each of the four models of assessment has strengths and weaknesses. Since some models concentrate on evaluating student learning directly while other models only imply student achievement, educators should carefully consider why assessment is conducted, what is to be measured, and why it should be measured. Furthermore, agreement should be reached regarding how, and in what context, assessments are to be conducted and how the resulting data are to be evaluated. Educators should avoid the common errors of assuming that all models of assessment produce the same results or reversing the sequence of considerations by first implementing assessment tools and techniques in hope they will somehow support an unspecified purpose for assessment. To be successful, strategies for an assessment of student learning should be based upon discussions and agreements within the college community and between the college community and the institution's publics concerning expectations, functions, and forms assessment will take in evaluating and documenting institutional and educational outcomes. In the end, however, what really matters to students directly, and to others more indirectly, is that the college conducts effective and meaningful evaluations of student learning that yield clear and compelling evidence of student achievement of explicitly stated knowledge, skills, and abilities.

Learning From the Learning Colleges: Observations Along the Journey

— Kay M. McClenney

McClenney, K. M. (2001). "Learning From the Learning Colleges: Observations Along the Journey." *Learning Abstracts* 4(2).

In January 2000, the League for Innovation launched The Learning College Project to assist community colleges around the world to become more learning-centered institutions. Twelve Vanguard Learning Colleges (VLCs) were selected by an international advisory committee to help develop model programs and best practices in learning-centered education with a specific focus on five key areas: organizational culture, staff recruitment and development, technology, learning outcomes, and underprepared students.

Between October 2000 and March 2001, three project staff members and the project's external evaluator got a glimpse of the work of these colleges in one-day site visits to the VLCs. These visits provide a basis for a preliminary set of observations regarding the challenges involved as colleges make the journey to become more learning centered. In making these observations, several caveats apply: (1) None of these observations apply to every college. (2) Most of the observations apply to many of the colleges. (3) Although a high degree of consensus exists, the observations may not reflect the views of every project staff member involved in the meetings.

The campus visits affirmed that the VLCs are leading community colleges where innovation is the norm and institutional pride is evident and justified; in these colleges innovation abounds. Led by committed and creative people and aimed almost exclusively at improving student service and student success, these innovations include outstanding programs in student advising, developmental education, faculty orientation and development, learning communities, project-based learning, applications of technology to improve teaching and learning, electronic portfolio development, Web-based registration and financial aid processes, call center customer service operations, Baldrige quality processes, and partnerships with businesses, community organizations, universities, and the public schools. At one college, a campus group identifies effective innovations and supports bringing them to scale within the college. This energy for innovation provided the backdrop for the campus visits, and from interactions during the visits emerged the significant crosscutting themes that follow.

Key Observations: A Baker's Dozen

1. The journey is long, the tasks are multiple, the challenges are conceptually and politically complex... The commitment to become a Learning College can be viewed as a long, arduous, and exciting journey to realign institutional priorities, policies, programs, practices, and personnel to focus on learning as the primary business of the college. This observation is not gratuitous information or rhetorical fluff; rather, it is an exclamation point. The visitors were reminded that talking and writing about major institutional transformation is easy, but making it happen is quite difficult.

2. The commitment to learning is not always a visible priority. All of the VLCs have a long history of commitment to learning, but this commitment is not always explicit in policies, programs, practices, and participation of college personnel in the educational enterprise. The reasons vary from campus to campus: In some cases, the focus on learning may still be one of several competing priorities; in others, the formal language of the institution does not appear to have caught up with its intentions and daily practice; in still others, disparate projects have not yet been blessed with an explicit unifying vision.

3. Innovations and projects abound, but they sometimes lack unifying goals or principles and frequently spawn reform fatigue. All of the VLCs are heavily engaged in a variety of innovations and projects, sometimes numbering more than fifty on a single campus. In some cases, no unifying principles or goals exist for the vast array of institutional activities, a phenomenon that produces a culture some staff members identify as unfocused and frenetic. As one VLC team member said, "This college is pathologically committed to innovation." Faculty and staff also identified a syndrome they call reform fatigue. Already dancing as fast as they can, they seek organizing principles and priorities as well as ways to reconfigure workloads and perhaps say no to some activities. Some of the VLCs are attempting to create a common set of principles, goals, and values focused on learning to help integrate and drive their work, and the Learning College concept is viewed by many leaders in the VLCs as an ideal umbrella under which to collect, unify, and focus college initiatives.

4. Effective ways to scale up innovations that demonstrably support student learning are greatly needed. Conversations about the plethora of projects under way in the colleges also yielded expressions of concern about the need to find effective ways to scale up successful innovations born through special projects. Too often, people at VLCs find that effective approaches remain marginal or even disappear from the institutional map once the inventor burns out or the grant runs out. By contrast, at least one VLC has established a process for bringing innovations to scale.

5. The language of learning (a) is increasingly reflected in key institutional documents, (b) needs action to match walk with talk, (c) is not yet broadly and fully understood, and (d) produces resistance and resentment in some quarters. As community colleges begin to use the language of learning in mission statements, program descriptions, policy statements, and titles of key staff, the Learning

College concept is in danger of being gently co-opted by the appearance of interest and support without the necessary hard and long effort to make the concept come to full fruition. This observation comes also with a counterpoint. That is, on some campuses there is a notable resistance to the language of the Learning College among at least some faculty and staff. Explanations of this phenomenon vary from complaints about education jargon to objections that "we have always been about learning here!" and a sense that past performance is being unfairly criticized.

6. There exists a continuing need for organizational teaching and learning—to gain common understanding and define common ground and then to develop new skill sets. An insight related to the language issue was articulated by one VLC faculty member in this way: There is still a significant need for internal teaching and learning, first to come to a collective and local understanding of the meaning of Learning College and then to develop new skill sets and attitudes. "Don't assume too quickly," he said, "that faculty actually know how to do things differently." That honest reflection can clearly be applied to other campus groups as well.

7. Learner-centered and learning-centered are still often used as though they were synonymous terms. Some of the VLCs are still using learner and learning as if they were synonymous concepts. Community colleges have historically been learner or student centered, and many of them take great pride in this focus as one of their core values. The Learning College also includes a focus on the learner as a core value but places priority on learning as the desired outcome for learners. This modification of perspective is subtle but can also be transformative in key areas of institutional policy and practice.

8. People foresee the need to consider significant changes in the roles of faculty and other professionals. With some anticipation and also a measure of dread, some interviewees noted that a serious focus on learning will bring colleges to consider significant changes in the roles of faculty and other professionals. The shift from deliverer of knowledge to facilitator of learning may be only the tip of the proverbial iceberg, as people consider possibilities as diverse as case manager roles, distance learning specialists, and the potential unbundling of instruction and the assessment of learning. Such changes, they say, should be dictated by evidence of what works in facilitating student learning.

9. The most challenging task is also the most essential task: defining, assessing, and documenting student learning outcomes. Most community colleges have had experience in this process in selected occupational programs, but the VLCs are finding it quite difficult to apply the process to all college courses, programs, and degrees. A number of the VLCs have defined learning outcomes for many courses and have embedded these in the curriculum, though general education courses and critical across-the-curriculum skills remain a challenge. Few VLCs are satisfied with their processes to assess the acquisition of skills and knowledge identified in the outcome statements,

and none of the colleges have created satisfactory models to document and transcript the learning outcomes. Clearly, substantial and important work needs to be done in this arena.

10. Companion to the assessment challenge is the work of developing a culture of evidence. Building a culture that addresses the demand for data about student learning, the capacity to produce and analyze that data, and the skills and commitment to use data for continuous improvement represents a significant departure from community college traditions of justification by anecdote. People in the VLCs are recognizing the value and the power of data-driven decision making.

11. Project evaluation at the campus level needs further attention. A significant amount of work still needs to be done within a number of the VLCs to establish clear and appropriate ways to evaluate outcomes of the project and achievement of project objectives. Community colleges have a fine tradition of becoming so involved in the work at hand that they overlook evaluation of its impact. It will take active commitment and public accountability to avoid that phenomenon in this project.

12. Project participation has reinforced college efforts to put learning first in related initiatives. The VLCs recognize the value of participating in this project and have used their participation to reinforce their efforts to place learning first in related initiatives such as accreditation, total quality management, and measurements of institutional effectiveness.

13. [reprise] The journey is long, the tasks are multiple, the challenges are conceptually and politically complex—and there is a significant distance yet to travel. The VLCs are accustomed to being recognized in the U.S. and Canada as outstanding community colleges, and they have created a culture of pride and high expectations for their work. They like to succeed, and they like to perform at very high levels of competency. Compared to an ideal model of the Learning College, the VLCs are certainly best in class. At this point in the journey, however, the participant colleges, each on its own path, have a considerable distance to travel in order to achieve the five major project objectives. The early moral of this story can therefore be appropriately summarized: "A Learning College has a lot to learn!"

Observations of Fellow Travelers

The project evaluator emerged from these campus visits enriched by her own learning—and with a notebook full of quotations from the Learning College pioneers. Asked to define the difference between a very good community college and a Learning College, one college staff member noted, "The difference is when you can provide credible and convincing evidence of learning." Another commented, "An important goal for us is the *planned abandonment* of low-priority, off-target, or ineffective programs." And, finally, one college staff member offered a fitting benediction when she revealed the extent to which the Learning College idea can be embedded in an institution: "Being learning-centered is like breathing for us."

Benchmarking Best Practices in the Learning College

— Kay M. McClenney

McClenney, K. M. (2003). "Benchmarking Best Practices in the Learning College." *Learning Abstracts* 6(4).

Across North America, increasing numbers of community and technical colleges are committing themselves to an important and timely challenge: the transformation of good or even excellent institutions into colleges that are powerfully and effectively focused on student learning. An example of this commitment is found in the work of 12 Vanguard Learning Colleges* that have been part of the Learning College Project at the League for Innovation.

Reflecting on their progress in becoming more learning-centered institutions, the faculty, staff, and administrators of these colleges strongly affirm the importance of benchmarking as a tool for transformation. Widely used in the private sector, benchmarking is generally defined as a process for identifying, understanding, and adapting outstanding practices from other organizations in order to help one's own organization improve its performance. In the case of the learning college, of course, the central focus is on improvement of student learning and persistence.

According to the American Productivity and Quality Center (APQC), some key themes characterize successful benchmarking and best-practice adoption efforts. Among them are these two:

1. Transfer is a people-to-people process; meaningful relationships precede sharing and transfer.

2. Benchmarking stems from a personal and organizational willingness to learn. A vibrant sense of curiosity and a deep respect and desire for learning may be the real keys. [See www.apqc.org]

The founder of APQC, Jack Grayson, says that benchmarking requires "being humble enough to admit that another [organization] is better at something and being wise enough to learn how to match or surpass it." The Vanguard Learning Colleges seized the opportunity to identify among their fellow institutions the exemplary programs and practices that seemed worthy of examination, adaptation, and then, perhaps, adoption on their own campuses. Unquestionably, there are other community colleges whose work deserves similar mention and similar attention in benchmarking work. The community college field needs to hear also about their practices—and the evidence of their effectiveness.

Promising Practices

Given the number of intriguing initiatives under way at the 12 Vanguard Learning Colleges, it is challenging to name a few that particularly stand out. However, a sampling of programs and practices that deserve serious attention would surely include the following:

Organizational Structure to Support Learning. Cascadia Community College (WA), organized around four major learning outcomes, and Community College of Denver, organized into "centers" that cut across traditional boundaries.

Strategic Plan Integration and Follow-Through. Moraine Valley Community College, Valencia Community College, Community College of Baltimore County (CCBC).

Cross-Functional Teams and Other Inclusive Approaches to Institutional Transformation. "Learning Dialogs" at Sinclair Community College and Moraine Valley Community College; the Council for Innovation and Student Learning (CISL) at Community College of Baltimore County; Valencia Community College's "Goal Teams," formed to monitor and report progress toward achievement of goals set forth in the college's strategic plan, titled "Learning First"; Kirkwood Community College's Student Success Council, which has been a significant force in establishing direction and follow-through for a variety of initiatives, including those focused on student orientation and advising.

Learning Strategies. Learning communities at Community College of Denver, Lane Community College, and elsewhere (e.g., the average retention rate for students in learning communities at CCD for spring/fall and fall/spring was 71 percent, compared with the college average of 55 percent); linkages between credit and noncredit programs and staffing pioneered at Moraine Valley; Process Learning at Kirkwood Community College, Madison Area Technical College, and Sinclair Community College; the College 101 (student orientation) course at Moraine Valley; and LifeMap, the outstanding academic advising model at Valencia.

Learning Outcomes and Assessment. Community College of Baltimore County (GREAT Project—GeneRal Education Assessment Teams); Cascadia Community College (building learning outcomes into the fabric of the institution; work on cross-cutting core "literacies"); the Community College of Denver's Computerized Study Skills Assessment Test (CCSAT), now being pilot tested at two other colleges; Kirkwood's Essential Skills Institute, a faculty-led institute that is exploring the option of offering vocational students a certificate in Essential Skills when they show competence in communication, teamwork, and computation skills; CCD's cross-functional curriculum development work, which addresses curriculum duplication among Information Technology, Graphic Design, Multimedia, Communication (radio/film/video), and Graphic Technology programs and

* The colleges that have participated in the Learning College Project are Cascadia Community College; Community College of Baltimore County (CCBC); Community College of Denver (CCD); Humber College; Kirkwood Community College; Lane Community College; Madison Area Technical College (MATC); Moraine Valley Community College; Palomar College; Richland College; Sinclair Community College; and Valencia Community College.

which started with the question, "What competencies do students need?"; Humber College's Generic Skills Resource Manuals, developed for Communications, Writing Across the Curriculum, Personal Skills, Interpersonal Skills, Thinking Skills, Mathematics, and Computer Skills; CCBC's and Kirkwood's learning outcomes assessment projects, engaging faculty in design and implementation of assessments; and the developing culture of evidence at Richland College, where there is a serious commitment to processes for quality improvement.

Programs and Services for Underprepared Students. Valencia's focus on student experience at "the front door" of the college; comprehensive academic and support programs for first-generation students at CCD; the Kirkwood Community College Learning Services department, nominated as one of the best programs in the country; and an intensive focus on improvement of programs and services for underprepared students at Madison Area Technical College.

Tracking Student Progress. Student tracking systems at CCBC and at Humber College; Community College of Denver's student tracking database (a work still in progress); information provided to faculty about students in their classrooms at Richland College.

Technology to Support and Enhance Learning. The Center for Interactive Learning at Sinclair; Cascadia Community College's Student ePortfolio and Employee ePortfolio (note that Palomar College has also done some work in this area); CCBC's Virtual Academy (for faculty who wish to teach distance learning courses); Kirkwood's use of learning technology to improve Surgical Technology student and program performance (all exams for the three-semester Surgical Technology program will be imported into the Perception online test-authoring system, and then test data on acquisition of program competencies will be analyzed and online tutorials created to address areas of weak learning); the new AtLas portal at Valencia, an online portal that connects students to tools needed to succeed at Valencia, enabling them to register and pay for classes, check their grades, email professors and classmates, see campus announcements, and search job sites. AtLas also connects students to the resources of LifeMap, Valencia's comprehensive system of student services and academic planning.

Faculty and Staff Recruitment and Development. A splendid new faculty orientation program at Moraine Valley; innovations in role definitions and staffing patterns at Richland College; Humber's impressive staff development program; MATC's revision of recruitment and selection processes to reflect learning-centered principles; CCBC's Virtual Academy, for faculty who wish to teach distance learning courses; the "teacher formation" program at Richland, based on Parker Palmer's *Courage to Teach*; CCD's faculty performance appraisal and pay-for-performance system.

Raising the Bar

Benchmarking is a strategy particularly beneficial in colleges where people are willing to focus their efforts on selected aspects of institutional practice, with an eye toward improvement; where value is placed on *evidence* of effectiveness; and where such evidence is an important factor in decisions about institutional policy, programs, and practices.

If benchmarking is to play its part in quality improvement, the community college field must increasingly insist on a meaningful benchmarking process, which particularly includes a rigorous definition of the term best practice. Reference to *best practices* in education quite clearly should be based on evidence that the practices produce improved results.

Unfortunately
for those who seek

it, the evidence we need does not always exist or may not endure rigorous scrutiny.

Unfortunately for those who seek it, the evidence we need does not always exist or may not endure rigorous scrutiny. In those cases, of course, community college people press ahead, relying still on critical judgment, the wisdom of experience, and a willingness to innovate. But the serious pursuit of quality in undergraduate education highlights the acute need for rigorous evaluation of educational practices, yielding models and strategies that are proven effective. The hallmark questions for the learning college are the two posed by Terry O'Banion: "How does this action promote and expand student learning?" and the tough one, "How do we know?"

Learning College Inventory

— Terry O'Banion, Cindy L. Miles, and Cynthia D. Wilson

O'Banion, T., Miles, C. L., and Wilson, C. D. (2000). Learning College Inventory. Created for the Learning College Project. Mission Viejo, CA: League for Innovation in the Community College.

This inventory is designed to help an institution assess its status as a Learning College* and to provide a tool with which it can monitor and direct its progress toward becoming more learning centered. This inventory comprises five critical areas in which institutions committed to becoming Learning Colleges are focusing their attention and resources: Organizational Culture, Staff Recruitment & Development, Technology, Student Learning, and Learning Outcomes. This inventory reflects the key characteristics and principles of a Learning College (outlined in the Appendix) as applied to these five focus areas.

Please indicate your employment category by circling one of the following categories:

FACULTY   SUPPORT STAFF   ADMINISTRATOR

Instructions: For each statement in the Learning College Inventory, indicate the LEVEL OF IMPLEMENTATION that your college has achieved regarding the item described by using the following scale:

? = **I DON'T KNOW** THE IMPLEMENTATION STATUS OF THIS ITEM AT OUR COLLEGE.

0 = **(NONE)** OUR COLLEGE HAS NOT YET ADDRESSED THIS ITEM.

1 = **(DISCUSSION)** OUR COLLEGE IS IN DISCUSSION STAGE BUT HAS TAKEN NO FURTHER ACTION ON THIS ITEM.

2 = **(PLANNING)** OUR COLLEGE IS IN PLANNING STAGE WITH THIS ITEM.

3 = **(PARTIAL IMPLEMENTATION)** OUR COLLEGE HAS TAKEN SPECIFIC ACTION ON THIS ITEM.

4 = **(FULL IMPLEMENTATION)** OUR COLLEGE HAS FULLY IMPLEMENTED ACTION RELATED TO THIS ITEM.

I. ORGANIZATIONAL CULTURE

Learning Colleges strive to develop an organizational culture where policies, programs, practices, and personnel support learning as the major institutional priority. The culture of an organization both shapes and reflects its values and practices and is often expressed in the ways decisions are made and resources are directed. This section of the survey deals with decision making, resource allocation, and activities designed to create a culture focused on learning.

1. Governing and Planning

a. The governing board has approved a college mission statement that reflects a commitment to learning-centered principles.
? 0 1 2 3 4

b. An institutionwide action plan guides implementation of the college's learning-centered mission.
? 0 1 2 3 4

c. All college stakeholder groups are involved in planning for and implementing learning-centered principles.
? 0 1 2 3 4

d. College stakeholders consider the following questions when making decisions:

(1) Does this decision improve and expand learning?
? 0 1 2 3 4

(2) How do we know this action improves and expands learning?
? 0 1 2 3 4

e. The college is talking with the state board to press for revised funding formulas that support nontraditional programs and practices that promote student learning.
? 0 1 2 3 4

2. Focusing Resources

Fiscal Resources

a. Budget processes and decisions are driven by a focus on learning (i.e., consideration of what will improve, expand, and document student learning).
? 0 1 2 3 4

b. Resources are allocated to support initiatives to make the college more learning centered.
? 0 1 2 3 4

c. Resources are allocated to improve or replace outdated college facilities to meet the needs of Knowledge Age learners.
? 0 1 2 3 4

d. Community and corporate partnerships are used to help the college improve and expand student learning.
? 0 1 2 3 4

e. The college devotes significant resources to research to identify, assess, document, and apply information about the learning outcomes of its students.
? 0 1 2 3 4

---

* A Learning College is defined as an institution dedicated to a focus on learning as outlined in *A Learning College for the Twenty-First Century* (O'Banion, 1997) and *Creating More Learning Centered Community Colleges* (O'Banion, 1997). See Appendix for listing of key characteristics and principles of a Learning College.

Staff Resources

a. Members of all college employee groups serve as resources to increase and expand student learning.
? 0 1 2 3 4

b. Practitioners and community volunteers serve as resources to increase and expand student learning.
? 0 1 2 3 4

c. Students serve as learning resources for other students and faculty.
? 0 1 2 3 4

d. The college uses nontraditional workload and faculty-student interaction models to improve and expand learning.
? 0 1 2 3 4

3. Creating a Culture Focused on Learning

a. College leaders demonstrate their commitment to creating a learning-centered institution.
? 0 1 2 3 4

b. College leaders are sufficiently knowledgeable of Learning College principles to lead the college toward becoming more learning centered.
? 0 1 2 3 4

c. Key college documents (e.g., mission and vision statements, college catalog, program descriptions, personnel policies, job descriptions) reflect learning-centered principles and practices.
? 0 1 2 3 4

d. The college's academic policies (e.g., registration, placement, attendance, academic standing) reflect priorities placed on learning.
? 0 1 2 3 4

e. The college community supports the major changes needed to make the college more learning centered.
? 0 1 2 3 4

f. The college regularly evaluates its progress toward becoming more learning centered.
? 0 1 2 3 4

II. STAFF RECRUITMENT AND DEVELOPMENT

The members of the college community bring life to Learning College principles. Staff recruitment and development procedures say much about the institution's commitment to "placing learning first" and are the first steps in building a community dedicated to student and organizational learning. For this learning community to be successful, all college stakeholders must be included in substantive conversations about what it means to focus institutional resources and activities on learning, and the outcomes of these conversations must be translated to action. [NOTE: "Staff" refers to all college employees.]

4. Selecting Staff

a. Job descriptions reflect staff behaviors and outcomes that promote student learning and success.
? 0 1 2 3 4

b. Selection committees are trained in how to apply a focus on learning in the hiring process.
? 0 1 2 3 4

c. Newly hired staff demonstrate a commitment to promoting student learning and success.
? 0 1 2 3 4

5. Defining Staff Roles

a. Roles and responsibilities for all employee groups explicitly relate to improving student learning and creating more effective learning environments.
? 0 1 2 3 4

b. College reward systems encourage staff to adopt these learning-centered roles.
? 0 1 2 3 4

c. College staff who model learning-centered roles are enlisted in plans for institutional change.
? 0 1 2 3 4

6. Developing Staff

a. Staff development programs are designed to prepare all staff to help the college become more learning centered.
? 0 1 2 3 4

b. Staff development programs reflect changes in student learning needs.
? 0 1 2 3 4

c. Staff development activities to promote and sustain learning-centered policies, programs, and practices are provided for all employee groups as follows:

(1) new employees
? 0 1 2 3 4

(2) administrators
? 0 1 2 3 4

(3) trustees/governing board members
? 0 1 2 3 4

(4) full-time faculty
? 0 1 2 3 4

(5) part-time faculty
? 0 1 2 3 4

(5) professional staff
? 0 1 2 3 4

(6) support/classified staff
? 0 1 2 3 4

d. Each year, an increasing percentage of employees participate in staff development activities focused on promoting learning-centered principles.

    ?   0   1   2   3   4

e. Employee evaluation processes and outcomes demonstrate a focus on learning-centered principles.

    ?   0   1   2   3   4

7. Holding Conversations About Learning

a. Collegewide conversations about learning (i.e., what it means to focus policies, programs, and practices on learning) are a routine practice.

    ?   0   1   2   3   4

b. Business, industry, and other community stakeholders are engaged in college conversations about learning.

    ?   0   1   2   3   4

c. College trustees/governing board members are engaged in college conversations about learning.

    ?   0   1   2   3   4

d. Outcomes from these conversations about learning are used to modify college policies, programs, and practices to improve and expand learning.

    ?   0   1   2   3   4

III. Information Technology

In the Learning College, information technology is used as a powerful tool to improve and enhance learning for students and staff. Technology is used to connect learners to information, resources, support services, learning facilitators, and other learners. Learning Colleges use technology as a means to give learners more control over their own learning and to make learning more effective and more efficient.

8. Planning for Information Technology

a. The college has a long-term strategic information technology plan that addresses technology purchase, upgrade, user support, and staff training.

    ?   0   1   2   3   4

b. The technology plan includes specific references to ways technology will be used to increase and expand learning for students.

    ?   0   1   2   3   4

c. The college monitors the degree and quality of access to technology for all members of the college community.

    ?   0   1   2   3   4

d. The college has a formal strategy to increase access to technology for all members of the college community.

    ?   0   1   2   3   4

e. The college routinely evaluates the efficacy of technology applications in facilitating student learning or success.

    ?   0   1   2   3   4

9. Applying Information Technology

The college consistently searches for better ways of using information technology to improve and expand student learning or success in the following areas across the institution:

a. Admissions	?	0	1	2	3	4
b. Orientation	?	0	1	2	3	4
c. Assessment	?	0	1	2	3	4
d. Advisement	?	0	1	2	3	4
e. Registration	?	0	1	2	3	4

f. Enrollment management

    ?   0   1   2   3   4

g. Creation of learning environments and experiences

    ?   0   1   2   3   4

h. Development of individualized student learning plans

    ?   0   1   2   3   4

i. Monitoring student progress

    ?   0   1   2   3   4

j. Student interactions with faculty and other students

    ?   0   1   2   3   4

k. Access to information resources

    ?   0   1   2   3   4

l. Documenting competencies and goals achieved

    ?   0   1   2   3   4

m. Technology-enhanced options for self-initiated student learning that require no assistance from college staff

    ?   0   1   2   3   4

n. Career planning and placement

    ?   0   1   2   3   4

o. 24-hour help desk to support students and staff

    ?   0   1   2   3   4

IV. Student Learning

Student learning is the goal and guiding principle of the Learning College. Inherent to the learning-centered college are anytime, anywhere, anyway options for learning; powerful learning environments and experiences; and collaborative learning opportunities. In the Learning College students are expected to take primary responsibility for their learning, and all students are offered support and resources to help them meet their learning goals.

10. Providing More Options

a. The college routinely inventories the learning options currently available to students and staff.

    ?   0   1   2   3   4

b. The college has a plan for increasing the learning options available for students and staff.

    ?   0   1   2   3   4

c. Anytime learning opportunities are available for all students.

? 0 1 2 3 4

d. Anyplace learning opportunities are available for all students.

? 0 1 2 3 4

a. Opportunities for experiential learning (e.g., service learning, internships, cooperatives) are available for all students.

? 0 1 2 3 4

11. Creating More Powerful Learning Environments and Experiences

a. Each student has an individualized learning plan designed to meet his/her learning goals.

? 0 1 2 3 4

b. Courses and learning experiences within the curriculum are designed to enable students to achieve expected learning outcomes for each program.

? 0 1 2 3 4

c. Each faculty member's teaching styles and approaches are documented and shared with students to help with selection of learning options.

? 0 1 2 3 4

d. Each student's learning style is assessed to help choose optimal learning options.

? 0 1 2 3 4

e. Student evaluations are used to improve learning environments and experiences.

? 0 1 2 3 4

12. Collaborating for Learning

a. The value of collaboration to promote learning is reflected in mission statements, program descriptions, course designs, course scheduling, and reward systems.

? 0 1 2 3 4

b. The college uses collaborative processes to plan for and promote student and organizational learning.

? 0 1 2 3 4

c. Collaborative learning experiences are available for students through a variety of options (e.g., learning communities, team learning, project-based learning, student mentoring, peer tutoring).

? 0 1 2 3 4

d. Models of collaborative learning with proven success for improving and expanding student learning are identified for replication.

? 0 1 2 3 4

13. Orienting Students to New Options and Responsibilities

a. All students are given training to help them take primary responsibility for their learning and navigate the variety of available learning options.

? 0 1 2 3 4

b. The college has identified standards and expectations for the student's role in his/her own learning process (e.g., making decisions, exploring options, signing agreements, undergoing assessments).

? 0 1 2 3 4

c. Expectations regarding students' responsibilities in the learning process are documented and communicated in all courses.

? 0 1 2 3 4

14. Ensuring Success of Underprepared Students

a. The college regularly assesses its programs for underprepared students to determine student success rates, program strengths, and program weaknesses.

? 0 1 2 3 4

b. Staff with responsibility for underprepared students undergo specialized development programs aimed at increasing success rates for this population.

? 0 1 2 3 4

c. Underprepared students have a variety of learning options proven to enhance success for this population.

? 0 1 2 3 4

d. Assessment, advising, placement, and orientation programs for underprepared students reflect strategies proven to enhance retention and success for this population.

? 0 1 2 3 4

e. Faculty use strategies proven to improve retention and success of underprepared students.

? 0 1 2 3 4

f. All students have equal access to college services and resources, regardless of academic preparation.

? 0 1 2 3 4

V. Learning Outcomes

Learning outcomes are the backbone of the Learning College. Only when learning can be measured and certified can an institution confirm that learning has occurred. Learning outcomes, as explored in this section, refer to core competencies (knowledge and/or abilities) that a learner may acquire and demonstrate independent of a traditional course or program.

15. Identifying and Agreeing on Learning Outcomes

a. College staff agree on the value of identifying student learning outcomes (i.e., core competencies measured beyond the learning experience).

? 0 1 2 3 4

b. A collegewide process for identifying and agreeing on student learning outcomes is used.

? 0 1 2 3 4

c. Faculty members in every program and department are engaged in identifying and agreeing on learning outcomes.

? 0 1 2 3 4

d. The institution provides resources (training, reference materials, time, consultants) to assist staff in identifying and assessing learning outcomes.

? 0 1 2 3 4

e. The college has defined a set of learning outcomes that students in each program must achieve.

? 0 1 2 3 4

16. Assessing and Documenting Learning Outcomes

a. College staff agree on the value of assessing and documenting student learning outcomes.

? 0 1 2 3 4

b. A collegewide process for assessing and documenting learning outcomes is used.

? 0 1 2 3 4

c. Assessment is used to identify the gaps between learners' knowledge and skills and their learning goals.

? 0 1 2 3 4

d. Successful models for assessing student learning outcomes are identified for others to follow.

? 0 1 2 3 4

e. College staff use innovative approaches for measuring learning outcomes not easily measured by traditional tests.

? 0 1 2 3 4

f. The college successfully documents student learning in ways other than grades and credit.

? 0 1 2 3 4

Appendix

Key Characteristics and Principles of the Learning College

I. *A Learning College Renews Its Focus on Student Learning*

- Places learning first in every policy, program, & practice

II. *A Learning College Overhauls the Traditional Architecture of Education*

- Moves from time-bound, place-bound, bureaucracy-bound, role-bound to anytime, anyplace, anyway learning options

III. *Key Learning College Principles*

1. The Learning College creates substantive change in individual learners.

2. The Learning College engages learners in the learning process as full partners who assume primary responsibility for their own choices.

3. The Learning College creates and offers as many options for learning as possible.

4. The Learning College assists learners to form and participate in collaborative learning activities.

5. The Learning College defines the roles of learning facilitators by the needs of the learners.

6. The Learning College and its learning facilitators succeed only when improved and expanded learning can be documented for its learners.

Accreditation and the Learning College: Parallel Purposes and Principles for Practice

— Ronald L. Baker and Cynthia D. Wilson

Baker, R. L., and Wilson, C. D. (2006). "Accreditation and the Learning College: Parallel Purposes and Principles for Practice." *Learning Abstracts* 9(3)

In the early years of the Learning College movement, those of us who were involved in projects focused on the Learning College repeatedly heard familiar reasons for resistance. The most popular of these focused on lack of resources and on resource allocation, but close behind them was a perception that the accreditation processes do not support the work of the Learning College. Regardless of where we were in the U.S. or Canada, and as paradoxical as it sounds, we heard a common refrain about accrediting bodies—and other external agencies—creating obstacles to keep these educational institutions from focusing on learning.

During the seven years since the launch of the League's major projects on the Learning College and learning outcomes, the conversation has changed significantly. As colleges involved in those projects examined themselves closely and honestly, many found that the obstacles to implementation were often the result of individual and collective attitudes more than external restrictions. The findings of the Learning College Project, for example, clearly indicated that becoming more strongly focused on learning is an issue of will rather than one of resources, and the resolute commitment of colleges to this movement during the devastating budget cuts that occurred in the early years of this decade are testament to that reality.

It may be a function of the maturation of the Learning College movement and the expansion of self-study options, but we rarely hear the kinds of concerns we once did about the impact of accreditation on Learning College practice. Conversations have shifted from frustrated declarations that *there is no way we can do this with all the accreditation requirements we have* to thoughtful consideration of ways the self-study process can be used to reinforce a strong, collegewide focus on and commitment to learning. Now, rather than complaints about accreditation, we hear questions: *How do we link our Learning College work and our self-study? What options are available to us in designing and conducting our self-study? What colleges are effectively coupling self-study and Learning College implementation?*

The current conversation indicates a realization that the principles of accreditation and the principles of the Learning College are not at cross purposes. Both efforts admit the inherent academic values of student learning achievement, institutional and program effectiveness, and continuous improvement. These values are clearly evident in community and technical college missions and in accreditation criteria. An examination of the principles on which accreditation and the Learning College are based reveals four common elements that are the focus of this discussion: student learning, effectiveness, improvement, and evidence.

Student Learning. Both accreditation and the Learning College place strong emphasis on the importance of identifying and articulating student learning outcomes. The Learning College concept is based on the fundamental principle that a learning-focused institution "creates substantive change in the individual learner" (O'Banion, 1997). This substantive change in students occurs through their learning experiences while interacting with the institution, its faculty and staff, and other learners. For educators to determine whether intended change occurs, that change—the outcomes of learning—must be clearly defined.

Regional accreditation requires that institutions identify intended learning outcomes, plan carefully the program of instruction leading to achievement of those outcomes, and evaluate the effectiveness of the educational program in terms of the change it brings about in students. After the outcomes are defined, learning experiences are developed to facilitate student achievement of those outcomes, and assessment strategies are devised to monitor student progress. Assessment is both formative, to foster and enhance learning, and summative, to evaluate achievements. Both types of assessment are used to document student achievement of the learning outcomes.

Effectiveness. Historically, effectiveness was based on institutional intentions and capacity, with judgments determined by reviewing institutional inputs, most notably infrastructures, processes, and resources. However, judgments based solely on capital and capacity are no longer adequate to meet expectations of external agencies. Effectiveness must be evaluated in terms of achievements and results. More than simply responding to external calls for accountability, institutions engaged in the Learning College movement increasingly find it in their interest to examine carefully the degree to which their accomplishments match their intentions.

> **Accreditation** and the learning college both stress assessment of intentions, practices, and achievements.

Accreditation and the Learning College both stress assessment of intentions, practices, and achievements. Only by carefully evaluating all three of these elements can institutions meaningfully evaluate their effectiveness in achieving stated outcomes. Accreditation agencies expect institutions to define their outcomes, set goals that lead to achievement of those outcomes, and develop and implement methods of assessing their effectiveness in achieving those outcomes. Similarly, Terry O'Banion's questions—Does this action improve and expand student learning? and How do we know?—place strong focus on the need for and analysis of data to determine whether actions are achieving desired goals and objectives.

Improvement. Continuous improvement is the core of the accreditation process and fundamental to the Learning College movement. However, using assessment, data collection, and data analysis to determine effectiveness can easily become a perfunctory, meaningless task if the results are not used to make improvements to enhance and sustain the achievement of intended outcomes. While summative assessment evaluates strengths and shortfalls, formative assessment encourages growth and improvement by providing a rich source of feedback related to the organic, evolving nature of teaching, learning, and educational practice. When assessment results are used in an ongoing manner to inform practice, the assessment process comes full circle.

Both the Learning College concept and the principles of accreditation emphasize an ongoing cycle of planning and evaluation. They require application of the review and revision cycle to all aspects of institutional practice: curriculum, pedagogy, and achievements. The cycle requires analysis of structures, processes, and practices, as well as synthesis of their roles and interrelationships, to understand their individual and collective influence on outcomes achievement and mission fulfillment.

Evidence. Any meaningful discussion of effectiveness requires a valid and useful response to a fundamental question: *How do we know?* Answering the question requires evidence, which then forms the basis for conclusions colleges and their employees draw about both the institution and the practices within it. Development of that evidence, in turn, requires the collection and analysis of assessment data.

Thus, the myth
that accreditation and
the learning college are

disconnected, unrelated

endeavors is debunked.

Considered in context with institutional values, missions, characteristics, philosophies, intended outcomes, and so on, this evidence provides insight into the institution's effectiveness in fulfilling its charge to improve and expand student learning.

In recognition of the diversity of institutional missions and characteristics, accreditation and Learning College principles do not prescribe the forms of that evidence. However, accredited and learning-centered institutions are expected to use information from their planning and evaluation processes to demonstrate evidence of outcomes achievement. In particular, they are expected to provide evidence that students achieve intended learning outcomes regardless of where or how instruction was structured and delivered. Further, institutions are expected to provide evidence that their assessment activities are substantive and ongoing, and lead to the improvement of teaching and learning.

Accreditation and the Learning College provide frameworks for continuous improvement and outcomes achievement that allow freedom of implementation to accommodate a variety of institutional cultures, characteristics, and circumstances. They both require assessment, analysis and evaluation of assessment data, and use of the results to improve practice. Grounded in core values of student learning achievement, institutional effectiveness, and continuous improvement, accreditation holds institutions accountable for fulfilling their own intentions. Similarly, the Learning College puts student learning at the center of the institution's work and requires that the organization provide in a meaningful, evidence-supported manner an answer to O'Banion's questions: *Does this action improve and expand student learning?* and *How do we know?*

Centered on student learning, effectiveness, improvement, and evidence, the principles of accreditation and the principles of the Learning College are parallel in purpose and in practice. Applied meaningfully and in tandem, accreditation and Learning College practices can help community and technical colleges evaluate fulfillment of their own intentions and assess achievement of their own outcomes. As a very useful byproduct, institutions will develop evidence for use within the organization to inform and improve practice and respond to calls for accountability from external sources. Thus, the myth that accreditation and the Learning College are disconnected, unrelated endeavors is debunked. The more closely they are examined, the more they are found to be compatible and mutually supportive of effective community and technical college practice.

Reference

O'Banion, T. (1997). *A Learning College for the 21st Century.* Phoenix: Oryx Press.

Double-Loop Learning in Higher Education

— John Tagg

Tagg, John. (2007 July/August). "Double-Loop Learning in Higher Education." *Change*. 36-41.

The scenario is familiar to us all: A college is conscientiously trying to improve its performance on the array of challenges that go by terms such as "assessment," "retention," "accountability," and "general education." The president of the college appoints a task force to address these many interrelated issues, the third or fourth such group on the campus over a period of 20 years. The general-education program has been revised twice. The college had offered departments a series of grants to develop assessment plans for the better part of a decade, but these disappeared in a year of cutbacks. It had offered several learning-community courses, which also disappeared when the faculty involved retired— although the college continues to offer a first-year program and an honors program. In short, the task force discovers that most of the ideas proposed in their first brainstorming session have already been tried on that campus.

However, the task-force members also discover that there has been no systematic attempt to track the results of these various experiments. In some cases, no data were gathered. In a few, studies were conducted for a year or so, then were discontinued once the program assumed permanent status. Overall, the institution has no evidence about what students learn in their courses or how long that learning lasts.

After two hours' discussion at their fifth meeting, a chemistry professor summarizes the situation as he sees it: "We're running in place. We take two steps forward, then slide back. Nothing we do makes any demonstrable difference." "But if that's true," says the director of information technology, "then how do we even know if we're doing a better or a worse job? We don't." The task force adjourns until the next week with the following question echoing in members' minds: Does anything we do make a difference?

The Learning Gap

The most fundamental problem of colleges is that, in some respects, the people within them don't learn very well. That is largely true of the students, to be sure. College students who do well on tests of short-term recall may quickly forget what they have supposedly learned. Students who don't get the grades they want may "study harder" and, as a result, improve their grades. But whether this effort has any long-term benefit depends on how they were studying in the first place and whether they study differently or just more. If "study" means trying to commit to memory discrete items of information that might appear on a test, then doing more of it will lead both to remembering more in the short term and forgetting more in the long term. Doing more is not doing better unless what you are doing makes an important difference.

Colleges have a similar problem. Dissatisfied with their completion rates, they may "study" how to improve the situation. The results of these efforts, however, will usually be like those of the student who spends extra hours cramming for the test.

Most faculty, staff, and administrators in higher education genuinely believe in the importance of undergraduate learning and want to improve it. And many colleges innovate a lot, frequently in an effort to make those improvements. But in the domain of its core activities, the college doesn't learn easily.

While faculty may innovate in their disciplinary research and may expand courses to cover new material or decide to offer new courses, when it comes to changing the basic pedagogy or the framework for student learning, faculty seem to have a learning disability. Diane Halpern, professor of psychology at Claremont McKenna College, and Milton Hakel of Bowling Green State University have studied the application of contemporary cognitive science to college teaching. "We have found precious little evidence," they report, "that content experts in the learning sciences actually apply the principles they teach in their own classrooms. Like virtually all college faculty, they teach the way they were taught." Even experts in learning can't learn in their role as agents of the college. Even the young dogs can't seem to learn new tricks. Why?

Theories-in-Use and Espoused Theories

A major part of the explanation resides in the nature of colleges and universities as organizations. Why do people in an organization find some subjects essentially "undiscussable," to the extent that they change the subject when those issues come up? Why do people new to an organization, even after reading the written rules and going through initiation rituals, find many practices confusing and need to observe the old-timers at work for a while before they "get it"? Why is it that veterans of an organizational culture can correct novices when they make mistakes but often can't explain why what the novices are doing is unacceptable? Why, in other words, do people in organizations often behave in ways that even they cannot explain? They do so for the same reason that people who advocate change in an organization's practices—for what seem to them good reasons—find that, even when no one opposes or disagrees with their ideas and even after months or years of careful planning and development, substantive change seldom happens. When things do turn out differently after a "reform," the results often exhibit a completely unforeseen and unplanned pattern of difference.

All organizations, not just educational institutions, operate using a set of tacit assumptions, often invisible even to those within them, about how people in the organization should behave. These assumptions are frequently at variance with the written mission. As organizational theorists Chris Argyris of Harvard University and the late Donald Schön of the Massachusetts Institute of Technology long ago pointed out, people's behavior in organizations is often governed by an unstated but systematic and logical set of rules, a *theory-in-use*, which can differ a great deal from what the same people would be willing to defend—their *espoused theory*. The result is that, as Argyris put it, "Managements, at all levels, in many organizations, create, by their own choice, a world that is contrary to what they say they prefer. ... It is as if they are compulsively tied to a set of processes that prevent them from changing what they believe they should change."

Single-Loop Learning and Double-Loop Learning

This is not to say, of course, that people in organizations—and colleges in particular—don't learn. Of course they do. But they learn most readily in a certain way and with certain constraints. Argyris and Schön, following Ross Ashby, a pioneering theorist in cybernetics and artificial intelligence, made an important distinction between two levels of organizational learning: single-loop learning and double-loop learning.

We act most of the time out of habit, and most of the time habitual actions produce the consequences we hope for, or a reasonable facsimile thereof. It is usually when they do not that we are called upon to learn. Learning is a process by which we discover how to achieve our objectives or to correct or redress negative consequences of our actions.

We embark upon every action with some (usually unstated and often unconscious) assumptions about what we want to achieve and what it is possible for us to do—our governing values. When we are acting in an organizational context, these governing values are implicit in the organization's theory-in-use.

If the action strategies we adopt within the constraints imposed by the governing values achieve the consequences that we seek, no learning is called for, except to the extent that a successful outcome tends to reinforce the strategies for action we have already adopted.

It is only when we do not achieve satisfactory consequences that we are called upon to revise our thinking and our actions—to learn something. Consider a very simple example, first posited by Ashby and elaborated by Argyris and Schön: a heating and cooling system governed by a thermostat. The thermostat is a very simple model of *single-loop learning*. The governing value in this system is the thermostat setting, say 76°. The "learning loop" as the thermostat changes the room temperature to the desired level might be diagrammed this way:

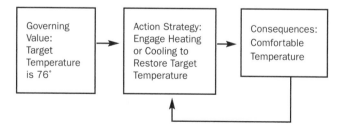

Under normal circumstances, the system will operate effectively in this way. But what if something from outside the system introduces a factor that the system's original assumptions did not allow for? For example, what if the humidity changes, so that what was a comfortable temperature yesterday becomes unpleasant today? Single-loop learning will no longer suffice.

When the single-loop approach fails to achieve a comfortable environment, the only way to get better results is to move up to double-loop learning. What needs to be adjusted now is not just the action strategy but the governing value itself. In the case of the thermostat, when 76° proves too warm for a muggy day with a room full of people, we need to adjust the governing value to 72°:

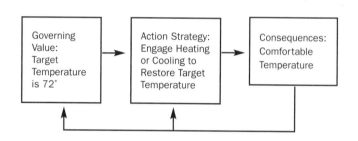

The distinction between single-loop and double-loop learning applies to much that we do in higher education. And it explains why most innovations, even those that produce unambiguously good results, fail to transform institutions. Most innovations alter action strategies without moving on to make the second loop and re-examine the governing values.

Organizational Habits as Governing Values

To find the values that govern a system's theory-in-use, don't ask people what they believe—watch what they do. The governing values that determine the institutional learning system are embodied in the standardized routines of educational practice. Some years ago, John Meyer and Brian Rowan, organizational theorists at Stanford University, characterized these routine practices as "ritual classifications." They include such things as the academic calendar, the class, the grading system, and the pedagogical practices. These are the operational components and metrics of the organization's theory-in-use.

These routine practices and formal classifications are largely invisible because we take them for granted. G. K. Chesterton's observation, "The things we see every day are the things we never see at all," is as true in organizational life as it is in personal life. These structural features and organizational habits are part of the theory-in-use of colleges but hardly even appear in the espoused theories of educators.

"One of the most difficult learning problems organizations face," says Argyris, "is to learn that they are not able to learn, and that the cause of this inability is the focus on what is taken for granted, namely, routines."

The Calendar

Consider the academic calendar, which at nearly all colleges is structured on either a semester or a quarter system. The semester or quarter imports into most academic processes a governing value that constrains the action strategies available—in this case, mandating that all students should learn all subjects in, say, 16 weeks. That is the functional implication of the formal routine that all courses are offered in a 16-week calendar.

Within the parameters set by this governing value, faculty will pursue a range of action strategies. They will develop syllabi for all of their courses that attempt to cover a body of material that the "average" student might be able to handle in 16 weeks, and they will develop assignments and assessments that can be paced over the 16-week period. Sometimes this will work fine—but sometimes the consequences will be disappointing:

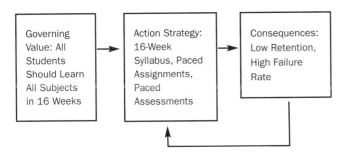

When the consequences are unsatisfactory, most teachers and institutions will take the single-loop approach by modifying the action strategies—changing the assignments and altering the assessments:

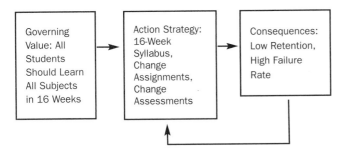

Sometimes these new action strategies will be effective. But many improvements will last only for the short run, and problems will recur.

When you consider yourself as a learner, you instantly recognize that you take longer to master some subjects than others. You may even recall the experience of being prepared for the final exam early in your math class, while you ardently wished for another two weeks to complete your term paper in philosophy. Or vice versa. Indeed, both the research and the rhetoric of higher education abound with the recognition of the cognitive and functional diversity of learners.

But that is our espoused theory. Our theory-in-use is tied to the governing value that tells us that all students are functionally alike. As long as we are constrained by that value, we will tinker around the edges without addressing the underlying problem. The situation calls for double-loop learning, for reconsidering the governing value:

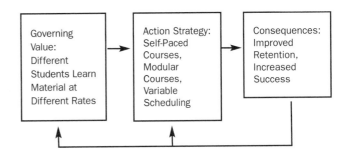

Modifying the governing value opens up a whole array of action strategies that were previously closed off. Mesa Community College in Arizona reorganized a "graveyard" math course into modules, allowing students to progress at their own pace but requiring them to successfully complete each module before advancing to the next. Students could take up to a year to complete the course, as long as they were making progress. The success rate in the course nearly doubled. At North Central Technical College in Wisconsin, one of its vocational programs allows students to move at their own pace, starting and completing courses when they get the work done without reference to the academic calendar. The experiment is still young, but it appears that different students take a range of different time periods to successfully complete the same sequence of tasks. California State University, Channel Islands, is giving students the option of selecting different amounts of time to complete a challenging gateway course.

All of these experiments have been successful; none has been expanded beyond a single course. Why? Because the theory-in-use in the institution as a whole, incorporated in the academic calendar, still prohibits the innovation. So it remains marginal, even when it works spectacularly well.

The Curriculum

The academic calendar is a formal framework for delivering instruction. The content of that instruction is the curriculum. If we look at the standardized routines that largely define the work of curriculum committees, we can see the governing value at work. Most curriculum committees operate under a theory-in-use that the curriculum is what teachers cover in their classes, so that is what the committees examine. This determines the action strategies available to those involved in developing and revising the curriculum:

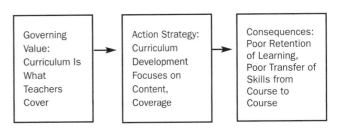

The curriculum is hotly contested on many campuses. Faculty members, administrators, and staff expend enormous effort certifying, organizing, and validating—according to the rules in place—the definitions and content of classes. But there is substantial evidence that, for many students, curriculum in this sense doesn't make much difference.

Consider general education—the only curricular program at most institutions that applies to all students. Alexander Astin, the long-time head of the Higher Education Research Institute at UCLA, examined the effect of various general-education programs on 22 outcomes directly relevant to the expressed goals of general education. He found that "the particular manner in which the general education curriculum is structured makes very little difference for these twenty-two outcomes." In other words, the whole curriculum process at many institutions is much ado about not very much in terms of the outcomes of the process for students.

A single-loop approach to curriculum reform is likely to perpetuate current difficulties into the indefinite future. Juggling the courses students are required to take, altering the subject matter covered, or increasing bureaucratic oversight—none of this will substantially alter the outcomes of the curriculum as a whole.

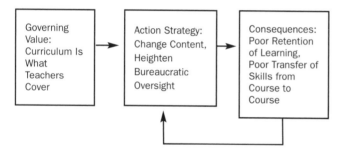

The fatal flaw resides in the governing value itself, which is embedded in higher education's standard routines. It is not the teachers who do the learning, it is the students. The only way to liberate the curriculum from the constraints of single-loop learning is to revise the governing value:

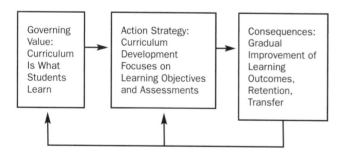

If we adopt in practice the governing value that the curriculum is what students learn rather than what teachers teach, it will dramatically change the way we make decisions about it. The emphasis will shift from what teachers are doing to what students are doing. We will have to ask what we want students to learn in a course, what we want students to be able to do during and after a course. The traditional curriculum committee questions will suddenly appear, at best, partial and sketchy. Instead, the means of

assessing student learning and providing feedback to both faculty and the students themselves will become central action strategies for executing the curriculum.

Alverno College, in Milwaukee, Wisconsin, made the second loop some decades ago and restructured its curriculum around the ongoing assessment of student learning. As Marcia Mentkowski and her colleagues at Alverno put it, the curriculum is not simply a set of courses, it is a description of "learning experiences organized as frameworks for learning." In other words, it is primarily about what students do and only secondarily about what teachers do. Kings College in Wilkes-Barre, Pennsylvania; Olivet College in Olivet, Michigan; and California State University, Monterey Bay are examples of other institutions that have taken the second loop and defined what the curriculum means in terms of student learning.

The Time Horizon of Learning

Faculty are apt to believe that the students coming into their classes are inadequately prepared. The solution generally is to propose changes in requirements and assessment to better prepare students for advanced work. But all of this innovation reflects a governing value embedded in both the calendar and the curriculum: that the goal of the classroom teacher should be to maximize what students know at the end of the semester or quarter, when the final exam is given.

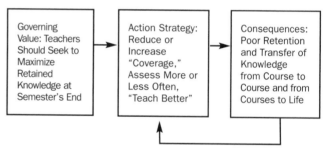

The issue here is what we might call the time horizon of learning. The time horizon that a person adopts in thinking about a decision or action depends on the answer to the implied question, "How long will I have to live with the consequences of this action?" We all invest less effort and involvement in choices that have a short time horizon than in choices that have a long one.

While a lot can be done by a single teacher in a single course, the time horizon for an isolated course is relatively brief. As long as the teacher's involvement ends with the term, students tend to see the course as ending with the final exam.

Of course, nobody in higher education espouses a short time horizon for learning. On the contrary, the term "lifelong learning" has gained such visibility in mission statements and presidential addresses that it has become a cliché. The phrase suggests a radically long time horizon for college-level learning. The double-loop route here, as elsewhere, is to introduce what we really believe into the governing value, to replace the organizational habit with the educational truth:

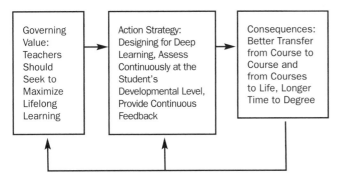

Here, taking the second loop will require a number of changes in organizational habits. We can best extend the time horizon of learning beyond the class by extending the framework of performance, feedback, and assessment. The student must be engaged in a project that will extend beyond the final exam. The feedback the student receives must be relevant to work that will carry on after the semester grade is in. Common assessments must be developed by teams of faculty rather than separately by individuals.

Portland State University in Oregon has developed a general-education program that exhibits double-loop learning. The general-education program there begins with a freshman learning community, which leads to a sophomore cluster of courses with a unifying seminar and then to the an upper-division cluster. The program concludes with the senior capstone, a collaborative project in which groups of seniors work under faculty supervision on community-based projects that result in a significant work product. Portland State is developing an electronic portfolio that will track the elements of the general-education program throughout the student's academic career. In this, they are following the example of colleges like Alverno and Olivet, which have used the portfolio as a means of extending the time horizon of student learning by seeing it in terms of long-term goals and tasks.

Staying Stuck

Meyer and Rowan pointed out that educational organizations get by only by adopting what they called "the logic of confidence"—assuming that if organizational habits are being followed, the organization is achieving its purpose. This obviates the need to examine either the work or its outcomes. So if classes are being taught, the formal rituals of education are being performed, and all is presumed to be going well.

But what are instructors actually doing in these classes? Nobody knows. Pedagogical practices are considered the private business of the teacher, protected by what Lee Shulman has called "pedagogical solitude." But there is almost certainly a lot of lecturing going on. Yet Ernest T. Pascarella of the University of Illinois at Chicago, and Patrick T. Terenzini of the Center for the Study of Higher Education at The Pennsylvania State University conclude in *How College Affects Students* "with striking consistency, studies show that innovative, active, collaborative, cooperative, and constructivist approaches shape learning more powerfully... than do conventional lecture-discussion and text-based approaches."

Pedagogical reforms bump up against what Argyris and Schön call organizational defensive routines. Argyris defines defensive routines as "any action or policy that prevents human beings from experiencing negative surprises, embarrassment, or threat, and simultaneously prevents the organization from reducing or eliminating the causes of the surprises, embarrassment, and threat." Among the most deeply embedded and intractable of organizational habits, defensive routines are the mechanisms by which the organizational theory-in-use protects itself from the espoused theories of the people who run the organization.

The logic of confidence leads colleges and universities to adopt a variety of defensive routines. Thus they reject even the most obvious ideas for solving the most obvious educational problems. Students can't do the work they need to in the semester? The obvious solution is to give them more time. Students who have completed the courses still don't have the knowledge and skills they need for more advanced work? Advance them on the basis of the demonstrated knowledge and skills instead of course completion. Students forget most of what they have learned within two months after the course is over? Assess them not just at the end of the course but on an ongoing basis. For all of these problems and many of the others that beset higher-education institutions, fairly clear and direct solutions exist that we fend off with our defensive routines.

The first step toward double-loop learning is to shine a light on what matters, the values built into an institution's operations.

Learning to Change, Changing to Learn

Colleges and universities today are assaulted by imperatives to increase access, decrease costs, increase diversity, manage athletics, work with high schools, and be accountable not merely to Tom, Dick, and Harry but also to their brother Mike, who serves in the state legislature. These issues are important.

But the core challenge that will determine our ability to address any of them is to see our own theories-in-use and reconsider them when our wheels are spinning on sand and we can get no traction to move forward.

The problem that colleges face is that their defensive routines cover up their theories-in-use and make their governing values sacrosanct. One reason it is so easy to deflect conversations and questions about the espoused values of institutions is that often there is no publicly available evidence about the college's results, as was true with the hypothetical college described at the beginning of this article.

In the venerable story of the drunk crawling around under the lamp post, looking for the keys he dropped, the bystander asks where he was when he dropped his keys. "Over there," he replies, pointing to a bench some distance away. "Then why," asks the bystander, "are you looking here?" "Because," the drunk replies, "it's too dark over there."

Like the drunk under the lamp post, colleges look where the light is, and the light is not shining on their real values and purposes. The first step toward double-loop learning is to shine a light on what matters, the values built into an institution's operations. And if they are not producing the results we want, the second step is to change them.

References

Argyris, C. *On Organizational Learning*. Cambridge, MA: Blackwell, 1992.

Argyris, C. *Overcoming Organizational Defenses: Facilitating Organizational Learning*. Upper Saddle River, NJ: Prentice Hall, 1990.

Argyris, C. and Schön, D. A. *Organizational Learning: A Theory of Action Perspective*. Reading, MA: Addison-Wesley, 1978.

Astin, A. W. *What Matters in College? "Four Critical Years" Revisited*. San Francisco: Jossey-Bass, 1993.

Halpern, D., and Hakel, M. "Applying the Science of Learning to the University and Beyond: Teaching for Long-Term Retention and Transfer." *Change*, July-August 2003: 36-41.

Mentkowski, M., and associates. *Learning That Lasts: Integrating Learning, Development, and Performance in College and Beyond*. San Francisco: Jossey-Bass, 2001.

Meyer, J. W., and Rowan, B. "The Structure of Educational Organizations." In J. V. Baldridge and T. Deal, *The Dynamics of Organizational Change in Education*. Berkeley: McCutchan Publishing Corp., 1983.

Pascarella, E. T., and Terenzini, P. T. *How College Affects Students, Volume 2: A Third Decade of Research*. San Francisco: Jossey-Bass, 2005.

Tagg, J. *The Learning Paradigm College*. Bolton, MA: Anker Publications, 2003.

Part IV.
An Architecture for Learning

The Wingspread Group's recommendation for "overhauling the traditional architecture of higher education" led many educators toward ideas for transforming the organizational structure, academic calendar, curriculum, job functions, and other workplace and classroom activities. Others, though, thought more literally, and focused on ways the physical structure of educational institutions could contribute to student learning and success. The first two articles in Part IV focus on the connection between the physical and metaphorical architecture for learning. William J. Flynn, who directed the Learning Paradigm Conference at Palomar College and assisted the League for Innovation in creating its Learning College Summit, has worked with colleges, architects, and furniture companies in designing and developing effective holistic environments for learning. In "Paradigm Shift: How Higher Education is Improving Learning," he connects the ideas of the Learning Paradigm to the functionality of the built environment, and offers examples of ways community colleges and other higher education institutions are working to "increase learning per square foot" by creating spaces that accommodate the new ways of teaching and learning (pages 177-181).

Others, though, thought more literally, and focused on ways the physical structure of educational institutions could contribute to student learning and success.

Michael Schoop, president of Cuyahoga Community College's Metropolitan Campus and The Cross Papers Fellow, 2007, based his fellowship monograph on the concept of teaching by design. In *From Classrooms to Learning Spaces: Teaching by Design* (The Cross Papers, Number 10), Schoop envisions comfortable, flexible learning space that promotes student engagement by providing ample space and configurations for active and collaborative learning. He encourages faculty to become involved in the innovative design of learning spaces and offers tips for educating administrators about the value of thoughtfully designed classrooms (pages 182-188).

The third and final article in this section returns to the discussion of organizational structure, as Terry O'Banion offers strategies for designing an institution focused on learning. In "Creating a New Architecture for the Learning College," he questions traditional structural elements—department, workload formula, grading system, late registration, and academic calendar—and invites educators to explore alternatives that are closely aligned with a strong, intentional, collegewide focus on learning (pages 189-193).

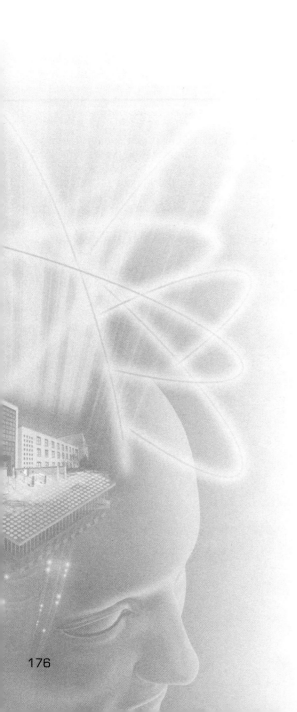

Paradigm Shift: How Higher Education is Improving Learning

— William J. Flynn

Flynn, W. J. (2006). "Paradigm Shift: How Higher Education is Improving Learning." Herman Miller, Inc.

There are increasing calls for change and improvement in the American educational system. The accountability movement, begun in an attempt to revitalize K-12 institutions, is now gaining momentum in postsecondary education. Governors, legislators, and coordinating or system boards are considering achievement on performance indicators as one factor in determining future campus allocations. To be truly responsive to the calls for accountability, institutions may have to rethink the core mission of undergraduate education and re-examine their central values. Many critics think education will have to place learning at the center of all its actions, decisions, and allocations in order to be truly and meaningfully accountable.

In the last 10 years, much of the impetus for a discussion on learning came from an article that appeared in the November/December 1995 issue of Change, "From Teaching To Learning: A New Paradigm For Undergraduate Education." The authors, Robert Barr and John Tagg, tapped into a deeply ingrained sense that something had to change. By applying to undergraduate education the theories of scientist Thomas Kuhn and futurist Joel Barker, they developed a simple and penetrating analysis of the current modus operandi in the classroom they called the Instruction Paradigm.

In this paradigm, the mission was to provide instruction to students, and the focus was on the teacher, who usually employed lecture as the primary method of delivering instruction. Learning was clearly the responsibility of the student, and its measurement was not a high priority. This centuries-old model of the scholar possessing knowledge and transferring it to eager students has changed little since before the invention of the printing press.

Other characteristics of the Instruction Paradigm were readily recognizable. Independent, discipline-centered departments were repositories of specialized and somewhat isolated knowledge. Significant resources and planning were committed to keeping teachers current in their disciplines through professional development programs. A subtle but perceptible caste system existed on many campuses in which the faculty were the "upper class" and other employees were identified as support staff.

Despite the significant body of literature on the value of collaborative or self-paced learning environments, the learning community movement, and assessment as a valuable pedagogical tool, there was little documentation of efforts to incorporate these approaches into the curriculum. There was agreement that students came to the campus with multiple learning styles and that critical thinking should be incorporated into every course, yet there was little concrete evidence that schools practiced what they preached.

Introducing the Learning Paradigm

Barr and Tagg argued that the very mission, vision, culture, and structure of a college must undergo a paradigm shift from the Instruction Paradigm to the Learning Paradigm, from being an institution that provided instruction to students to an institution that produced learning in students. Once that shift is made, everything has the potential for change.

In the new scheme, faculty become the designers of powerful learning environments, and every college employee, not just faculty, has a role to play and a contribution to make in maintaining a learner-centered environment. Curriculum design is based on an analysis of what a student needs to know to function in a complex world rather than on what the teacher knows how to teach. Colleges are encouraged to reconfigure the ways in which they interact with students. The name of the game is learning, not instruction.

In the view of Barr and Tagg, colleges and faculty were prisoners of a system, structure, and history not of their creation, one that prevented meaningful collaboration among campus stakeholders. Archaic and discriminatory grading practices continue, in some cases predefining how letter grades will be distributed in a class without concern for the prior preparation, abilities, or academic potential that an individual student possesses. Given the nature of colleges and universities—their history and traditions, their commitment to shared governance and consensus building, and a substantial institutional culture that seems to resist change—the impediments to an organizational shift suggested by the Learning Paradigm are formidable.

> Curriculum design is based on an analysis of what a student needs to know to function in a complex world rather than on what the teacher knows how to teach.

Since the arrival of the article by Barr and Tagg, there has been a measurable movement to embrace learning as the focus of undergraduate education. As the concept spread rapidly throughout education, a new emphasis on learning began to appear. Every new book, conference program, and website echoed the concept: learning college, learning communities, learning organizations, learning outcomes, brain-compatible learning, surface learning versus deep learning, and teachers as learning facilitators.

Other Voices for Change

Movements such as Management by Objective, Total Quality Management, behavioral objectives, learning outcomes, and the student development movement of the 1970s all have chipped away at the traditional education system with moderate success. The literature on institutional change began to gather momentum in the early 1990s, as more critics weighed in on what was wrong with undergraduate education. The Wingspread Group on Higher Education (1993) offered a concise statement on the implications of change in academia and the impact of that change:

> Putting learning at the heart of the academic enterprise will mean overhauling the conceptual, procedural, curricular, and other architecture of postsecondary education on most campuses.

> Hastening the potential for that overhaul was the emergence of information technology as an essential dimension of institutional infrastructure and the impact of the Internet on instruction. If today's student has a choice of accessing information and learning electronically anywhere and at any time by means of the World Wide Web or televised courses, and the provider of this educational experience can be the local community college or a university thousands of miles away, what competitive advantages do local colleges have when they require students to battle freeways and confront crammed parking lots in order to sit in crowded, uncomfortable lecture halls to acquire the same knowledge? The student no longer has to go to a "place" to learn; learning now comes to the student.

Challenge to the Classroom

For many faculty, the classroom is a familiar and comforting environment. However, as William Plater observed, even though the metaphor of the classroom is a powerful one, this "most basic and fundamental unit of academic life—the sanctity of the classroom and the authority of the teacher in it—is about to be turned inside out."

In Plater's view, readily available access to information means that the traditional classroom might lose its place of primacy as the central location where knowledge is acquired. This, in turn, may force educators to rethink the teacher-student relationship. Faculty, in addition to their subject expertise, need to be trained in identifying learning styles, developing modular curriculum, and mastering instructional technology and methodology in order to become effective assessors of a student's abilities and potential, as well as designers of learning environments and systems. In turn, colleges and universities need to revisit how they design, update, renovate, and equip current classrooms to make the most of teacher-student interaction.

Implicit in this analysis is an emphasis on the environment, the physical space, as a contributor to enhanced learning.

Barriers to Learning

Terry O'Banion, another contributor to the literature of change, echoed and expanded upon the Wingspread Group's view of the primacy of learning. In O'Banion's perspective, educational institutions face four limitations. First, they are bureaucracy-bound with restrictions embedded in education codes, procedures manuals, state master plans, legislatively driven budgets, and organizational cultures that tend to perpetuate business as usual.

Second, faculty are role-bound, working in isolation in their own classrooms, portrayed as the "expert" filling up the empty vessel of the student by using the lecture as the primary delivery mechanism.

Third, colleges and universities are time-bound. College offerings are atomistic and compartmentalized. In this metaphor, the atom is the 50-minute lecture period and the molecule is the three-credit course offered in a 15-week semester or a 10-week quarter. In this environment, time is constant while learning varies from class to class.

Lastly, institutions are place-bound. The very concepts of the campus, the classroom, the library, the laboratory are all "places you go to learn." The historic one-room schoolhouse has left an imprint on current educational facilities. Many standard classrooms lack flexibility and are not the most conducive locations for meaningful learning to occur. Too often the layout, furnishings, and design of a classroom are the result of budgetary necessity failing to provide the flexibility, comfort, and atmosphere that can contribute to an enhanced learning environment. While all four limitations put potential restrictions on the ability to design a learner-centered environment, it is in the area of place that colleges and universities have the most opportunity to make a difference.

A Place for Learning

Among critics, there is a growing sense that "formal education" (listening, taking notes, reading, taking exams) is not effective, and the locus of traditional education, the classroom, is perhaps one of the causes for this deficiency. This is perhaps a corollary of Barr and Tagg's Learning Paradigm—that a room designed to house the transfer of information from teacher to student is not conducive to deep learning and retention. Rather, it is informal education (collaboration, peer interaction, mentoring, reflection, coaching) that can provide a basis for academic success.

As Tagg observed in a subsequent book, colleges provide instruction in classes. When this methodology doesn't work, the remedy is to offer more courses. When students fail to learn, it is regrettable but the system doesn't change. In the Learning Paradigm, the approach is to diagnose the reasons for the failure to learn and create an environment that addresses the problem. Learning is continually assessed and the environment is regularly modified to produce more learning. Implicit in this analysis is an emphasis on the environment, the physical space, as a contributor to enhanced learning.

New Students, Old System

Today's students are changing far more rapidly than the colleges and universities that recruit them. They have a preferred mode of activity and interaction that is not in sync with an educational system that is showing its age. "Net Gen" students, as author and consultant Marc Prensky calls them, are not interested in large lecture halls, preferring informal, small-group discussion, often through text messaging or e-mail, as a means of gaining understanding of curriculum content. They want a learning space in which they can get to know one another, engage in dialogue, work independently or in groups on projects, get or provide feedback, and, in general, they seek a collaborative environment that fosters understanding and learning.

Colleges that create new classroom buildings are hoping for a long life for those facilities, and their hopes usually will be realized. However, while a building will last 50 or more years, its mechanical and electrical functions will need replacement long before the building's useful life is over. Cabling and IT hardware has a shorter shelf life, and software will become obsolete even sooner. Furniture, decor, variable lighting, and flexibility are often afterthoughts in the design process. What should be addressed in the planning process are questions on the pedagogical approach to be taken in a given space, layout, functionality, flexibility, access to technology, and the human needs of the room: lighting, temperature, acoustics, adaptability, comfort.

The highly regarded book, *Student Success in College: Creating Conditions That Matter*, offers insight into strategies that promote student success. Based on the Documenting Effective Educational Practice (DEEP) project at Indiana University, the book investigated common features of 20 institutions and their cultures. Among the institutions' shared values were a "living" mission, strong focus on student learning, and shared responsibility for educational quality and student success. Joining these essential indicators of success was, "environments adapted for educational enrichment."

Each institution in the project has a unique campus setting, both natural and/or constructed. Each college understands the value of "place," a realization that its unique geography, layout, and architecture could be made an active part of the learning equation. Each was quick to alter the physical environment in order to enhance a potential learning situation. For example, Evergreen State College used its Puget Sound location and surrounding wooded preserves to study plants, ecosystems, and marine life. Ursinus College redesigned facilities to put "interaction areas" near faculty offices, enhancing and strengthening collaboration between teacher and student. George Mason University situated its Johnson Center at the heart of the campus, with its library, food court, movie theater, retail outlets, student support offices, and small-group study spaces attracting students literally around the clock.

Many DEEP institutions had strong ties with the community, extending learning opportunities into surrounding municipalities, increasing the number of "virtual labs" while providing service learning opportunities with real-life people and organizations. Testimony documented that signage, landscaping, architecture, and the physical environment influenced student's feelings of engagement, self-worth, and belonging, leading to increased retention.

George Kuh, principal author of *Student Success in College* is also the Director of the National Survey of Student Engagement (NSSE), an annual assessment of information supplied by colleges and universities on student participation in programs. Since the inception of the survey, more than 844,000 students at 972 four-year colleges and universities across the country have reported their college activities and experiences to the NSSE, making the program a leading authority on the improvement of undergraduate education, enhancing student success, and promoting collegiate quality. Among its most recent findings: The single best predictor of student satisfaction with college is the degree to which students perceive the college environment to be supportive of their academic and social needs. Another recent study of the impact of facilities on recruitment and retention of students gave some clues about the growing emphasis on the quality of learning environments. The research, published by APPA (Association of Higher Education Facilities Officers), went beyond the considerable research done on factors that impact a student's decision to attend or not choose a particular college or university.

Two-thirds of the respondents indicated that the "Overall Quality of the Campus Facilities" was "Essential" or "Very Important" to their decision.

The research, conducted among APPA member institutions, included a total of 16,153 students responding from 46 institutions across the U.S. and Canada. Understandably, the top five characteristics cited by students focused on academics, indicating that the students wanted a quality educational experience. Two-thirds of the respondents indicated that the "Overall Quality of the Campus Facilities" was "Essential" or "Very Important" to their decision. Half of the respondents indicated that the "Attractiveness of the Campus" scored in those upper-end categories as well.

Re-examining the Built Environment

What are colleges and universities doing to enhance learning through commitment to innovative campus construction or renovation? Here are some examples.

Estrella Mountain, one of the ten colleges that comprise the Maricopa Community College District in Arizona, recently had the opportunity to renovate two liberal arts classrooms. Prior to the project, school officials had developed three principles for designing learning spaces: leverage of physical space, engaging stakeholders, and a concept they called "radical flexibility"—the desire to make faculty and students unencumbered by either the space in which they interacted or the technology used in the learning process.

As part of this project, classrooms were transformed into "learning studios," featuring ergonomic furniture, wireless technology, mobile teaching stations, wall writing areas, and informal learning spaces within the formal instructional setting. Based on positive feedback from users of these two spaces, the college recently opened Ocotillo Hall with 22 learning studios based on the feedback from the original prototypes.

The movement toward studios and away from traditional classrooms is seen in other institutions as well. Due to its variable geometry, flexible seating arrangements, and use of enhanced technology, the studio concept allows for a variety of pedagogical options. With all furnishings moveable, classes can spontaneously reconfigure the spaces to match the day's subject matter and presentational or interactive style. A room with no front engenders creative reconfiguration. Contemplation, engagement, collaboration, and reflection are all possible and encouraged. The resultant learning is dynamic rather than static.

The studio concept has also been successfully expanded into the residential-life experience. The University of Dayton has developed twenty-first-century residential facilities that mix living and learning to expand student engagement. The first phase of ArtStreet, completed in the fall of 2005, includes six two-story townhouses and five loft apartments sitting above performance spaces, artist studios, group discussion spaces, a multimedia room, exhibit spaces, the campus radio station, and a recording studio, all anchored by a cafe that serves as a gathering place for the "neighborhood."

A room
with no front
engenders creative
reconfiguration.

ArtStreet is just one component of the university's ambitious Learning Village concept, in which collaboration, connectivity, and community are the hallmarks of an all-encompassing commitment to place learning at the forefront of every endeavor. Housing 400 first- and second-year students, Marianist Hall is another unique facility where learning studios, faculty and campus ministry offices, a two-story bookstore, post office, credit union, food emporium, and 60-seat chapel are all integrated under one roof.

The Ryan C. Harris Learning Teaching Center continues the theme of collaboration and connection. One feature of the Center is "The Studio," an experimental classroom and laboratory for inquiry-based teaching and a place where faculty can try new pedagogies and share their experiences with other faculty in a collaborative and supportive setting. The aim is to stimulate a community of practice among participating faculty around teaching and student learning and to produce useful outcomes for students and learning for faculty. With mobile furniture and white boards on ceiling tracks, the room can be quickly configured to small-group discussion, then back to full-class presentation. Wireless technology enhances the connectivity of all participants.

Increasing Learning Per Square Foot

The intelligent use of technology has opened new doors to innovative facilities use at other institutions. MIT's TEAL classroom (Technology-Enabled Active Learning) is a case in point. The TEAL format, piloted in 2001 in an introductory physics class in electromagnetism, combines lecture, recitation, and hands-on laboratory experiments into one classroom experience. To successfully accomplish this, the classroom had to be rethought. Through imaginative positioning of tables, projection screens, white boards, laptops, an instructor's station, and discussion areas, active-engagements methods such as desktop experiments and collaborative exercises are incorporated into the traditional college course.

In a similar vein, The SCALE-UP project at North Carolina State goes after a different target—large-enrollment classes. SCALE-UP stands for Student-Centered Activities for Large Enrollment Undergraduate Programs and seeks to deliver a learning environment that is highly collaborative, hands-on, computer intensive, and interactive. Rather than being seated in a large lecture auditorium, students face each other across small tables. Instead of standing behind a lectern, the teacher roams the room, answering questions, monitoring progress, occasionally giving a mini-lecture among, instead of in front of, the class. Students share laptops, complete impromptu assignments, and collaborate on projects. The setting is described on the project website as "very much like a banquet hall, with lively interactions nearly all the time."

To document the advantage of designing a collaborative learning environment, North Carolina State University (NCSU) has conducted evaluations of learning attainment in parallel classes, one in the SCALE-UP model, and the other in a more traditional pedagogy. A wide array of quantitative and qualitative methods, including classroom observers taking field notes as well as video recorders capturing classroom interactions, were employed to evaluate the educational impact of the SCALE-UP pedagogy. Data were compiled from over 16,000 NCSU students over a five-year span from 1997 to 2002. Failure rate ratios were calculated by dividing the percentage failing traditional courses by the percentage failing in SCALE-UP. Overall, students were nearly three times as likely to fail in a traditionally taught section as in an equivalent SCALE-UP section of the course.

Using SAT scores as a way of identifying students at risk of failure in traditional physics, researchers found there was no difference in passing rates for those students with Math SAT scores above 500. But of those students whose Math SAT was less than 500, 83 percent of the SCALE-UP students passed Engineering Statics compared to only 69 percent in traditional sections. The SCALE-UP website summarizes their findings as follows: Ability to solve problems is improved, conceptual understanding is increased, attitudes are improved, and failure rates are drastically reduced, especially for women and minorities.

In addition to efforts by single institutions, there are some promising collaborative ventures among higher education partners. NITLE, a partnership of the National Institute for Technology and Liberal Education and three other consortia, is one example. With almost 100 participating colleges, many of them with prestigious reputations, the organization fosters experimentation with emerging technologies and how they can produce an enriched learning experience. Projects include 3D visualization, podcasting, wiki open editing, and wireless computing, all breaking down the traditional lecture hall format and encouraging students to explore and experiment with PDAs, pocket PCs, and cell phones. As a result of this mobile technology, students are beginning to alter their study and social habits, which in turn causes their colleges to rethink the physical environment they must provide and the technology to support it.

Space: The Final Frontier

With this growing movement to revitalize the learning environment, colleges and universities are revisiting the comfortable paradigms of the conventional classroom. New design and renovation strategies are emphasizing easily reconfigured, multiple-use spaces to permit small group discussion, collaborative learning exercises, and maximum individualized interactions with faculty who have appropriate presentational technology to enhance their efforts.

In recent years, technology has significantly affected our world, and its presence is strongly felt in education. While virtual learning has an increasing role to play in the future, there is no reason to eliminate the place-bound campuses and locations in which institutions have invested. But the likelihood of massive new capital construction funding is small. Instead they must find ways to respond to critics by demonstrating that deep and meaningful learning takes place in their facilities. More institutions must move from the comfort of the Instruction Paradigm to the challenge of the Learning Paradigm, daring to transform twentieth century classrooms into twenty-first century learning environments.

References

Alfred, Richard and Patricia Carter. *Reaching for the Future*. Ann Arbor, MI: Consortium for Community College Development, 1997.

Barr, Robert B. and John Tagg. "From Teaching to Learning: A New Paradigm for Undergraduate Education." *Change 27*, (6), 1995.

Beichner, Robert J. and Jeffrey M. Saul. "Introduction to the SCALEUP (Student-Centered Activities for Large Enrollment Undergraduate Programs) Project. Paper submitted to the Proceedings of the International School of Physics, "Enrico Fermi," Varenna, Italy, (July 2003).

Brown, Malcolm. "Learning Spaces." in Educating the Net Gen, ed. Diana G. Oblinger and James L. Oblinger. Boulder, CO: EDUCAUSE, 2005.

Hunt, James B. Jr. and Thomas J. Tiemey. "American Higher Education: How Does It Measure Up for the 21st Century?" National Policy Center on Higher Education report #06-2.

Johnson, Chris and Cyprien Lomas. "Design of the Learning Space." *EDUCAUSE Review*, July 2005.

Long, Phillip D. and Stephen C. Ehrman. "Future of the Learning Space." *EDUCAUSE Review*, July/August 2005.

National Research Council, John D. Bransford et al., eds. *How People Learn: Brain, Mind, Experience, and School*. Washington, D.C.: National Academy Press, 2000.

O'Banion, Terry. *A Learning College for the 21st Century*. Phoenix, AZ: Oryx Press, 1997.

O'Banion, Terry. *Creating More Learning-Centered Community Colleges*. San Francisco, CA: The League for Innovation in the Community College and PeopleSoft, 1997.

Oblinger, Diana and Oblinger, James. "Is It Age or IT: First Steps toward Understanding the Net Generation." In *Educating the Net Gen*, ed. Diana G. Oblinger and James L. Oblinger. Boulder, CO: EDUCAUSE, 2005.

Plater, William M. "Future Work: Faculty Time in the Twenty-First Century." *Change* (May/June. 1995).

Prensky, Marc. "Digital Natives, Digital Immigrants." *On the Horizon*, vol. 9, no. 5 (October 2001).

Tagg, John. *The Learning Paradigm College*. Bolton, MA: Anker Publishing, 2003.

Wedge, Carole C., and Thomas D. Kearns. "Creation of the Learning Space," *EDUCAUSE Review*, July/August 2005.

Wingspread Group on Higher Education. *An American Imperative: Higher Expectations for Higher Education*. Racine, WI: The Johnson Foundation, 1993.

For information on the National Survey of Student Engagement, visit http://nsse.iub.edu/pdf/NSSE2005_annual_report.pdf

For information about NITLE, visit http://www.nitle.org/index.php/nitle

For information on the TEAL classroom, visit http://icampus.mit.edu/

Photos of SCALE-UP installations are available at http://www.ncsu.edu/PER/SCALEUP/Classrooms.html

From Classrooms to Learning Spaces: Teaching by Design
The Cross Papers, Number 10

— Michael Schoop

Schoop, M. (2007). *From Classrooms to Learning Spaces: Teaching by Design*. The Cross Papers, Number 10. Phoenix: League for Innovation in the Community College.

Foreword

In 1993, the Wingspread Group described the failings of the American system of higher education, recommending that its traditional architecture be changed to better meet the needs of learners. The next decade saw the community college field responding to that call by proposing alternatives to the architecture. Leaders in community college education focused on organizational transformation and changes in the role of teaching and learning across the institution. Applying principles of the learning organization, they asked us to change our mental models; introducing the learning paradigm, they distinguished between teaching-centered and learning-centered institutions; and proposing the learning college, they urged us to put learning first and provide learning experiences any way, any place, and any time.

> Beyond our own desire to improve, however, are compelling shifts in the landscape of higher education that argue for change.

The physical space of learning was caught up in the movement as we saw the development of one-stop shops for student services and the growth of teaching and learning centers for campus-based professional development. Advances in technology led to the creation of smart classrooms, cyber cafes, and other innovative uses of teaching and learning spaces. More recently, interest in the physical architecture of learning spaces has increased as community colleges celebrating silver and golden anniversaries face renovation and expansion in the context of 21st century learning.

In this volume of The Cross Papers, Michael Schoop considers physical architecture and space design as vital elements in promoting and facilitating learning. He not only encourages faculty to join the conversation about learning space, but also suggests resources they can use to experiment and innovate in their current—perhaps traditional—classrooms. Schoop provides several steps faculty can take to garner support from their faculty colleagues and college administrators to ensure that renovated and newly built classroom space is appropriate for today's and tomorrow's learners and teachers. From his perspective as a former teacher and current campus president, Schoop also offers tips for talking with administrators about the use and design of physical space for learning.

For ten years, The Cross Papers have been a prominent voice in the conversation about learning that began in response to *An American Imperative*. K. Patricia Cross was initially commissioned by the League to write The Cross Papers, an annual volume for community college faculty that would synthesize teaching and learning theory, identify effective practice in teaching and learning, and prompt discussions among faculty about innovation in teaching and learning. After writing seven of the volumes, Pat Cross retired, and she generously gifted the League with an endowment to continue this important work through The Cross Papers Fellowship. The League is grateful for her support, and to the legions of community college faculty whose dedication to learning helps to improve the lives of their students every day.

Cynthia Wilson
Vice President, Learning and Research
League for Innovation in the Community College

From Classrooms to Learning Spaces: Teaching by Design

This essay is designed as guidebook and resource to support innovative teachers—those early adopters who know their field, are confident about their abilities, and yet are always striving to discover emerging techniques and tools to help their students learn more. In addition to a set of teaching and learning design resources, this essay offers strategies to enlist colleagues in the formidable task of creating and exploring learning environments that, for both intellectual and political reasons, can only be realized through collaboration. Although grounded in the literature on teaching and learning, the essay sees research as informing the specific tactics of a larger strategy to, as one commentator puts it, "make the revolution happen in the schools that we all kind of know should happen" (Schank, n.d.).

Beyond our own desire to improve, however, are compelling shifts in the landscape of higher education that argue for change. Old calls for reform are receiving new audiences and the pressure for change is mounting.

More than a decade ago, a group of college presidents, scholars, and policy makers gathered at a retreat in Wisconsin to reflect on the state of higher education in America. The Wingspread Group, as they came to be known, drafted an open letter to the American public. Titled *An American Imperative*, it declared higher education to be under threat and proclaimed that "[p]utting learning at the heart of the academic enterprise will mean overhauling the conceptual, procedural, curricular, and other architecture of postsecondary education on most campuses" (1993, p. 14). Thirteen years later, U.S. Secretary of Education Margaret Spellings echoed these concerns, issuing a report recommending that

> America's colleges and universities embrace a culture of continuous innovation and quality improvement. We urge these institutions to develop new pedagogies, curricula, and technologies to improve learning, particularly in the areas of science and mathematics. (p. 5)

The policy makers are not the only source of pressure on higher education. In the intervening years between *An American Imperative* and the Spellings Report, we have seen dramatic changes in who goes to college, how they are taught, and who provides those opportunities. So-called nontraditional students now make up 53 percent of the enrollment at community colleges (Horn, 2006). And the growth of for-profits has increased competition for those adult students, while challenges to traditional modes of instruction from asynchronous, network-mediated teaching have broken the monopoly of time and place previously held by colleges and universities. The revolution demanded by policy makers is well under way. In response to both the internal and external pressures on higher education, theorists such as Peter Smith and Terry O'Banion see the need for colleges and universities to become dynamic, flexible, and adaptable to the emerging needs of multiple audiences. Following the work of Peter Senge, O'Banion (1997) called for the creation of learning colleges, which he defined as those that: (1) create substantive change in learners; (2) ask learners to be responsible for making choices about their education; (3) offer learners options; (4) document the change in learners; (5) provide a collaborative learning experience; and (6) adapt the roles of facilitators to the needs of learners (p. 47). A number of institutions have moved toward implementing O'Banion's principles and becoming learning colleges.

The question you may be asking is, "What does all this have to do with teachers?" The answer is that at the center of any college—learning or otherwise—are its classrooms. Classrooms, although they are almost never designed by teachers, both influence and are emblematic of our default model of teaching. Even as we acknowledge the value of the rest of the college experience, the classroom is the place where we hope and believe we will affect students most. It is also the place that receives the least attention in our discussion of teaching. Our model of teaching, whether sage on the stage, guide on the side, teacher-centered, or learner-focused, is a craft model. Good teachers are expert, highly skilled, highly motivated individual craftspeople. We close the classroom door and are responsible for everything from soup to nuts—writing assignments, duplicating assignments, lecture, lessons, classroom management, discipline—until the door opens again.

Classroom Scenes: The Architecture of Teaching and Learning

Every teacher has an ideal class. Usually, it is that class you have in your mind just before you begin the semester. You can see the experience in vivid detail like a movie in your mind. My movie goes like this: The students all show up, on time, on the first day, ready to learn. Before long, the room is buzzing with activity. A trio of students stands at the board sketching out possible solutions to a problem. A crimson-haired woman with a nose-ring explains an idea while a guy wearing a backwards baseball cap throws his head back and gets the "ah, I see" look as a wave of recognition washes over him. Two young women sit at a table deep in animated conversation, their laptops side by side. Gestures and comments punctuate the steady

clicking as their fingers dance across the keyboards. A small group gathers in front of a projection on the wall, pointing to various elements as they toss suggestions back and forth about what works in the design and why. There is laughter, camaraderie, a real sense of excitement. Everyone knows what to do and they are doing it. Now picture this far more common scene: Students slowly file in and take their seats facing the whiteboard. Occasional greetings are punctuated by the thump of books as they are unloaded on the desks. A few eager souls sit in the first row; the rest sit in the middle or the back, doing their best to blend in with the beige walls. The students who know each other chat about homework and social lives. As the minutes tick by, the students look around the room and start to glance toward the door.

They are waiting for the class to begin.

The first scenario represents many of the best practices used by effective teachers and supported by research (Chickering and Gamson, 1987). Some of the features are obvious: the students are interacting with peers; they are spending their time actively engaged in tasks associated with learning the subject matter; the feedback on their work is immediate; the class offers a variety of ways of learning. Less obvious are the high expectations associated with a class of self-directed learners. The only thing missing from the picture is a teacher.

In the second scenario, the absence of the teacher is even more noticeable. The sense of expectation is triggered by the belief that class does not begin until the teacher arrives. The idea of the teacher at the center of classroom is fostered not only by centuries of acculturation but by the room itself. The architecture of traditional classrooms is built around a nineteenth-century model of instruction that is "place-bound, role-bound, time-bound, and efficiency-bound" (O'Banion, 1997). The typical classroom has seats arranged in rows facing the front of the room. The front is marked by a desk or podium and defined with black- or whiteboard. The most common type of seating is the arm-tablet chair, designed for an individual student to have just enough space to rest textbooks, notes, and supplies. The tablet is often slightly inclined toward the student, a useful convenience for writing, but a precarious surface for computers.

There are just two social roles: student and teacher. The student sits in her seat, listens to the lecture, takes notes, raises her hand, answers teacher-directed questions, and does her homework. The teacher sets the agenda, delivers the lecture, writes on the board, hands out the assignments, and grades the results. Classes and course schedules are built around 50- to 75-minute time blocks to meet contact-hour requirements that are often enacted in state codes regulating colleges and universities. Because of the cost of operation and maintenance, idle classroom space is expensive. Indeed, a number of states have space utilization as part of their funding formula for community colleges (ECS, 1999). So space planners and administrators have powerful incentives to support the creation of generic, general purpose classrooms rather than more specialized spaces. Yet, just as Barr and Tagg (1995) alerted educators to the need to shift our focus from teaching to learning, so architects, college planners, presidents, provosts, deans, and others are beginning to recognize that the physical space on a campus needs to reflect not only the requirements of a discipline but also the needs of the learner (Van Note Chism, 2002; Oblinger, 2004.) Faculty members can play an indispensable role in the learning revolution by becoming more involved in the design of formal and informal settings in which students learn. In the learning college, the traditional role of the teacher evolves into that of a designer, an architect of learning environments.

Some 413 of the nation's 1,171 community colleges were built in the decade between 1960 and 1970, the same period during which a generation of faculty was hired. Many of those campuses have reached an age where major renovation is needed. Current faculty members have an opportunity to design learning environments and activities that will likely affect generations to come (Witt et al., 1994, p. 185).

Teaching by Design

Computing and the Internet challenge us to ask two fundamental yet largely unarticulated questions: first, what can be done in a physical space that cannot be done anywhere else, and second, what can human beings do that computers cannot? That second question is a focal point for both skepticism and anxiety. Many of us distrust the techno-hype, the belief in computers as a cure-all for the limitations of the current system or as a gateway to an imagined educational nirvana where education is inexpensive, quick, and fun. A good education in the real world, we insist, requires expertise, experience, and the hard work of good teaching. There are no shortcuts. Yet if we see teaching as just a matter of transmitting information—the so-called banking model—clearly computers have greater capacities than human beings.

While in a
conventional classroom

there are only two roles, teacher and student, a studio imagines many roles from the painter or sculptor of the artist's studio, to the engineer, writer, producer, actor, and director of a television studio.

The classroom is notoriously resistant to change, but that is where we must focus our efforts. That is where, presumably, we have the greatest institutional control and, we hope, the greatest effect on students. We as teachers have acquired habits over a lifetime. We teach as we were taught; our models of good teaching are the ones that worked for us as students, and many of us were good at school.

I no longer teach for a living, but I still think of myself as a teacher. Based on the experience of working with a team to design and build a new kind of classroom, and based on classroom experience, my concept of what it means to be a teacher has evolved and continues to evolve. The metaphor that shaped those design efforts can be an important instrument for others who wish to use collaborative design as one strategy in response to the persistent problem of improving student performance with limited resources. We live in a time of challenge and disruption, but also of opportunity, of the promise upheld by a growing body of

research on how people learn and can use well-designed environments and digital devices to work together more effectively and make each other smarter. At the heart of all that follows in this story is the fundamental claim that there are some kinds of experience that we simply cannot create as teachers by ourselves.

The Studio Metaphor

Over the last century, the growth of higher education in the United States gave birth to campuses that bear the unmistakable marks of modern industrial design: bland, sturdy, standardized classrooms with mass-produced furniture for large numbers of people. This was not always so. In the Renaissance, the great works of art attributed to individual geniuses such as da Vinci and Michelangelo were often the result of collaborations between master and apprentice. The Renaissance studia, from which we derive the word studio, flourished as a form of education well into the 19th century and it survives in the contemporary fields of plastic and performing arts. Outside the academy, the archetypal modern studio is in television production where technology—derived from the Greek word techne, meaning art—and creative purpose are an intrinsic part of the activity. The present design project hearkens back to that history in taking studio as its guiding metaphor to reimagine the classroom.

Given the origin of studio in the creative arts, it is perhaps surprising that contemporary use of the concept for classroom design has been most conspicuously realized in the sciences. Jack M. Wilson, former dean of undergraduate education at Rensselaer Polytechnic Institute (RPI), is cited frequently as one of the early adopters of the concept and the use of the phrase "studio classroom" in U.S. higher education. Led by Wilson, RPI redesigned introductory science courses that had previously been conducted using the traditional lecture-laboratory format into studio classes that integrate lecture and lab. Wilson, a physicist, reviewed the literature on physics teaching and discovered the limited effectiveness of the lecture method at colleges and universities at every level. As an administrator, Wilson was interested in finding more effective teaching methods while controlling costs. The innovation addressed both issues by redesigning introductory physics courses to integrate lecture and laboratory in the same space.

The resulting courses employ what Brown, Collins, and Duguid (1989) describe as "cognitive apprenticeship," a method in which students are asked to assume tasks, roles, and responsibilities that are authentic professional practices. Students in the redesigned courses reported higher satisfaction and showed improved performances compared to conventional courses. The studio classes proved so effective that Wilson and his colleagues at RPI were recognized with the prestigious Theodore Hesburg Award for programs that enhance undergraduate teaching and student learning. Institutions ranging from MIT and American University to Piedmont Technical College and Wake Technical Community College have successfully advanced the design of studio classrooms.

Researcher and teacher Stanley Pogrow argues that "metaphor is much more important to the design of sophisticated programs than research and theory" (1996). Because studio classrooms are not limited to specific disciplines or technologies, it is worth considering how studio metaphor differs from our conventional conception of a classroom. While in a conventional classroom there are only two roles, teacher and student, a studio imagines many roles from the painter or sculptor of the artist's studio, to the engineer, writer, producer, actor, and director of a television studio. Typically, we imagine a classroom as spartan and orderly in furnishing—desks, chairs, podium, blackboard—rather than having the richness and clutter of a studio where a variety of raw materials—clay, paint, costumes, props, video tape—may be close at hand to be deployed in creative work. Perhaps the most significant difference between the default notion of a classroom and that of a studio is the underlying motive. If we are honest, we would acknowledge that most students come to class, at least initially, to fulfill a requirement, to get a grade, to get credits, to get a degree. The fundamental motive is social obligation. The motive for a studio is to engage in creative work that produces a tangible object.

The studio model integrates all of Chickering and Gamson's (1987) seven principles of good practice, which were "distilled findings from decades of research on the undergraduate experience" (Chickering and Ehrman, 1996). The design of studio classrooms recognizes that while form follows function, function also follows form. Students will collaborate more easily when they are not isolated in arm-tablet chairs; teachers will feel more comfortable with an environment where computers do not block lines of sight and literally get in the way. More importantly, however, the studio makes the use of computing, information, and presentation a routine part of the classroom, just as they are in other work environments. The studio model also easily accommodates many of the strategies associated with effective teaching, including problem-based, collaborative, and experiential learning. The design follows the philosophy that the most powerful learning environments are those that enable the learner to engage in guided practice and reflection in the context of authentic activities. The model of teaching embedded in the studio is the "cognitive apprenticeship" described by Brown, Collins, and Duguid (1989). Rather than simply completing exercises designed to develop specific skills, students are asked to assume tasks, roles, and responsibilities that are recognized professional practices.

Perhaps the most intriguing aspect of the studio model is its potential to move the learning revolution to the space at the heart of our institutional activities: the classroom. Because of the rich array of computing and information resources available in studio classrooms, we can collect data and monitor routine student performance in real time. Each studio has the potential to become a repository of data on applied cognition, a laboratory for learning. Within that environment, the teacher's role shifts from that of performer to that of researcher, analyst, and designer. The role of the learner changes, too, as the classroom is transformed from a performance space for the teacher to a work place where students and teachers collaborate and create products that have intrinsic value. In this sense, the studio model has the potential to enhance dramatically the creativity that is at the heart of every good classroom.

Other Creative Learning Environments

Although studio classrooms are perhaps the most dramatic innovation in the design of spaces where students learn, college campuses have always had a range of space types representing a variety of activities.

Learning studios. Learning studios are flexible spaces designed to allow students and teachers to easily reconfigure the room depending on the requirements of the activities on any given day. Wireless access, laptop computers, and movable whiteboards and chairs allow the room to be rearranged for individual work, small groups, seminar-style discussions, or presentations (Lopez and Gee, 2006). Unlike a studio classroom, a learning studio may or may not have been developed with a particular curriculum in mind.

Information commons. The information commons is the Knowledge Age successor to the library. It locates books, computers, networks, and access to other information appliances in spaces that allow for informal interaction. An information commons often features food and beverage areas, comfortable seating, and soft, indirect lighting. Rather than traditional stacks and rows of tables, curved pathways and a variety of seating arrangements encourage interaction among patrons.

> The design follows the philosophy that the most powerful learning environments are those that enable the learner to engage in guided practice and reflection in the context of authentic activities.

Designing the Future

In the past, it was typical for the planning of buildings to be left to administrators, planners, and engineers. More recently, architects and experts on space design have offered excellent guidance on the kinds of processes that would more productively connect capital projects to teaching and learning. Taking an institutional view of design, Wedge and Kearns (2005) suggest that the principal steps in a successful process are identifying and involving various campus constituencies, defining the goals of a space, surveying existing resources, projecting future needs, exploring alternatives, and making recommendations. Although designing from the broad campus perspective can be an important element in garnering support for large changes, such a process tends to focus on the management and allocation of resources rather than on learning. For many faculty members, the design process is more likely to center on his or her own classroom. From that perspective, Johnson and Lomas (2005) describe a process that begins with the institutional context but then immediately turns to the learning principles as a guide to learning activities, and from those derives a set of design principles, requirements, and an evaluation methodology for the learning environment that is being envisioned.

Educational research summarized in the "Seven Principles for Good Practice in Undergraduate Education" and elsewhere has provided ample guidance on how people learn. New generations of learners for whom computing and information appliances are commonplace will pressure us to apply the principles creatively, using computing and communications devices as instruments for collaboration and co-creation of knowledge in classrooms. For faculty members beginning the journey toward creating a new kind of learning experience, the process of designing innovative learning spaces depends upon providing a catalyst not only for students, but also for colleagues and the organization to learn. The following are seven steps faculty members can take to begin redesigning their learning environments from the inside out.

Know the institutional constraints. As you are planning, consider basic operational questions such as, when is the semester course schedule printed? When are faculty loads assigned? When are rooms assigned? How and by whom? The timing of operations in the academic year is a powerful determinant of how willing people are to collaborate and plan.

First who, then what. Although knowledge and learning are clearly interdisciplinary, the curriculum, our thinking, and academic culture are driven by disciplines. The easiest place to start, then, is to look for a team in your own discipline. That said, the next criterion for a team member is willingness to experiment and be part of a team. Belonging to a team builds political support within your department for curricula changes and, more importantly, establishes a community of practice that reinforces a culture of innovation.

Focus on collaboration. The research demonstrates unequivocally that collaboration is the best way to learn (Cross, 2000; Pascarella and Terenzini, 2005). That finding applies not only to students. The most effective collaborative strategies in the classroom involve tasks requiring cooperation to succeed. Learning-space design is a model of such projects. Involving IT staff and student services professionals in the conversation early will not only extend the knowledge of available resources, but also provide important insight on possible constraints.

Experiment in your own classroom. Along with you, experience is a great teacher. Start with a few manageable changes in your own class. A number of web-based resources provide excellent starting points:

- The TLT Group's Resource Page offers a large repository of teaching strategies that employ easy-to-use technology to implement the "Seven Principles for Good Practice in Undergraduate Education" in classroom activities. Visit www.tltgroup.org/programs/seven.html.

- MERLOT (Multimedia Educational Resource for Learning and Online Teaching) is a peer-reviewed, online archive that includes many collaborative, active-learning assignments supported by technology.

- The PT3 Pathways Project features Real World Learning Objects—RWLOs—and a wealth of source materials to support a redesign of part or all of an existing course. Visit www.rwlo.org.

Educate your administrator. Because of the substantial resource commitment required to design and build learning spaces, securing support from the campus leadership early is essential. Volunteering to help organize, but not necessarily lead, a committee on classroom and space design is a good place to start. Prior to launch, plant a few seeds about space design through conversation and select articles from the literature. Cultivate the fine art of letting the plan be someone else's idea. See "How to Talk With Administrators" (below) for additional, specific tips.

Start where people are. What are the departmental or college initiatives? How does this project solve someone else's problem or advance his or her agenda? Co-opting builds support and reduces the chances that colleagues will see the design of innovative learning spaces as yet another item to be added to a long to-do list.

Form follows function; funds follow flexibility. Flexible space helps fulfill the administrative need to satisfy as many constituencies as possible and make best use of scarce physical resources by making them available for as many kinds of classes as possible.

How to Talk With Administrators

Suppose you have read all the literature, you've gathered a team of like-minded teachers, and you are ready to leap into designing and teaching in a studio environment. Now you have to convince an administrator to commit the financial and other resources to get it done. In other words, you have to educate your administrators. As with other learners, the best place to begin is where they are.

From an administrator's point of view, this project is one among many competing demands for time, attention, and money. Although we are theoretically part of a professional culture in which the best ideas triumph, a number of much more practical considerations are far more likely to determine whether your project gets support. Chief among these considerations is to what degree you have made it easy for the administrator to say "yes" by answering her questions about the project. Naturally, she will want to know about the pedagogical advantages of this investment, but student learning is just the starting point. How much each classroom will cost to build and how long it will take, how it will be scheduled, what it will cost to maintain, how teachers will be trained to use it, and what kind of technical support might be required are questions to which most administrators will want answers before they embrace construction of a project.

Peer recruitment. As with any project, choosing the right people is essential. Crafting an open invitation to all members of the faculty in the form of a request for proposals can help administrators avoid political problems down the road. That strategy does not, however, preclude encouraging people who already have reputations for being creative teachers to respond to the call and join the team. The talent of the individual teacher, however, is not the only consideration. The success of a project and its long-term sustainability as a model depends on a creating a team. Having a balance of nurturers with goal-setters, organizers with creators, and planners with improvisers fosters the creative tension essential to the design process. It lays the foundation for a community of professional practice that can develop and grow to become part of the mainstream culture at an institution.

Resources. The first lesson for any administrator is that the easiest place to find resources is to look at the people and the money you already have. Reallocating resources, however, almost always comes with a political price tag because it trades someone else's priorities for your own. You can negotiate release time during the design process for yourself and your colleagues based on the additional work necessary to integrate space and curricular design. The team is not creating a single room for an individual teacher or group of teachers, but a model for a flexible learning environment that can be replicated and scaled across a campus.

From Classrooms to Learning Spaces

O'Banion's evocative description of most educational reform as "trimming the branches of a dying tree" belies some hard, cold, brick-and-mortar realities for colleges and universities. While O'Banion refers to dead-end organizational structures, even the more extreme predictions about the changing nature of the higher education industry do not suggest that college campuses will disappear. Yet evolutionary pressures may well redefine the meaning of place in education. In the face of challenges to the "economic foundation of the present system" from the "changed flow of information due to electronic communications," Eli Noam (1995) sees campuses becoming less important as repositories of knowledge (para. 20). Noam continues:

> This suggests a change of emphasis for universities. True teaching and learning are about more than information. Education is based on mentoring, internalization, identification, role-modeling, guidance, and group activity. In these processes, physical proximity plays an important role. Thus, the strength of the future physical university lies less in pure information and more in college as a community. (Noam 1995, para. 21)

Noam's claim that community is a key element of learning is supported by the research (cited in Cross, 2000). It also begins to address a growing question in the Internet age: What is it that we can do in a physical space that we cannot do anywhere else? Creating community—social and intellectual connections—is at the heart of what should happen in classrooms and other learning spaces.

The recent report from the Secretary of Education's Commission on the Future of Higher Education (2006) concludes, "The future of our country's colleges and universities is threatened by global competitive pressures, powerful technological developments, restraints on public finance, and serious structural limitations that cry out for reform" (p. 26). Those sentiments echo the message expressed more than a decade ago by *An American Imperative* (1993), which warned:

> A disturbing and dangerous mismatch exists between what American society needs of higher education and what it is receiving. Nowhere is the mismatch more dangerous than in the quality of undergraduate preparation provided on many campuses. The American imperative for the 21st

century is that society must hold higher education to much higher expectations or risk national decline. (para. 1)

Even if the reports of the demise of traditional higher education are exaggerated, much work remains to be done as we face the challenges of a rapidly changing landscape. No one group can face those challenges alone. Successfully cultivating the emerging model of higher education will require the efforts of students, administrators, staff, community members, and the faculty. But faculty members have a special role to play in designing physical environments that foster communities defined by curiosity, creativity, and a common interest in learning. More so than administrators or researchers, innovative faculty members can lead the way to designing new campus and pedagogies both by continuing to model the creativity and spirit of experimentation that sets their teaching apart and by seeking out projects that require the support and involvement of their colleagues. In a sense, that is the greatest unknown of the emerging age—whether teachers can use the instruments of computing and communication to work not only with students, but also with each other.

References

Barr, R., and Tagg, J. (1995 Nov/Dec). From Teaching to Learning: A New Paradigm for Undergraduate Education. *Change, 27*(6). Retrieved January 7, 2006, from http://critical.tamucc.edu/~blalock/readings/ tch2learn.htm.

Beichner, R., Bernold, L., Burniston, E., Dail, P., Felder, R., Gastineau, J., Gjertsen, M., and Risley, J. (1999 July). Case Study of the Physics Component of an Integrated Curriculum. *American Journal of Physics, 67*(7), S16-24. Retrieved April 28, 2006, from ftp://ftp.ncsu.edu/pub/ncsu/beichner/RB/IntegratedCurriculum.pdf.

Belcher, J. (2001). Studio Physics at MIT. Physics Department Newsletter. Massachusetts Institute of Technology. Retrieved April 28, 2006, from http://www.del.univpm.it/MIT/visualizations/resources/PhysicsNewsLetter.pdf.

Brown, J. S., Collins, A., and Duguid, P. (1989). Situated Cognition and the Culture of Learning. *Education Researcher, 18*(1), pp. 32-42. Retrieved April 26, 2006, from http://www.sociallifeofinformation.com/Situated_Learning.htm.

Cataldo J., and del Cerro, G. (2001). The Pilot Design Studio-Classroom. *Proceedings of the 2001 American Society for Engineering Education Annual Conference & Exposition.* Washington, DC: American Society for Engineering Education. Accessed January 25, 2007, from http://www.asee.org/acPapers/00775_2001.PDF.

Chickering, A. W., and Ehrmann, S. C. (1996). Implementing the Seven Principles: Technology as a Lever. *AAHE Bulletin, 49*(2), pp. 3-6. Retrieved October 1, 2003, from http://www.tltgroup.org/programs/seven.html.

Chickering, A. W., and Gamson, Z. F. (1987). Seven Principles for Good Practice in Undergraduate Education. *AAHE Bulletin, 39*(7), pp. 3-7.

Collins, A., Brown, J. S., and Hollum, A. (1991). Cognitive Apprenticeship: Making Thinking Visible. Reprinted from the Winter 1991 issue of *American Educator*, the quarterly journal of the American Federation of Teachers. Accessed at http://kenton.k12.ky.us/DL/General/Readings/Collins_CogApp.pdf.

Cross, K. P. (2000). *Collaborative Learning 101*. The Cross Papers, Number 4. Mission Viejo, CA: League for Innovation in the Community College.

Education Commission of the States. (2000 November). State Funding for Community Colleges: A 50-State Survey. Denver: Center for Community College Policy, Education Commission of the States. Retrieved August 13, 2003, from http://www.ecs.org/clearinghouse/ 22/86/2286.pdf.

Flynn, W. J. (2003 January). The Learning Decade. *Learning Abstracts 6*(1).

Gonsalvez, C., and Atchison, M. (2000 December). Implementing Studios for Experiential Learning. *Proceedings of the Australasian Conference on Computing Education*, 8. ACSE '00. Retrieved April 28, 2006, from http://delivery.acm.org/10.1145/360000/359386/p116gonsalvez.pdf?key1=359386&key2=4141246411&coll=GUIDE&dl=GUIDE&CFID=70432544&CFTOKEN=90738076.

Horn, L., and Nevill, S. (2006). *Profile of Undergraduates in U.S. Postsecondary Educational Institutions 2003-2004* (NCES 2006-184). U.S. Department of Education. Washington DC: National Center for Educational Statistics, p. 9.

Lopez, H., and Gee, L. (2006). Learning Studios Project: Estrella Mountain Community College. In D. G. Oblinger, Ed., *Learning Spaces*, pp. 19.1-19.7. Washington, DC: Educause. Retrieved August 1, 2006 from http://www.educause.edu/ir/library/pdf/P7102cs6.pdf.

Johnson, C., and Lomas, C. (2005, July/August). Design of Learning Space: Learning and Design Principles. *Educause Review*, pp. 16-28.

Noam, E. (1995). Electronics and the Dim Future of the University. Columbia Business School Virtual Institute of Information. New York: Columbia University. Accessed from http://www.vii.org/papers/ citinoa3.htm.

O'Banion, T. (1997). *A Learning College for the 21st Century*. Phoenix: Oryx Press.

Oblinger, D. (2004 October). Leading the Transition From Classrooms to Learning Spaces. A National Learning Infrastructure Initiative White Paper. Washington, DC: Educause. Retrieved August 1, 2006 at http://www.educause.edu/LibraryDetailPage/666&ID=NLI0447.

Pascarella, P. T., and Terenzini, E. T. (2005). *How College Affects Students: A Third Decade of Research*. San Francisco: Jossey-Bass.

Pipes, R. B., and Wilson, J. M. (1996). A Multimedia Model for Undergraduate Education. *Technology In Society, 18*(3), pp. 387-401. Accessed from http://ciue.rpi.edu/pdfs/mmModelUGed.pdf.

Pogrow, S. (1996). Reforming the Wannabe Reformers: Why Education Reforms Almost Always End Up Making Things Worse. *Phi Delta Kappan, 77*(10), pp. 656-663.

Schank, R. (n.d.). Hear Roger Schank Introduce Engines for Education. *Engines for Education*. Institute for the Learning Sciences, Northwestern University. Audio-stream accessed January 25, 2007, at http://www.engines4ed.org/hyperbook/nodes/intro-zoomer.html.

Senge, P. M. (1990). *The Fifth Discipline: The Art and Practice of the Learning Organization*. New York: Doubleday.

Smith, P. (2004). *The Quiet Crisis: How Higher Education Is Failing America*. Bolton, MA: Anker.

U.S. Department of Education. (2006, August 18). A National Dialogue: The Secretary of Education's Commission on the Future of Higher Education—Draft Report. Retrieved September 1, 2006, from http://www.ed.gov/about/bdscomm/list/hiedfuture/reports/0809-draft.pdf.

Van Note Chism, N. (2002). A Tale of Two Classrooms. *New Directions in Teaching and Learning, 92*(Winter), pp. 5-12.

Wedge, C., and Kearns, T. (2005, July/August). Creation of the Learning Space: Catalysts for Envisioning and Navigating the Design Process. *Educause Review*, pp. 32-38.

Williams, P. J., MacLatchy, C., Backman, P., and Retson, D. (1997). Studio Physics at Acadia Univeristy. *Physics in Canada 53*(2), pp. 96-101. Retrieved April 28, 2006, from http://aitt.acadiau.ca/research/science/studiophysics.pdf.

Wilson, J. M. (2001). The Development of the Studio Classroom. In P. S. Goodman, Ed., *Technology Enhanced Learning: Opportunities for Change*. Mahwah, NJ: Lawrence Erlbaum Associates.

Wingspread Group on Higher Education. (1993). *An American Imperative: Higher Expectations for Higher Education*. Racine, WI: The Johnson Foundation. Accessed at http://www.johnsonfdn.org/AmericanImperative/hiexp.html.

Witt, A., Wattenbarger, J., Gollattscheck, J., and Suppinger, J. (1994). *America's Community Colleges: The First Century*. Washington DC: Community College Press.

Creating a New Architecture for the Learning College

— Terry O'Banion

O'Banion, T. (2007 September). "Creating a New Architecture for the Learning College." *Community College Journal of Research and Practice, 31*(9), pp. 713-724.

The publication of *A Nation at Risk* in 1983 triggered a series of major reform efforts in education that are still evolving. As part of the reform efforts, leaders began to refer to a Learning Revolution that would "place learning first by overhauling the traditional architecture of education." The old architecture—time-bound, place-bound, role-bound, and bureaucracy-bound—was an artifact of earlier eras when school was designed for an agricultural and an industrial economy. It was easy for educational leaders to "place learning first" by changing their language. Vice Presidents of Academic Affairs became Vice Presidents of Learning; Learning Outcomes became the universal goal; the institutions became Learning Colleges. New mission and value statements began to appear in community college catalogs to reflect the new emphasis on learning. The American Association of Community Colleges joined the revolution with a new mission statement: "Building a nation of learners by advancing America's community colleges." The really hard work was to "overhaul the traditional architecture." This brief article takes a first step in suggesting what that "overhaul" might look like for departmental structures, workload formula, grading, late registration, and some of the time-bound artifacts. It is noted that the five examples are but the tip of the iceberg if community colleges are to fully engage the Learning Revolution.

A Learning Revolution is spreading rapidly through all sectors of education, and the community college has become the most visible crucible in which the concepts and practices of this revolution are being forged. First articulated in the early 1990s by Robert Barr, John Tagg, and George Boggs as a new Learning Paradigm, this fresh approach to educational reform leads educators away from fixing educational problems by the process of adding on a new program, new staff, and more technology to a traditional core of programs and services. The new approach suggests that the old models of education are no longer functional and that they even stand in the way of changes that would substantially improve student learning. Pat Cross (1984) has recognized the problem for many years: "After some two decades of trying to find answers to the question of how to provide education for all the people, I have concluded that our commitment to the lock-step, time-defined structures of education stands in the way of lasting progress" (p. 171).

The basic concepts of the Learning Revolution were best expressed in the work of the Wingspread Group on Higher Education (1993): "Putting learning at the heart of the academic enterprise will mean overhauling the conceptual, procedural, curricular, and other architecture of postsecondary education on most campuses." These two key concepts—(a) place learning first (b) by overhauling the traditional architecture of education—charted a new direction for educational reform and launched a revolution in the way we think about the core business and basic structures of education.

It was not difficult to "place learning first," at least in the language of education. Many educational institutions began embracing the language of "learning," and community colleges were among the early adopters. Ironically, mission and value statements had to be revised to make explicit that learning was the central purpose, the institution's first priority. Deans of Instruction became Vice Presidents for Learning. The accrediting associations pressed for colleges to identify and measure learning outcomes. Colleges claimed to be Learning Organizations creating Learning Communities for their students and for their staffs. Strategic plans were revised to include the core principles of the Learning College. Learning became the mantra of educational reform throughout the 1990s.

Earnest and eager to "place learning first" in every policy, program, and practice, and in the way they use their personnel, the early leaders of the Learning Revolution found it relatively easy to change the language of education. However, they began to run into problems reflected in Roger Moe's (1994) keen observation that "Higher education is a thousand years of tradition wrapped in a hundred years of bureaucracy." It was the second key concept of the Learning Revolution—"overhauling the traditional architecture of education"—that was the real challenge.

The traditional architecture of education was designed in an earlier time to meet the needs of an agrarian and an industrial economy; it was not designed to improve and expand student learning. At the end of the 1800s, schools were based on an agricultural economy that accommodated the needs of farmers who depended on their children to work on the farms. Schools were designed to end in the middle of the afternoon so that students could be home before dark to milk the cows, gather the eggs, and feed the hogs. School closed down for the summer to allow students to attend to major farm chores: harvesting crops, tilling new land, building barns, and repairing tools and fences. "Everyone recognizes it (the academic calendar) for what it is: a relic of an agrarian society in which all able-bodied men and women were needed in the fields at certain times of the year" (Lovett, 1995, p. B1).

When the nation changed in the 1920s and 1930s from an agricultural to an industrial economy, the old school structure remained as the foundation but was updated and streamlined to fit the new industrial organizational model.

> ## It was the
> ### second key concept
> of the Learning Revolution—
> "overhauling the traditional
> architecture of education"—
> that was the real challenge.

"Scientific management" and hierarchical organization, the bedrock principles of bureaucracy, were introduced in the schools, in part to socialize youth in the virtues of order and discipline. More importantly, the modern factory, pioneered by Henry Ford in the production of automobiles, appealed to educators as an ideal model on which to structure the schools. Organize students into groups of 35 and move them through 55-minute periods of instruction in a 16-week term; the school bell echoed the factory whistle that kept everything moving on time. "America's schools still operate like factories, subjecting the raw material (students) to standardized instruction and routine inspection" (Alvin and Heidi Toffler, 1995, p. 13).

Today, this inherited architecture of education places great limits on a system struggling to redefine and transform itself into a learning-centered enterprise, one that can continually deepen learning and improve student success. The school system, from K to Gray, is time-bound, place-bound, bureaucracy-bound, and role-bound. These bonds must be broken and a new, more fluid architecture created that places learning first and enables the institution to become ever smarter and better at improving its outcomes if the Learning Revolution is to come to full fruition. The Wingspread Group on Higher Education (1993) defined the Learning Revolution and pointed the way for ensuring its success: "The nation that responds best and most rapidly to the educational demands of the Age of the Learner will enjoy a commanding international advantage in the pursuit of both domestic tranquility and economic prosperity. To achieve these goals for our country, we must educate more people and educate them far better. *That will require new ways of thinking*" (p. 7, Italics added). The 12 Vanguard Learning Colleges in the League for Innovation's Learning College Project have been struggling with new ways of thinking about how to implement the concepts called for in the Learning Revolution—concepts expressed in the Learning Paradigm and the core principles of the Learning College. They have been particularly interested in exploring how to "overhaul the traditional architecture of education" so they could more substantively "place learning first" and improve it. Beginning in January of 2000, the Vanguard Learning Colleges agreed to work together over a three-year period to create new architectural forms that would allow them to place learning as their first priority. Teams from the 12 colleges have met for intensive seminars for the past three summers and in special sessions at the League's annual conference on innovations. In addition, the colleges have shared an active network of communication facilitated through the Learning College website at www.league.org. Some promising "new ways of thinking" about an architecture to support learning are beginning to emerge from the work of these colleges. The early outlines of this new architecture—new practices and key questions—in five selected areas will be of interest to many colleges struggling to implement the Learning Revolution.

How can
technology enhance
the communication required in some disciplines without organizing the entire college around disciplines?

Departmental Structures

Community colleges inherited the departmental/divisional structures for organizing faculty into discipline groups from the universities. Some educators believe that such an organizing structure serves to reinforce the culture of the discipline guilds over larger institutional values, especially community college values that may be different in some important ways from the values of the university. One example is that by organizing around disciplines, the vocational faculty and the liberal arts faculty in community colleges tend to be isolated from one another when they need to forge curriculum and instructional alliances to enhance student learning.

In the 1960s, a number of new community colleges experimented with an organizational architecture designed to enhance communication across faculty disciplines. The Novato Campus of the College of Marin (California) organized faculty into "Houses" that represented a very broad view of the knowledge and skills the college valued. At Santa Fe Community College (Florida), faculty were organized into "Units" of 16. Each unit included representatives from a wide range of disciplines. The unit's leader attended to the needs of members and guided them in the creation of a community that addressed larger institutional values that, at Santa Fe, were quite different from those of other community colleges. Faculty met in discipline groups when they needed to select textbooks, agree on common assessment, and make curriculum decisions, but their primary physical and philosophical commitment was to the "Unit."

Cascadia Community College (Washington) is currently organizing its faculty and staff around four fundamental learning outcomes. Learning Outcome Teams (LOTs) involving all faculty, staff, and administration are the funded units that create college initiatives and projects, act as communication outlets, and select their own methods and priorities for ensuring that students achieve the desired outcome. Creating such a structure is easier when a college is new, but it can be done even in established colleges. Sir Sandford Fleming College (Ontario) eliminated the traditional departmental structure and created six new "Centres of Specialization" managed by faculty teams. The centers are organized around natural resources, community development and health, law and justice, management and business studies, interdisciplinary studies, and applied computing and information technology. The new structure was supported by the faculty union, and both management and the union agree that, to date, the new model is working extremely well.

If a college wished to continue with a discipline-oriented structure, how would it be organized to best represent new fields of knowledge while enhancing cross-disciplinary communication? How can technology enhance the communication required in some disciplines without organizing the entire college around disciplines? Is it necessary to organize faculty and staff into any kind of groupings? Why? And, if so, how could they be organized to best meet the rationale posed in the answer to why? Is there an organizational structure for faculty and staff that would communicate that a college is truly learning centered and that would ensure a focus on improving learning?

The Workload Formula

The bureaucracy-bound historical architecture has created one of the most limiting practices in educational culture with the concept of the workload formula. The long shadow of education's adaptation to the industrial economy is clearly evident in the formula that the best way to use faculty resources is to assign full-time faculty to teach five courses a semester as their load, an apt term for this inefficient and educationally ineffective practice. All other faculty assignments are keyed to this formula. Many faculty are permitted to teach one or two courses more as an "overload." This practice of allowing faculty to teach an "overload" raises very serious but unaddressed questions about the validity of the load concept—or at least the formula that five courses represent tasks truly equivalent to at least a 40-hour work week. Some faculty are released from teaching one or more courses to do other things, and the time assigned is based on the workload formula. Part-time faculty are hired and assigned to teach courses according to the workload formula when there are not enough full-time faculty to teach all the courses offered.

The fact that the workload formula is so deeply embedded in the culture of most educational institutions is testimony to the value placed on institutional efficiency over improving and expanding learning for students. How faculty time is allocated is more important than student time. If institutions placed a priority on learning, they would design many variations in terms of structures to accommodate student needs. Indeed, many institutions experiment with such variations as independent study, learning communities, service learning, cooperative education, etc.; but the workload formula is ever present to cast its long and restrictive shadow over these innovations. The workload formula enslaves faculty in a structured system in which they do not often have opportunities to contribute their greatest talents and creativity to the educational enterprise. The innovators have adapted to the system. Like the "A" students who have learned to negotiate the traditional architecture, faculty innovators have learned to be subversive and cunning in getting around the system. They do this in order to create environments that work better for learning. If the workload formula was changed faculty would not have to waste their energies working around its limiting structures; what could faculty accomplish in their roles as the facilitators of learning if they were freed from the workload formula?

Since education has been such a labor-intensive enterprise, there will be no major reforms and little increased productivity on the part of the faculty until we free ourselves from the tyranny of the workload formula. We need to change the conversation from "my load, my classes, my students" to "How can we realign our resources to improve and expand learning for our students?" We begin by defining resources not on the basis of a formula that assumes full-time faculty load equals learning produced in students. We do it by determining what we want our students to learn and then figuring out how to use the vast resources available to us: classified staff, students, community volunteers, administrators, educators in other institutions, technology, full-time faculty, and part-time faculty.

Ask the faculty what ways other than teaching five classes they can identify to make a significant contribution to improving and expanding learning. If number of classes or number of students is not the basis for faculty contributions to the educational enterprise, how is the learning they produce to be calculated? Need this be calculated at the individual faculty or staff member level? What kind of architecture is needed to implement the concept of the faculty member as a "manager of learning"? What kinds of creative alliances would emerge in the institution to accommodate the needs of the "boundless" faculty? If the roles of learning facilitators are to be determined by the needs of the students, what implications does such a practice have for workload? What kind of architecture can support clearly defined learning facilitator roles that are based on clearly defined student learning needs?

> If institutions placed a priority on learning, they would design many variations in terms of structures to accommodate student needs.

The Grading System

The grading system of A through F is one of the most powerful elements of the historical architecture of education. Grades begin to stamp a person's value in the early years of schooling and accumulate weight with each passing (or failing!) year. Eventually grades are pooled into a grade point average (GPA) and stick with the student, like the Scarlet Letter, for the rest of his or her life. The GPA influences participation in athletics and social events, plays a key role in determining high school graduation and admission to college, influences decisions regarding scholarships and financial aid, and becomes an issue in social standing and parental approval. Grades are the coin of the realm as sectors of education trade in student lives for the good of society.

It is a little discouraging, therefore, when we come to understand that "The course grade is an inadequate report of an inaccurate judgment by a biased and variable judge of the extent to which a student has attained an undefined level of mastery of an unknown proportion of an indefinite material" (Dressel, 1983, p. 1) No wonder that two teachers grading the same piece of work cannot agree on the grade to be assigned. Teachers receive little or no training in assessment and the grading process and, thus, may assign grades as a measure of punctuality, a measure of gain or growth, a measure of place in a distribution, a measure of dishonesty, a measure of extra work, a measure of attendance, a measure of writing skill, a measure of motivation or perseverance, a measure of social class, a measure of political statement, or as a measure of the teacher's health or emotional state the day a grade is assigned. Pooling grades from various courses—an A in Russian literature has as much value as an A in Volleyball—from various teachers to create a grade point average creates a witches' brew, and we would rather not know the specific origins of the ingredients.

Educators generally agree that grades are a poor measure of what a student knows and understands about a body of knowledge, and there have been numerous attempts to redress the wrong by creating alternative systems of proficiencies, competencies, skills, standards, or outcomes. There is a great deal of attention focused on these alternatives at the moment as educational leaders and critics call for a "culture of evidence" to replace a culture that assumes learning takes place because something has been taught. A League for Innovation project captures this rising tide of concern in a project that assists community colleges in defining learning outcomes, teaching learning outcomes, assessing learning outcomes, and documenting learning outcomes. Accrediting associations are embedding the concept of "learning outcomes" deeply into revised accreditation processes, laying the foundation for a new educational architecture that places learning first.

Faculty
abhor late
registration—and
with good reason.

How can we create a common understanding and a common system for documenting what a student has learned during his or her formal schooling? Can we agree on learning outcomes for every planned educational experience, on ways to determine levels of proficiency for the outcomes, on ways to assess the acquisition of the outcomes? How can we strike a balance between the supposed efficiency of the GPA and the cumbersome lists of skills achieved at some level of proficiency? How do we measure what a student knows in contrast to what a student can do with that knowledge? What responsibility does the student have in participating in this process that is so important to future success?

Late Registration

Almost every institution of higher education in the country engages every term in a practice that plays havoc with the goal of creating an effective learning environment for students—late registration. The practice emerged to provide opportunities for students and for the institution. During the late registration period, usually the first week of class of a 16-week term, students are allowed, with some restrictions at some colleges, to change class schedules as they seek more accommodating times, more useful courses, and better teachers. In some cases, students may be seeking easier courses or teachers. For the institution, the purpose is to increase the number of enrolled students and hence revenue through a funding formula based on full-time equivalent students or average daily attendance: the more students, the more money. Late registration is an educationally ineffective architecture deeply embedded in the culture of institutions of higher education.

Faculty abhor late registration—and with good reason. Most faculty recognize that the first day of class may be the most important as they begin to create an expectation and a climate to entice students to master the course. Faculty give careful consideration to orienting students, welcoming

students, creating a sense of class community, providing course overviews, introducing themselves and their perspectives, and making beginning assignments—all on the first day and in the first week. This initial groundwork early in the term is the key to subsequent success for many students, but the preparation process is constantly interrupted by the comings and goings of late-registering students. Thus, many teachers do not even try to use the first day and the first week in any substantive way, and often dismiss students from class early. In these situations there develops a cynical collusion between both students and the faculty member that communicates that learning is really not very important at this institution. A climate of cynicism begins to pervade the institution as faculty realize that administrators are more interested in head count and the increased income than they are in supporting faculty efforts to create an effective learning environment.

What can colleges do to market registration as an opportunity that ends the day before the first class begins? What compromises can faculty and administrators make to ensure that the institution enrolls the maximum number of students who wish to register but does so in time to take advantage of the special arrangements faculty create for the first day and first week of class? How can the late registration issue be addressed as an opportunity for students to take responsibility for improving and expanding their own learning?

Time-Bound Artifacts

The class hour, the three-hour credit course, the semester or quarter term, and the school year are the building blocks of an architecture created for agricultural and industrial economies. They may have been useful building blocks in earlier times and understandings of our mission, but today they are impediments to creating the most powerful learning environments possible.

Recognizing that schools suffer from a time-bound mentality, the U.S. Department of Education, in 1992, appointed a national commission to study the issue. Addressing the time issue primarily in K-12 schools, the commission noted, "Unyielding and relentless, the time available in a uniform six-hour day and a 180-day year is the unacknowledged design flaw in American education. By relying on time as the metric for school organization and curriculum, we have built the learning enterprise on a foundation of sand" (National Education Commission on Time and Learning 1994, p. 8).

Herding groups of students through one-hour sessions five days a week in high schools and three days a week in college flies in the face of everything known about what works to improve and expand learning. No one believes that 30 different students arrive at the appointed hour ready to learn in the same way, on the same schedule, all in rhythm with each other and the teacher. The National Education Commission of Time and Learning concluded, "Learning in America is a prisoner of time. For the past 150 years, American public schools have held time constant and let learning vary…Time is learning's warden" (1994, p. 7).

The time framework is particularly pernicious when it is extended to credit hours per course. "The vast majority of college courses have three or four hours of credit. Isn't it a coincidence of cosmic proportions that it takes exactly the same billable unit of work to learn the plays of Shakespeare and differential calculus? Or maybe the guest has been amputated to fit the bed" (Peters, 1994, p. 23). The National Education Commission on Time and Learning reports that, "no matter how complex or simple the school subject—literature, shop, physics, gym, or algebra—the schedule assigns each an impartial national average of 51 minutes per class period, regardless of how well or poorly students comprehend the material" (1994, p. 7).

The unit of measure must be changed to reflect mastery instead of time in the seat, recognizing what is universally understood: human beings learn at different rates. Students should not have to serve time in schools. Students able to learn fast are held back and bored. Students needing more time are denied it. School time should be redesigned to serve the learning needs of students.

What time-free alternatives can colleges create to better serve the learning needs of students? How can entrance and exit competencies be used to design a time-free architecture? How can technology be used to free students and teachers from the old time-bound architecture? How does a college maintain some time-bound structures that work for some students and create time-free structures that work for other students?

Conclusion

These five examples are but the tip of the iceberg of the challenges colleges face in overhauling the architecture of education to place learning first and to embarking on the path of creating ever more powerful learning experiences and environments. The old architecture restricts what works for learning in every nook and cranny of the institution—in the governance and management structures, in the divisions between instruction and student services, in the buildings constructed in earlier times, in the design of student seats and faculty desks, in the dominance of the lecture, in the academic policies: the residue of "a thousand years of tradition wrapped in a hundred years of bureaucracy" (Moe, 1994, p. 1).

If we can, however, begin redesigning our inherited architecture one brick at a time we may begin to learn the skills and attitudes necessary to creating a new architecture. In the process, we may discover that the pieces are connected in such a way that changing one brick affects many others. We will need to be agile to ensure that dislodging one brick does not bring the entire house down on our heads. We may need to create temporary structures to hold up a sagging program until we can fortify the new architecture. As we put on our hard hats and enter the danger zones, we must keep in mind that the purpose is not just the destruction of the old but the creation of the new for one reason: improving and expanding learning and success for our students.

References

Cross, K. P. (November 1984). The Rising Tide of School Reform Reports. *Phi Delta Kappan*.

Dressel, P. (1983). Grades: One More Tilt at the Windmill. In A. W. Chickering (Ed.), *Bulletin*, Memphis State University Center for the Study of Higher Education.

Lovett, C. (November 24, 1995). Small Steps to Achieve Big Changes. *The Chronicle of Higher Education*.

Moe, R. (January 1994). Cited in Armajani, B. et al. *A Model for the Reinvented Higher Education System: State Policy and College Learning*. Denver: Education Commission of the States.

National Education Commission on Time and Learning (April 1994). *Prisoners of Time*. Washington, D. C.: U. S. Government Printing Office.

O'Banion, T. (Fall 1995). Community Colleges Lead a Learning Revolution. *Educational Record, 76*(4), 23–27.

Peters, R. (November-December 1994). Some Snarks are Boojums: Accountability and the End(s) of Higher Education. *Change*.

Toffler, A. & Toffler, H. (March-April 1995). Getting Set for the Coming Millennium. *The Futurist*.

Wingspread Group on Higher Education. (1993). *An American Imperative: Higher Expectations for Higher Education*. Racine, WI: The Johnson Foundation.

Part V.

The Future of the Learning College

Among those promises is one made as a result of the Learning College movement, an overt promise many community colleges have made to focus on learning.

On the heels of the Learning College Project and the 21st Century Learning Outcomes Project, and with support from The Atlantic Philanthropies, Inc., the Education Commission of the States and the League for Innovation partnered in a project focused on the future of the community college. The organizations commissioned five working briefs to be used by the principal author, Kay McClenney, in preparing an essay articulating the serious challenges faced by community colleges as they worked to fulfill their missions. That essay, "Keeping America's Promise: Challenges for Community Colleges," (pages 197-206) launches the final section of this volume. It includes trends that are still relevant for community colleges as well as promises these institutions are still trying to keep. Among those promises is one made at least in part as a result of the Learning College movement, an overt promise many community colleges have made to focus on learning.

As colleges continue exploring ways to keep their promises to improve and expand student learning, Cindy Miles and Elisa Robyn, in "Passing the Learning College Test: Courage and Innovation" (pages 207-213) challenge institutions not only to question their approaches to learning, but also to question the very questions they are asking. Miles and Robyn suggest that the reasons the solutions have not worked isn't that the answers are wrong, but that the wrong questions are being asked. More than an intellectual exercise, Miles and Robyn provide a recipe for creative and innovative explorations of the work colleges do, of the ways that work is done, and of the results—intended and actual—that are the effects of that work.

Finally, in "The Learning College: How Do We Know?" (pages 214-217), Cynthia Wilson summarizes what has been learned in the years since the Barr and Tagg article appeared in *Change*, and she turns the Learning College's most fundamental question back on itself. She explores possible ways to find answers to the how-do-we-know question, and determines that although progress has been made, the journey is far from over.

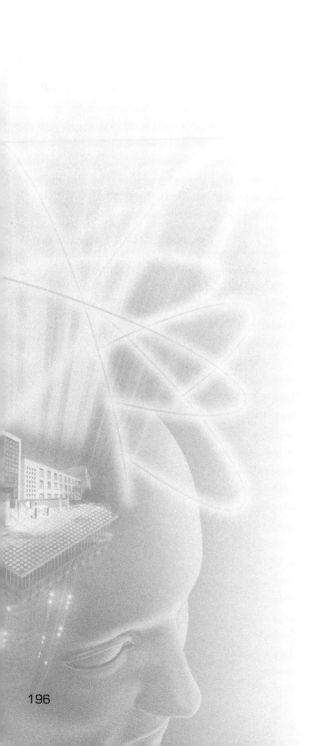

Keeping America's Promise: Challenges for Community Colleges

— Kay M. McClenney

McClenney, K. M. (2004). "Keeping America's Promise: Challenges for Community Colleges." In K. Boswell and C. D. Wilson, Eds., *Keeping America's Promise: A Report on the Future of the Community College*, pp. 7-18. Denver: Education Commission of the States.

America and Americans make a lot of promises, about a lot of different things. Just for the fun of it, I googled "keeping the promise." There will be no surprise about the array of things I found: promises of instant wealth through questionable real estate transactions and instant organizational effectiveness through IT outsourcing; promises and reminders of promises about public school reform, full funding of the global AIDS act, equal access for the differently abled, deposit insurance reform, and prescription drugs for older Americans.

There's more, though. In the email inbox I find promises of many things. A cure for baldness. Get rich quick by laundering money for a stranger in Africa. Sexual virility. Lose 50 pounds or gain three inches. Then there are the personal promises, made to ourselves and those closest to us: When I grow up.... You'll understand when you're older (my son reminded me of that one). I promise to do my duty to God and my country. I'll call you next Sunday. The check's in the mail. Happily ever after. In the year 2004, I resolve.... 'Til death do us part.

There are the political promises, remarkably plentiful in this election year, but always with us. Securing Social Security. Reducing class size. Ending welfare as we know it. Finding weapons of mass destruction. Peace in our time. No Child Left Behind. There are promises that cut across the cultural, commercial, personal, and political aspects of our lives. I pledge allegiance to the flag. Hard work will be rewarded. A chicken in every pot. A laptop in every lap. America has made many promises. In the Constitution, "we the people" committed to one another to "promote the general welfare" and to "secure the blessings of liberty to ourselves and our posterity." Consider these American promises, too: "Give me your tired, your poor, your huddled masses yearning to breathe free." "Life, liberty and the pursuit of happiness." "Liberty and justice for all." One man, one vote. Equal treatment under the law. And to the victims and survivors of the World War II Holocaust: "Never again. Never, never again."

The most fundamental American promises, though, are the promises of opportunity and equity for every individual. Every individual. This is the land where a person born in humble circumstances, if she is willing to work hard, can rise to the highest level, can grow wealthy and secure, can contribute, can become President.

Opportunity = Education. Perhaps one of the most fundamental developments at the end of the 20th century is this: *Opportunity in this country is more and more a function of education*, and that reality is something that sets America apart. As Tony Carnevale has observed:

In today's economy, access to postsecondary education or training has become the threshold requirement for individual career success.... Unlike the European welfare states that guarantee access to income and benefits irrespective of individual educational performance, our increasing reliance on education as the arbiter of economic opportunity allows us to expand opportunity without surrendering individual responsibility. As a result, we emphasize equality of educational opportunity rather than equality of economic outcomes. (Carnevale, 2004, p. 39)

Evidence of the country's commitment to educational opportunity has come, over the years, through some major public policy commitments. The preeminent examples include the Morrill Act of 1862, establishing the land grant colleges; the GI Bill, which was invented as a way to do something productive with all of those World War II veterans who were coming home and flooding the labor market, but which also effectively assailed the notion that higher education was only for the elites; the Truman Commission, which in 1947 called for the establishment of a national network of low-cost public community colleges; and Pell Grants, our most important source of need-based financial aid for college students.

> The most fundamental American promises, though, are the promises of opportunity and equity for every individual.

Through these commitments, America has worked to keep its promises of opportunity and of education that opens doors to opportunity. It is time now to revive the discussion of this nation's important promises, in particular the promises related to American higher education and especially the promises involving people committed to the work of the nation's community colleges. What are the promises we, as a nation, have made? What are the promises we ought to make? Are they empty promises, pipe dreams? Or, are they real, meaningful commitments? If we are to keep these promises, what are the challenges ahead?

Trends That Matter

To begin, it will be useful to take a quick look at the context within which we are all working. Obviously, the multiple developments in our global and local environments provide a plethora of forces that community college leaders must take into account. But for the present purpose, it will suffice to highlight briefly four trends that matter significantly in understanding both our promises and our challenges in keeping them.

Trend 1. Escalating Demand for Postsecondary Education. This is a reality that is well known: In the 21st century, America's ability to educate its people "will increasingly determine its economic competitiveness as the country shifts from an industrial to an information economy" (Carnevale and Desrochers, 2004, p. 39). To put it bluntly, the fastest-growing and best-paying jobs in the American economy are those that require at least some college experience. And as Tom Mortenson (2004) says, "Those who get this education can participate. Those who don't can't."

Furthermore, there is a companion reality that presidents, governors, and other political leaders increasingly understand; that is the fact that "increases in a country's overall level of educational attainment cause corresponding increases in its overall rate of economic growth. *Increasing a country's average level of schooling by one year can increase economic growth by about 5 to 15 percent*" (Carnevale and Desrochers, 2004, p. 39, emphasis added).

Carnevale and Desrochers (2004) paint a powerful picture of future workforce needs:

> As the baby boomers with postsecondary education retire over the next 20 years, it will be difficult to produce a sufficient number of Americans with postsecondary education or training to meet the economy's needs. Shortages of workers with some college-level skills could increase to more than 14 million by 2020. (p.42)

In addition to the increasingly urgent needs of the economy, the baby-boom echo will boost the numbers of high school graduates through most of the current decade. There will be state and regional variations in the impact on higher education, but generally, even if current college participation levels are simply maintained, community colleges across the nation will likely see about a 13 percent increase in enrollment over 2000 levels by 2015. If efforts to increase participation rates to the level achieved in the highest-performing states are successful, that enrollment increase could be as much as 46 percent (Martinez, 2004).

Civil Society and Quality of Life. As Carnevale and Desrochers correctly assert, "postsecondary education is about more than dollars and cents. It does more than provide foot soldiers for the American economy" (Carnevale and Desrochers, 2004, p. 39). In fact, an individual's educational attainment level is powerfully correlated with many of the things that we as Americans care most about in our society.

The more educated a person is, the more likely she is to be gainfully employed, to pay taxes, to participate in civic life and democratic processes, to vote. At the same time, he is less likely to be dependent on public support, less likely to be on welfare or in prison, and more likely to be able to provide for the educational and health-related needs of his children.

Trend 2. Continuously Changing Student "Mix." Community college students are diverse already, as these institutions serve about half of all of the minority undergraduates in the U.S. Still, though, the student population will become increasingly diverse in every way: more students of color, more English language learners, more first-generation college students, more adult students, more students from low-income families.

Figure 1. Benefits of Education

More likely to...	Less likely to...
• Be gainfully employed • Pay taxes • Participate in civic life and democratic processes • Vote • Be able to provide for education and health of children	• Be dependent on public support • Be on welfare • Be in prison

Source: Carnevale and Desrochers, 2004

According to the National Center for Education Statistics (2002), the definition of a nontraditional student is one who is financially independent, attends part-time, works full time, delays enrollment after high school, has dependents, is a single parent, or does not have a high school diploma.

Under that definition, in the 1999 academic year, almost 90 percent of all community college students were nontraditional (Hamm, 2004). Here are representative facts describing the student population:

- About two-thirds of community college students are part-time students, compared to about a quarter of students in baccalaureate institutions (Voorhees as cited in Hamm, 2004).

- 54 percent of community college students work full time (Hamm, 2004).

- 34 percent have dependents, 16 percent are single parents, and 23 percent spend 6-20 hours a week commuting to their college classes (CCSSE, 2003).

- Over 45 percent of community college enrollees are first-generation college students (Wilson, 2004).

- Almost 44 percent of community college students are 25 or older (Wilson, 2004).

Trend 3. Going to College: Not What It Used to Be. In the not-too-distant past, going to college typically meant going off to college, generally an 18-year-old leaving home to live on or near campus, attending classes full time and, usually, earning the degree four years later at the place where he started. In stark contrast, Americans now use higher education in much different ways.

Figure 2. Community College Student Characteristics

Work full time	54%
Have dependents	34%
Are single parents	16%
Commute to class 6 to 20 hours a week	23%
Are first-generation college students	45%
Are 25 or older	44%

Sources: CCSSE, 2003; Hamm, 2004; Wilson, 2004

How students go to college. Many of today's students attend part-time, often going to multiple institutions before attaining a credential, enrolling in two or more institutions simultaneously, stopping in and out, transferring in all directions, and so on. In fact, only one in six current undergraduate students in the U.S. is 18 to 24 years old, attends school full time, and lives on campus.

According to the Community College Survey of Student Engagement (2003), 35 percent of community college students began their college studies somewhere other than their current institution. More and more are concurrently enrolled in high school and community college (12,000 in New York City, for example, and at least 3 percent nationally); a significant proportion already have a degree (about 16 percent on average, but the numbers go up to around 20 percent or more in some locations); and at least another 6 percent take courses simultaneously at another college or university.

Generally, students have more choices available to them, involving more delivery options on campus, in the workplace, or online. They are shopping for educational experiences and trying to piece them together in ways that make sense. Or not.

Why students go to college. With regard to educational goals, it is now increasingly well understood that community college students have many different goals; that an individual student often has more than one; and that, especially if the college does its job right, the goals are likely to change over time. Among the goals students cite for their college attendance are these:

- 62 percent want to obtain knowledge in a specific area

- 58 percent aspire to obtain an associate degree

- 47 percent plan to transfer to a 4-year institution

- 59 percent want to obtain job-related skills

- 35 percent aim to complete a certificate

- 33 percent need to update their job skills

- 28 percent want to change careers

- 23 percent say they are taking courses for self-improvement (CCSSE, 2003)

Where students go to college. Community colleges today enroll almost half of all undergraduate students in the U.S. However, for-profit institutions now award at least 10 percent of all associate degrees, and their share of the two-year college market is 28 percent, up from 19 percent in a decade (Kelly as cited in Hamm, 2004). This growth occurs despite the significantly higher costs to students. Furthermore, there are now more than 2,000 corporate universities in the U.S. alone, many of them offering associate and baccalaureate degrees. Motorola University, for example, has 400 full-time faculty and 800 part-timers at 99 sites in more than 20 countries, serving 100,000 students a year (Talisayon as cited in Hamm, 2004).

Rapid escalation in the numbers of students taking online courses is changing the face of the higher education enterprise. According to the U.S. Department of Education, about 54,000 online courses were offered in 1998, with 1.6 million students enrolled. Seventy-two percent of public two-year institutions offered distance education courses (Carnevale, 2000). If this looks like a complex, dizzying picture, then it helps lead to an understanding of the talk about "swirling students," and the myriad implications for needed changes in institutional work.

Figure 3. Nontraditional Learning Options

For-Profit Institutions	Corporate Universities	Online Courses
• 10% of all associate degrees • 28% of community college market	• 2,000+ in U.S. • associate and baccalaureate degrees	• 54,000 online courses • 1.6 million students enrolled • 72% of public associate-degree granting institutions offered distance education options

Sources: Hamm, 2004; Carnevale, 2000

Trend 4. Funding Squeeze. Here's a sobering thought: As enrollment continues to grow, funding will continue to fail to keep pace with either inflation or the number of students being served (Martinez, 2004). In high-enrollment states like California, for example, community colleges for some time have been serving large numbers of students for whom they do not receive enrollment-based funding from the state. Furthermore, there are features of state funding mechanisms across the country that either fail to support or are downright hostile to important aspects of the community college mission. Examples include fiscal policy related to remedial education and to financial aid, or more accurately, the lack of it, for part-time students. In other words, there are few financial incentives for community colleges to do the work that society most needs them to do.

Community College Promises

With this context in mind, consider the important promises that community colleges have made to their students and their communities.

Promise 1. Provide and Promote Access to College. "Well, of course," is the common response. "That goes without saying." But the influx of aspiring students may well mask some issues that demand attention. The truth is that college access in America is deeply at risk. In particular, the income-based disparities for both participation in higher education and degree completion in this country are scandalous. The threats have to do with finance, to be sure. But inadequate academic preparation for college and disparities across groups are just as serious.

Financing Higher Education. Funding remains a critical issue in higher education access, evidenced by these facts:

- Higher tuition rates and slashed state appropriations denied at least 250,000 prospective students access to college in the 2003-2004 fiscal year, according to the National Center for Public Policy in Higher Education.

- Among high school graduates, 77 percent of high-income students enroll in college immediately after high school versus 50 percent of students from low-income families (Price, 2004).

- The shifts from grants to loans and from need-based to merit-based aid (that is, toward middle-class entitlements), together with the lack of financial aid for part-time students, conspire to make participation and success an ever-greater challenge for low-income students.

There is another possibility that may create even deeper dilemmas. As traditional baccalaureate institutions continue both to increase tuition and to limit enrollments, there may be a shift to community colleges of more highly qualified students who are seeking a lower-cost alternative. This prospect might be welcomed by some faculty, and it could also be seen as an easy way of improving performance for accountability reporting. After all, the easiest way for a college to look better is to be more selective in accepting students; that's what Harvard does. But simply serving the more-qualified students will not keep the promise.

Academic Preparation. Almost 50 percent of all first-time community college students are assessed as underprepared for the academic demands of college-level courses (Roueche and Roueche, 1999). The challenges in this regard are, of course, typically more acute for low-income students and students of color—those whose previous schooling has served them least well.

Racial and Ethnic Disparities. Among the population of Americans age 18 to 24—the traditional college-age group—39 percent of Whites were enrolled in college versus 30 percent of African Americans and 19 percent of Hispanics (Price, 2004). Also, 66 percent of White high school graduates enrolled in college immediately after high school versus 56 percent of African Americans and 49 percent of Hispanics (Price, 2004).

Figure 4. College Enrollment Trends by Race/Ethnicity, 1999

African Race/Ethnicity	White	African American	Hispanic
18-24 year olds enrolled in college	39%	30%	19%
Enroll immediately after high school	66%	56%	49%

Source: Price, 2004

And the men. Men are underrepresented by a growing margin, comprising only 43 percent of community college enrollment.

Promise 2. Improve Student Attainment. Painted in summary form, the community college picture looks like this: Community colleges have inarguably the toughest job in American higher education. These are open-admissions institutions. They serve disproportionately high numbers of poor students and students of color. Many of their students are the ones who were least well served by their previous public school education and therefore most likely to have academic challenges as well as fiscal ones. Community college students are three to four times more likely than

students in four-year colleges to reflect factors that put them at risk of not completing their education. To support services for these students, the community colleges on average charge only 37 percent of the tuition and fees charged at four-year institutions and receive a fraction of the per-student appropriations of state dollars. And these students are likely to be coming to community colleges in ever higher numbers over the next decade at least, even as higher education appropriations as a proportion of state budgets continue to decline. Add all of this to the college attendance patterns described earlier, including the fact that students come to community colleges with many different goals and certainly not always intending to attain a degree or to transfer.

This is a reasonable description of the community college reality, and *it is the truth*. It is a truth those of us in community college education have become expert in articulating to policy makers and the media. It is a truth that provides important context for understanding institutional performance and accountability. Nonetheless, it is essential to communicate a tough message: *Community college educators too often hide behind that truth.* With that truth as a shield, we too often fail to look hard at our record with regard to student attainment, too often don't ask ourselves the hard questions about how we are doing and what we could do better.

The American Council on Education recently issued a statement with sector-by-sector statistics on graduation and persistence rates, with this report about community colleges:

> One-quarter of students who entered a public two-year institution in 1995-1996 with the goal of earning a degree or certificate had attained a credential at that institution by 2001 [six years later]. However, it is important to note that many students enter community colleges with educational goals other than degree attainment, and nearly 60 percent of entering students attend half-time or less. In addition, nearly one-third (31 percent) of students who began at these institutions transferred to other institutions. After considering transfer students, 39 percent of beginning students who entered at a public two-year institution had earned a degree or certificate within six years. More than 17 percent of students who entered community colleges in 1995-1996 were still enrolled six years later, resulting in an overall persistence and attainment rate of 56 percent. (ACE, 2003)

This is a fairly balanced statement, and ACE was apt in applying the rationale that we in community colleges have practiced so well. The question we have to ask ourselves, and to discuss seriously with colleagues on campus, is whether this is good enough. *I would answer that it is not.*

There is a more alarming piece, though. Another analysis shows that 38 percent of White students who began at a community college earned a degree or certificate within six years versus 26 percent of African Americans and 29 percent of Hispanics (Price, 2004).

Figure 5. Six-Year Completion Rate by Race/Ethnicity

White	38%
African American	26%
Hispanic	29%

Source: Price, 2004

With regard specifically to retention, for community colleges nationally, the drop-out rate from the first to the second year is around 50 percent. A closer look reveals that low-income and minority students are too often the ones most likely to drop out. Another important truth is that we in education know about educational practices that contribute to higher levels of student persistence and learning. We need to do more of what we know.

Promise 3. Focus on Learning. Thanks to Terry O'Banion, to Bob Barr and John Tagg, and to many others in the higher education field, there has been a near tidal wave of interest in work that helps colleges become more powerfully and effectively focused on student learning. Of course, just about every college likes to think that it is "learning centered." After all, educators ask, "Isn't that the business of higher education?"

Of course, the honest answer to that question is, "Sure, well—maybe—sometimes." The colleges that seriously take on the concept of "the learning college" realize that there is substantial and challenging work involved. A piece written for the American Association of Higher Education describes six fundamental characteristics of a learning-centered institution:

1. The institution has clearly defined outcomes for student learning.

2. The institution systematically assesses and documents student learning.

3. Students participate in a diverse array of engaging learning experiences aligned with required outcomes and designed in accord with good educational practice.

4. Data about student learning typically prompt reflection, decisions, and action.

5. The institution emphasizes student learning in its processes for recruiting, hiring, orienting, deploying, evaluating, and developing personnel.

6. Key institutional documents and policies, collegial effort, and leadership behavior consistently reflect a focus on learning (McClenney, 2003).

Assuming Collective Responsibility for Student Learning. It is important to mention one of the most significant cultural changes that must occur in this work. By and large, the business of teaching and learning in American colleges and universities has traditionally been a dramatically isolated and individualistic enterprise. The faculty member designs his own course, develops her own tests, sets his own standards, and gives her own grades, all the while declaring, "My classroom is my kingdom." Collective responsibility for student learning is not something most faculty members learned to value in graduate school.

But the League for Innovation in the Community College's Learning College Project revealed that it is precisely that sense of collective responsibility, cutting across classrooms, disciplines, departments, and divisions, that is requisite to development of a learning-centered college. At the end of the three-year project, a member of one of the college teams said, "The big answer to, 'What's new here?' is that people are taking more collective responsibility for student learning."

A serious focus on learning almost inevitably leads to other challenging questions among colleagues. One such question is, What *kind* of learning are we trying to achieve? Is it the kind of learning that too often results from the lecture method and multiple choice exams, what the cognitive scientists are calling surface learning? That's the learning that lasts until approximately 20 minutes after the final exam, at which time it is literally dumped from the brain. Or do we seek to produce deep learning, the kind of learning that only occurs through application and performance, through transfer to and use in new situations? That's the learning that lasts.

There is yet another important question: "How good is *good enough*?" What are our standards for student learning and student academic progress? A few real examples illustrate the pertinence of the question:

- The three-year graduation rate for students at College X is 14 percent, which is about average for similar colleges.

- The success rate for Introductory Biology students at College Y is 30 percent.

- In College Z, 50 percent of the students who begin developmental education courses in September are still enrolled at the end of the semester.

If 86 percent of our students are not graduating, if 70 percent are not successful in an introductory science course, if half of the students who begin developmental education have withdrawn from the college by the end of the term, is this good enough? In the end, "Is this good enough?" is a question that must be asked and answered by the faculty and administrative leaders in every college. And when the discussions take place, those faculty and those administrators are defining the meaning of quality at that college, defining the meaning of the associate degree.

Promise 4. Embrace Accountability. No longer a news flash for most higher education leaders is the fact that accountability is here to stay. The actions of state legislatures and the work on reauthorization of the federal Higher Education Act assure that as postsecondary education becomes more important to the economy and resources become tighter and tighter, there will be a continuing and escalating level of interest in the results that higher education produces with the public's money.

This is, or can be, good news. Accountability is not just inevitable; it is a good thing. It is a good thing because it is in the public interest. Community colleges, overwhelmingly, are public institutions. Community colleges are making public promises. And community colleges have an obligation to publicly report results. The urgent priority for these institutions is to be involved in shaping accountability systems so that they are appropriate to community college missions and students, and so that they serve rather than thwart the access and attainment promises.

One healthy challenge is proactively to define appropriate indicators of performance, and there is important work occurring on this front in Florida, Massachusetts, and other states around the country, as well as in several foundation supported initiatives.

Promise 5. We Must—and We Will—Close the Gap. As made clear by data cited above, there remains in American higher education a significant gap in educational attainment between students from high socioeconomic levels and students who are poor, between White students and their African-American and Hispanic peers. The gap is dangerous. It is intolerable. It is a blight on America's future. And it is worse in community colleges than elsewhere in higher education.

Of course, the students who come to community colleges are the students who are already most at risk. They experience three to four times the risk, in fact, of their peers in traditional baccalaureate institutions. But guess what? These are the students we in community colleges serve. Community colleges signed up for the open-door admissions policy. Community colleges take these students' tuition money (or the aid money that pays it) and count them as FTEs. And it is crucially important, both to the individual students and to wider society, that they be successful in reaching higher levels of educational attainment.

Furthermore, community college educators are confronted with the fact that for the most part, we cannot blame the students. Some colleges are demonstrating that the gaps can be closed. The Community College of Denver deserves the kudos it continues to receive for having turned possibility into reality. Other colleges now are signing on for the task. Under Chancellor Irving McPhail's leadership, The Community College of Baltimore County conducted an analysis of student outcomes, including retention and graduation, that revealed stunning gaps between White and African-American students. Rather than filing that report quickly and quietly in the bottom drawer, or talking about all the reasons they couldn't do anything about it, college leaders decided to acknowledge the gap, discuss it openly, and publicly commit to closing it. They have set goals, established timelines, identified strategies, and now at least four other community colleges in Maryland are joining a consortium to attack the problems together.

There is no more important work in American society than this work. Furthermore, it may be said with conviction that *to be successful in this work is not just a professional challenge. It is a moral obligation.*

Making Good on the Promises

No one ever said that keeping a promise was easy, but then, an African proverb advises that, "Smooth seas do not make skillful sailors." What is it going to take to make good on these promises? Truthfully, it is going to take serious, focused, collaborative, and sustained effort over a considerable period of time. A handful of inescapably necessary strategies would include the ones described below:

1. Create Stronger Connections with K-12 Education. There are many examples of such efforts around the country. The League's College and Career Transitions Initiative currently involves 15 site partnerships across the U.S. These are community colleges working with high schools and employers to carve meaningful career pathways for students. In addition, the middle-college model now is being even more widely adapted to create "early colleges," thanks to significant foundation support, particularly from the Bill and Melinda Gates Foundation. Beyond those models, there are other promising efforts, like the Ford Foundation's Bridges to Opportunity Initiative; and there are community colleges like those in the City University of New York system, where educators have created an astonishing array of collaborative efforts with the public schools, from the thousands of high school students who are concurrently enrolled in college, to the grade school on campus for the children of welfare moms, to the co-located high school, to the Diploma Now program, which provides early morning GED preparation classes for high school students who otherwise would be dropping out. Whatever the model, the structure, or the form of governance, the clear need is to create multiple pathways for students both to and through the community college.

2. Build A New Culture of Evidence in Community Colleges. For three years, 12 Vanguard Learning Colleges—already fine institutions—participated in the League's Learning College Project, taking on the tough work of focusing their colleges more powerfully and effectively on student learning. In the course of that work, it became evident that the single most powerful lever for change resided in the second of two questions continuously posed by Terry O'Banion. The first question is, "How will this decision/action/program/policy improve and expand student learning?" And that second, more powerful question is, "*How do we know?*"

For a long time, a lot of community college people have lived reasonably comfortably in a culture of anecdote. Those anecdotes are important parts of the culture of our institutions, but by and large, they are stories about the best student experiences rather than the typical student experiences. So there is a very important promise that we need to make to ourselves: *We will tell ourselves the truth about what happens to our students.*

To be specific, we will decide what questions need to be answered about student progress, student attainment, and student success in our institutions. We will identify the critical performance indicators that will tell us how we're doing. We will collect clear and credible evidence of institutional performance on those indicators. *And we will break down the data by race and ethnicity, income, gender, and age* so that we will have a genuine understanding of how student groups may differentially fare in our colleges. Then we will use the data and our understandings of it to target improvements in the work we do with students.

The problem here is not that colleges don't have data. We have lots and lots of data. The problem is that we usually don't ask the right questions of the data, don't display it in ways that make sense to most reasonably alert adults, and therefore don't see or hear the story that it can tell us about our students' experiences and the efficacy of our work.

But one of our gravest oversights is that we usually do not break down the data in ways that will depict the likely reality of systematic differences in outcomes for different groups of students. In colleges where people have had the courage to do this, the first time they disaggregate data, they are almost inevitably distressed by what they learn.

Pertinent here is the work of Estela Bensimon, who directs the Diversity Scorecard Project at the University of Southern California. Bensimon (2004) is addressing this issue head on, working with 14 two- and four-year colleges and universities in the Los Angeles area. In general, the process used in each college is for a cross-functional group she calls the "evidence team" to create equity indicators and benchmarks that comprise the "diversity scorecard" for the institution. The premise is that for institutional change to occur, "individuals must see, on their own, and as clearly as possible, the magnitude of inequities (*awareness*). They then must analyze and integrate the meaning of these inequities (*interpretation*), so that they are moved to act upon them (*action*)" (p. 46).

This is not just an exercise in collecting data. Bensimon (2004) and her colleagues "regard the act of *developing equity* indicators and *creating* the Diversity Scorecard as the intervention that prompts institutional change" (p. 46). This effect may be witnessed in college after college. As noted earlier, the problem is rarely a lack of data. The problem is also rarely a lack of good intentions. By and large, community college people work in these institutions precisely because they want to do good work. They want to help change people's lives. They want to *teach*; and they're both perplexed and distressed when, as one faculty member said, "It finally came to me—the inescapable conclusion that students just weren't learning what I thought I was teaching." There is nothing particularly easy about building a culture of evidence. Truth to tell, in the early going, evidence causes problems. It challenges assumptions and traditions. It disrupts informal power structures. It threatens the *status quo* and suggests needs for change. It comforts the afflicted, but it afflicts the comfortable.

On the other hand, it also helps chart a course to excellence; and a collective willingness to insist on, examine, and use evidence builds the credibility and integrity of community college work. As a science instructor said: "I look at it as polishing chrome versus fixing the engine. For too long, we've been really busy polishing the chrome."

3. Provide Effective Remediation. According to McCabe (2000), 67 percent of high school students earn a diploma, but only 43 percent of those students are prepared for college-level work. And 41 percent of all community college freshmen enroll in remedial classes (Voorhees, 2000).

One hoped-for solution is to shift remediation to the high schools, "where it belongs." This, of course, is much to be desired. Right now, though, it is also wishful thinking. While we need to be hopeful about and supportive of high school reform, we also must acknowledge that for as far as we

can see into the future, there is going to be a continuing and critical need for community colleges to be engaged in a significant amount of remedial education. Contributing factors are these:

- the slow rate of change in the quality of high schools, notably in those urban areas where the graduation rates, particularly for students of color, are much lower than the averages;

- the continuing influx of immigrants of all ages;

- the average age of community college students (about 29), which means that even if high schools were perfect tomorrow, the adults who had unsuccessful experiences there will continue to arrive at the doors of community colleges for the next decade; and

- the needs of adults more generally, i.e., people coming from the welfare system, from the criminal justice system, from low-paying or obsolete occupations, or those whose jobs have been outsourced to India.

There are too many policy makers and too many educators who want to believe that the need for remediation is going to go away and, therefore, that they don't have to pay for it, or make policy to support it, or hold institutions accountable for doing it well, or reward the ones that do. *Effective* remediation is a huge bargain. As McCabe (2000) points out, most students who successfully complete the prescribed remedial course sequence become productively employed, 16 percent as professionals, 54 percent in mid-level white-collar or technical positions, 20 percent as high-skill blue-collar workers. Only 9 percent remain in unskilled or low-skill jobs.

For all of these reasons, the crucial need is for community colleges to do remedial education *both unapologetically* and *exceedingly well*. The plain truth of the matter is that if students don't succeed in developmental education, they simply won't have the opportunity to succeed anywhere else. They won't take the advanced courses in literature and history that faculty members love to teach, they won't graduate, they won't transfer, and they won't land one of those high-demand, high-wage jobs. On the contrary, they are all too likely to land on welfare or in jail. Education or incarceration? That does not seem like a difficult choice.

It is the level of effective performance in developmental education that is the legitimate issue. There are some few colleges that can document doing an exceptional job in developmental education, working with challenging and diverse student populations so that participation in developmental education actually becomes a predictor of student persistence, graduation, and transfer. That takes away many of the excuses for poor performance.

On the other hand, of the half million academically underprepared students who enter community colleges each year, a substantial portion never make it out of remedial education, and only half go on to enroll in a baccalaureate degree program. For students of color, that figure is less than 20 percent (Lumina, 2004).

Sometimes it is necessary to acknowledge that while there are questions about whether students are ready for college, there are equally serious questions about whether some of the colleges committed to open admissions are really ready for the students.

We can do better.

4. Strengthen Student Engagement in the Community College Learning Experience. The research on undergraduate learning is unequivocal on this point: The more engaged students are, the more connected—to one another, to faculty and other college people, and to the subject matter—the more they will learn and the more likely they will be to persist to attainment of their educational goals.

Results from the Community College Survey of Student Engagement point to the critical importance of focusing squarely on the classroom, however it might be defined. What community college educators can do now to enhance retention and learning is the purposeful redesign of student learning experiences. In that redesign process, educators need to incorporate more of what is now known about effective educational practice and how students learn.

Thankfully, there is an expanding array of strategies for teaching and learning that seems to fill the bill: the burgeoning development of learning communities, as exemplified by the Seattle Central Community College, La Guardia Community College, Lane Community College, and many others; the expanding uses of process learning, of culturally mediated instruction, of project-based learning and service learning. All of these strategies—and some others as well—help to create what Carol Kasworm (2003) has called "the connecting classroom." She's not referring to the Internet; she's talking about approaches that promote connection among classmates, connections between faculty and students, connections made between students' lives and work and the subject matter of the course.

In particular, we need to redesign those gatekeeper courses. Every college has them—the high-enrollment courses that also have high failure rates and mark the end of many students' college careers. At Richland College in Dallas, a group of faculty members took a look at student outcomes for one of their introductory science courses and didn't like what they saw. As a consequence, they undertook a collaborative redesign process. Every college should consider doing the same. Carol Twigg's work at the Center for Academic Transformation offers a terrific collection of ideas about how to redesign these courses with two objectives in mind: to increase student learning while also lowering costs.

There's an important caveat to this enthusiasm about innovations in teaching and learning. Pat Hutchings (2004), in a recent online essay in Carnegie Foundation Perspectives, reminds us of the Tibetan Buddhists' idea of the "near enemy," the recognition that "any virtue has a bad cousin." The bad cousin in this case—the downside of these encouraging developments—is "the potential for a kind of insularity and balkanization, with the various teaching camps each going their own direction, in isolation from the others."

This is a pertinent point, because the community college phenomenon is that we collect innovations. We're like kids in Toys "R" Us: "Ooh, that's very cool—I want one of those. And this, too. Oh, and I just have to have this because Sinclair Community College has one!" In another example of competition among institutions, a dean of a college in a multicollege district described the intensity of the institution's rivalry with another college in the district: "You know," he said, "if they had a tornado over there, we would insist on having one, too."

5. Rethink and Redesign. If we are to deal with our realities and keep our promises, we are going to have to rethink some of our most basic assumptions, question our familiar structures and practices, and gore some favored oxen. A bit of relevant wisdom, offered on the menu at the Café des Artistes in New York, is this: "Tradition is often just a form of conspiracy to keep the future from happening."

This redesign effort is the work of transformational change in our institutions. It is conceptually difficult, politically dangerous, and demanding of a long-term commitment. Those who are really committed to it could lose their jobs. Those who are good at it may never get the credit. It is best that we learn to think of this as fun. And it is essential that we think of it as a team sport.

What kinds of tasks might be on this list for change? For example, colleges will need to:

- Focus attention and resources on the "front door" of the college. Community colleges lose half of their students in the first year and untold numbers before the census date of the first semester. We know that we need to connect early, connect often. We know that we need to help students set goals and milestones so that they can see possibilities, so that they have reasons to come back to school on Monday, in January, next year.

- Get rid of late registration and other firmly entrenched institutional practices that are more about revenue generation, bureaucratic folderol, or faculty convenience than they are about student learning and success.

- Remediate our own pervasive but fallacious assumption that any group of adults will learn a set of knowledge and skills at the same rate. We have to figure out how to insist that time will be the variable and learning the constant.

- Create more coherent and rigorous sub-degree certificates or modules of knowledge and skills, some of them in general education areas like quantitative reasoning, writing, and the like, and some linked to emerging career clusters.

- Become expert in the assessment and certification of learning, wherever it occurs; this is the growth industry of the future.

- Develop and employ far more portable mechanisms for documenting learning, such as smart cards and electronic portfolios.

- Construct class schedules not as a list of pet courses taught by individual instructors at their convenience but of linked learning experiences taught by teams of instructors and counselors who assume collective responsibility for a cohort of students.

- Reconfigure staffing to align with commitments to keep the promises, and to acknowledge that all the forms of expertise required for the classroom focus on learning and attainment—instructional design, content expertise, curriculum development, technology applications, multiple teaching strategies, assessment of learning, and student advising—may not frequently reside in a single individual.

6. Exercise Leadership. This will be done in a lot of different ways and at many different levels in the college organizations. But this transformational work is hard, and it certainly will not happen by itself. It requires continuous acts of courage to put data in front of an institution and ask hard questions about what must be learned from it. It requires continuous acts of will to make and support decisions that put resources where rhetoric is. And it requires truly relentless focus to avoid all of the possible diversions, the cool gadgets of educational innovation, the easier wins—and to keep all eyes on the Promise.

So keeping the promises will require all of this work and more. In sum, it's going to take

- more effective public and policy advocacy;

- tough questions and truth telling;

- rethinking, redefining, redesigning;

- letting go of things that feel comfortable but don't work;

- scaling up the things that do work; and

- charting a course through the often rough seas of institutional change.

Promises Worth Keeping

In a leap year, we get one extra day for Black History Month, and this year provided that benefit. It is appropriate, then, to recall the perspective on America's promise that was expressed by Martin Luther King, Jr., on the steps of the Lincoln Memorial in 1963:

> When the architects of our republic wrote the magnificent words of the Constitution and the Declaration of Independence, they were signing a promissory note to which every American was to fall heir.... This note was a promise that all men would be guaranteed the inalienable rights of life, liberty, and the pursuit of happiness.

King went on to decry the obvious—that America had defaulted on the promise "insofar as her citizens of color are concerned," that America had delivered a check that came back marked "insufficient funds." "But," he said, "We refuse to believe that the bank of justice is bankrupt. We refuse to believe that there are insufficient funds in the great vaults of opportunity in this nation." And he went on with those famous words: "No, no, we are not satisfied, and we will not be satisfied until justice rolls down like waters and righteousness like a mighty stream." Today we acknowledge again, more than 35 years after Dr. King's death, that even in a society as powerful and wealthy as ours, even as good as we think we try to be, there are people who are not living the American dream. Still there are young people who do not believe that the dream is their dream. Still there are people who should be in our colleges but are not. And there are people who are there now but won't achieve their goals. There are promises that have been broken and promises that just haven't been kept...yet. As we contemplate the challenges ahead, it is appropriate to give thanks.

To the students—those who learn from us and those who teach us; those so quick we struggle to keep up and those who struggle because we move too quickly; those who know exactly where they're headed, and those who still believe that the only reason they're in college is because someone made a terrible, wonderful mistake; to those who skip class to care for a sick child, run to class because the bus was late, or simply march to a different drummer; to those who challenge us and those whose courage touches our souls. To each and every student, we say, "Thank you." We are thankful to know them, even if just a little. And we are grateful to them for the opportunity, with their participation and sacrifice and hard work, to make good on America's promise.

To the people of our community colleges—faculty, staff, administrators, presidents—who daily undertake what should be recognized as some of the most important work in America, we say, "Thank you." If we keep our promises, we will be indispensably helpful in ensuring that America keeps hers. We all have promises to keep. And miles to go before we sleep. And miles to go before we sleep.

References

American Council on Education (2003 August). Student Success: Understanding Graduation and Persistence Rates. *ACE Issue Brief*. ACE Center for Policy Analysis. Washington, DC: Author.

Bensimon, E. (2004 January/February). The Diversity Scorecard. *Change, 36*:1(44-46).

Carnevale, D. (2000 January 1). Survey Finds 72% Rise in Number of Distance-Education Programs. *The Chronicle of Higher Education*, p. A57.

Carnevale, A. P., and Desrochers, D. M. (2004). Why Learning? The Value of Higher Education to Society and the Individual. *Keeping America's Promise*. A joint publication of Education Commission of the States and League for Innovation in the Community College. Denver: Education Commission of the States.

Community College Survey of Student Engagement (2003). *Engaging Community Colleges: National Benchmarks of Quality*. Austin, TX: Author.

Hamm, R. E. (2004). Going to College: Not What It Used To Be. *Keeping America's Promise*. A joint publication of Education Commission of the States and League for Innovation in the Community College. Denver: Education Commission of the States.

Hutchings, P. (2004 January). Building a Better Conversation About Learning. *Carnegie Foundation Perspectives*. Accessible at www.carnegiefoundation.org/perspectives.

Kasworm, C. (2003 April 21). What is Collegiate Involvement for Adult Undergraduates? In D. Kilgore (Moderator/Reactor), *What Does Research Suggest About Effective College Involvement of Adult Undergraduate Students?* Symposium conducted at the 2003 Annual Meeting of the American Educational Research Association, Chicago, IL.

King, M. L., Jr. (1963 August 28). I Have a Dream. Address delivered at the March on Washington for Jobs and Freedom. Available: The Martin Luther King, Jr. Papers Project at Stanford University (http://www.stanford.edu/group/King/publications/speeches-Frame.htm).

Lumina Foundation Newsletter (2004 January 27). www.luminafoundation.org.

Martinez, M. (2004). High and Rising: How Much Higher Will College Enrollments Go? *Keeping America's Promise*. A joint publication of Education Commission of the States and League for Innovation in the Community College. Denver: ECS.

McCabe, R. H. (2000). *No One to Waste: A Report to Public Decision Makers and Community College Leaders*. Washington, DC: Community College Press.

McClenney, K. (2003 Spring). The Learning-Centered Institution: Key Characteristics. *Inquiry & Action, 1*(5-6). American Association of Higher Education.

Mortenson, T. (2003 November). Undergraduate Degree Completion by Age 25 to 29 for Those Who Enter College—1947 to 2002. *Postsecondary Education Opportunity*, 137. http://www.postsecondary.org/ti/ti_15.asp

Price, D. V. (2004). Defining the Gaps: Access and Success at America's Community Colleges. *Keeping America's Promise*. A joint publication of Education Commission of the States and League for Innovation in the Community College. Denver: Education Commission of the States.

Roueche, J. E., and Roueche, S. D. (1999). *High Stakes, High Performance: Making Remedial Education Work*. Washington, DC: Community College Press.

Voorhees, R. (2000). Financing Community College for a New Century. In M. Paulsen & J. Smart (Eds.), *The Finance of Higher Education: Theory, Research, Policy and Practice*. Edison, NJ: Agathon Press.

Wilson, C. D. (2004). Coming Through the Open Door: A Student Profile. *Keeping America's Promise*. A joint publication of Education Commission of the States and League for Innovation in the Community College. Denver: Education Commission of the States.

Reprinted with permission.

Passing the Learning College Test: Courage and Innovation

— Cindy L. Miles and Elisa S. Robyn

A chronic challenge for America's community colleges is how best to measure and demonstrate the significance and value of our institutions. Size still matters when we describe ourselves to our constituents and colleagues. Most "About Our College" narratives boast tallies of students, buildings, campuses, and awards; the span of our campus footprint and service region; and, though shrunken in these days of revenue nosedives, the magnitude of our budgets and endowments. Even so, after marching to two decades of accountability pipers, few of us limit our narratives to such input measures. We genuinely care what happens to our students, and we increasingly strive to report our success in terms of the success of our students.

Even so, we perennially debate whether our success is rightfully defined by measurements of matriculation, retention, persistence, GPA, course progression, graduation, transfer, goal attainment, job acquisition, student satisfaction, or improved financial status of our graduates and communities. "Our students come to us for many reasons!" we assert, so we muster all-of-the-above answers to chronicle our worth. Nonetheless, we know that, all told, these metrics offer an inadequate tale of how well we meet society's demands. We know we improve the lives of many students, yet we also know, or suspect, how many we fail and how much more we wish we could do. Friends and critics alike remind us of our low student success rates and growing dissatisfaction among employers and policy makers in both the quality and quantity of our graduates (Bailey & Morest, 2006; Bok, 2005; Friedman, 2009; Mellow & Heelan, 2008). We are making progress, but our best efforts seem inadequate, underrepresented, or both.

Over the last decade, many community colleges have turned to the Learning College movement as a guidance system for navigating the twin issues of how to prove and improve student success. A number of colleges have found direction in the six "Learning College principles" defined by Terry O'Banion in the seminal work, *A Learning College for the 21st Century* (1997):

1. The Learning College creates substantive change in individual learners.

2. The Learning College engages learners in the learning process as full partners, assuming primary responsibility for their own choices.

3. The Learning College creates and offers as many options for learning as possible.

4. The Learning College assists learners to form and participate in collaborative learning activities.

5. The Learning College defines the roles of learning facilitators by the needs of the learners.

6. The Learning College and its learning facilitators succeed only when improved and expanded learning can be documented for its learners.

To keep their eyes on the prize of learning, colleges are encouraged to examine every action (decision, hire, plan, curriculum, policy, resource allocation, procedure, etc.) through the lens of two persistent questions offered by O'Banion as the quintessential Learning College criteria:

• Does this action improve and expand student learning?

• How do we know?

The Learning College Test Bank

Our colleges are under fire to show evidence of success. Institutions striving for high marks as Learning Colleges can choose from an array of options in their test bank of evaluation approaches: formative and summative, objective and subjective, formal and informal. More and more colleges are choosing performance-based measures aimed at continuous progress improvement, but sometimes their greatest need is to simply and plainly demonstrate that they are Grade A institutions.

Curiously, how a college dedicated to the Learning College journey assesses its progress—how it grades itself on its own Learning College test—may reveal more about the institution's culture, values, and leadership than its actual contributions to student learning. A common response from colleges aiming to become more learning centered is to cut to the chase—to the ends that the six principles portray for an idealized Learning College—and tackle them as a hopeful rubric for measuring their success.

Some colleges limit their selections from the Learning College test bank and adopt one or two of the principles as their success mantras. They tackle a short-answer version of the Learning College test, like this figurative institution fixated on Principle #3: "Mountain Valley College is a Learning College where learning happens anywhere, anytime, anyway."

Other institutions approach the Learning College challenge as a matching test or scavenger hunt, striving to check off as many items as quickly as possible and claim "Been There, Done That, Got the Learning College T-Shirt." They scour their programs and processes for verification of each principle:

1. Change in learners? Done! Ninety-one percent of our graduates agree or strongly agree that attending our college improved their lives.

#3. Learning options? You bet! We have day, evening, weekend course offerings; the tutoring center is open weekdays until 10 p.m. and half a day Saturday and Sunday; online learning is up 15 percent; we have 20 new hybrid courses.

#4. Collaborative learning? Check! We've got 12 learning communities each semester.

Finally, a number of institutions excel in the essay test approach by producing a flood of publications espousing Learning College goals and values, new vision and mission statements about being learning centered, and inscriptions of Learning College principles in course syllabi, catalogs, websites, and marketing materials. In classic "thought, word, deed" sequence, language is often the forerunner in an organizational change initiative. The challenge, of course, is to match our walk to our talk.

Appraisals of our Learning College successes are somewhat susceptible to grade inflation. We may amplify our progress to send constructive messages about the hard work under way or to keep motivation levels of faculty and staff high. Sometimes we suffer from good old-fashioned self-deception. This may be a natural reaction, akin to our responses to performance appraisal queries about how well we work with colleagues. No doubt,

An agenda
for measuring and

documenting student learning can easily lose out to budget cuts, accreditation demands, and enrollment issues, even among institutions highly committed to the Learning College journey.

we all give ourselves high points for collegiality and collaboration. Who would claim to be uncooperative or unresponsive? We might admit to being a trifle tenacious or stubborn regarding weighty issues, but we know we mean well.

Truth be told, our natural tendency is to judge ourselves based on our circumstances and intentions, while we judge others based on their actions and outcomes (Pronin, 2007). We tend to believe we are making significant gains because we know our intentions are good, even in the face of contrary evidence, such as slipped deadlines or fractional improvements in student achievement. We feel even more comfortable when we look around and conclude we are doing about as well as everyone else, and better than some.

With the rising higher education hubbub about institutional report cards and national accountability systems, our tendency may be to accentuate our successes and tweak a program here or a policy there to match the Learning College answer key. Undoubtedly, any of the Learning College test approaches help make student learning a sharper focus of institutional attention. The trouble is that too often all we produce is an isolated change or ancillary program that improves the lot of comparatively few students. Small-scale solutions cannot change the reality that for decades we have been losing half our entering students each term and few ever reach graduation. Never mind our inability to ensure that what students learn with us is what they need to thrive in their further schooling, work, and life.

Staying on Course

Launching a full-scale approach to elevate student learning to the forefront of the institutional enterprise is not for the fainthearted. Colleges that set off on the Learning College journey soon recognize the complexity of the expedition. Tremendous institutional energy is needed just to reach consensus that the current rate of student success is something that can and should be changed. Agreeing on actions and motivating participation requires even more time and finesse, and the risk of stalling out or losing direction intensifies in the face of countervailing pressures. Like sailors seeking a port upwind, we often must chart counter-intuitive routes back and forth, seemingly away from our target, to make incremental progress toward it. The trick is to remember where we are ultimately trying to go:

> The only way to sail upwind is to take a zigzagging course that keeps the sails full and the ship moving…. You sail slightly upwind in one direction or "tack," heading sideways to, but always slightly toward your goal, for a very long time. Then you turn and tack the other way. These shallow angles allow you to sail into the wind toward your goal. While you are tacking, you are never perfectly on course (i.e., aimed directly at your destination) until your final tack….
>
> Tacking upwind has risks. For one, you must remember to turn. This sounds silly, but getting caught up in your tack and forgetting your true mark is a common mistake. If you are on a very long tack you may begin to feel like the direction your nose points is where you are actually headed…. It is easy to confuse the tack with your true course. (Robyn & Miles, 2006)

A college aimed at becoming more learning centered might take a long tack toward Learning College Principle #6: documenting improved and expanded student learning by launching a student learning outcomes (SLO) initiative. Anyone involved with SLO work knows the laborious steps involved: reaching institutional consensus on a set of desired SLOs; determining whether to implement SLOs at the individual, course, program, or institutional level; undertaking curriculum mapping of where SLOs are addressed at identified levels of mastery across the curriculum and in co-curricular activities; cultivating faculty interest and skills in writing and using SLOs; developing effective rubrics and authentic assessments; choosing software to track assessments and outcomes; and agreeing on how to use and report results.

Such complexities point to why SLO initiatives are rarely institutionalized in fewer than three years. It is abundantly common to head off on any one of the individual jaunts of the SLO voyage, get caught up in that complex work, and forget to tack back toward the overall goal of student learning and success. Colleges sailing into SLO headwinds toward sunny shores of improved student achievement face a world of typhoons, doldrums, rocky shoals, mutinies, sirens, and sea monsters that challenge all but the most hardy captains and crews.

Of the original institutions included in the League for Innovation in the Community College's two major projects launched in 2000 to advance Learning College activities, the Learning College Project, with 12 colleges, and the 21st Century Learning Outcomes Project, with 16 colleges, only a handful remain on the same path. Many of these initiatives got off to a big-bang start and fizzled out over time. The chief academic officer at one of the institutions recently remarked, "We had to start all over again last year. Too many of the folks who had gotten the program started have retired or left, and too many faculty didn't see the value in what we were doing." In a number of cases the initiative lost steam when the president retired or moved on to another institution.

The perfect storm of seismic demographic and economic shifts pounding our institutions in the last decade has made it even harder to steer major institutional changes. An agenda for measuring and documenting student learning can easily lose out to budget cuts, accreditation demands, and enrollment issues, even among institutions highly committed to the Learning College journey. Plus, the lag time between implementing a learning initiative and being able to measure noticeable gains in student or institutional success can leave a college stalled in the doldrums of uncertainty.

Too often, daily demands of our institutional lives win the "urgent versus important" battles for our attention and resources (Covey, 1990). Add to this the fact that our funding and policy systems are not built to promote outcome-based success measures, and it is clear that odds are stacked against making big organizational changes that establish the primacy of learning. The coin of the higher education realm in most states remains enrollment, enrollment, enrollment.

Those tenacious institutions that have stayed the course sagely remind us to view the Learning College as a journey rather than a destination and to devise systems that help us regularly revisit our original inspirations for setting sail. Undoubtedly, on any long, arduous voyage, we are prone to forget why we set out in the first place.

Finding Our Big Why

So, why would a college dedicate itself to learning? The question seems tautological or even insulting. What are colleges about, if not learning? American higher education has long ridden the twin rails of advancing our economic prosperity as well as our democratic society. Learning may open minds, but college opens doors to personal and societal success. As President Bill Law of Tallahassee Community College puts it: "Access changes self-perception. Degrees and certificates change lives."

Community colleges—democracy's colleges—have served more than a century as pragmatic champions of egalitarian ideals and gateways to the American Dream. People come to our colleges full of expectation and hope, but often bring crushing challenges along with them. More than ever before, our students are underprepared for college work, distracted by work and family demands, and impatient to get in and out of our institutions. Frequently, learning seems to be the least of their concerns.

Despite the array of reasons students come to us, one they all share is to somehow make their lives better. Seldom do we fully understand the motivational state of our students as they entrust us with their personal and career aspirations. Much of the complex, human-intensive work we do is to engage students' attention in the learning process long enough for them to make choices to succeed. Research tells us that we do this best by getting to know their capabilities and desires; by promoting their meaningful engagement with content, colleagues, and mentors; and by holding them to standards high enough to foster pride in accomplishment. Sometimes we help our students learn and succeed by believing in them more than they believe in themselves.

As America's open door to higher education, community colleges are known for our anyway, anyhow commitment to serve all comers. Recently, though, we have begun to sag under the weight of our idealistic image of offering instant learning for a stunningly varied and underprepared onslaught of students. Leaders from the White House to the Lumina and Bill & Melinda Gates Foundations are raising the bar even higher with calls for us to help keep America's workforce competitive and economy viable by doubling our college graduation rates by 2020. Never mind that these expectations mount as our funding streams melt like 4th of July popsicles.

A Learning College approach can help keep an institution grounded in the face of such unprecedented challenges. Most of the "Big Why's" offered by members of institutions dedicated to becoming Learning Colleges speak to our fundamental values:

- It keeps us honest and in alignment with what we say we're here for.
- It keeps our resources focused on what's most important.
- It makes the way you get A's in college relevant to getting A's in life.
- It matches the architecture of the institution to the complex architecture that students are being prepared to work and live in.
- It shifts the focus from "what's convenient for the college" to "what's good for the student."
- The world is changing, learners are changing, and we need to keep up.
- It brings to life the belief that all students can learn what they need if given the proper tools, feedback, and support.
- It democratizes the learning process by giving more power—and responsibility—to learners for their own learning and success.
- "[It] helps students make passionate connections to learning." (O'Banion,1997)

Students are not the only beneficiaries in learning-centered institutions. Faculty and staff also report various intrinsic rewards from joining the Learning College journey:

- It shifts the organizational culture to a focus on learning for everyone—everyone gets to keep being a learner.
- It removes some of the institutional barriers to learning we have been railing against for years.
- It frees us to explore and experiment with new energy and conviction.

- Faculty get to fall back in love with their discipline.

- You get permission to not have to know it all, to not have to always be the expert.

- It reinvigorates us about why we came to the community college in the first place.

- It gives us all a clear, shared purpose for working here—student learning!

Transformational Learning

Whether learning is the goal or by-product of college, its results are frequently transformational. One of the highest test scores attainable is that associated with the golden fleece of the primary Learning College principle: creating substantive change in individual learners. Such learning is sometimes described as transformative, a type of learning that extends beyond garnering knowledge or skills to being altered in meaningful ways by what one learns (Mezirow, 2000). These fundamental changes may involve shifting personal perspectives, questioning unspoken assumptions, and even redefining one's place in the world.

Research tells us that our students thrive and learn best in enlivened, relevant, engaging learning environments. As educators, our greatest exhilaration is to create the magical learning formula that flips the switch in students' motivation from perfunctory pursuit of the grade to impassioned drive for new ideas and understanding. For our part, we must make whatever change is necessary to keep the machinations of our academic processes from eclipsing the power of learning as a human and societal improvement process.

In the miasma of our budget processes, enrollment management systems, or outcomes reports, we can lose sight of how much more our students want from learning, and how much more we want on their behalf. We do not want our individual students to get lost in the institutional effectiveness data that we aggregate around retention, GPA, and graduation measures. Certainly, we want them to pass their classes and graduate. But we also want them to experience the transformational power of learning. What we want most is for them to feel the excitement for learning that author Pat Conroy (2002) described in his memoir *The Losing Season*: "Goose bumps marched the length and breadth of my body and the back of my neck tingled as I knew for the first time that learning itself could carry the sting of divine inextinguishable pleasure."

Our highest hope is to support them in becoming empowered communicators, thinkers, and leaders who enrich their families, businesses, and communities and keep our economy and society strong. We must not get so busy with our bricklaying that we lose sight of the cathedrals we are building.

Better Questions

We might advance our Learning College test scores by asking better questions. Einstein was once asked what he would do if he had an hour to save the world in a dangerous situation. He replied that he would spend 55 minutes discovering the correct way to frame the question, then 5 minutes finding the solution (Michalko, 2001). Following

this lead requires recognizing, first, that we may not have instant answers, and second, that what we think we know might actually prevent us from discovering a better solution. To borrow another Einstein tenet, the thinking that got us into the problem is not likely to get us out of it.

What questions might free us from our usual mindset and push us to a deeper level of learning-centered thinking? We could try turning our typical questions inside out. Rather than asking why students leave the college, perhaps we should ask who stays and why they stay. When we hear students say that they left for financial reasons, we might pause over our instant solution to provide more scholarships, grants, loans, or work study. Perhaps when we talk with Marcos, who checked the "financial issues" box on the exit survey, we find out he left because he felt he didn't fit in socially. Maybe Charlotte will tell us she checked the same box because she happily got a new job. Maybe we learn about the frustrations of many students who did not even try to fill out the forms because they were so overwhelming. Maybe the students who thought about dropping out, but stayed, can teach us how to shape our retention programs.

We can ask better questions about how to structure our learning environments, even those seemingly supported by good data. We have plenty of evidence, backed by more than 15 years of research on learning communities, that students learn better and are more successful in cohorts. Unfortunately, many colleges have trouble getting students to sign up for blocks of learning community classes. Each term we ask, "How can we get more students to sign up for our learning community courses?" Perhaps we might more profitably ask, "What other ways can we build student cohorts?" or "What is it about cohorts that helps students learn and succeed, and how else might we offer these experiences?"

Our old-school questions seem to be all about changing student behaviors to match our systems. A number of perennial issues cry out for new questioning:

Old School Questions How do we get students to…	Inside-Out Questions
…come to class?	How can we make class as engaging as hanging out and talking with friends about interesting ideas? What can those who don't come to class tell us?
…go to advising?	Where do students like to go for answers? How can we make getting good academic advice part of the learner's responsibility? How can we offer the proven features of holistic advising to all students?
…participate in student clubs and activities?	What are students already doing together that can be leveraged? What activities offer students multiple values—social, economic, educational—all at once?
…buy their textbooks?	What is the cost/benefit analysis of the text? How else can we provide the needed information at a lesser cost? What motivated those who bought the text?

Perhaps the most pertinent inside-out question of all is "How do we involve students in answering these questions?"

Spandrels and Evolutionary Change

The Learning College test teaches us to recognize how our institutions function as answers to problems from a prior era. Today, we still hire faculty and staff, determine workloads, design the number of chapters in textbooks, determine when students take vacations, manage our facilities and resources, and measure our success using systems of work based on manufacturing assembly lines that were adapted to education over a hundred years ago (O'Banion, 1997). These vestigial systems are our college equivalents of architectural spandrels, features designed for a function they no longer serve, like the spaces between the pillars of bridges left from construction that are used by the homeless for sleeping (Buss, et al., 1998). Spandrels may be useful, but no longer for their original purpose.

Evolution of our organizations rarely keeps up with learning-centered test questions. Too many colleges remain bogged down in debates over whether students can learn enough in a short-term class, or whether hybrid and online classes are good learning models, or how to track contact hours when learning occurs outside the classroom. We know these are not our most evolved inquiries. We know learning is not restricted to time on task. We remember the thrill of accelerated learning when we were highly engaged by a new activity, event, person, or idea. Too rarely do we pay attention to the elements that make great learning experiences work.

Deeper questioning may lead us into the dark realm of unpredictable answers and elemental change. From a biological systems perspective, change is experienced by an organism as a wound to be healed or an invasion to be thwarted. Whether confronting a new psychological or physical element, the organism's reaction is the same. The basal, instinctive response to an agent of change is to avoid it, control it, isolate it, or extinguish it before it can harm or disturb one's personal ecosystem. Even the thought of change can prompt responses such as fear, anxiety, or mental paralysis.

Organizations tend to react to change in the same fashion as organisms (McMurtry, personal communication, 2008). As well-educated members of college bionetworks, we like to believe we are open to change. Generally, however, this proves true only if the change makes sense to us individually and we get a say in how fast and in what way it enters our world order. Otherwise, we engage our primal defense mechanisms to wait it out, wall it off, or kill it.

Learning is the most fundamental form of change. Without careful introduction, students may experience changes inherent in learning as disruptive and unsafe rather than welcoming and enriching. Done well, learning can feel more like falling in love than fighting for survival. If we succeed in providing a learning culture for our students, they can begin to move more comfortably to unfamiliar rhythms without tripping over outdated institutional structures and tempos.

Examining whether our policies and programs are based on evidence about what helps people learn is uncharted territory for most colleges. An honest investigation of student achievement may signal a need to redesign organizational processes, launch new programs, revise or eliminate outdated offerings, or realign budgets with learner's needs. However, the mere whisper of these thoughts generally summons such torrents of territorialism and protectionism that many colleges avoid the conversation altogether. Innovative, learning-focused architectural designs promoting collaborative learning, integrated lecture/lab studios, and even accidental opportunities for student engagement are increasingly common in our building projects. But the social, procedural, and curricular architecture of our academies evolves much more slowly.

Courage, Curiosity, and Liberal Education

Despite the colossal challenges associated with devising adequate and agreeable metrics for measurement, few educators would deny that the ultimate test of college effectiveness is student-level success. Individual student learning is our *raison d'être* and our definitive Learning College evaluation.

It takes courage for a college to scrutinize what happens over time to individual students who attend our institutions. Even more resolve is needed to dig into deeper questions about differences that appear when data are disaggregated by a variety of variables, such as college readiness, attendance patterns, gender, ethnicity, and income. So many studies have told us so repeatedly that underprepared, low-income, minority students have lower attendance and success rates at all levels of schooling that we risk being inured to these findings. No longer surprised, we may slip into our own learned helplessness when these data cross our desks or monitors.

With practice, we can ask deep questions, listen to responses we might not want to hear, and resist our instincts to stifle the unfamiliar or undesirable.

Great concentration is needed to stay awake to the nuances and possibility in the detailed profusion of information increasingly available to guide our decisions and actions. These numbers and trend lines hold powerful truths about our institutional history and values. They also serve as petroglyphs of our students' experiences as they pass through our real or virtual halls, charting their successes and failures as well as our engagement in advancing their hopes and dreams.

Currently, the most daring collective work aimed at using data to promote student success in community colleges is led by the national Achieving the Dream (ATD) initiative, a multi-organizational partnership of foundations, educational organizations, and research and policy centers. At this writing, more than 100 community colleges in 22 states have joined the ATD network and are busy conducting unblinking assessments of how their students are doing. These institutions commit to an organizational focus on inquiry and using evidence to make changes to promote student retention and graduation, with a special eye toward students of color and low-income students. Since the path to standard goal completion—a degree or certificate—is lengthy for many community college students, ATD institutions measure key milestones along the journey: completing developmental courses; enrolling in and completing college-level or gatekeeper courses such as math and English; finishing courses attempted; and persisting from one term to the next. ATD's network of institutions is altering the community college landscape and doing more to promote use of real-time and longitudinal data to advance learning-centered precepts than any previous project or initiative.

Community colleges are also devising ways beyond standard course, program, and degree completion rates to measure important learning competencies such as critical thinking, communication, ethical thinking, civic responsibility, information literacy, aesthetic appreciation, teamwork, problem solving, and cultural competency. A number of two-year colleges have joined initiatives like the Association of American Colleges and Universities Liberal Education and America's Promise (LEAP) program, which challenges the notion that college students must choose between a "practical" or a "liberal" education. LEAP institutions emphasize "high-impact educational practices"—first-year seminars, learning communities, undergraduate research, service learning, capstone projects—as well as use of "assessment to deepen learning and establish a culture of shared purpose and continuous improvement."

Learning is increasingly recognized as a complex and mercurial matter, not circumscribed neatly by simple measures. Increasingly, even innovation, creativity, and curiosity are seeping into the outcomes conversation as critical competencies for our global playing field. It was, after all, Einstein who argued for curiosity as an essential learning element:

> The important thing is not to stop questioning. Curiosity has its own reason for existing. One cannot help but be in awe when one contemplates the mysteries of eternity, of life, of the marvelous structure of reality. It is enough if one tries merely to comprehend a little of this mystery every day. Never lose a holy curiosity.

Beyond the Grade

We understand our students' pragmatic temptation to do only enough to get the grade, especially those heroically balancing family, work, and school demands. Yet we know we must try to sell them on the superior value of deep, liberal learning for its longevity and even utility in today's knowledge economy, over cheap, fleeting surface learning sure to fade after they pass the test. Making the same case to our institutions is similarly challenging. How do we argue the value proposition of engaging in the strenuous work of developing a transformational Learning College culture to already stressed administrators, faculty, and staff? Surely the array of notable services they provide every day despite shrinking resources and growing demands is meritorious enough to earn them an A.

In a curiously interdependent way, the answer to motivating a higher-order focus on learning is exactly the same for our colleges as for our students. In both cases, we call for staying engaged in the learning process long enough and deeply enough to achieve a grade that truly matters. It takes stubborn diligence to hone in on what we value most, to develop precise, evidence-based measures to track our progress, and to keep our eye on the prize long enough to succeed.

As we "perched at the millennium" in 1998, Kay McClenney offered a Buddhist beginner's mind perspective of idealized 21s century community colleges that would rely on evidence rather than anecdote for decision making, strive to build learning capacity rather than address learning deficiencies, design learning systems based on learners' needs rather than institutional interests, and gauge success in terms of student learning rather than teaching inputs. McClenney listed the tools needed for such transformational colleges as "will, vision, focus, data, and guts."

More than a decade later, hundreds of community colleges are using these simple, potent tools and showing significant gains on their tests of student success. They mark progress by closing gaps in achievement scores traditionally found along demographic lines, by working with middle and high schools to reduce remediation needs of incoming students, by redesigning curriculum and support programs to accelerate students from developmental to college-level courses, by promoting higher order learning attainment that prepares students to succeed in a global economy, and by increasing the number of students earning college certificates and degrees.

The Long and Short Way

Paradoxically, to pass the Learning College test with the highest score means we must frequently slow down and do less. We cannot critically examine complex data and make thoughtful strategic decisions in fly-by, multitasking, one-minute-manager meetings. Our more-with-less treadmills hamper institutional learning in the same way that student learning suffers when a teacher tries to cover too much material in a class. Howard Gardner (1999), father of multiple intelligences, argues against instructional cramming to cover "Plato to NATO" as nonsensical and useless. He contends, "The greatest enemy of understanding is coverage."

To translate our institutions into environments that foster deeper, more meaningful learning, we must slow our own learning production line enough to more fully explore our students' optimal learning conditions. We become transformational learners ourselves as we wrestle with questions of what works and why. We deepen our discernment and improve our practice when we are willing to open ourselves to what may be uneasy truths or exhilarating epiphanies about the learning experiences and achievements of our students. Reflection—the precious commodity of taking time to think—is essential to higher learning. True for students. True for Learning Colleges.

In the end, the simple success formula is to keep a clear eye on and a fire in our bellies for what brought us to this journey in the first place. This spirit of the Big Why is included in the postscript that one of the authors includes in all her course syllabi:

> Now that we have reviewed all the rules, regulations, standards, and plans, I would like to tell you my personal goal for this course. I am not interested in being a score keeper, hounding you to turn in work so that you can pass. I am interested in making you mentally hungry, inspiring you to look at the world around you, and your place in it, in a different, more informed and involved way. If you leave this class with more questions than you walked in with, with a hunger to know more, with a sense that your choices in this world make a difference, then I have succeeded. I hope to ignite a renaissance of thought in each of you. My job, then, is to facilitate this process. It is your responsibility to choose how much you wish to learn, and at what level you wish to perform. In essence, your choice will determine your grade.

As Learning College aspirants, it helps to practice a "power of *and*" approach (Miles, 2002), and strive to be compassionate *and* strong, builders of bridges *and* holders of standards, teachers *and* learners, idealists *and* pragmatists, career-builders *and* academics. Fortunately, most community colleges have the vitality and diversity needed to launch a culture of inquiry and learning. We take pride in our humanitarian ideals and resilient spirits. These traits will come in handy for nurturing the cognitive courage to ask better questions, examine disturbing data, and wrestle with thorny circumstances so that we might truly reform ourselves into the ideal crucibles for learning first called for fifteen years ago (Barr & Tagg, 1995; O'Banion, 1997).

Our decisive test is how well we fulfill the Learning College foundational principle to measurably improve and expand substantive student learning. In navigating our Learning College journeys toward this big final exam, we can take a cue from the Talmud lesson that the shortest distance to one's destination is not always apparent: *The short way is longer and the long way is shorter.* Our students need us now because their lives and the world cannot stop. At the same time, we must slow down enough to engage our college community in building purposeful habits of individual and institutional learning capable of transforming minds and lives. There is no singular or swift path, neither is there a shortcut around the truth that we will pass our Learning College test only when all our students succeed and the evidence of their success is abundantly clear to us all.

References

Bailey, T. & Morest, V.S. (eds). (2006). *Defending the Community College Equity Agenda*. Baltimore, MD: Johns Hopkins University Press.

Barr, R.B., & Tagg, J. (1995). From Teaching to Learning: A New Paradigm for Undergraduate Education. *Change, 27*(6), 13-25.

Bok, D. (2005) *Our Underachieving Colleges: A Candid Look at How Much Students Learn and Why They Should Be Learning More*. Princeton: Princeton University Press.

Buss, D.M., Haselton, M. G., Shackelford, T.K., Bleske, A.L., & Wakefield, J. C. (1998). Adaptations, Exaptations, and Spandrels. *American Psychologist*. 53, 533-548.

Conroy, P. (2002). *My Losing Season*. New York: Nan E. Talese/Doubleday.

Covey, S. (1990) *Seven Habits of Highly Effective People*. New York: Simon and Schuster.

Gardner, H. (1999) *The Disciplined Mind: What All Students Should Understand*. New York: Simon & Schuster.

McMurtry, J., (Oct. 2008). Personal communication.

McClenney, K. (1998). Community Colleges Perched at the Millennium. *Learning Abstracts*. 11(8).

Mellow, G. O. & Heelan, C. (2008). Minding the Dream: *The Process and Practice of the American Community College*. Lanham, MD: Rowman & Littlefield.

Merisotis, J. (October 14, 2009) The Howard R. Bowen Lecture, Claremont Graduate University, Claremont, CA. http://www.luminafoundation.org/about_us/president/speeches /2009-10-14.html

Mezirow, J. (2000). *Learning as Transformation: Critical Perspectives on a Theory in Progress*. San Francisco: Jossey Bass.

Michalko, M. (2001). *Cracking Creativity*. Berkeley, CA: Ten Speed Press.

Miles, C. (2002). "Organizational Readiness: Middle Age and the Middle Way." In N. Thomas (Ed.), *Perspectives on the Community College*. (pp.19-22). Phoenix: League for Innovation in the Community College

O'Banion, T. (1997). *A Learning College for the 21st Century*. Phoenix: Oryx Press.

Pronin, E. (2007) Valuing Thoughts, Ignoring Behavior: The Introspection Illusion as a Source of the Bias Blind Spot. *Journal of Experimental Social Psychology*. 43, 565-578.

Robyn, E. & Miles, C. (2006). *Pirate Wisdom*. New York, NY: iUniverse.

The Learning College: How Do We Know?

— Cynthia D. Wilson

As I sit down to write this closing chapter for *Focus on Learning: A Learning College Reader*, it has been over 15 years since Bob Barr and John Tagg challenged the status quo with their seminal article, "From Teaching to Learning: A New Paradigm for Undergraduate Education." In that time, much has been written about the Learning College, and colleges around the world have committed to becoming more learning-centered institutions. The Learning College has been the focus of countless books, articles, conferences, workshops, in-service programs, demonstration projects, presentations, and conversations. But what have we learned? More importantly, how do we know the Learning College improves and expands student learning?

In early years, when questions were raised about the effectiveness of the Learning College as a framework for improving student learning, the answer was easy: the concept was too new, too untried, for us to know. And that worked, for a while. But 15 years on, even accounting for the unhurried pace at which higher education institutions traditionally change, that response is no longer adequate.

During these years, we have learned some lessons. The League's Learning College Project and 21st Century Learning Outcomes Project provided ample evidence of what we suspected—this work is hard—and gave us insights into what it takes to become a learning-centered institution. But those projects ended almost a decade ago, and 15 years after the first works on the Learning Paradigm and the Learning College appeared, it is time for us to answer the Terry O'Banion questions about the concept itself: Does the Learning College improve and expand student learning? How do we know? In considering answers to these two questions, it is helpful to review what we have learned; it is also helpful to review what we have gained since *An American Imperative* was published.

What We Have Learned

Working with numerous colleges in the past decade and reviewing the collection of articles reproduced here have reaffirmed for me much of what we learned through the League's early learning-focused projects: This work takes solid commitment.*

Commitment of leadership. The commitment to becoming a college with a strong, conscious, overt focus on learning manifests itself in committed leaders—both formal and informal—and board members. The importance of presidential commitment to the Learning College philosophy and to the institution's journey should not be understated, and leaders demonstrate their commitment to a strong focus on learning in substantive as well as symbolic ways, always emphasizing the importance of the college's commitment to learning. Sadly, we have also learned that when these committed presidents resign or retire, they are sometimes replaced with leaders who abandon the learning initiative, allowing it to wither and die. The commitment of informal leaders to this work is also important. Engaging them early in the conversations and activities around the Learning College can help secure their support. Including board members on cross-college teams that lead the effort (see "Commitment to collaboration," p. 215) helps establish support from college boards to embed the focus on learning in every aspect of college life and work.

Commitment of resources. Lamenting the lack of resources to support the work necessary to intensify a college's focus on learning is a common refrain in the early stages of this work; however, as colleges make progress, even during economic downturns, their perspectives change. Becoming more focused on learning is often described not as a matter of money, but as a matter of will. The use of O'Banion's two fundamental questions—"Does this action improve and expand student learning?" and "How do we know?"—in budgeting and decision-making processes can help ensure that resources support the focus on learning.

Commitment to professional development. Aligning staff development offerings to support the college's learning-centered focus is a prudent use of professional development funds, time, and other resources. Extending professional development and staff training to all employees models the focus on learning and helps staff and administrators, as well as faculty, better understand their roles in the Learning College.

Commitment to innovation. In a recent study of the nature of innovation in the community college (www.league.org/natureofinnovation), researchers found that an environment where leaders encourage and promote innovation is an important trait of a culture that values innovation. Exploring new ways of working, teaching, and supporting student learning necessitates risk by individuals who try new strategies and by the organization as it moves forward. An environment of trust provides the freedom to implement new ideas in a safe place that encourages thoughtful experimentation, celebrates successful attempts, and learns lessons from failure that help ensure success in the next effort.

---

* A description of lessons learned from the Learning College Project is available in Wilson, C. (2005). "Beyond the Rhetoric: The Learning College in Action." In C. J. McPhail, Ed., *Establishing and Sustaining Learning-Centered Community Colleges*. Washington, DC: Community College Press.

Commitment to collaboration. Developing a cross-college working team to lead the Learning College initiative is an effective strategy. Teams that include the president, a board member, chief academic and student services administrators, and formal or informal faculty and support staff leaders can be a major factor in moving the work throughout the college. Cross-functional teams allow various perspectives to be included in the organizational conversation and help ensure champions to support and encourage the work across the institution. Team members learn about and work together in overcoming challenges and issues faced by various areas. The team also helps eliminate isolation and territorialism as people come together in a collective focus on learning.

Commitment to discourse. The focus on learning can be promoted through collegewide conversations that engage all members of the college in discussions of learning-related issues and challenges. They may be formal conversations with full participation on a single topic, or they may be informal conversations on various topics. These conversations can help in defining the Learning College and its terminology in the local college context, and achieving a common focus and understanding of the college's goal.

Commitment to self-examination. Candid self-examination is a fundamental and routine aspect of the Learning College. For the colleges that examine themselves closely, the findings are not always pleasant. Through honest self-examination, the college can identify, revise, or eliminate programs and practices that are not effective. As colleges engage in self-examination, they can begin to discover and acknowledge discrepancies between words and deeds. Self-examination can also lead to a fundamental question of integrity: Are we doing what we say we're doing?

Commitment to learning and evidence. With the powerful focus on learning and collecting evidence of that learning, these two traits—learning and evidence—represent the core work of the Learning College. In seeking answers to the ubiquitous how-do-we-know question, colleges emphasize the use of data about learning in planning, in creating and assessing teaching and learning environments and experiences, in supporting the learning process to ensure learner success, and in every other aspect of the college's life. Using evidence mindfully to improve courses, programs, and the entire institution, colleges examine their strengths and weaknesses—in some cases, raising questions about the usefulness of data that is collected.

Commitment to defining and documenting student learning. By clearly defining the learning and demonstrations of learning required for student success, all participants in the learning process are informed of and can be focused on offering appropriate learner support. The work of learning outcomes has been generally regarded the most difficult and challenging part of the journey. Despite the difficulty, colleges do make progress, often slow progress. In response to the sixth learning college principle, "the learning college and its learning facilitators succeed only when improved and expanded learning can be documented" (O'Banion, *A Learning College for the 21st Century*, Oryx Press, 1997, p.

47), colleges are experimenting with ways to provide a thorough record of learning for students seeking employment or transfer, such as electronic portfolios and annotated transcripts.

Commitment to collective responsibility for student learning. One of O'Banion's (1997) six principles of the Learning College includes the student taking primary responsibility for his or her own choices about learning. Many community college students, though, come through our open doors unprepared for college-level work, and may be unlikely candidates for taking that degree of responsibility for learning. By making students "full partners in their own learning" (O'Banion, 1997, p. 47), learning becomes a joint venture between the learner and the rest of the college, with everyone—faculty, staff, administrators, other students, even community members—contributing in some meaningful way to learner success. Strategies such as individual education plans, early alert processes, and case management approaches can help students become lifelong learners.

What We Have Gained

In its 1993 landmark report, *An American Imperative*, the Wingspread Group on Higher Education issued a signal call for major reform: "Putting learning at the heart of the academic enterprise will mean overhauling the conceptual, procedural, curricular, and other architecture of postsecondary education on most campuses" (p. 14). This was a call for sweeping change in American higher education, and the Learning Paradigm and the Learning College were the most visible responses to that call. Other answers and actions complemented these influential ideas, of course, but it was primarily the work around the Learning Paradigm and the Learning College that provided community college educators with an array of resources for use in the continuing work of moving colleges to a more learning-centered perspective. We, as educators from all levels of higher education, are among the beneficiaries of these years of reform.

We have tools. We have several tools in this volume alone, including the self-assessment appended to *An American Imperative*, the League's Learning College Inventory, the benchmarks identified by Kay McClenney, the not-necessarily-rhetorical questions posed by Terry O'Banion and others, and the questioning strategies suggested by Cindy Miles and Elisa Robyn. We also have the anticipation of other questions that are bound to arise when conversation groups read and discuss any of the works in this volume, or any of the many other writings on such topics as learning theory, assessment, evaluation, organizational transformation, effective practices in teaching and learning, or cultures of learning and evidence. We have other tools, also, such as the Community College Survey of Student Engagement and others in the suite of surveys available through the Center for Community College Student Engagement—all focused on learning. We have Renate Krakauer's Learning College inventory.

We have project research. We have the results of innovative projects such as AAC&U's Greater Expectations, Alverno College's Innovation and Inquiry for Student Learning, the League's College and Career Transitions

Initiative and Significant Discussions Project, and the successful strategies and results from Achieving the Dream. We have the Carnegie Foundation's Scholarship of Teaching and Learning and projects such as Strengthening Precollegiate Education in Community Colleges. We have SRI International's work on domain-specific assessment. We have more than 35 dissertation studies on Learning College topics.

We have curriculum models. We have high-quality curriculum from open educational resources projects such as those produced by the Monterey Institute for Technology and Education (MITE), including the National Repository of Online Courses and Hippocampus; and we can look forward to results of the work MITE is now doing in developmental math. We have NCAT and course redesign. We have Ruth Stiehl's primers on curriculum development, curriculum mapping, and assessment.

We have quality-enhancement processes. We have AQIP, QEP, and other accreditation reaffirmation and self-study processes based on quality enhancement and focused on learning outcomes, processes that are designed more for continuous improvement than for decennial reporting.

We have professional development models. We have campuses with their own centers for teaching and learning, and a burgeoning effort to expand the offerings of these centers to include professional development opportunities for all college employees. We have professional development resources such as LENs and Getting Results.

We have student learning and support models. We have one-stop centers, both online and on site. We have tools developed by nonprofit and for-profit vendors, with all the many features of course and learner management systems. We have accurate assessment and placement instruments, learning-centered tutorials, and brain-based learning. We have real-world models of organizational structures for learning; of effective student services, teaching and learning strategies, learning communities, and first-year experience programs; and of the physical architecture of learning.

We have each other. We have colleagues around the world who are eager to learn and eager to share their own experiences, partners in the U.S., Canada, New Zealand, Scotland, the Netherlands, Australia, Jamaica, Turkey, Singapore, and elsewhere. We have learning-centered gatherings, from the League's Innovations conference and Learning College Summit to events sponsored by local, state, national, and international organizations, where we celebrate what works and seek remedies for what doesn't. We have a vast network and a tremendous amount of knowledge and experience, if we choose to use it.

The Unanswered Question: How Do We Know?

Still, and with all these resources and many others, how do we know the Learning College is working? The goal of the Learning College Project was to create a network of community colleges focused on becoming more learning centered. The network was created, and the League has expanded and nurtured it through publications such as *Learning Abstracts*, and through the annual Innovations

conference and Learning College Summit. The project goal was achieved. Building and nourishing a network can help a movement grow, but that doesn't tell us whether the movement is effective. Adherents of the Learning College would not accept the argument that our colleges are effective because students keep coming to them, so we can hardly say the Learning College is effective because institutions keep joining the caravan. The questions ring: What impact has the Learning College had? Has it been effective? How do we know? How can we know? The hard truth is, we think it is working, but our evidence is primarily anecdotal. And for people who have been preaching with evangelical zeal the necessity of a culture of evidence, anecdote alone is unacceptable. Following some of the advice often given to colleges that start the journey may be one way to find out, or begin finding out, how successful the Learning College is.

Gather up the innovations. In his presentations to institutions beginning the Learning College journey, Terry O'Banion advises leaders to "gather up the innovations." He suggests using the Learning College as a kind of umbrella under which to collect and inventory all the effective, discrete practices, programs, and processes scattered around any college. For the broader learning-focused movement, the list just provided may be a start, but what else is out there? How can we find it? If a central repository is not feasible, what about a central directory? Do current structures, such as ERIC, fill the need? Would such a repository be useful? How would it be used, and who would use it?

Talk to colleagues. Conduct a meaningful focus-on-learning survey of community colleges to determine the degree to which colleges have become more attentive to the core philosophy of the learning-centered movement. To what extent do colleges depend on evidence over anecdote? Analyze and slice data in revealing ways? Use findings to inform actions and decisions? Document substantive change in learners in meaningful ways that go beyond traditional grades and course credit?

Create the map. Early in this work, its leaders advised that there is no map; each college has to find its own way. At that point, no one really knew the lay of the land. We have more knowledge now, and for colleges that are just beginning the journey, or beginning it again, a map might be useful. By now we may know enough to create one, complete with super highways and back roads, scenic views and rush-hour traffic, construction zones and caution signs, free parking and dead ends. Is a map necessary? Would it be useful to colleges new to the journey? What about veteran Learning Colleges that may have encountered detours or gotten lost? Could they use a Learning College GPS or alert system they can access for help? Would they?

Ask the right questions. Let the Learning College movement learn from its own advice, asking itself the two questions: Does the Learning College improve and expand student learning? How do we know? Apply the primary Learning College principle to the movement as a whole: Does the Learning College create substantive change in individual learners? Follow that question with the persistent how-do-we-know question. This kind of assessment of the concept in action has not been conducted. Should it be? What might be the value of such a study?

Evaluate, Evaluate, Evaluate. What strategies could be used to determine whether the Learning College has been effective? Do we need to re-examine the early inventories? Will we find them still relevant? Still helpful? Do they need to be revised? Do others need to be developed for colleges that are further along on the journey? Used widely, would these inventories reveal any truths about the effectiveness of the Learning College? If not, what would?

Can We Get There From Here?

For more than 15 years, community colleges have consciously, overtly taken the path to become more learning centered, and as the litany of questions in the preceding paragraphs suggests, now it is time to stand back, to assess, to see what progress we have made. *An American Imperative* was published almost two decades ago, but it still rings true. With all the money, time, expertise, and effort that has been poured into higher education reform and the focus on learning, overall retention rates are still lower than we want them to be. The current emphasis on and attention to completion are welcome, even as they add to the already intense pressure colleges are under to produce effective, large-scale developmental education programs, and to improve capacity to meet the needs of students who are juggling low-wage full-time jobs, child care, substandard housing, calculus, and English as a second language. With all the work community college educators have to do, and there is plenty, do they even have time to ask—much less answer—the questions the Learning College poses?

Yes, they do. One gift of the Learning College movement is that it has made asking such questions an everyday priority at community colleges and their counterparts around the world. The Learning College concept gives community college educators the gift of practical inquiry, a framework in which to question the practices, structures, motives, and even integrity of their institutions—and to act on the answers, especially when those answers reveal unpleasant realities. Through this inquiry process, the Learning College framework liberates community colleges from tired, ineffective programs, policies, and ways of thinking, thereby freeing resources—time, energy, funds, creativity, innovation—for the development of improved learning opportunities for students.

Educational reform efforts come and go, trendy strategies with alliterative monikers grab our attention for a while before fading out of memory, but an educational movement that has at its core an institutional and individual focus on improving and expanding learning seems worthy of longevity. Becoming a more learning-centered institution is a process, and the "Learning College journey" gives that process a recognizable name. What the process is called may change over time; in fact, individual colleges are encouraged to define their own language of learning. Some have intentionally avoided the terms "Learning College" and "Learning Paradigm," preferring instead to use language that better fits their culture.

At this point, the answer to the how-do-we-know question about the broader Learning College movement is general and anecdotal; a proper, evidence-based response is work for a major study and beyond the scope of this volume. However, that the Learning College movement is still with us, and that it still resonates with so many community college administrators, faculty, and staff, is a reflection of the substantive framework it establishes for individual institutions. What may be most significant at this stage is that colleges continue to engage in the practical inquiry that enriches their focus on learning, and that they do this to improve the learning and the lives of the students and communities they serve. The questions raised by the learning-centered movement are exactly the kinds of questions community colleges needed to be asking themselves 15 years ago, and they are the questions these institutions need to keep asking themselves today. Indeed, one of the most important outcomes of the work with the Learning Paradigm and the Learning Colleges is that we have learned to ask these absolutely essential questions: *Does this action improve and expand learning? How do we know?*

These two questions are a solid place to start, and colleges that adopt them as a mantra are finding ways to remove existing barriers to learning; to implement policies, programs, and practices that enhance student success; and to rely on meaningful data, beyond anecdotal evidence, to demonstrate they are improving and expanding student learning. But these questions are only a starting point; more pointed, more substantive, more productive questions are sure to arise, questions with answers that will help not only our community colleges, but also other educational institutions and our society as a whole to sharpen the focus on learning.